DATE DUE

George W. Bush, War Criminal?

GEORGE W. BUSH, WAR CRIMINAL?

The Bush Administration's Liability for 269 War Crimes

Michael Haas

Foreword by Benjamin B. Ferencz
Former Chief Prosecutor, Nuremberg Military Tribunals

PRAEGER

Westport, Connecticut
London

Library of Congress Cataloging-in-Publication Data

Haas, Michael 1938–
    George W. Bush, war criminal? : the Bush administration's liability for 269 war crimes / Michael Haas ; foreword by Benjamin B. Ferencz.
        p. cm.
    Includes bibliographical references and index.
    ISBN 978-0-313-36499-0 (alk. paper)
    1. War on Terrorism, 2001—Law and legislation. 2. War on Terrorism, 2001—Law and legislation—United States. 3. International offenses. 4. Bush, George W. (George Walker), 1946– I. Title.
    KZ6795.T47H33 2009
    341.60973—dc22   2008032931

British Library Cataloguing in Publication Data is available.

Library of Congress Catalog Card Number: 2008032931
ISBN: 978-0-313-36499-0

First published in 2009

Praeger Publishers, 88 Post Road West, Westport, CT 06881
An imprint of Greenwood Publishing Group, Inc.
www.praeger.com

Printed in the United States of America

The paper used in this book complies with the Permanent Paper Standard issued by the National Information Standards Organization (Z39.48-1984).

10 9 8 7 6 5 4 3 2 1

Dedicated to the journalists who have exposed the truth, the attorneys who fight to preserve our rights, and the innocent victims of unjust treatment.

CONTENTS

CONTENTS

TABLES AND APPENDICES

FOREWORD

Ever since the American colonies broke away from the British Crown, the created nation has been inspired by the doctrine that no man is above the law. Engraved above the portico of the marble Supreme Court building in Washington is the promise: "Equal Justice under Law."

When the highly esteemed Associate Justice Robert M. Jackson took temporary leave of the Supreme Court to serve as U.S. chief prosecutor at the Nuremberg war crimes trials following World War II, he repeatedly made clear that law must apply equally to everyone. "To pass these defendants a poisoned chalice," he said, "is to put it to our own lips as well." His successor as chief of counsel for another dozen war crimes trials at Nuremberg, Brigadier General Telford Taylor, a Harvard Law School graduate who later became a professor of law at Columbia University and Cardozo Law School, put it more succinctly: "Law is not a one-way street."

These guiding juridical principles of our nation, which earned worldwide respect for our country, are being tested today. When, in his courageous book *George W. Bush, War Criminal?*, Professor Dr. Michael Haas dares to challenge the legality of many deeds by the current Bush administration, he is acting in the finest traditions of our democratic nation. His book deserves respectful and careful consideration.

The compendium of 269 war crimes attributed to the Bush administration is impressive. Dr. Haas acknowledges that the factual and legal arguments he has meticulously assembled are derived from other published materials. Indeed, the publication of the secret "Downing Street Memo" in the *Sunday Times* of London on July 23, 2003, blew the whistle that the Bush administration had already decided to invade Iraq and was engaged in a campaign of public deception to gain support for the war. The UN Charter, which legally binds all nations, prohibits the use of armed force except in very limited conditions of self-defense, which were inapplicable. Without UN Security Council authorization, a good argument could be made that the U.S. invasion of Iraq was unlawful.

In addition to the crimes of aggression, which the International Military Tribunal at Nuremberg and Justice Jackson described as "the supreme international crime," Haas identifies a host of specific crimes committed in the conduct of war, as well as the illegal mistreatment of prisoners and failure to hold accountable those who violated standards designed to protect military personnel of all nations. Several appendices outline and list sources for each of the crimes attributable to various members of the Bush administration.

It is the declared goal of the author, writing as a scholar, to draw attention to the enormity of injustices and illegalities that must be addressed before America's tarnished reputation in the world can be restored. It must be recalled that a fundamental tenet of our system of justice under law is to insist that all accused are presumed innocent and no one can be convicted of crime without proof of guilt beyond reasonable doubt. Certainly these rights belong to the president of the United States and those who serve him. However, there is also an obligation on the part of the president in a democracy to make all of the relevant facts available to the public. The Bush administration has thus far failed to do so. Haas suggests that Congress appoint a "truth commission": to ascertain the sworn and verified truth. Until that is done, it will be unavoidable that suspicions will remain and that criminal allegations and civil lawsuits against the suspected parties will inevitably continue.

Our nation must reassert its traditional respect for the rule of law, as articulated at Nuremberg, to regain its stature as a moral leader in the world. The reputation of the United States has been soiled by its staunch opposition to the International Criminal Court and to allowing any international or foreign tribunal to try American nationals for aggression or any other war crimes. In June 2008, Congressman Dennis Kucinich of Ohio introduced a comprehensive House Resolution to impeach President George W. Bush. This book by Professor Haas provides additional information and moves in the right direction. It will be up to the public to demand that the elected leaders comply with the existing laws and the great American traditions that Professor Haas, Congressman Kucinich, and many other patriotic Americans seek to uphold.

Benjamin B. Ferencz, J.D.
Harvard Law School, 1943
Nuremberg Military Tribunals
"The *Einsatzgruppen* Case"
New Rochelle, New York
www.benferencz.org

PREFACE

While I was writing the chapter on war crimes for my *International Human Rights: A Comprehensive Introduction* (2008), I reviewed the texts of the Hague and Geneva Conventions and many other international agreements. What astonished me most were the war crimes that were then being committed by the United States around the world in the aftermath of the attack on the World Trade Center and the Pentagon on 9/11. Although news reports focused mostly on mistreatment of prisoners, I became curious about how many provisions in the various international legal documents were also being violated with impunity. The result of my research is the present volume.

As a political scientist, not a lawyer, I interpret the legal agreements as a delineation of specific war crimes. I have sought to identify each offense from a careful reading of the texts, while wording each war crime in a manner that would be intelligible for the ordinary reader. I have done little investigative research but instead have mined existing writing on the subject by eyewitnesses, government officials, journalists, lawyers, and other observers. I have engaged in what is literally known as "research"—that is, I have looked back at what has been recorded in order to sort firsthand and secondhand statements into a comprehensive listing of war crimes.

When I first drafted the title for chapter 1, I knew that almost the entire top rank of lawyers in the Department of Justice, including one-time Attorney General Ashcroft, had at one time threatened to resign over legal shenanigans being concocted at the White House. I was then unaware of a comment made in 2004 by James Comey, Deputy Director of the Department of Justice's Office of Legal Counsel, about a memo by John Yoo, Comey's predecessor, at the White House. In the presence of David Addington, Chief of Staff to Vice President Dick Cheney, according to a *New York Times* article by Scott Shane, David Johnson, and James Risen, Comey confidently asserted that "no lawyer" would ever endorse Yoo's analysis. In response to Addington's riposte—that he was a lawyer, and he found the analysis convincing—Comey is supposed to have blurted out, "No *good* lawyer." Clearly, we were thinking along similar lines.

Likewise, I was the first to propose a truth commission to sort out the war crimes of the Bush administration. A few weeks after circulating a draft of my book in New York and Washington, a well-respected journalist proposed such a body in print.

The present volume offers little new factual information, preferring instead to link information gathered by others to specific crimes derived from legal texts. Although some journalists and writers make that connection, most do not. The result is that readers around the world view barbarous events in emotional and moral terms but do not fully understand the juridical and political implications. For today the globe is being transformed into an unchecked superpower playpen where might appears to make right. Hundreds of years of human rights progress are in serious jeopardy as long as governmental war criminals live blissfully in the knowledge that they will never be accountable for their crimes. Insofar as decision makers feel free to violate well-established norms of proper conduct, terrorists have been emboldened and have easily attracted volunteers. The surreal symbiosis between war criminals in Washington and terrorists around the world makes everyone less secure.

One value of an encyclopedic enumeration of war crimes and relevant evidence is to present an informal codification of war crimes so that readers will realize the legal significance of daily reports in the press. Ideally, journalists will sharpen their reporting of incidents when they know whether what is happening may be a war crime. The more the public observes reference in the news to possible war crimes violations, the more decision makers will be accountable. Otherwise, the impunity of high Bush administration officials for the immense violations documented in the pages below threatens to turn back the clock on human progress by shredding the Magna Carta, the American Constitution, the Universal Declaration of Human Rights, the Hague and

Geneva Conventions, and similar agreements that have advanced humanity from barbarism toward civilized behavior.

The Sources section contains abbreviated citations for each war crime. Full citations appear in the References section, which also lists sources for statements in the narratives outside the discussion of specific war crimes. Nevertheless, keyword Internet search engines can locate the various references much faster than old-fashioned footnote hunting. Because some citations for war crimes may perhaps contain questionable information, I provide corroborated references so that the thesis of the volume—that war crimes have been amply documented—will be thickly rather than thinly supported. Those who may object that I have cherrypicked evidence should reflect that prosecutions of criminals do just that. Nevertheless, I welcome criticism and challenge detractors to consider all the independently collected evidence.

The task of assembling a compendium of war crimes of the Bush administration has been daunting and demanding. Accordingly, I have asked for assistance along the way. I am particularly grateful to e-mail responses to queries from fellow political scientist Eric Herring, law professor Herbert Margulies, Reprieve attorney Clive Stafford Smith, and journalist Carol Williams. In presenting papers based on some of the chapters at various academic conferences, I have benefited from the feedback. Robert Hutchinson, Praeger's senior acquisitions editor, deserves particular credit for backing me throughout the final months of the project. Indefatigable literary agent Charlotte Gusay, in addition to supplying many marketing ideas and support for the project, provided a timely Internet article. My longtime friend Geoffrey Commons, an attorney, has also assisted by assuring me that my opinions and statements are "not even close to being causes for potential legal action." I invite controversy and disagreement, and I certainly have no intention to impugn the integrity or reputation of those whose sincere actions and beliefs I question.

Because I felt that the completed publication should be available before George W. Bush leaves office, I quit my position as a college instructor to devote full time to the project at my Hollywood Hills home. I now await considered responses.

Michael Haas
Los Angeles, California
www.USwarcrimes.com

Part I

INTRODUCTION

A specter is haunting the world—the specter of war crimes. Civilized people of the world agree on the need to exorcise this specter, including the Pope and UN Secretary-General, conservative FBI agents and ultra-liberal democrats, French radicals and German Jewish Nazi survivors. And many others.

Where are those in opposition to war crimes who have been decried as "soft on terrorism" by their opponents in power? Where is the opposition that has hurled back the branding reproach of "war criminals"?

Two things result from these facts:

1. War crimes are already acknowledged by civilized peoples to have been committed by George W. Bush and his fellow conspirators on behalf of the United States.

2. It is high time that those who believe that war crimes should be prosecuted must openly, in the face of the whole world, publish their evidence and meet this specter of war crimes with a thorough indictment of all the offenses that have been committed so that those responsible can be brought to justice.

To this end, good people of many nationalities call out for action. They do so in a manner far more openly than when similar words appeared 160 years ago on behalf of an ideology that has been long since discredited. And now, in the pages below, the evidence of 269 war crimes will be presented.

Chapter 1

A PRESIDENT WITHOUT
A GOOD LAWYER

The attacks on September 11, 2001, were monstrous, unprovoked crimes, clearly violating domestic and international law because of the indiscriminate use of violence against innocent civilians. Congress and the President felt vulnerable, believing that additional attack waves might be imminent. When Bush asked Congress to grant him almost unlimited emergency powers, the Senate rejected his proposal on September 14. Instead, Congress adopted the USA Patriot Act on October 25, and the president signed the law on October 26.

Meanwhile, rather than negotiating with Congress for more latitude, Bush swallowed the conclusion in a secret Justice Department memo dated September 25 that he had the authority to take "any means necessary, anywhere, against any enemy as long as the [country] was at war." Advised that Congress could do nothing to impede the president in wartime, Bush then proceeded to take action that might later be judged as illegal. His advisers felt that in time of war the need to provide national security trumped constitutional, legal, and international restrictions on presidential conduct. Thus, the Bush presidency may be viewed as a watershed in which the White House attempted to reinvent the Constitution in order to eliminate the checks and balances so carefully crafted by James Madison and others in Philadelphia during 1787.

Soon the United States attacked Afghanistan and Iraq, thousands of suspected terrorists were arrested around the world, and American residents at home were under a wide dragnet of surveillance. In the process, the Bush administration unnecessarily violated American statutes and international requirements in treaties that establish the law of warfare.

THE SUPREME COURT RULES: A WAR CRIME
HAS BEEN COMMITTED

Vice President Dick Cheney, Defense Secretary Donald Rumsfeld, and others in the Bush administration believed that international law placed unrealistic restrictions on the need for the United States to defend itself. On September 11, 2001, Bush is quoted by former head of the National Security Counter-Terrorism Group Richard Clarke as saying, "I don't care what the international lawyers say. We are going to kick some ass."

On January 25, 2002, as prisoners were being sent from Afghanistan to Guantánamo, Counsel to the President Alberto Gonzales issued a memorandum agreeing with Justice Department officials that the Geneva Conventions were "quaint" and "outmoded," and therefore inapplicable to suspected terrorists being collected and imprisoned by the United States. In the opinion of Jack Goldsmith, who later headed the Justice Department's Office of Legal Counsel, the January 25 memo constituted a "conspiracy to commit a war crime."

Bush's first defeats in the Supreme Court came in 2004. In *Rasul v Bush* and *Hamdi v Rumsfeld*, the court ruled that those held in an American prison, including Guantánamo, had the right to contest their detentions by filing a writ of habeas corpus. Shafiq Rasul was a British citizen, Yaser Hamdi an American. Only one justice sided with Bush in both cases. Justice Sandra Day O'Connor, in the majority opinion in *Hamdi*, declared that a "state of war is not a blank check for the President."

In 2006, the Supreme Court of the United States ruled in *Hamdan v Rumsfeld* that Donald Rumsfeld, then Secretary of Defense, had violated Article 3 of all four Geneva Conventions of 1949. The offense was refusing to allow a prisoner under the custody of the U.S. military to be tried in a regularly constituted court. In so doing, the justices by implication identified George W. Bush—the author of the executive order of November 13, 2001, which established the unconstitutional court—as a potential war criminal. The court also reminded Bush that he did not have a "blank check" from Congress.

Neither Bush nor Rumsfeld was on trial in either case, since the role of the Supreme Court was, as usual, to clarify principles to be applied at the trial court level. However, anyone cited by the Supreme Court for violating a provision of the Geneva Conventions might subsequently be sued as a war criminal. Indeed, as documented later in this volume,

269 war crimes were committed during the era of the Bush administration. Many bear Bush's personal fingerprints.

Under American and international law, heads of government cannot be hauled into court for criminal offenses while in office. When they leave office, however, they can be prosecuted.

January 20, 2009, is the last day of Bush's presidency. Among his legacies is the fact that the United States lost world leadership on human rights. One reason is the widely publicized abuses committed at Abu Ghraib and Guantánamo. From that day in January, lawsuits can be filed against Bush. In fact, several plaintiffs sued Bush and Rumsfeld before that date.

BUSH'S LEGAL ADVICE

George W. Bush does not have a law degree, so he relied on legal advice. When legal opinions differed, he counted on his own judgment. Bush is fully aware that he and others in his administration may have committed one or more war crimes. Bush could have had the best possible legal advice in the world. As president, he was in a position to hire the cream of the crop. However, presidents who value loyalty over competence avoid employing persons with independent judgment. Those who dissented from the White House consensus were marginalized from the decision-making process.

Among his legal advisers (Table 1.1), Alberto Gonzales and Harriet Miers had no previous experience with international law. John Ashcroft and James Comey quit after their legal opinions were not accepted. Colin Powell also resigned, having been repeatedly ignored about the need to affirm the Geneva Conventions. Jack Goldsmith, who withdrew legal opinions written by Jay Bybee and John Yoo for conflating common law with international law in badly crafted memos, also quit when he realized that his advice was unwelcome in the White House. Coalition Provisional Authority administrator for Iraq, J. Paul Bremer III, accepted Douglas Feith's legal opinion in firing hundreds of thousands of Iraqis, thereby providing many with a motive for joining the insurgency. Michael Mukasey, Bush's last Attorney General, engaged in sophistry before Congress in trying to avoid admitting that Bush had broken the law when he authorized torture.

In 2004, perceptive journalist Anthony Lewis characterized Bush's legal advice as similar to that of a "mob lawyer to a mafia don on how to skirt the law and stay out of prison." According to international

Table 1.1
Bush's Lawyers and Advisers

Name	Position During Critical Years of the Bush Administration
David S. Addington	Legal Counsel to the Vice President, 2001–2005; Chief of Staff to the Vice President, 2005–2009
John D. Ashcroft	Attorney General, 2001–2005
Diane E. Beaver	Lieutenant Colonel and Staff Judge Advocate, Guantánamo Naval Base, 2002–2003
J. Paul Bremer III	Coalition Provisional Authority Administrator, 2003–2004
Jay S. Bybee	Assistant Attorney General, 2001–2003
Richard B. Cheney	Vice President, 2001–2009
James B. Comey	Deputy Attorney General, 2004–2005
Lieutenant General Bantz J. Craddock	Commander, U.S. Southern Command, 2004–2006
Robert J. Delahunty	Special Counsel, Office of Legal Counsel, Department of Justice, 2001–2004
Daniel J. Dell'Orto	Principal Deputy General Counsel, Department of Defense, 2000–2009
Major General Michael E. Dunlavey	Commander, Joint Task Force, Guantánamo, 2002
Douglas J. Feith	Undersecretary of Defense for Policy, 2001–2005
Timothy E. Flanigan	Deputy Counsel to the President, 2001–2002
Jack Goldsmith	Director, Office of Legal Counsel, Department of Justice, 2003–2004
Alberto R. Gonzales	Counsel to the President, 2001–2005; Attorney General, 2005–2007
William J. Haynes II	General Counsel, Department of Defense, 2001–2008
General James T. Hill	Commander, Southern Command, 2002–2004
Harriet E. Miers	White House Counsel, 2005-2007
Major General Geoffrey D. Miller	Commander, Joint Task Force, Guantánamo, 2002–2003; Deputy Commanding General for Detainee Operations for Multinational Forces in Iraq, 2003–2004
Michael B. Mukasey	Attorney General, 2007–2009
General Richard B. Myers	Chairman, Joint Chiefs of Staff, 2001–2005
Lieutenant Colonel Jerald Phifer	Director, J2, Department of Defense, Joint Task Force, Guantánamo, 2002–2003

(*continued*)

Table 1.1 (*continued*)

Name	Position During Critical Years of the Bush Administration
Patrick J. Philbin	Deputy Assistant Attorney General, 2003–2005
General Colin L. Powell	Secretary of State, 2001–2005
Condoleezza Rice	National Security Adviser, 2001–2005; Secretary of State, 2005–2009
Donald H. Rumsfeld	Secretary of Defense, 2001–2006
George J. Tenet	Director, Central Intelligence Agency, 1997–2004
Paul D. Wolfowitz	Deputy Secretary of Defense, 2001–2005
John C. Yoo	Deputy Assistant Attorney General, 2001–2003

lawyer Philippe Sands, the conspiracy among some of Bush's lawyers calls to mind the clique of judges whose legal opinions were cited to convict them of war crimes at the Nuremberg War Crimes Trials in 1948, a trial that inspired the film *Judgment at Nuremberg* (1961).

In the panic after 9/11, Bush and his entourage received considerable public support in the quest to prevent further terrorist attacks. Although the sense of hysteria dissipated in time, the Department of Homeland Security nevertheless tried to hype the sense of danger by changing various color codes, the latter a feature familiar to viewers of the zany television series *Get Smart*. Some fantastic plots, we now know, were fabricated by suspected terrorist leaders who were being tortured and wanted the cruelty to end.

In any case, Congress and the public expected that President Bush would exercise careful judgment in following the Constitution and the law, despite the sui generis situation of a country under potential catastrophic attack from unknown persons. Americans wanted to prevent future terrorist attacks while their government preserved a long tradition as the foremost advocate of human rights. Americans expected a judicious balance between liberty and security.

Today, nearly a decade later, the threat of terrorism seems much less imminent. Bush's violations of the Constitution as well as domestic and international law have besmirched the reputation of the United States. In so doing, they have accomplished a goal of which the al-Qaeda terrorists only dreamed—to transform the United States into a rogue nation feared by the rest of the world and loved by almost none.

THE BUSH DOCTRINE

"History begins today," said George Bush on September 12, 2001, perhaps imagining that his role resembled those in Paris who declared that the first year of the French Revolution was Year One. He was perhaps unaware that he was also aping the proclamation of the genocidal Khmer Rouge in Cambodia that its first year of rule was Year Zero.

Based on bad legal advice, Bush launched a comprehensive reinterpretation of American international policies. At the domestic level, Bush ignored the Declaration of Independence, the Constitution, and American domestic laws.

As carefully prepared by Thomas Jefferson, a major portion of the Declaration of Independence attacked King George III for unjust decisions, yet George W. Bush reenacted some of those very grievances: In particular, President Bush authorized mistreatment of aliens on American soil, established military commissions without Congressional approval, dispatched "swarms of officers" (in the words of the Declaration) to harass American residents, made the military supreme over civilian methods of dealing with terrorism, deprived detainees of trial by jury, engaged in extraordinary rendition, ignored American law and Congress, hired mercenaries for military roles, and otherwise refused to address grievances based on the rule of law. For many Americans, Bush betrayed the principles of the American Revolution. For others, he was fighting valiantly to defend the country.

At the international level, before 9/11 Bush had already embarked on a unilateralist withdrawal from interest in several international treaties and disregarded international law, which the United States had sponsored for more than two centuries. The "new paradigm," known as the "war on terror," was to be fought with new rules, which are collectively known as the Bush Doctrine (Table 1.2).

The formulation of the Bush Doctrine began with the initial view that the 9/11 attack was an "act of war" to which the appropriate response was to take preemptive action, including war against Afghanistan and later Iraq. Over time, the Bush Doctrine developed more complexity. Bush soon claimed that he could identify anyone as an "enemy," that his designation would be conclusive, and that no court had authority to review his decision. Accordingly, questionable executive orders and legal opinions were issued to authorize torture of Americans as well as foreigners (Appendix 1.1). Bush gave such wide

Table 1.2
The Bush Doctrine and Successful Court Challenges

Elements of the Bush Doctrine	Successful Court Challenges
Countries allowing terrorist organizations on their soil may be attacked.	
Hostile countries with weapons of mass destruction may be attacked preemptively.	
Bold, unilateral action deters terrorism.	
The United States must refuse to talk to countries that follow "bad policies."	
Democracy must be exported abroad.	
The United States must ignore international bodies that respond slowly to emerging threats.	
Important presidential decisions may be kept secret.	
The president has the right to violate previous executive orders.	
The president does not have to disclose any violation of executive orders or laws.	
The president may ignore provisions in congressional laws by issuing signing statements that qualify their applicability or meaning.	
The president has "blank check" authority to determine what his powers are in wartime and cannot be questioned by Congress or the courts on his actions.	*Hamdi v Rumsfeld* (2004); *Hamdan v Rumsfeld* (2006)
The president's legal opinions must guide all members of the executive branch.	
Department of Justice legal opinions exonerate presidents from prosecution.	
The president has the authority to arrest anyone in the world and torture them for information, even American citizens.	
The president can authorize the assassination of any suspected terrorist.	
Executive conversations and documents do not have to be disclosed to Congress.	*Judiciary Committee v Miers (2008)*
The United States may extend unlimited communication surveillance over the entire world, including domestically.	

(continued)

Table 1.2 (*continued*)

Elements of the Bush Doctrine	Successful Court Challenges
Terrorist suspects abroad are "unlawful enemy combatants," unprotected by the Geneva Conventions.	*Hamdan v Rumsfeld* (2006)
Alien terrorist suspects may be abducted and flown to secret prisons for torture.	
Aliens have few, if any, rights in American courts.	*Zadvydas v Davis* (2001)
Alien terrorist suspects may be held indefinitely until the "war on terror" ends.	*Rasul v Bush* (2004)
Alien terrorist suspects lack the right of writ of habeas corpus.	*Rasul v Bush* (2004); *Boumediene v Bush* (2008)
Alien terrorist suspects lack the right of counsel.	*Hamdi v Rumsfeld* (2004)
Lawyers for foreign detainees may be denied private conversations with clients.	*Bismullah v Gates* (2007)
Terrorist suspects may be confined secretly.	*Associated Press v Dept. of Defense* (2006)
Terrorist suspects may be confined indefinitely.	*Hamdi v Rumsfeld* (2004)
Terrorist suspects may be tried in secret.	*Hamdan v Rumsfeld* (2006)
Terrorist suspects may be tried with evidence based on hearsay.	
Terrorist suspects may be tried with evidence extracted from torture.	*In re Guantánamo Detainees* (2005)
Terrorist suspects enjoy no attorney-client privileges.	*Al-Odah v U.S.* (2004)
To gain release, a prisoner must first sign a statement indicating satisfaction with the treatment during confinement.	
The state secrets doctrine bars judges from receiving evidence that might either convict or exonerate defendants.	*Associated Press v Dept. of Defense* (2006)
Resident aliens can be deported from the United States without a hearing, even for minor offenses or casual associations.	*El-Maghraby v Ashcroft* (2005); *Lopez v Gonzales* (2007)

(*continued*)

Table 1.2 (*continued*)

Elements of the Bush Doctrine	Successful Court Challenges
Nonresident aliens have no rights under American law.	*Rasul v Bush* (2004)
E-mailing a website of a suspected "terrorist group" is illegal.	*Al-Hussayen v U.S.* (2004)
Facilitating the receipt of cable TV channels operated by terrorist groups is illegal.	
Organizations may be designated "terrorist groups" without administrative or legal challenge.	*Humanitarian Law Project v Dept. of the Treasury* (2006)
Assets of "terrorist groups" may be confiscated without administrative or legal challenge.	*Humanitarian Law Project v Dept. of the Treasury* (2006)
Assets of persons alleged to support terrorism may be confiscated without administrative or legal challenge.	*Humanitarian Law Project v Dept. of the Treasury* (2006)
The military may arrest its own citizens abroad, torture them, and either detain them indefinitely in an American-run prison or turn them over to a foreign court.	
The government can conduct searches for records without a warrant.	
The government can demand American agencies, organizations, and residents to surrender records without a warrant or benefit of legal advice.	*Doe v Gonzales* (2005)

latitude to subordinates that presidential authorization in many cases may be considered to have been pre-approved for those who acted on his behalf.

The concept of the "war on terror" was itself an odd neologism, as war is ordinarily considered to be armed aggression between opposing militarized forces. Accordingly, the term appears in quotation marks throughout the following pages.

The Bush Doctrine, insofar as it was at variance with established domestic and international law, was soon challenged in court. In some cases, Bush prevailed. In June 2006, the Supreme Court's ruling in *Hamdan v Rumsfeld* came as a shock, telling Bush that he had authorized war crimes.

On September 6, 2006, President Bush expressed such concern that he and other administration officials were guilty of war crimes that he asked Congress to amend the War Crimes Act of 1996 in order to decriminalize certain acts, even retroactively. Among the war crimes that he thereby implicitly admitted authorizing in the past were disappearances, extrajudicial imprisonment, torture, transporting prisoners between countries, and denying the International Committee of the Red Cross access to prisoners. Foolishly, he asked Congress to change the law in order to exempt members of the military from prosecution, but they were already subject to possible courts-martial and were never covered by the War Crimes Act in the first place.

On the same day, Bush ordered that fourteen persons detained in secret prisons be flown to Guantánamo for trial. He thereby admitted that he had been supporting American gulags overseas. On July 20, 2007, Bush also backtracked on treatment of prisoners in an executive order that banned sexual abuse and required conformity with many Geneva Convention standards at Guantánamo.

Bush thus was fully aware that international law imposed constraints which, if exceeded, might result in his prosecution. He felt that the American people wanted a commander-in-chief who would place protection from another 9/11 attack as a higher goal than conformity to what his advisers perceived as a minefield of vague domestic and international legal restrictions. His lawyers exploited what they thought were gray areas in the law, and Bush took the regal approach in believing that he had considerable latitude to do whatever he felt necessary.

As a result, President Bush was unable to give clear direction to subordinates in order to avoid war crimes. Warlords in Afghanistan rounded up hundreds of persons on the flimsiest of evidence, and American military personnel placed them in various prisons for an indefinite period and even abused them. Lieutenant General Raymond Odierno reportedly sanctioned middle-of-the-night roundups of hundreds of innocent Iraqis with marginal justification and had them sent to Abu Ghraib. Bush dispatched J. Paul Bremer III to head the Coalition Provisional Authority in Baghdad without any legal basis—neither an executive order nor an act of Congress—and Bremer then proceeded to brush aside Geneva Convention requirements governing the postwar occupation of Iraq.

Bush indicated the desirability of closing Guantánamo after the world learned that his subordinates mistreated prisoners, but he never followed through. A half dozen military attorneys resigned rather than continuing their roles in what they perceived as Guantánamo's "kangaroo court," as Bush had already pronounced the prisoners guilty before a trial and his judgment was heard down the chain of command.

There is considerable evidence to suggest that Bush's culpability for war crimes was intentional. Although several military personnel have been disciplined for misconduct, some observers believe that those accused thus far were merely scapegoats so that the misconduct of senior officials would not be investigated. In some cases, military personnel have received light sentences, albeit appropriately, but skeptics interpret lax accountability to mean tacit approval of their offenses from much higher up the civilian and military hierarchy.

OUTLINE OF THE BOOK

The purpose of this volume is to ascertain whether George W. Bush and members of his administration could be charged and convicted as war criminals. Accordingly, the four chapters in Part II delineate 269 war crimes, citing documentary sources. The two chapters in Part III indicate which tribunals might place those accused on trial, who might be tried, and whether war crimes trials are desirable.

Part II

IDENTIFICATION OF WAR CRIMES

There are four basic war crimes, as I define them. They focus on: (1) the legality of war, (2) the conduct of war, (3) treatment of prisoners, and (4) the conduct of the postwar occupation. I have merged "crimes against humanity" and "crimes against peace" into the single concept of "war crimes." Several international agreements govern each category of war crimes. Within each category, there are many specific offenses.

During 2001, the terrorist group al-Qaeda clearly violated international norms by first plotting and then, on September 11, carrying out indiscriminate attacks on innocent persons. Many of the plotters have been arrested though not yet convicted of war crimes and remain accountable for their actions, as they should be within a legal framework that has developed for more than a century.

George W. Bush, as commander-in-chief, launched two wars. Judged by the same standards, he is accountable for the wars that he commanded in Afghanistan and Iraq and related actions inside and outside both countries. Although previous studies have decried war crimes of earlier American administrations, what is different here are the crimes committed in mistreating thousands of prisoners and in occupying two countries.

In the next four chapters, all four types of war crimes that may be attributed to Bush, directly or indirectly, are identified with reference to various agreements. There could be several counts for each crime; that is, separate incidents relevant to each category. Nevertheless, the enumeration herein is of types of crimes rather than a count based on incidents.

For example, waging aggression in Afghanistan and Iraq constitutes a single war crime rather than being counted separately as two war crimes. Whereas 269 war crimes are identified in the next four chapters, the count would be much higher if perpetrators of each specific incident were cited as distinct war criminals. Millions of victims of the crimes may nevertheless come forward to seek justice based on what George W. Bush and his subordinates have brazenly done to violate the international law of warfare.

Evidence for each specific war crime, as identified in the following four chapters and cited in the appended Sources, comes from several books, court cases, monographs, newspaper accounts, and photographs. The References section has full citations, occasionally annotated.

Chapter 2

CRIMES OF AGGRESSION

George W. Bush begins Cabinet and other meetings with prayer, asking for divine guidance and support. One might therefore expect that he would listen to Judaeo-Christian teachings relevant to matters of foreign policy, which include the Mosaic prohibition "Thou shalt not kill!" After Moses, Bush should know, theologians have critiqued various justifications for war to develop the doctrine of "just war."

THE CONCEPT OF "JUST WAR"

According to fifth-century theologian St. Augustine, "A just war... avenges wrongs, when a nation or state has to be punished, for refusing to make amends for the wrongs inflicted by its subjects, or to restore what it has seized unjustly." When the objective of a war is to punish on a false pretext, the war is unjust according to St. Augustine.

Thirteenth-century Christian philosopher Thomas Aquinas derived four principles from Augustine's doctrine, and seventeenth-century legal philosopher Hugo Grotius further developed a set of criteria for evaluating whether war could be justly waged (Table 2.1). Their ideas inform debates on whether the reasons for the wars in Afghanistan and Iraq were just.

INTERNATIONAL LAW OF WARFARE

"Just war" notions of Augustine, Aquinas, and Grotius first began to be encoded into international law in 1648, when the Thirty Years' War ended in two treaties known as the Peace of Westphalia. Since wars that had engulfed Europe from 1618 to 1648 were principally fought

Table 2.1
Principles of Just War Theory

Theorist	Principle	Explication
Thomas Aquinas (1225–1274)	Just authority	Only rulers have the power to start a war, since they are required to maintain order. Private warfare is outlawed.
	Just cause or rightful intention	There is a right to stop gross evil and to promote good.
	Military necessity	The use of force should be a response to an aggressor, whose actions are certain, grave, and lasting.
	Last resort	Efforts to resolve a conflict must exhaust all peaceful means before contemplating war.
Hugo Grotius (1583–1645)	Defense	Wars are just when they defend the national interest.
	Indemnity	Wars are just if they recover damages inflicted by another state.
	Punishment	Wars are just if they stop a gross, ongoing injustice.
	Last resort	Wars are just only if peaceful methods fail to resolve an interstate conflict based on the preceding three pretexts.

between rulers who tried to impose Catholic or Protestant state churches on their populations, the Peace of Westphalia outlawed war waged on the basis of how a ruler governed his or her subjects. Today, however, we live in a post-Westphalian world in which the world community might approve a war to stop ongoing genocide.

A more ordinary prohibition came in 1814, when a treaty was drawn up after the end of the Napoleonic Wars. Leaders of Britain, France, Prussia, and Russia agreed in the Final Act of the Congress of Vienna that France improperly violated the Treaty of Tilsit of 1807, which guaranteed peace with Russia, when Napoléon's troops marched into Russia in 1812. In other words, international law disallows war in violation of a treaty.

In 1899, during the administration of President William McKinley, the first of several treaties adopted at the International Peace Conference at The Hague established the option of having international conflicts between two countries resolved peacefully through the intervention of third parties, but without any mandatory requirement. President Theodore Roosevelt was particularly active in having the Hague conference reconvene in 1907, when the 1899 treaty was strengthened by having countries agree in principle to accept third-party intervention.

Aggressive war was first declared to be illegal in the General Act for the Renunciation of War, a multilateral treaty negotiated in 1928 by American Secretary of State Frank Kellogg and French Foreign Minister Aristide Briand during the administration of President Calvin Coolidge. Aggression was also outlawed in the United Nations Charter in 1945 as well as in the charters governing war crimes trials at Nuremberg in 1945 and Tokyo in 1946 while Harry Truman was president. The International Criminal Court was established in 1998, while Bill Clinton was president, as a permanent war crimes tribunal (Appendix 2.1).

RIGHT OF REPRISAL AND RIGHT OF SELF-DEFENSE

International law allows a right of reprisal and a right of self-defense. After the wanton attacks on 9/11, which may qualify as war crimes, both measures were contemplated.

For *self-defense* to be justified, however, a state must obtain permission from the United Nations Security Council. The permission must be explicit, not implicit, and only when an attack is demonstrably imminent, leaving no time for negotiations.

For a *reprisal* to be lawful, the injured state must first give notice of displeasure and request compensation or cessation of ongoing harmful action. When the hostile party makes no response, an act of redress is acceptable, provided that the response is proportionate to the injury suffered.

Since President Bush did not consider bombing empty al-Qaeda training camps in Afghanistan to be a proportionate reprisal, he wanted stronger action. He declared the existence of the "war on terror." But the 9/11 attack did not involve an invasion force or ground troops, and the attack did not immediately emanate from a military base that could be bombed. Instead, the 9/11 attack was an isolated incident within a larger game plan, not the first wave in a series of attacks. The Bush administration, nevertheless, was fearful of future aggression by unknown persons in unexpected locations. The degree of hysteria was most visible in the appearance of David Addington, Cheney's Chief of Staff, before Congress in mid-2008, when he was clearly unable to countenance any alternative to allowing the end to justify the illegal means.

Those who flew into the World Trade Center towers and the Pentagon committed criminal acts that could have been prosecuted in civilian courts, but they were dead. Although most of the 9/11 conspirators never entered the United States, Zacarias Moussaoui was arrested in Minnesota on August 16, 2001, for immigration violations and indicted on December 11, 2001, for a role in the 9/11 plot. Convicted in a federal criminal court, he was sentenced to life in prison. He is the only foreigner thus far to face judgment in a federal court for an offense related to 9/11, though other foreigners (Uzair Paracha and Richard Reid, for example) have been convicted of terror-related offenses. One might, therefore, ask why those arrested in the "war on terror" outside the United States were not processed for violations of federal crimes?

The Federal Bureau of Investigation (FBI), having been blamed for not preventing the attacks, was assigned a lesser role and has arrested very few suspected terrorists in the United States. Instead, the military option advanced by the Department of Defense (DOD) and the Central Intelligence Agency (CIA) prevailed when Bush considered the 9/11 attacks to be salvos in his "war on terror" and asked the military to respond.

On September 17, 2001, George W. Bush claimed the right to have the CIA arrest anyone in the world, deposit them in a secret prison, and torture them on his personal order as long as he wanted, just on suspicion that the person was a member of an Islamic terrorist organization, not just al-Qaeda. The claim is in a secret directive that was later exposed by Human Rights Watch.

Even in 2008, a Senate report indicated that Bush had filled only two of twenty-four critically needed FBI senior intelligence officer positions authorized by Congress, and the FBI reported vacancies in one-third of its counterterrorism positions. Many FBI agents originally assigned to work alongside the CIA and DOD intelligence agents objected to the CIA interrogation methods, which involved torture. FBI officials then withdrew from their assignments.

Instead of a criminal justice approach, which might focus on trying terrorists, Bush placed a military template over the tragic events and declared the 9/11 attack to be an "act of war." One reason may be that Osama Bin Laden had been quoted as having declared war on the United States in 1996, followed up by various violent incidents on American property overseas—notably, on U.S. embassies in two African countries during 1998 and on the U.S.S. *Cole* during the year 2000.

However, those who planted a car bomb in the basement of the World Trade Center during 1993 were tried and found guilty in federal court. In 2003, Spanish judge Baltazar Garzón indicted three 9/11 accomplices along with thirty-two other al-Qaeda operatives, including Osama bin Laden. In 2005, when most were convicted of terrorist offenses in a Spanish court, the prosecutor told the press that the proceedings proved the superiority of the legal approach to "wars and detention camps," obviously commenting on Bush's military approach to the same terrorist threat. Indeed, a RAND Corporation study, based on terrorism cases over the years, concluded that militarization of counterterrorism is counterproductive.

In accordance with the criminal justice approach, Ahmad Ghailani was indicted in federal court for his role in the American embassy bombing in Tanzania during 1998. But after he was captured in Pakistan during 2004, he was sent to a secret prison to be tortured and then flown in 2006 to Guantánamo to be tried by a military commission rather than by the court in New York that had original jurisdiction.

Having taken a military approach, beyond the international law dealing with reprisal, Bush opened himself to the possibility that he would commit war crimes. In a press briefing on February 13, 2004, Deputy Assistant Secretary of Defense Paul Butler curiously opined that "the law of armed conflict governs what we're doing."

THE BASIC WAR CRIME: AGGRESSION

International law imposes definite restrictions on the use of military force. Accordingly, the discussion below identifies crimes under international law associated with the decisions to go to war in Afghanistan and in Iraq. Texts of relevant agreements are highlighted to provide the legal context. Sources of information are primarily from accounts by former White House Press Secretary Scott McClellan as well as journalists Tom Ricks, Ron Suskind, Bob Woodward, and many others.

Kellogg-Briand Pact, 1928, Art. I. The High Contracting Parties solemnly declare in the names of their respective peoples that they condemn recourse to war for the solution of international controversies, and renounce it, as an instrument of national policy in their relations with one another. **Art. II.** The High Contracting Parties agree that the settlement or solution of all disputes or conflicts of whatever nature or of whatever origin they may be, which may arise among them, shall never be sought except by pacific means.

War Crime #1. Waging Aggressive War. War with Afghanistan began on October 7, 2001. War with Iraq started on March 19, 2003. When Bush publicly contemplated war with Afghanistan, the Taliban authorities in Kabul reportedly offered to hand over Osama Bin Laden, the leader of al-Qaeda, for trial, since the foreign, Arabic-speaking al-Qaeda enjoyed little support among the Pushtu-speaking Taliban. Because the Taliban first required proof from Washington that Bin Laden was responsible for the 9/11 attacks, Bush deemed the response insufficient and considered the government in Kabul to be a "failed state" that lacked the power to cooperate with the American reprisal against al-Qaeda. Later, Saddam Hussein offered to resign his position and leave Iraq in exchange for a $1 billion payment, but Bush was unimpressed. The United States attacked both countries without adequately seeking an alternative or peaceful way to resolve differences. In the case of Afghanistan, the war came quickly after 9/11, and the UN was not given a proper role. As for Iraq, which had no connection with 9/11, the Security Council might have authorized a no-fly zone over the entire country, thereby grounding Saddam Hussein's aerial defenses against domestic efforts to topple his regime, but Bush was impatient.

In both cases, Bush claimed the right to engage in "preemptive war." His justification came from a memo written by Justice Department official John Yoo on September 25, 2001. Bush believed that the United States could lawfully launch a preemptive war against any hostile country in the world without UN approval. Yet some six decades earlier, the Nuremberg War Crimes Tribunal disapproved of Germany's attacks on Denmark and Norway, which the Nazi regime had argued were necessary to prevent the two countries from serving as Allied launching pads for invading Germany.

Neither Afghanistan nor Iraq attacked the United States, so neither war was based on self-defense. Preemptive war is not an accepted form of self-defense under international law.

Al-Qaeda, based in Afghanistan, planned the 9/11 attack on the United States. Because the ruling Taliban harbored al-Qaeda, Bush arrogated to himself the right to topple the entire Afghan government, despite the reported willingness of the Kabul government to hand over Osama Bin Laden.

A justification for the war in Iraq, the failure of Saddam Hussein to comply with UN resolutions over the years, evaporated when Bush decided not to ask the Security Council for approval to go to war on that or any other basis. Indeed, a German court in 2005 ruled that the Iraq War was illegal under international and German law. First Lieutenant Ehren Watada made the same claim in refusing to serve the United States in Iraq. Although a military court refused to accept his claim as a legitimate defense, his case ended when the judge declared a mistrial on procedural grounds.

Convention on Duties and Rights of States in the Event of Civil Strife, 1928, Art. 1. The Contracting States bind themselves to observe the following rules . . . To forbid the traffic in arms and war material, except when intended for the Government, while the belligerency of the rebels has not been recognized, in which latter case the rules of neutrality shall be applied.

War Crime #2. Aiding Rebels in a Civil War. American support for the Northern Alliance in Afghanistan was clearly aid to one side of a civil war. And millions were paid to persuade warlords in the south to attack the Taliban with Bush's specific approval.

Civil war in Iraq was a goal as early as 1998, during the presidency of Bill Clinton, and President George W. Bush agreed to continue funding rebel groups when he took office. Yet Bush did not sponsor Iraqi armed units to drive Saddam Hussein from power in 2003.

By 2004, civil war broke out between Shi'ite and Sunni groups in Iraq. Nevertheless, the American military was continuing to train and equip the Iraqi national army, then composed primarily of Kurds and Shi'ites, in order to fight Sunni insurgents.

In 2006, the United States secretly supported one faction in the civil war in Somalia on the basis of intelligence that the country harbored al-Qaeda members. Later, the United States approved an invasion of that country by Ethiopian troops.

In August 2007 and spring 2008, American helicopters targeted members of Muqtada al-Sadr's Mahdi Army, one of the major militias in the ongoing intrasectarian civil war in Iraq, thereby benefiting the Badr faction of Prime Minister Nuri al-Maliki. Nevertheless, the Iraqi army and police, which the United States had been training and arming, was infiltrated by members of the Mahdi Army, many of whom refused to participate in attacks on Sadr's militia. In May, Major General Kevin Bergner claimed that American attacks were targeted at criminals, not Sadrists, though al-Sadr had declared war on American troops in April, so Bergner's statement was not easy to accept.

In 2008, the United States was accused of backing the People's Mujahadin of Iran as a counterterrorist force. The Iraq government had branded the group, which was confined to Camp Ashraf by the American military, as terrorist and wanted to expel its members from the country. Once again, Washington backed one faction over another in Iraq.

Some of the above may rise to the level of war crimes. There has been no outcry against American actions because the opponents were not held in high repute.

UN Charter, 1945, Art. 2(4). All Members shall refrain in their international relations from the threat or use of force against the territorial integrity or political independence of any state, or in any other manner inconsistent with the Purposes of the United Nations. **Art. 39.** The Security Council shall determine the existence of any threat to the peace, breach of the peace, or act of aggression and shall make recommendations, or decide what measures shall be taken . . . to maintain or restore international peace and security. **Art. 51** Nothing in the present Charter shall impair the inherent right of individual or collective self-defense if an armed attack occurs against a Member of the United Nations, until the Security Council has taken measures necessary to maintain international peace and security. Measures taken by Members in the exercise of this right of self-defense shall be immediately reported to the Security Council and shall not in any way affect the authority and responsibility of the Security Council under the present Charter to take at any time such action as it deems necessary in order to maintain or restore international peace and security.

War Crime #3. Threatening Aggressive War. A long-standing principle of international law is that any country can undertake a reprisal against an individual hostile action, so the American bombing of a presumed al-Qaeda training camp in 1998 was doubtless an appropriate response to the embassy attacks in Africa earlier that year. Two full-scale wars is clearly an overreaction to 9/11.

No UN approval was granted for either war. On September 15, 2004, UN Secretary General Kofi Annan declared that the Iraq War, because in violation of the UN Charter, was illegal. Former President Jimmy Carter subsequently agreed with that judgment. Policy deliberations in the White House, according to journalist Bob Woodward's *Bush at War*, never mentioned international law, the UN Charter, or any of its provisions.

Although the General Act for the Renunciation of War of 1928 outlawed war itself, the UN Charter goes beyond by providing an institutional channel and a set of procedures for resolving conflicts peacefully. Article 51 of the Charter, for example, permits countries to engage in immediate self-defense in response to an ongoing armed attack before approaching the UN Security Council. Instead, the United States made demands on the rulers of Afghanistan and Iraq, threatening war if certain conditions were not met. The United States asked the Afghan government to close all terrorist training camps and to hand over every terrorist to "appropriate authorities." President Saddam Hussein was asked to resign and leave the country.

Neither Afghanistan nor Iraq posed imminent threats to the United States. Under the right of reprisal, the United States could have applied a measured response to the 9/11 attack. But a claim to prevent war by threatening war is contrary to the UN Charter when there is no imminent threat.

On January 29, 2002, in his State of the Union address, Bush claimed the right to make war on any country "while dangers gather"—that is, on any country deemed hostile to the United States. Since the United Nations did not authorize the war with Afghanistan or Iraq, Bush thereby became an international outlaw defying international law. His repeated references to military options in dealing with Iran also qualify as war crimes.

> **Nuremberg Charter, 1945.** Crimes against peace: namely, planning, preparation, initiation or waging of a war of aggression, or a war in violation of international treaties, agreements or assurances, or participation in a common plan or conspiracy for the accomplishment of any of the foregoing . . .

War Crime #4. Planning and Preparing for a War of Aggression. After 9/11, Defense Secretary Donald Rumsfeld said, referring to the Muslim world, "We have a choice—either to change the way we live, which is unacceptable, or to change the way that they live, and we chose the latter." Bush considered the attack on September 11, 2001, as a pretext for attacking Afghanistan. CIA operatives were inside the country before 9/11, and their numbers increased shortly afterward. One day after Bush issued an ultimatum to the Taliban government in Kabul, he talked to General Tommy Franks about war plans to invade Afghanistan.

According to former Treasury Secretary Paul O'Neill, preparations for war on Iraq had been undertaken at the first National Security Council meeting on January 30, 2001. Indeed, as a candidate for president, George W. Bush in May 1999 intimated that he was interested in invading Iraq if he became president. He requested an Iraq war plan from Rumsfeld on November 21, 2001. Bush first declared the "preemption doctrine" on September 12, 2002, whereby the United States would attack Iraq sooner to prevent an Iraqi attack later.

In the opinion of Senator Robert Byrd, war with Iraq was being considered "not as a last resort but as a first resort." Indeed, several Bush advisers immediately blamed the 9/11 attack on Saddam Hussein, lacking as they did an understanding of the existence of al-Qaeda. Privately, Bush decided on war with Iraq on January 13, 2003. The rush to war in Iraq without proper military planning was opposed by many military officers as "amateurish." Indeed, several military units were withdrawn from Afghanistan while al-Qaeda was still on the run and could have been cornered. The same units were redeployed to Iraq.

War Crime #5. Conspiracy to Wage War. Plotting among several persons to wage war constitutes conspiracy. Secretly shifting $700 million appropriated by Congress for the Afghan War to the forthcoming war in Iraq is more evidence of conspiracy.

Another way to define "conspiracy" is illegal action taken in concert with more than one country. The plot to invade Iraq was conceived by Britain and the United States. President George W. Bush and Prime Minister Tony Blair jointly planned the war by July 2002, according to notes in what has become known as the Downing Street Memo. London was prepared to join Washington in waging war on Iraq regardless of the outcome of international diplomacy in the United Nations.

Other countries were also involved. Troops entering Afghanistan came from Uzbekistan, and those marching into Iraq started from Kuwait. A dozen countries allowed American warplanes to enter their airspace, and American warships docked at the ports of Qatar and other countries. The air war was directed from Saudi Arabia. Turkey, however, refused access.

A later conspiracy dates from November 5, 2007, when President Bush promised Turkish Prime Minister Recep Tayyip Erdogan that the United States would assist Turkey in fighting Kurdish rebels inside Iraq. Then on December 1, on the basis of American intelligence, Turkish fighter jets bombed villages containing Kurdish rebels in northern Iraq. Another counterinsurgency bombing on December 16 was described by one reporter as "the largest known cross-border attack since the American invasion in 2003."

On December 17, 2007, despite a condemnation of the aerial campaign by the parliament in Baghdad, there was an incursion by some

300 Turkish ground forces. More attacks followed in the spring over the objections of the Iraqi government. They could only have been launched with the permission of the United States, which controlled Iraqi airspace and was the occupying military power. Indeed, American military intelligence was provided before and during the December operation. Nevertheless, on February 27, 2008, the United States urged Turkey to end the offensive quickly, and the Iraqi and Turkish governments finally agreed to cooperate in July 2008.

Civil & Political Rights Covenant, 1966, Art. 20(1). Any propaganda for war shall be prohibited by law.

War Crime #6. Propaganda for War. War advocacy based on falsehoods was evidenced by the constant drumbeat from Washington about weapons of mass destruction that Saddam Hussein supposedly possessed. The Pentagon recruited retired military officers, some with ties to future contractors, to offer themselves as military experts on television news programs as part of what former Deputy Press Secretary Scott McClellan has characterized as a "propaganda" campaign. I, for one, was suspicious of the monotonous rhetorical drumbeat.

Two nonprofit journalism organizations have counted at least 935 false statements that were issued by President Bush and officials in his administration from September 11, 2001, to September 11, 2003, including 259 by Bush personally. Most statements alleged that Iraq had links to al-Qaeda or had weapons of mass destruction. The most famous are the "axis of evil" speech to Congress on January 29, 2002, and the West Point speech of June 1, 2002. According to journalist Bob Woodward, Bush was well aware that claims about weapons of mass destruction were exaggerated. Jeremy Greenstock, former British Foreign Secretary, attests that Bush knew that there was no truth to a nuclear threat from Saddam Hussein. On October 1, 2002, a confidential CIA report assured that Saddam Hussein did not pose a military threat to the United States. When the document was summarized for public release on October 4, that reference was deleted. Then on October 7, Bush's speech identified Saddam as posing a serious military threat, clearly contradicting the intelligence on which he pretended to rely. Also, on October 7, while Bush loudly proclaimed that Iraq posed a serious security threat to the United States, CIA Director George Tenet said the opposite in a letter to the Senate Intelligence Committee.

Since the rhetoric was not only inaccurate but deliberately false, by having "intelligence and facts...fixed around the policy" rather than the reverse (in the words of the Downing Street Memo), the inference is that speeches by Bush constituted official propaganda rather than reasoned judgments based on solid evidence. A record of a conversation between Bush and Spanish Prime Minister José María Aznar on November 22, 2002, known as the Crawford Memo, further demonstrates that the president was engaging in propaganda to shape public opinion, that is, to manufacture consent for a war in Iraq that otherwise would not have been supported by Congress.

Although the attack on Afghanistan was premised on changing the regime harboring al-Qaeda, many observers wonder about the real reason for the war in Iraq, as so many discredited pretexts were offered. Bush, however, megalomaniacally confided to Bob Woodward in *Bush at War*, "I'm the commander...see, I don't need to explain. I do not need to explain why I say things. That's the interesting thing about being the president. Maybe somebody needs to explain to me why they say something, but I don't feel like I owe anybody an explanation." But he does.

In support of the view that the motive instead was to ensure American and Western control of Iraq's oil, Paul O'Neill reports that, while Secretary of the Treasury, he saw a secret document dated March 5, 2001, with the title "Plan for Post-Saddam Iraq and Foreign Suitors of Iraqi Oilfield Contracts." The document, made public by Judicial Watch after a Freedom-of-Information Act request, listed oil companies of thirty countries that might gain concessions over various Iraqi oilfields. In January 2008, Bush's signing statement of the military appropriations bill states that he would not obey that law's prohibition against "United States control of the oil resources of Iraq." Regarding Afghanistan, an alternative view is that a gas pipeline through the country had been blocked by the Taliban.

A prominent explanation for the two wars is that Bush at first listened to conflicting arguments among his advisers and agreed to give priority to a war in Afghanistan because that is where al-Qaeda was located. The decision to go to war with Iraq, according to one narrative, was made after Bush took sides in a turf battle between the caution of Secretary of State Colin Powell and the aggressive advocacy of Vice President Dick Cheney and Secretary of Defense Donald Rumsfeld. Indeed, within hours of the 9/11 attacks, Cheney and Rumsfeld were speculating that Saddam Hussein, not al-Qaeda, was responsible. Later, they tried to connect Saddam Hussein to al-Qaeda and used the claim about Saddam's supposed weapons of mass destruction to trump Powell's caution.

According to Scott McClellan, then Bush's press spokesperson, the official explanations were the "gathering danger" of Saddam Hussein's alleged weapons of mass destruction and the supposed linkage of Hussein with al-Qaeda. Privately, he says, Bush accepted the naïve scenario that a future democratic Iraq would serve as a model for a transformed Middle East.

Bush also gave the following explanation to Palestinian Prime Minister Mahmoud Abbas, as quoted on June 24, 2003, in the Israeli newspaper *Ha'aretz*: "God told me to strike at Al Qaeda and I struck them, and then he instructed me to strike at Saddam, which I did." And in July 16, 2004, the *Lancaster New Era* reports that Bush confided to an Amish group: "God speaks through me. Without that, I couldn't do my job."

Bush and his advisers occasionally pointed to human rights justifications for the two wars—the mistreatment of women by the Taliban and the massacres of Kurds and Shi'ites by Saddam Hussein in Iraq. How ironic it is that the person most responsible for making Saddam Hussein's execution possible is now himself accused of war crimes. According to Paul Wolfowitz, human rights concerns did not enter into Bush's thinking in the invasions of Afghanistan and Iraq. In Afghanistan, the fundamentalist Taliban was simply replaced by the fundamentalist Northern Alliance and various fundamentalist Pushtu warlords in the south.

Whatever the motive, Bush sought the toppling of governments in Afghanistan and Iraq. Chasing Osama Bin Laden evidently was of secondary importance, as General Tommy Franks refused a lower-level request for firepower to block exit trails to Pakistan.

CONCLUSION

Congress voted to approve the "war on terror" but was largely silent from 2001 as the above six war crimes were committed. Deference to the president's objective of rooting out terrorism prevailed in the invasion of Afghanistan. The Iraq War was marketed to the American people without a genuine public debate based on the facts. Other countries, however, saw things differently.

Whereas Bush believed fervently in a best-case scenario about bringing democracy to the Middle East, he discounted the worst-case scenario of endless tribal insurgency. The result was a lack of contemplation—in other words, self-delusion.

Then scandalous photographs from the American-run Abu Ghraib prison in Iraq were revealed in 2004. Ever since, the news media and political officeholders have provided such lengthy celluloid and paper trails to document so many varied war crimes that the press and the public have lost track of their enormity. The following chapters, accordingly, provide a comprehensive delineation of war crimes committed in the conduct of war, in the treatment of prisoners, and in the occupation of Afghanistan and Iraq.

Chapter 3

CRIMES COMMITTED IN THE CONDUCT OF WAR

When Chinese President Hu Jintao visited George W. Bush in 2006, he bestowed a gift of Sun-Tzu's *The Art of War*, a classic written 1,600 years ago. If Bush had carefully read the book, he would have learned that "shock and awe" destruction violated the principle that violence used in war should be no more than what is necessary to win.

Indeed, theorists have long argued that wars must be waged humanely. The Hindu Code of Manu (200 BC) prohibited the killing of innocent civilians and surrendering soldiers, destruction of towns, and the use of certain loathsome weapons.

In the seventh century, the prophet Mohammed counseled warriors not to harm innocent women and children and not to destroy the homes and livelihoods of those who are conquered. In 643, Abu Bakr, the first Muslim caliph, banned the slaying of older persons, urging those in battle to be merciful. When the Crusaders violated these principles four centuries later, Muslims were shocked, as they are today by what Bush's wars have wrought in Afghanistan and Iraq.

Aquinas and Grotius, who developed "just war" theory, also proposed principles for determining when armed aggression crossed the line into unacceptable barbarism (Table 3.1). For example, Grotius proposed a ban on all warfare conducted on the high seas so that international commerce would be immune from violence.

In 989, a Catholic synod sought to prohibit attacks on children, clergy, merchants, peasants, and women. In 1027, a Catholic council banned warfare on religious holidays. Another council banned the crossbow in 1139.

Richard II of England proclaimed in 1386 that the death penalty would be invoked on those who would in wartime attack women and

Table 3.1
Principles of Just Means of War

Theorist	Principle	Explication
Thomas Aquinas (1225–1274)	Humanity	There should be no unnecessary violence; prisoners should be captured and humanely treated.
	Chivalry	The use of defensive force should not involve dishonorable means, expedients, or conduct; no war should produce evils greater than those providing the pretext to war.
	Proportionality	Violence should be only enough to stop an evil and end in peace.
Hugo Grotius (1583–1645)	Discrimination	Combat should not be directed at civilians.
	Humanity	Enemy soldiers should be captured respectfully.
	Proportionality	The scope of the war should be minimal, calibrated only to the end sought.

unarmed priests, burn houses, and desecrate churches. Similar provisions were adopted by King Ferdinand of Hungary in 1526. King Gustavus II of Sweden in 1621 decreed in the country's Articles of War a ban on killing women, children, the clergy, the elderly, and female servants.

The first treaty regulating warfare was signed in 1675 between France and Germany (then called the Holy Roman Empire). Known as the Strasbourg Agreement, the two countries agreed never to use poison or toxic bullets. Subsequently, international law on the conduct of war grew considerably (Appendix 3.1), with the United States in the forefront of that legal development.

The Constitution of the United States, as written in 1787, gives Congress the power to "define and punish piracies and felonies committed on the high seas and offences against the law of nations" (Article I, Section 8). Pirates, the terrorists of the day, were interrupting shipping from the Caribbean to North Africa and beyond. At first, the American government paid tribute to the Barbary States to stop attacks by the pirates, but from 1801 to 1815 Congress authorized military campaigns to root out the pirates as war criminals.

During the American Civil War (1861–1865), President Abraham Lincoln asked Professor Francis Lieber of Columbia University to draw up a guide for the humane conduct of warfare so that he could legitimate the role of the North as the Union army fought the South and established martial law over the territory increasingly occupied. In 1863, Lincoln issued *Instructions for the Government of Armies of the United States in the Field*, known as the Lieber Code, which covered nearly all aspects of warfare. Based on international custom, that is, practices accepted by civilized nations, a major concept was the principle of "military necessity," that is, that no more force should be employed than necessary in war. The Lieber Code is the foundation for the Army Field Manual.

Subsequently, the Red Cross was formed, the Hague and Geneva conventions were adopted, and other agreements have established crimes under international law to govern the conduct of war. The aim is to provide everyone some protection in time of war by placing limits on human suffering and by preventing the chaotic devastation resulting from modern methods of warfare. Topics range from the treatment of the wounded to prohibited weapons to a ban on killing innocent civilians to prohibiting mercenaries.

MANAGEMENT OF THE AFGHANISTAN AND IRAQ WARS

The war in Afghanistan began on October 7, 2002. Following a somewhat ordinary war plan, the American military assisted the Northern Alliance of anti-Taliban warlords to prevail over the Taliban-controlled government.

The war in Iraq began on March 20, 2003, primarily with massive "shock and awe" bombing. The Kurds were not allowed to open a northern front, and Turkey did not allow passage of American troops, so the primarily Anglo-American invasion began from Kuwait.

In both cases, the capital cities were seized as a sign of victory. The first resistance came in the form of guerrilla-type activities. After

Baghdad fell, an insurgency arose in which Ba'athists, Saddamists, Sunnis, and later al-Qaeda supporters launched attacks. Saddam Hussein had previously distributed videotapes of *Black Hawk Down* (2001) to demonstrate how to defeat an American invasion force. He and al-Qaeda also relied on their external networks to finance the insurgency.

At first, Rumsfeld denied the existence of the insurgency, but in time counterinsurgency operations were mounted. In 2004, the most significant counterinsurgency offensive occurred when the American military conducted two campaigns against Falluja in Iraq. Aerial bombardments and a ground campaign left the city in ruins and hundreds of innocent civilians dead.

In 2006, the insurgent strategy changed. By leaving fingerprints of the insurgent Sunni on the destruction of the Shi'ite Samara Mosque, al-Qaeda fomented a civil war. While Bush at first denied the existence of the civil war, calls for withdrawal from Iraq were legion. The military, under the capable leadership of General David Petraeus, then embarked in 2007 on the "surge," an escalation of American military forces to stop ethnic cleansing, while offering funds to Sunni tribal leaders to drive out the forces of "al-Qaeda in Iraq." Military operations, in short, have presented challenges in a messy situation, for which restraint based on the Geneva Conventions was not always viewed favorably in the White House.

Throughout both wars, Defense Secretary Donald Rumsfeld acted as micromanager, to the chagrin of many senior military officers. Rumsfeld thereby implicated himself and his immediate superior, President Bush, as possible war criminals for violations of the international laws governing warfare that are detailed below.

The basic principle of humane warfare, avoidance of unnecessary destruction to persons and property, has been repeatedly violated. One reason is that insufficient troops have been augmented by airstrikes, and the aerial warfare has repeatedly hit civilian targets. The aim has been to minimize American military casualties, but the result has been to maximize Afghan and Iraqi civilian casualties.

The analysis below categorizes crimes in the conduct of war in terms of prohibited targets and weapons, misconduct by soldiers and their commanders, and unlawful uses of mercenaries. Relevant events are the initial invasions as well as subsequent military campaigns in dealing with insurgent forces. Sources of information come primarily from the accounts of journalists Rajiv Chandrasekaran, Seymour Hersh, Tom

Ricks, and Bob Woodward as well as nongovernmental organizations Human Rights First, Human Rights Watch, and the Red Cross.

PROHIBITED TARGETS

The laws of warfare limit death and destruction to certain targets. The principle is that certain persons and places should be neutral, left outside the scope of combat. Using high-altitude aircraft and Cruise missiles located on warships has meant few American casualties but imprecision in targeting.

> **Red Cross Convention, 1864, Art. 1.** Ambulances and military hospitals shall be acknowledged to be neutral, and, as such, shall be protected and respected by belligerents so long as any sick or wounded may be therein.

War Crime #7. Failure to Observe the Neutrality of a Hospital. In 2001, the children's hospital in Kabul was bombed, and the hospital in Herat was targeted, resulting in about one hundred deaths. The al-Nouman Hospital in Baghdad was hit in the initial bombing in 2003, resulting in the deaths of five persons. A tank shell destroyed the generator of the Yarmouk Hospital in Baghdad. Central Health Center was bombed during the assault on Falluja in November 2004, killing thirty-five patients and twenty-four hospital employees. The Nazzal Emergency Hospital in Falluja, run by a Saudi Arabian Islamic charity, was reduced to rubble. The incidents certainly gave new meaning to the term "surgical strike." American troops ordered the evacuation of hospitals in Falluja just when they were urgently needed.

> **Hague II, 1899, Art. 25.** The attack or bombardment of towns, villages, habitations or buildings which are not defended, is prohibited.

War Crime #8. Destruction of Undefended Targets. Both in Afghanistan and Iraq, high-explosive bombs were dropped in crowded urban areas. The Falluja assault that began on April 4, 2004, devastated a city of at least 250,000 inhabitants. Some 700 airstrikes damaged or destroyed 18,000 of Falluja's 39,000 buildings. In 2007, airstrikes in Iraq increased sevenfold over 2006, including 500-pound bombs dropped in neighborhoods where insurgents blended in with residents, resulting in the destruction of many homes and shops.

> **Hague II, 1899, Art. 27.** In sieges and bombardments all necessary steps should be taken to spare as far as possible edifices devoted to religion, art, science, and charity, hospitals, and places where the sick and wounded are collected, provided they are not used at the same time for military purposes.

War Crime #9. Bombing of Edifices Devoted to Art, Charity, Religion, and Science. "Shock and awe" bombing, as approved by Rumsfeld, razed the museum in Tikrit during 2003. In 2004, a fireball ripped through the al-Hassan Mosque in Falluja, reportedly killing four theology students, and forty worshippers were killed when a 500-pound bomb demolished the Abdul-Aziz al-Samarrai Mosque. At least sixty mosques have been destroyed by American forces in Iraq.

> **Hague IV, 1907, Art. 3.** A belligerent party which violates the provisions of the said Regulations shall, if the case demands, be liable to pay compensation. It shall be responsible for all acts committed by persons forming part of its armed forces.

War Crime #10. Failure to Compensate. Approximately 75 percent of Iraqi compensation claims have been rejected. Only $1.5 million has been paid for civilian deaths and property damage out of an estimated billions of dollars of destruction of prohibited targets. Civilians have been told that their claims are unfounded because they heedlessly remained in locations of military action, though the action was most often carried out without warning.

> **Hague IX, 1907, Art. 1.** The bombardment by naval forces of undefended ports, towns, villages, dwellings, or buildings is forbidden.

War Crime #11. Naval Bombardment of Undefended Buildings, Dwellings, Towns, and Villages. In Afghanistan, an estimated 70 percent of the bombing was by naval aircraft. Part of the "shock and awe" strategy involved firing 400 Cruise missiles on Iraq targets on each of the first two days of the war. Many civilians died in the attacks on al-Dura Farm, which were explicitly approved by Bush, as well as the districts of al-Karrada and al-Mansur in Baghdad and the al-Tuwaisi district of Basra.

> **Hague V, 1907, Art. 1.** The territory of neutral powers is inviolable.

War Crime #12. Bombing of Neutral Countries. So-called precision bombs landed on both Iran and Turkey during March 2003. Although the attack on Turkey, an ally, may have been inadvertent, the bombing of an Iranian Oil Ministry building may have been deliberate. There is no record of apologies to either country.

Iran's charge that the United States supports attacks launched from northern Iraq has been denied in Washington, yet in 2005 rules of engagement permitted attacks on Iran as well as Syria by the American military. Unmanned airstrikes, to eliminate supposed members of al-Qaeda in Bush's larger "war on terror," have hit Pakistan and Somalia as well.

Pakistan President Pervez Musharraf believed that Deputy Secretary of State Richard Armitage threatened him in the following terms: "Be prepared to be bombed. Be prepared to go back to the Stone Age," a threat that Armitage has denied. Yet Pakistan is an American ally.

Although Musharraf granted permission for aircraft to bomb Osama Bin Laden inside Pakistan, the government has consistently protested deliberate bombing in recent years, aimed at eliminating al-Qaeda members hiding out across the border from Afghanistan. At least a dozen civilians died in bombing on January 12, 2006, whereupon protests were widespread throughout the country. Other incidents occurred in 2007 and 2008, when at least one hundred civilians and eleven paramilitary personnel were killed by bombing inside Pakistan. Decisions to drop bombs at specific targets in recent years, which appear to have been made at the highest levels of the American government, recall the events of 1965, when American troops widened the war by crossing from Vietnam into Cambodia, which served to accelerate the rise of the Khmer Rouge to power. On June 22, 2008, some of the dissidents in Pakistan began firing rockets back at NATO bases, doubtless with the support of many Pakistanis who resent incursions into their country. In July, Bush secretly authorized American ground attacks inside Pakistan. After the first such offensive on September 3, the Islamabad government condemned the raids and ordered counterattacks.

> **Geneva Convention, 1929, Art. 9.** The personnel engaged exclusively in the collection, transport and treatment of the wounded and sick, and in the administration of medical formations and establishments, and chaplains attached to armies, shall be respected and protected under all circumstances. If they fall into the hands of the enemy, they shall not be treated as prisoners of war.

War Crime #13. Failure to Observe the Neutrality of Hospital Employees. During the Falluja Massacre of 2004, American soldiers entered the city's General Hospital, forced all hospital employees and patients to lie on the ground, and tied their hands behind their backs. In addition, snipers reportedly targeted medical personnel.

> **Geneva Convention, 1929, Art. 10.** The personnel of Voluntary Aid Societies, duly recognized and authorized by their Government, who may be employed on the same duties as those of the personnel mentioned in the first paragraph of Article 9, are placed on the same footing as the personnel contemplated in that paragraph . . .

War Crime #14. Failure to Respect the Neutrality of a Voluntary Aid Society. Clearly marked Red Cross warehouses were bombed on three occasions in the Afghan War during October 2001. Leaflets dropped during the war warned that cooperation with al-Qaeda and the Taliban would jeopardize the continuation of international aid, which led Médecins Sans Frontières to object that their neutrality was compromised. During the siege of Falluja in November 2004, the American military refused to allow members of the Red Cross and the Red Crescent Society access to the city.

> **Cultural Property Convention, 1954, Art. 4(1).** The High Contracting Parties undertake to respect cultural property situated within their own territory as well as within the territory of other High Contracting Parties by refraining from any use of the property and its immediate surroundings or of the appliances in use for its protection for purposes which are likely to expose it to destruction or damage in the event of armed conflict; and by refraining from any act of hostility, directed against such property.

War Crime #15. Hostile Acts on the Ground Directed at a Museum. While taking control of Baghdad, American troops broke down the door to the Iraqi National Museum in Baghdad rather than securing the structure from Iraqi looters. Afterward, the museum was allowed to burn, and soldiers were not ordered to put out the fire.

> **Protocol 1, 1977, Art. 51(4).** Indiscriminate attacks are prohibited. Indiscriminate attacks are: (a) those which are not directed at a specific military objective; (b) those which employ a method or means of combat which cannot be directed at a specific military objective; or (c) those which employ a method or means of combat the effects of which cannot be limited as required by this Protocol; and consequently, in each such case, are of a nature to strike military objectives and civilians or civilian objects without distinction. **(5)** Among others, the following types of attacks are to be considered as indiscriminate: (a) an attack by bombardment by any methods or means which treats as a single military objective a number of clearly separated and distinct military objectives located in a city, town, village or other area containing a similar concentration of civilians or civilian objects . . .

War Crime #16. Indiscriminate Attacks Against Civilians. During the 2001 offensive in Afghanistan, at least 1,000 civilians died, many from carpet bombing. During 2008, aerial bombing once again resulted in killing innocent civilians and destroying several houses. More civilians have been killed by American forces in Afghanistan than during the reign of the Taliban.

The strategic decision to employ the "shock and awe" strategy in Iraq was the brainchild of Rumsfeld and approved by Bush. However, members of the military did not want to be put on trial later as war criminals for killing civilians without authorization. Bush and Rumsfeld therefore agreed to approve personally targets with high levels of "collateral damage" (the euphemism for civilian casualties), after they had been vetted by military lawyers. The threshold was thirty or more civilian deaths.

The first "shock and awe" on Baghdad during 2003 consisted of 1,000 Cruise missiles, a Hiroshima-sized attack. At least 10,000 were killed during the initial invasion. Later, casualties mounted. The Iraq Body Count group estimates that 85,000 Iraqi civilians died from the beginning of "shock and awe" hostilities until midyear 2008.

During the early phase of the insurgency in Iraq, the standard operating procedure for responding to a single hostile incident in a town, known as Operation Iron Hammer, was bombing, nighttime raids, and mass arrests. Rules of engagement permit shooting first whenever there is positive identification that a target either has hostile intent or has committed a hostile act, but according to one observer, "indiscriminate tactics had become the norm." Instead of responding to discrete threats in a village, attacks on entire villages resulted in massacres, notably in Haditha, Ishaqi, Karandeeb, Mahmoudiya, Nasariya, and (in Afghanistan) at Nangahar and Shinwar.

Outrage over the savage killing of four American civilian contractors in Falluja on March 31, 2004, eclipses the fact that the four were killed in retaliation for the slaughter of about a dozen Iraqi civilians. Among the 600 civilians killed during the American attack on Falluja the following week, half were women and children, including peaceful demonstrators. Their dead bodies were shown on Al-Jazeera Television throughout the Arabic-speaking world.

Checkpoints around Baghdad, with or without makeshift signs in English, have asked Iraqis to stop vehicles for inspection. Startled Iraqis have often been shot as a result of the confusion. One estimate is that 10,000 have been killed by nervous American soldiers, though only 1,000 ever fired back.

Airstrikes in Iraq killed more than one hundred innocent civilians from November 2007 to July 2008 during the "surge." In several cases, none of the increased American ground troops were spared to go to the locations of the targets, some of which were civilian checkpoints where Iraqis were being paid $10 per day each to screen vehicles as they traveled along a road. As a result, many civilians abandoned the checkpoints.

In April 2008, President Hamid Karzai complained that too many civilians were dying in the continuing American aerial effort to root out resurgent members of the Taliban. In July 2008 alone, 78 civilians died, more than half of whom were bombed at a wedding party in Nangahar. Although the aerial command center for Afghanistan and Iraq posted legal representatives from Judge Advocate General staff on twenty-four-hour duty, discretion still remained in the hands of field commanders.

Protocol 1, 1977, Art. 52(3). In case of doubt whether an object which is normally dedicated to civilian purposes, such as a place of worship, a house or other dwelling or a school, is being used to make an effective contribution to military action, it shall be presumed not to be so used. **Art. 53.**

continued

> Protection of cultural objects and of places of worship without prejudice to the provisions of the Hague Convention for the Protection of Cultural Property in the Event of Armed Conflict of 14 May 1954, and of other relevant international instruments, it is prohibited: (a) to commit any acts of hostility directed against the historic monuments, works of art or places of worship which constitute the cultural or spiritual heritage of peoples...

War Crime #17. Failure to Protect Cultural Property. In April 2003, after American troops broke into the locked doors of the National Museum, they stood by while Iraqis looted the museum. At least thirty-three major pieces and 15,000 artifacts were stolen. According to Abdul Zahra Talaqani, media director for the Iraqi Ministry for Tourism and Archaeology, "The American forces, when they entered...protected all the oil wells...but...paid no attention to Iraq's heritage." One month later, Interpol sponsored an international conference to assess the losses.

PROHIBITED WEAPONS

Because some weapons cause horrific injury to combatants and non-combatants, they have been banned. The planet itself might be in jeopardy if nuclear bombs were dropped, but that has happened only twice.

> **Hague II, 1899, Art. 23.** Besides the prohibitions provided by special Conventions, it is especially prohibited:... To employ arms, projectiles, or material of a nature to cause superfluous injury...

War Crime #18. Use of Arms and Projectiles to Cause Superfluous Injury. During the invasion of Iraq, airplanes and artillery dropped an estimated 10,782 cluster bombs, that is, canisters the size of automobiles containing dozens or hundreds of small explosives that can spread out to the length of two football fields. Subsequently, they exploded on many civilians, killing or maiming them; one estimate is that 372 Iraqi civilians died as a result. Even American military personnel on the ground have been wounded whenever they have encountered unexploded ordnance from cluster bombs. Cluster bombs were also used to combat the Iraq insurgency in areas where civilians live. A treaty specifically banning cluster bombs was signed on May 30, 2008.

Also in Iraq, airplanes dropped at least eleven 15,000-pound "daisy cutters," projectiles that obliterate the ground and thereby clear space for helicopter landing strips. Bullets that expand inside the body were also used.

Both cluster bombs and daisy cutters were also used in Afghanistan. The top brass (admirals and generals) are likely to have approved the weapons.

> **Protocol 1, 1977, Art. 55(1).** Care shall be taken in warfare to protect the natural environment against widespread, long-term and severe damage. This protection includes a prohibition of the use of methods or means of warfare which are intended or may be expected to cause such damage to the natural environment and thereby to prejudice the health or survival of the population.

War Crime #19. Use of Napalm. A hill outside Basra was napalmed during the initial invasion of Iraq. So were two bridges south of Baghdad.

> **Incendiary Weapons Protocol, 1980, Art. 2(1).** It is prohibited in all circumstances to make the civilian population as such, individual civilians or civilian objects the object of attack by incendiary weapons. **(2).** It is prohibited in all circumstances to make any military objective located within a concentration of civilians the object of attack by air-delivered incendiary weapons.

War Crime #20. Use of White Phosphorous. During November 2004, white phosphorous, a chemical that can cause serious burns, was used as an antipersonnel airborne weapon in Falluja, according to several American military officers. General Peter Pace, who headed the Joint Chiefs of Staff, defended the use of white phosphorous to illuminate targets at night but denied any war crimes violation.

> **Radioactive Waste Convention, 1997, Art. 11.** Each Contracting Party shall take the appropriate steps to ensure that at all stages of radioactive waste management individuals, society and the environment are adequately protected against radiological and other hazards.

War Crime #21. Use of Depleted Uranium Weapons. Some 2,000 tons of depleted uranium bullets and shells, which can combust into a ball of fire measuring 10,000 centigrade degrees, were utilized in the invasion of Iraq. At least 200 tons were used after the invasion.

MISCONDUCT BY FIELD SOLDIERS

While in combat, conscientious soldiers may act barbarously. Rules of warfare seek to restrain their often difficult split-second decisions on the battlefield. Yet their battlefield commanders evidently did not stress the international law of warfare because Bush and Rumsfeld told them to ignore the Geneva Conventions.

> **Hague II, 1899, Art. 23.** Besides the prohibitions provided by special Conventions, it is especially prohibited: ... To kill or wound treacherously individuals belonging to the hostile nation or army ...

War Crime #22. Killing or Wounding Civilians Treacherously. When fifteen-year-old Omar Khadr was first picked up from a battlefield in Afghanistan during 2002, he had two bullets in his back. He had been shot by an American soldier and was nearly executed when a Special Forces soldier told the soldier to stop firing at the boy.

Several Iraqis have been shot after capture because they tried to escape. The likely way for that to happen, as at Thathar Lake in May 2006, is for guards deliberately to allow them to escape so that they can be shot in pursuit.

In spring 2007, three Iraqis were killed in an apparent "baiting" program in which American soldiers planted weapons and other material on a street and then shot those who tried to pick them up. An AK-47 rifle was planted on one dead man's body to cover up a murder. In a trial of an army sniper, accused of the shooting, the Army refused to allow classified evidence on his behalf, thus suggesting that the program was sanctioned much higher up the chain of command.

War Crime #23. Failure to Accept the Surrender of Combatants. During the war in Afghanistan, low-level members of al-Qaeda who decided to surrender were executed on the spot by American soldiers, possibly following what they supposed was the subtext of Bush's "dead or alive" injunction stated September 17, 2001. Perhaps the most extraordinary blunder of the Iraq war was the refusal to accept a surrender offer from 500 Sunni insurgents in early 2004.

> **Hague II, 1899, Art. 47.** Pillage is formally prohibited.

War Crime #24. Pillage. Residents of Baghdad looted museums, offices, and universities during the fall of Baghdad in 2003. What is less well understood is that American troops, in plain view, took cash, printing presses, weapons, and other objects from some buildings before allowing Iraqis to seize whatever they wanted.

During the high point of the insurgency in Iraq, soldiers who searched houses sometimes took cash that they saw lying around. Lieutenant General Ricardo Sanchez, the commanding officer, never apologized for or returned what was stolen. Indeed, the problem of looting was summarily dismissed by Defense Secretary Rumsfeld.

Saad Eskander, director of the Iraq National Library and Archive, has recently sought the return of thousands of documents that he believes were illegally shipped to the United States. Although the Department of State has officially denied responsibility, the files are now located at the Hoover Institution at Stanford University.

> **Geneva I, 1949, Art. 3(2).** . . . The wounded and sick shall be collected and cared for.

War Crime #25. Failure to Attend to the Wounded. On March 4, 2007, Marines at Jalalabad, Afghanistan, left the battlefield without attending to those whom they had wounded. Similarly, on October 23, 2007, a helicopter fired on a group of persons who were carrying a wounded insurgent in a town near Tikrit, Iraq, thereby killing not only the man but also several women and children. In July 2008, American soldiers blocked Afghan villagers from rescuing wounded civilians so that they could go to a nearby hospital.

> **Geneva I, 1949, Art. 17.** Parties to the conflict shall ensure . . . that the dead are honorably interred, if possible according to the rites of the religion to which they belonged . . .

War Crime #26. Failure to Provide Proper Burials to Enemy Soldiers Killed in Combat. In November 2001, Northern Alliance commander Abdul Rashid Dostum captured some 35,000 persons who had peacefully surrendered at Konduz, Afghanistan. Offered $5,000 per head by American military forces, Northern Alliance forces stashed and shipped them in container lorries that were sealed and left to stand in the sun for many days. Those who survived benefited from machine-gunned holes in the metal exterior. When they were carted to Sherberghan Prison after a trip of eighty miles, most had died of asphyxiation and thirst, as portrayed in Jamie Doran's film *Afghan Massacre: Convoy of Death* (2002). American soldiers then dumped the dead into ditches.

On October 1, 2005, the bodies of two Afghan insurgents were burned by two American soldiers, contrary to the Muslim custom of burial. A few hours later, two psychological operation officers broadcast a message over a loudspeaker in which they challenged the Taliban to bury their dead and fight in the open. Subsequently, they received a reprimand, not a court-martial, for committing war crimes. In 2007, Marines reportedly fled after a battle at Jalalabad without burying dead Afghans.

Protocol 1, 1977, Art. 51(4). Indiscriminate attacks are prohibited. Indiscriminate attacks are: (a) those which are not directed at a specific military objective; (b) those which employ a method or means of combat which cannot be directed at a specific military objective; or (c) those which employ a method or means of combat the effects of which cannot be limited as required by this Protocol; and consequently, in each such case, are of a nature to strike military objectives and civilians or civilian objects without distinction. **(5).** Among others, the following types of attacks are to be considered as indiscriminate: ... (b) an attack which may be expected to cause incidental loss of civilian life, injury to civilians, damage to civilian objects, or a combination thereof, which would be excessive in relation to the concrete and direct military advantage anticipated.

War Crime #27. Excessive Targeting of Civilians. Bombing or raiding a house to kill a single enemy combatant while massacring innocent women and children in the process has been repeated on several occasions. A recent occurrence was in Ghazni, Afghanistan, where one civilian and nine Afghan police were killed by American ground and air troops on January 24, 2008. The Afghan police officers, who were looking for insurgents, were killed because American soldiers assumed incorrectly that they were forces of the Taliban. Subsequently, 200 villagers protested the raid by blocking the route to the nearby airport.

On May 11, 2008, thousands of Afghans blocked a road after an overnight raid killed three civilians. To clear the road, American troops killed two more civilians and wounded seven.

Soldiers on the ground also have been known to use hand grenades on an indiscriminate basis, such as to clear a room in a house before entry. A British officer complained that "American troops do shoot first and ask questions later." In Iraq, "shock and awe" bombing was far from a series of "surgical" strikes.

MISCONDUCT BY COMMANDERS

Field soldiers can receive unlawful orders. Thus, they can be disciplined either for obedience or disobedience. Under the principle of "command responsibility," high-ranking officers are required to restrain themselves and their subordinates from committing war crimes.

> **Hague II, 1899, Art. 26.** The Commander of an attacking force, before commencing a bombardment, except in the case of an assault, should do all he can to warn the authorities.

War Crime #28. Failure to Notify Authorities of Bombardments. At the beginning of both the Afghanistan and Iraq wars, there were no warnings to the governments about bombing targets by American military commanders. Recent airstrikes have not always been approved by the friendly Afghan, Pakistani, and Iraqi governments.

> **Hague IX, 1907, Art. 5.** In bombardments by naval forces all the necessary measures must be taken by the commander to spare as far as possible sacred edifices, buildings used for artistic, scientific, or charitable purposes, historic monuments, hospitals, and places where the sick or wounded are collected, on the understanding that they are not used at the same time for military purposes.

War Crime #29. Indiscriminate Naval Bombardments. "Shock and awe" was so massive that sites previously identified as off limits were destroyed. Twenty "high collateral damage" targets were hit in Iraq, some from American ships at sea. All targets with considerable civilian casualties were reportedly approved in advance by President Bush.

> **Hague IX, 1907, Art. 6.** The commander of the attacking naval force, before commencing the bombardment, must do his utmost to warn the authorities.

War Crime #30. Naval Bombardments Without Warning. Leaflets dropped in eastern Afghanistan on January 8, 2002, warned of bombing wherever Taliban weapons were visible but did not give information about the location of sanctuaries to avoid being hit. In Iraq, some leaflets dropped in Iraq did warn of specific locations to be targeted, but no such announcements were feasible during initial "shock and awe" bombing.

> **Civil and Political Rights Covenant, 1967, Art. 6.** No one shall be arbitrarily deprived of his life... **Art. 14(2).** Everyone charged with a criminal offense shall have the right to be presumed innocent until proved guilty according to law.

War Crime #31. Extrajudicial Executions. According to the Intelligence Authorization Act of 1991, the president must specifically authorize covert operations. Bush's effort to kill high-ranking civilian officials of the Afghan and Iraqi governments, including Osama Bin Laden and Saddam Hussein personally, is well known. Military intelligence estimates of their exact locations guided airstrikes, but intelligence was incorrect, resulting in unnecessary civilian casualties.

On November 3, 2002, a Hellfire missile from an unmanned Predator drone operated by the CIA reportedly killed senior al-Qaeda plotter Qaeda Senyan al-Harthi. The same type of executions continued unabated through 2008.

One war aim was to "decapitate" both regimes, leaving no government in place to surrender. President Bush specifically authorized bombing of Dora Farms, a location where intelligence information indicated that Saddam Hussein was present. Bombing as a substitute for traditional military action on the ground has accounted for about two dozen planned extrajudicial executions since 9/11, with few persons eliminated.

In the early stage of American occupation of Iraq, the "deck of cards" manhunt program was designed as a gimmick for capturing more than fifty Ba'athist leaders. Airstrikes of locations where they were presumed to gather proved fruitless. After the arrival of John Negroponte, onetime American ambassador to Honduras, the manhunt was organized in the form of death squads.

In December 2006, in *Public Committee Against Torture in Israel v Government of Israel*, the Israeli Supreme Court ruled that targeted assassinations of terrorist suspects are contrary to international law. The exceptions are when information is reliable, the subject is actively engaging in hostilities, and a normal arrest is too risky. Few if any of the American decapitation airstrikes have met that test.

Protocol 1, 1977, Art. 51(6). Attacks against the civilian population or civilians by way of reprisals are prohibited.

War Crime #32. Reprisals Against Innocent Civilians. Journalists Hersh and Woodward trace various "dead or alive" campaigns directly to President Bush's desire to retaliate against the terrorist attacks on 9/11. In Afghanistan, an estimated 800 members of the Taliban were killed immediately after capture. From 2003 to 2005, 94 percent of all "pacification operations" in Iraq were in retaliation for imagined or perceived threats of future insurgent attacks.

Praised by many as the voice of a free press in the Middle East, Al-Jazeera's coverage of the Iraq War and playing of videotapes from Osama Bin Laden were not appreciated by the White House, which said so numerous times. Bush's hostility to the television network is consistent with the bombing of the Al-Jazeera television headquarters in Kabul on November 12, 2001, and in Baghdad on April 8, 2003. Indeed, Al-Jazeera gave the coordinates of its broadcast facility in Iraq to American military authorities just before the war to avoid any mistake. One Al-Jazeera reporter died, and others were wounded in the latter attack. The house of a prominent Al-Jazeera journalist was apparently bombed after unfavorable coverage of the Falluja Massacre in 2004.

During the early days of the Iraq insurgency, civilian homes were demolished. In one village, a commanding officer ordered the bulldozing of date palms and fruit trees, contrary to a basic Islamic and Judaic principle of warfare, after residents failed to inform on the identities of insurgents. The doctrine of preemptive aggression, in other words, devolved into preemptive assault merely on suspicion.

On March 31, 2004, four unarmed workers of the private contractor company Blackwater were ambushed in Falluja while delivering kitchen equipment. Two of their bodies were burned, and the other two corpses were dragged through the streets and hung from a bridge over the Euphrates River. Marines were sent into the city to retaliate on April 4, 2004, resulting in what has become known as the Falluja Massacre. The massacre forced thousands from their homes and resulted in the deaths of at least 600 civilians but only 184 of an estimated 400 insurgents. In response, Minister of Human Rights Abd El-Basit Turki resigned in protest. The murderers of the Blackwater guards were never found.

The Falluja retaliation, characterized by UN representative Lakhdar Brahimi as "collective punishment," was planned as a reprisal at the highest level. President Bush demanded a quick response, saying, "Kick ass! ... If somebody tries to stop the march to democracy, we will seek them out and kill them! We must be tougher than hell!" When American forces assaulted Falluja in November, they destroyed half the homes in the quest to root out insurgents.

The Afghan Independent Human Rights Commission protested the firing of machine-gun rounds along a ten-mile route near Jalalabad on March 4, 2007. The incident was a reprisal after a car bomb attack at a particular point along a route, but firing at least 200 machine-run rounds for the next ten miles went far beyond a return of alleged enemy fire. As a result, nineteen Afghan civilians died and thirty-three were injured in what is known as the Shinwar Massacre.

Protocol 1, 1977, Art. 54(1). Starvation of civilians as a method of warfare is prohibited. **(2)** It is prohibited to attack, destroy, remove or render useless objects indispensable to the survival of the civilian population, such as food-stuffs, agricultural areas for the production of foodstuffs, crops, livestock, drinking water installations and supplies and irrigation works, for the specific purpose of denying them for their sustenance value to the civilian population or to the adverse Party, whatever the motive, whether in order to starve out civilians, to cause them to move away, or for any other motive.

War Crime #33. Depriving Civilians of Food and Drinking Water. The United States ignored pleas from Mary Robinson, UN High Commissioner for Human Rights, for a pause in bombing so that Afghans could receive food packets during the initial Afghan War. Prior to attacks on Falluja, Najaf, Samarra, and Tall Afar in 2004, electricity and running water facilities were cut to the civilian population. Water was also denied to civilians as they fled Falluja and Tall Afar.

> **Protocol 1, 1977, Art. 57(2).** With respect to attacks, the following precautions shall be taken: (a) those who plan or decide upon an attack shall: (i) do everything feasible to verify that the objectives to be attacked are neither civilians nor civilian objects and are not subject to special protection but are military objectives . . ., and that it is not prohibited by the provisions of this Protocol to attack them; (ii) take all feasible precautions in the choice of means and methods of attack with a view to avoiding, and in any event to minimizing, incidental loss of civilian life, injury to civilians and damage to civilian objects; (iii) refrain from deciding to launch any attack which may be expected to cause incidental loss of civilian life, injury to civilians, damage to civilian objects, or a combination thereof, which would be excessive in relation to the concrete and direct military advantage anticipated . . .

War Crime #34. Excessive Military Force. The initial carpet bombing in Afghanistan and the "shock and awe" bombardment of Baghdad were disproportionate to the extent of military resistance. Bombing at high altitudes obviously diminishes target accuracy.

Attacks on Falluja in 2004 were clearly excessive in relation to the military objective. On one occasion, after residents were told to evacuate, an entire high-rise building was razed to eliminate a single sniper. During 2006, eighteen Iraqi cities were struck by warplanes, causing hundreds of civilian casualties.

> **Protocol 1, 1977, Art. 82.** The High Contracting Parties at all times, and the Parties to the conflict in time of armed conflict, shall ensure that legal advisers are available, when necessary, to advise military commanders at the appropriate level on the application of the Conventions and this Protocol and on the appropriate instruction to be given to the armed forces on this subject.

War Crime #35. Failure to Provide Battlefield Officers with Appropriate Legal Advice. Bush's advice has been to ignore the Geneva Conventions, which the military have been trained to uphold. Although Lieutenant General Ricardo Sanchez asked for legal advisers so that he would not deviate from Geneva Convention standards, his request was denied. The commanding officers cited for dereliction of duty in the next five war crimes evidently received appropriate legal advice only after mistakes were made.

Protocol 1, 1977, Art. 86(1).....Parties to the conflict shall repress grave breaches, and take measures necessary to suppress all other breaches, of the Conventions or of this Protocol which result from a failure to act when under a duty to do so. **(2).** The fact that a breach of the Conventions or of this Protocol was committed by a subordinate does not absolve his superiors from penal or disciplinary responsibility, as the case may be, if they knew, or had information which should have enabled them to conclude in the circumstances at the time, that he was committing or was going to commit such a breach and if they did not take all feasible measures within their power to prevent or repress the breach.

War Crime #36. Failure to Prosecute Commanding Officers for Failure to Stop Battlefield Offenses. On December 31, 2007, the Marines dropped the charge of unpremeditated murder against Staff Sergeant Frank Wuterich for failing to stop the squad under his command while a massacre was ongoing in the town of Haditha. Instead, Wuterich's offense was reduced to involuntary manslaughter. His principal defense was that he was following rules of engagement established by superior officers. Few charges have been filed after the various massacres. After all, forensic evidence is rarely available in a battle zone.

Protocol 1, 1977, Art. 87(1).....Parties to the conflict shall require military commanders, with respect to members of the armed forces under their command and other persons under their control, to prevent and, where necessary, to suppress and to report to competent authorities breaches of the Conventions and of this Protocol.

War Crime #37. Failure of Commanding Officers to Report Battlefield Offenses to Their Superiors. On November 19, 2005, after an improvised explosive device caused the death of Lance Corporal Miguel Terrazas, members of his Marine unit killed at least fifteen unarmed Iraqis in Haditha, including eleven women and children. Some unarmed civilians were shot in a nearby vehicle. Marines went inside nearby houses without any clear evidence that they were connected to the bomb and gunned down the occupants. Pictures were taken of the Iraqis killed at Haditha, but battalion intelligence officer First Lieutenant Andrew Grayson reportedly ordered a subordinate to destroy the photos. Subsequent requests to report and investigate the deaths were rejected by superior officers. Because a subordinate eventually came forward to testify, Grayson was charged with making false official statements and obstruction of justice but later acquitted. One general and two colonels were reprimanded for failing to investigate the incident. Others were initially indicted for the killings, but charges against most had been dropped by early 2008.

> **Protocol 1, 1977, Art. 87(2).** In order to prevent and suppress breaches . . . Parties to the conflict shall require that, commensurate with their level of responsibility, commanders ensure that members of the armed forces under their command are aware of their obligations under the Conventions and this Protocol.

War Crime #38. Failure of Commanding Officers to Ensure That Subordinates Understand Geneva Convention Obligations Regarding the Conduct of Warfare. Staff Sergeant Wuterich evidently did not inform his squad at or before the Haditha Massacre that retaliatory action against innocent civilians would be a war crime. Instead of investigating first and shooting later, he believed the opposite after he heard gunfire that he thought emanated from a nearby house and led the entry into the house. Because he failed to consider the matter to be isolated gunfire, Wuterich was charged with leading an attack that would have been more appropriate had considerable and sustained gunfire come from the house.

But Bush and Rumsfeld spread confusing signals about the relevance of the Geneva Conventions. As a result, Wuterich and others have relied on surreal exculpatory defenses.

> **Protocol 1, 1977, Art. 87(3).** The High Contracting Parties and Parties to the conflict shall require any commander who is aware that subordinates or other persons under his control are going to commit or have committed a breach of the Conventions or of this Protocol, to initiate such steps as are necessary to prevent such violations of the Conventions or this Protocol, and, where appropriate, to initiate disciplinary or penal action against violators thereof.

War Crime #39. Failure of Commanding Officers to Prevent Subordinates from Plotting War Crimes on the Battlefield. In addition to a manslaughter charge, Wuterich was accused of dereliction of duty for not forbidding his squad from taking retaliatory action. Instead, he allegedly led them to take action that resulted in civilian deaths.

War Crime #40. Failure of Commanding Officers to Discipline or Prosecute Subordinates Who Commit War Crimes on the Battlefield. Civilian deaths were rarely investigated until April 2006, when the word went out that investigations were required whenever American military operations injured or killed Iraqis or damaged property worth more than $10,000. Neither apologies nor compensation have been offered in most cases. Of sixty-nine soldiers charged with killing Iraqi civilians in combat by early 2008, twenty-two were convicted of murder, negligent homicide, or voluntary manslaughter.

Deaths of civilians have been reported up the chain of command but have rarely resulted in timely courts-martial. Lieutenant Colonel Jeffrey Chessani, battalion commander at the time of the Haditha Massacre, was charged with failing to order a war crimes investigation. When he cited evidence that his failure resulted from political pressure from General James Mattis, his commanding officer, his charges were dismissed. A two-star general and two colonels received letters of censure for not investigating the incident.

Investigation began in early 2008 for those involved in the Shinwar Massacre. Six Marines were granted immunity to testify. Their testimony served to exonerate those not granted immunity, thereby infuriating Afghanistan's human rights commission.

PROHIBITED COMBATANTS

The law of warfare bans the use of mercenaries, that is, paid civilian combatants who are not members of regular armed forces. As of early 2007, the 180,000 civilian contractors in Iraq, which outnumbered the 160,000 troops in uniform, performed such functions as providing armaments, food, laundry, logistical support, reconstruction, security, and translation. An estimated 48,000 civilians from various countries have worked as military police, thereby replacing soldiers in uniform who could then be assigned to other tasks. Chilean mercenaries, many trained during the era of dictator Augusto Pinochet, have been assigned to guard the Baghdad airport, a defensive role. But the problem has been that civilian contractors have been employed in offensive military roles.

Mercenaries Convention, 1993, Art. 5(1). States Parties shall not recruit, use, finance or train mercenaries and shall prohibit such activities.

War Crime #41. Funding War Mercenaries. The first use of mercenaries was in Afghanistan. Funds went to the Northern Alliance, and various warlords were given CIA bribes to defect from support for the Taliban. Subsequently, CIA payments were made to warlords in Afghanistan, including to Hazrat Ali, for the capture of Osama Bin Laden. Reportedly, Ali was one of the warlords who helped him escape, as al-Qaeda apparently offered even more bribe money.

Civilian contractors operate independently of military authorities, answerable only to the Departments of Defense and State in Washington, D.C., which hire but do not supervise them. Civilian contractors working in Abu Ghraib were implicated in the abuse and torture of prisoners, but the military exercised no supervision over them.

Some security personnel have been paid from $500 to $1,500 per day. From 2003 to 2004, the Defense Department paid $2.7 billion for private security, the State Department $2.4 billion. In Iraq, the CIA's Scorpions unit consisted of four Iraqis who were paid to engage in sabotaging the insurgents. The United States has also paid Iraqis $10 per day to serve in security roles, including the operation of checkpoints.

From 2007, Sunnis have been paid to fight al-Qaeda. While Iraq is beset with militias that its government wants to disband, the United States supported the largest militia of all—the 90,000 Sunnis known as the Sons of Iraq. The legal way, to provide funds so that the Iraqi government could put them on the official payroll, was not pursued until September 2008.

> **Mercenaries Convention, 1993, Art. 3(1).** A mercenary ... who participates directly in hostilities or in a concerted act of violence, as the case may be, commits an offence for the purposes of the Convention.

War Crime #42. Mercenaries Have Engaged in Combat. Armed mercenaries have on several occasions engaged in combat even before being fired upon. On April 4, 2004, Blackwater forces were the sole forces engaged in combat with insurgents near Kut, and they commanded regular army troops during the Battle of Najaf.

Some contractors have died in combat. By one account, Blackwater acted offensively during 163 out of 195 firings on civilians (84 percent of the time) from 2005 to mid-September 2007. Crescent Security reportedly has continued to fire preemptively while passing through a town north of Baghdad because, once upon a time, that was the location of a roadside bomb. Other civilian contractors, armed with machine guns, have been reported to open fire, as if in an amusement park, while en route on highways where there is not a single sign of resistance.

According to one observer, "Western contractors fire at or into Iraqi vehicles on a regular basis," though only 10 percent of the Iraqis have ever shot back, thereby indicating that the shootings have been unprovoked. The American ambassador in Baghdad has whisked away from Iraq some contractors responsible for wanton attacks on civilians.

In September 2007, a videotape filmed Blackwater contractors firing machine guns for no apparent reason in al-Nisoor Square, Baghdad, resulting in the deaths of eleven civilians and injuries to twelve others. When the tape was played on television, there was an outcry. Although the Interior Ministry demanded that Blackwater should submit those responsible for trial in an Iraqi court, under suspected pressure from Washington, Prime Minister Nuri al-Maliki countermanded the request. Families, after being offered $3,000 in compensation payments by the American Embassy in 2008, refused what they considered "blood money." They wanted an apology first.

When asked whether private military contractors were regulated by American law, Defense Secretary Rumsfeld expressed the belief that the Iraq government had full jurisdiction, whereas the Defense Department's Office of General Counsel issued an opinion that the contractors were covered by American law. To clear up the ambiguity, in November 2006 Congress passed a law that placed civilian contractors under the Uniform Code of Military Justice, which means that they are immune from prosecution in civilian courts and can only be tried in military tribunals. The first such case, involving a Canadian contractor who stabbed a fellow contractor, was resolved in June 2008 when he pled guilty to stealing and disposing of the knife as well as lying about the incident. Nevertheless, an American woman claiming that she was raped by a civilian contractor in Iraq was permitted to file a lawsuit in federal court during 2008.

After the role of Blackwater in murdering Iraqi civilians generated much publicity in fall 2007, similar problems in Afghanistan came to light. Civilians have been killed by mercenaries in several combined aerial and ground campaigns in recent years.

CONCLUSION

The wars in Afghanistan and Iraq were conducted with insufficient troops to accomplish the basic goal of warfare—to seek and vanquish the enemy. Rather than using ground forces to oppose troops on a battlefield with air and naval support, bombing campaigns were launched to shock enemies into ceasing resistance. In other words, the initial wars were conceived largely as aerial campaigns, sometimes using weapons banned by international treaties. When military intelligence was wrong, as was too often the case, civilians died needlessly.

The goal of decapitating both regimes precluded the possibility of orderly surrender. The streets of Baghdad lacked police to stop lawlessness when civilian Iraqi authorities abandoned the city in fear of their lives. Looting occurred unabated, followed by insurgency and ethnic cleansing as the conflict spun out of control.

When the insurgency emerged in Iraq, a military approach was followed rather than a "hearts and minds" campaign to legitimate the role of foreign personnel. Soldiers, not trained for careful police work, clumsily and sometimes brutally interfered with the lives of innocent people until General Petraeus provided new leadership.

Mercenaries imported to fill the gap in military personnel were not subject to strict military discipline. Paying Iraqi militias from 2007 often meant that the United States was financing further killing in a civil war. Meanwhile, terrorists from Europe and elsewhere went to Iraq for military action and training.

From a larger perspective, Bush rejected the concept of a peace process to end any of the wars that he waged. There has been no peace conference involving adversaries, friends, and neutrals, and there has been a consistent refusal to negotiate. Instead, the wars have dragged on with an endless militarization of every issue.

In sum, Bush's aggression in Afghanistan and Iraq maximized the possibility of war crimes. Civilian deaths in the tens or hundreds of thousands compare with fewer than five thousand American deaths. American soldiers tragically sought to do their duty, sometimes heroically, in conflicts that were badly conceived. The future safety of American troops can no longer be assumed, if captured, due to the impact of the torture and other abuses meted out to prisoners collected by American forces, as described in the following chapter.

Chapter 4

CRIMES COMMITTED IN THE TREATMENT OF PRISONERS

Prisoners captured in war should be treated humanely during war and released at the end of war, according to the Hindu Code of Manu. The principle of chivalry, cited by Aquinas, is that noncombatants should not be harmed. Grotius's principle of humanity is that the sick and wounded should be cared for, and prisoners should be treated respectfully.

A major event in the American effort to develop international law occurred on December 25, 1775, when General George Washington insisted that mercenaries (Hessian prisoners) captured during the Battle of Trenton should be treated "with humanity." His goal, to win over the loyalty of the Hessians to the American cause, was successful.

Later, the Lieber Code of 1863 codified principles to govern treatment of captured persons during America's Civil War that were subsequently adopted by many countries in Europe. A significant advance in international law regarding the treatment of prisoners was the Red Cross Convention of 1864, which was adopted after nurse Florence Nightingale visited the battlefield in the Crimean War (1853–1856) and reported with horror that wounded soldiers were usually left unattended to die on the battlefield. Many international treaties have updated the 1864 treaty (Appendix 4.1).

APPLICABILITY OF THE GENEVA CONVENTIONS

Confusion exists over which laws cover prisoners in American-run prisons outside the United States after 9/11. The Third Geneva Convention applies to those picked up on battlefields while war is ongoing. The Fourth Geneva Convention focuses on those arrested by occupation authorities after war concludes. However, military operations have continued in Afghanistan and Iraq to the present, the United States has provided occupation forces in both countries, and the "war on terror" has not ended.

General Tommy Franks, who headed Central Command and thus oversaw the invasions of Afghanistan and Iraq, ordered his subordinates on October 17, 2001, to follow the Geneva Conventions in dealing with prisoners while war was ongoing. After initial fighting ended, and the regime in Kabul was toppled, Franks was countermanded by executive orders on November 13 from President George W. Bush, who accepted various legal opinions that classified some persons as "enemy combatants," not prisoners of war—in other words, outside the scope of the Geneva Conventions. Bush evidently hoped that Secretary of Defense Donald Rumsfeld and those in uniform might be shielded from criminality under domestic and international law for the way in which CIA and Special Operations military personnel were planning to treat prisoners.

In mid-2003, when the insurgency emerged in Iraq, Lieutenant General Ricardo Sanchez authorized mass arrests to obtain intelligence. Prisoners captured from insurgent attacks were then mixed together with civilians suspected of complicity in the Baghdad prison known as Abu Ghraib. Interrogation officials were unsure how to proceed when most Iraqis professed no knowledge about the insurgency.

On three grounds, all flawed, Bush accepted the premise that the Geneva Conventions were inapplicable. He listened to his closest advisers, some of whom tried to shout down dissent rather than having a serious debate on how to treat prisoners.

First, Bush asserted, because those detained were not in uniform, they were not covered by the Third Geneva Convention. But the document confers no such immunity from coverage. All those not taking an active part in hostilities, including those captured or surrendered in war, are initially protected (Article 3).

Second, Bush claimed an exemption because terrorists, both individually and collectively, have not ratified the Geneva Conventions and thus cannot claim protection. Nevertheless, there is no such reciprocity requirement. All signatories to the Conventions are unilaterally bound by the provisions (Article 2).

Third, Bush's lawyers argued that Article 5 of the Fourth Geneva Convention had a loophole, namely, that provisions were inapplicable "while the armed conflict continues" and where "absolute military security so requires." However, the exception is only intended to be "applied in individual cases of an exceptional nature." Instead, thousands were indiscriminately rounded up in Afghanistan and later Iraq. Some were not even screened for months.

Bush hoped that five types of prisoners were outside Geneva Convention protections:

(A) persons arrested on the battlefield fighting for the Taliban or members of the Taliban;

(B) those turned over to American authorities by bounty hunters in Afghanistan, Pakistan, and elsewhere as suspected members of al-Qaeda or affiliated terrorist organizations;

(C) persons captured around the world by the CIA as possible members of al-Qaeda;

(D) high-ranking members of the former regime of Saddam Hussein; and

(E) belligerents in the postwar Iraqi insurgency.

Guantánamo received some persons in categories A and B. Those in category C ended up in secret prisons. Some members of category D, who remained in Iraq, have been tried for war crimes, notably Saddam Hussein. That left category E as one to which Geneva Convention requirements might apply; accordingly, few Iraqis were sent to Guantánamo.

Although Bush declared on January 18, 2002, that belligerents in the Afghan War were covered by the Geneva Conventions, he insisted contradictorily that members of al-Qaeda and the Taliban were not to be treated as prisoners of war. Presumably, Taliban detainees were to stay in Afghanistan, while al-Qaeda suspects were shipped to Guantánamo, but the line was blurred. Bush also declared that the Geneva Conventions applied to Iraq, but Rumsfeld ignored him by authorizing extraordinary interrogation techniques in memos that he sent down the chain of command to Special Operations officers with Bush's authorization (Appendix 1.1).

What Bush's advisers failed to tell him was that Article 5 of the Third Geneva Convention considers *all* detainees from war initially to be prisoners of war (POWs) until lawful hearings are held to determine their status—hearings not held at Guantánamo until 2007, using procedures that are still in dispute.

Those collected from places other than battlefields would ordinarily have been tried for criminal acts, outside the scope of the Geneva Conventions, but none were at that time. Instead, Bush suspected all detainees of being enemies in the "war on terror." He considered the "battlefield" to be everywhere. Hoisted by his own petard, he should have considered all detainees as potential POWs until hearings mandated by the Geneva Conventions proved them to be participants in his self-proclaimed "war on terror." But he did not.

Bush openly disparaged Geneva Convention protections. Accordingly, subordinates assumed that no prisoners had any rights. But the Supreme Court has yet to confirm that anyone imprisoned at Abu Ghraib, Guantánamo, or elsewhere by the United States has been lawfully processed.

COLLECTING PRISONERS

Soon after 9/11, more than 200 suspected terrorists were rounded up by the CIA from more than forty countries around the world and held in secret locations, an effort that continued throughout the Bush administration. Journalist Ronald Kessler claims that some 5,000 suspected terrorists were eventually seized.

In Afghanistan, from as early as 2002, Deputy Secretary of Defense Paul Butler has admitted that some 10,000 persons were picked up, either as government soldiers fighting for the Taliban or as suspected members of al-Qaeda. Most were captured by warlords, who were paid by the American authorities from $50 to $25,000 for each person captured, with $15,000 the going rate for Afghans, and $25,000 the incentive price for those from Arabic-speaking countries. Some of those seized were Afghans whom the warlords disliked. Others were considered suspicious simply because they spoke Arabic.

Pakistani authorities likewise turned over suspicious foreigners, mostly from Arabic-speaking countries in the same price range, though $500,000 was paid for Abdullah Khadr, $5 million for Abu Talha al-Sudani, and $25 million for Abu Zubaydah. Pakistan President Pervez Musharraf boasted in his autobiography that bounties brought tens of millions of dollars to his country. Soufian al-Hawari and three others were sold by members of the Russian Mafia in Georgia for $100,000.

When those captured were sorted out, nearly 800 were sent to the American-held facility at Guantánamo Bay, Cuba, starting on January 11, 2002. The rest have remained at various sites in Afghanistan, were placed in secret prisons, or were released.

After American soldiers entered Baghdad in spring 2003, there was a manhunt for loyalists of Saddam Hussein. When the insurgency began in Iraq during midsummer 2003, the army arrested thousands more, some on the basis of $1,000 bounties, in order to gain information about the insurgents. At least 600 were considered "security detainees," allegedly playing a role in the insurgency. Although the conditions of their arrest—without a warrant from a civilian authority—are analyzed as violations of their rights under military occupation in chapter 5, their treatment in prison after arrest applies to the present chapter.

In the initial phases of their capture, the prisoners should have been interrogated carefully to determine whether they were indeed "enemies" of the United States. If not, they should have been released promptly. If determined to have knowledge about the insurgents, they might have been interrogated to determine whether they had knowledge of future hostile operations. Warriors on the opposite sides of a battlefield, after all, are expected to have committed hostile acts in accordance with a coherent battle plan. Following timely interrogation regarding plans afoot, those captured would ordinarily be held until the end of the war or, if warranted, they could be tried for war crimes, that is, for conduct not permitted on the battlefield under international law. But there was no such orderly process.

Abdurahman Khadr, who agreed to be a spy and mingled with Guantánamo detainees to gather information for the Americans, concluded in an April 21, 2004, public television *Frontline* interview, only "10 percent of the people … are really dangerous." The Red Cross has said the same. Erik Saar, who was a military translator from December 2002 to June 2003, estimated on *60 Minutes* on May 1, 2005, that only a "few dozen" at Guantánamo had any connection with terrorism. Major General Michael Dunlavey, who was in charge of the interrogation program when prisoners first arrived at Guantánamo, estimated that half of the detainees had no intelligence value. The Denbeaux study at Seton Hall University, which examined charges against prisoners at Guantánamo, concluded that 95 percent had been picked up by bounty hunters, not by American soldiers in the field. A taxi driver named Dilawar, charged with setting off a bomb that killed American soldiers, was discovered by documentary filmmaker Alex Gibney to have been handed over to American authorities by the very persons who were responsible for the bomb!

One of many puzzles surrounds the Chinese Muslims at Guantánamo. Known as Uighurs or Turkestanis, they are members of a movement to achieve freedom from China for a province that has long sought independence. They had escaped to Afghanistan, where bounty hunters picked them up. Rather than granting them asylum, American military authorities sent them to Guantánamo, though they were never alleged to have committed any offenses against the United States. The patently false pretext was that their separatist group is affiliated with al-Qaeda. Two, who petitioned a federal court to grant a writ of habeas corpus, were released to Albania in 2006 just three days before the court was to hear their case. Albania accepted three others, but the remaining seventeen were still at Guantánamo in mid-2008.

Some 774 persons ended up in Guantánamo. When those captured were determined not to be enemy personnel, about 500 were released. Of 60 who may be tried, 20 have been charged and are slated for trial. Some 70 are eligible for release, leaving the rest in limbo as of mid-2008. In *Boumediene v Bush* (2008), the Supreme Court agreed that the rest (possibly 144) can file habeas corpus petitions, whereupon the government would have to file charges or release them.

The Bush administration decided to use six main detention facilities—two in Afghanistan, three in Iraq, and the one at Guantánamo Bay. Estimates of those held in American-run prisons in Afghanistan range from 1,300 to 2,000. Journalist Nir Rosen estimated in March 2008 that some 24,000 were being held in American-run prisons in Iraq without charges. Together with the 274 at Guantánamo, the total worldwide was about 27,000 during mid-2008.

In addition, there have been at least eleven secret prisons run by the CIA. As of August 25, 2006, some 14,000 persons were being held secretly in detention worldwide, though 14 were sent to Guantánamo in 2007. The current number is unknown.

GUIDELINES FOR TREATING PRISONERS

Because of the lengthy detention of many prisoners, some entirely innocent of any hostile act or suspect association, considerable attention has been directed toward the mishandling of prisoners during interrogation and confinement. In the mid-1970s, when Britain attempted to hold suspected members of the Irish Republican Army (IRA) indefinitely, the very practice of indefinite detention served as a recruitment tool for the IRA. Bush was evidently unmindful of that lesson as well as the fact that Israel has never operated any parallel to Guantánamo after decades of coping with terrorism.

The FBI's standard procedures for interrogation involve psychological methods to obtain information from those arrested, consistent with American law. Nearly a thousand FBI agents were dispatched to Afghanistan,

Guantánamo, and Iraq and to various secret prisons from 2001 to 2004. The Army's field manual *Intelligence Interrogation* (1992) also provides a standard set of interrogation procedures after prisoners held have been deemed to possess valuable information (Appendix 4.2), incorporating Geneva Convention constraints. Prior to 9/11, the Army's procedures had been demonstrated to be 95 percent effective in extracting information from prisoners. But the Bush administration sought to blur the distinction between army intelligence gathering and the CIA's methods of interrogation.

The CIA, not under the jurisdiction of the Department of Defense, has a manual entitled *Counterintelligence Interrogation*, which principally focuses on psychological torture but does not follow Geneva Convention standards. Whereas the FBI and the armed forces have manuals that require Geneva Convention compliance so that untainted information can be used in court, the CIA's techniques can render a prisoner's statements inadmissible and therefore will serve to prevent a successful prosecution for war crimes and other offenses.

In 2002, Bush advanced the term "enemy combatant," a neologism with no status under either American or international law. One immediate aim was to obtain information about future terrorist acts through interrogations outside the Army and CIA manuals. The term was not defined until July 7, 2004, when Deputy Defense Secretary Paul Wolfowitz issued an administrative order.

Green lights for violating Geneva Convention standards regarding treatment of prisoners were found in memos issued by Bush and his subordinates, who in turn issued corresponding directives (Appendix 1.1). When American military police in Afghanistan were surprised in mid-November 2001 that Bush did not want to apply the Geneva Conventions to prisoners under their control, they awaited new military-established guidelines for handling prisoners, including interrogation methods. Similarly, Brigadier General Rick Baccus sought to apply Geneva Conventions standards to the first batch of prisoners at Guantánamo, but he was later relieved of his command.

While a debate about new guidelines took place in Washington, military intelligence officers thought that they could ignore the regulations explained during their military training, which evidently no longer applied, and do almost anything they wanted to obtain information about terrorist personnel and plots. It is an important legal principle that those in command who fail to provide clear orders are negligent and legally responsible for the acts of their subordinates.

Some of Bush's subordinates were pressured to deliver important revelations from the interrogations that were not immediately forthcoming. The first memos authorizing torture (Appendix 1.1) were written while anticipated information was not being extracted through normal interrogation. Captain Carolyn Wood, who was in charge of interrogations in Afghanistan from July 2002, decided to expand procedures to include barking dogs, prolonged nudity, and shackling in stress positions.

Major General Michael Dunlavey, commanding officer of the prison at Guantánamo, sent a memo on October 11, 2002, proposing four categories of techniques (Table 4.1). Whereas his memo appears to be a request to upgrade the harshness of interrogation, international lawyer Philippe Sands infers that he was pressured to author the document by those higher up the chain of command. In November, Major General Geoffrey Miller replaced Dunlavey and proceeded to try new techniques to extract information from prisoners, most of whom had nothing useful to disclose.

On December 2, 2002, Rumsfeld approved Dunlavey's Category 1 (deceiving and harassing inmates), Category 2 (forced stress positions) with the modification that standing could be for longer than four hours, and mild physical contact from Category 3 (threats of extreme pain). Techniques employed at Guantánamo with Rumsfeld's approval were also adopted for use in Afghanistan, though others were applied without

Table 4.1
Brigadier General Michael Dunlavey's Proposed Interrogation Techniques

Category	Examples
1	Yelling and deceiving inmates
2	Various forms of stress (standing for up to four hours, isolation up to 30 days, hooding during transportation and questioning, 20-hour interrogations, removal of religious items, forced nudity and grooming, and manipulating phobias, such as fear of dogs)
3	Threatening extreme pain or death of inmates or their families, hypothermia brought on by exposure to cold weather or cold water, waterboarding (using a wet towel and dripping water on a blindfolded prisoner to suggest drowning), and mild physical contact (grabbing, poking in the chest with the finger, and light pushing)
4	Extraordinary rendition

Source: Margulies, *Guantánamo and the Abuse of Presidential Power*, 97–99

authorization. Category 4 (extraordinary renditions), meanwhile, was kept secret and implemented entirely by the CIA outside Guantánamo.

Admiral Alberto Mora, then the Navy's General Counsel, expressed serious reservations, stopped the torture of Mohammed al-Qahtani at Guantánamo from proceeding beyond fifty-four days, and complained to Rumsfeld about Geneva Convention violations. On January 15, 2003, Rumsfeld changed his mind and rescinded the use of Categories 2 and 3. Enforced nudity, which Rumsfeld had approved on December 2, was thus disallowed six weeks later in a memo, but word of the change apparently did not get through to soldiers in detention facilities.

Rumsfeld then appointed members of a working group to study the issue further. Meanwhile, Lieutenant General Dan McNeill, commander of American forces in Afghanistan, dropped five of the unauthorized techniques on February 27, 2003, after learning that their use had resulted in two deaths at Bagram Air Force Base, Afghanistan.

On March 6, 2003, Rumsfeld's working group issued a report recommending thirty-five techniques from the Army field manual plus some techniques previously banned. On April 16, 2003, Rumsfeld accepted twenty-four of the thirty-five techniques recommended by his working group, though he never revealed which were dropped. Several revisions of interrogation procedures followed.

In August 2003, Miller was transferred to Abu Ghraib, where he met Wood, who also took up a new assignment there that month. She proceeded to post a list of interrogation procedures used in Afghanistan, most of which were from the Army field manual, but she also included others (Table 4.2), clearly with approval from Rumsfeld, whose signature appeared at the bottom. At the top, in the same Rumsfeldian scrawl, appeared the words, "Make sure this happens!"

Upon arrival in Baghdad, Miller asked Lieutenant General Ricardo Sanchez, commanding officer of American troops in Iraq, for an updated

Table 4.2
Posted Extraordinary Interrogation Procedures at Abu Ghraib

Technique	Duration
Isolation	Longer than 30 days
Presence of military working dogs	No minimum or maximum
Sensory deprivation	72 hours maximum
Stress positions	45 minutes maximum

Source: Miles, Oath Betrayed, 52

list of techniques. Sanchez quickly obliged with guidelines based on the Geneva Conventions, but modified them in September and October 2003. According to the investigative report of Major General George Fay, subordinates at Abu Ghraib believed Sanchez's guidance to be ambiguous, thereby giving them considerable discretion in handling prisoners.

Both the Army and the CIA assumed incorrectly that those undergoing interrogation had already been identified as possessing important information. There were insufficient military personnel to screen those captured in order to identify candidates for special interrogation techniques, so hundreds languished in detention facilities without knowing why they were there.

In *Chain of Command*, journalist Seymour Hersh reveals that Rumsfeld operated a special interrogation program under the specific authority of President Bush, who reauthorized the program monthly. That program, which operated in Afghanistan and Abu Ghraib outside the normal military command structure, ordered military police to play rough in preparing detainees for interrogation without providing clear guidelines. The prison commander at Abu Ghraib, Brigadier General Janis Karpinski, had no authority over interrogations and claimed to be unaware that intelligence officers were improperly giving orders to her prison guards.

Methods used by Army interrogators and the CIA were useless on those with no information to provide. When individuals in custody did not provide useful information, abuses were employed. When authorized types of abuse did not work, unauthorized techniques were tried.

Whereas Sanchez had originally ordered the military to comply with the Geneva Conventions, he had no authority over interrogations by the CIA or Special Operations personnel supplied by Rumsfeld. Nevertheless, Sanchez loaned some of his interrogators to the CIA and the Special Operations team for a week or two. When Sanchez's interrogators returned to his command, they had been exposed to techniques contrary to the Geneva Conventions and began to import them into how they handled prisoners at Abu Ghraib. As a result, the unauthorized "enhanced techniques" were applied to more and more prisoners. Inevitably, prisoners either provided false confessions to stop unbearable treatment or were punished for supposed noncooperation.

THE ABU GHRAIB SCANDAL

On April 28, 2004, grisly photographs from prisons in Iraq were displayed on the television program *60 Minutes*. Most snapshots came from

CRIMES COMMITTED IN THE TREATMENT OF PRISONERS   67

Abu Ghraib, though some may also have been taken at Camp Bucca, near Basra, or Camp Cropper near Baghdad. Testimony from various prisoners, including some who were sent home from Guantánamo and from secret prisons, also provided personal accounts about the use of strange techniques (Appendix 4.3). Soon there was an outcry around the world. A democratic country that had long criticized dictatorships for violating human rights lost its innocence and was charged with being a terrorist nation.

Several official investigations were then conducted at Abu Ghraib and Guantánamo. Some were whitewashes. Others had details about possible Geneva Convention violations by American personnel. Interrogation techniques were again revised, and disciplinary action was taken against some of those responsible at the lowest levels of the chain of command, though no one was ever specifically charged with torture at either location. (Two persons were convicted of torture at Bagram Air Force Base, however.) Abu Ghraib was transferred to Iraqi control in 2006.

The most controversial procedures, characterized as "torture," are prohibited in the Army field manual as well as by the Constitution, in American law, and in many legal precedents. Bush, despite saying, "We do not torture," never defined what he meant.

Congress, in response to the Abu Ghraib scandal, passed the Detainee Treatment Act of 2005, banning torture by the military but not the CIA. President Bush's signing statement indicated that he might authorize a violation of the law whenever he wanted. A secret memo written at the time by Attorney General Alberto Gonzales was rumored to have approved specific techniques, including waterboarding.

Bush's executive order on July 20, 2007, appeared to require the CIA to adhere to the interrogation techniques in the Army field manual. In so doing he implicitly admitted that he had condoned treatment outside the bounds of the manual right up until he signed the executive order.

On February 6, 2008, White House press secretary Tony Fratto stated that there were procedures in place to permit Bush to authorize the CIA to torture a detainee whenever there was a strong belief of an imminent attack. He argued that some waterboarding was not torture if conducted only for a few seconds. He was trying to stop Congress from passing a law that would explicitly ban waterboarding, but Congress passed the law anyway. On March 8, Bush vetoed that law, thereby assuming personal culpability for one of the most obvious war crimes. On April 11, he admitted that earlier he had approved torture.

MILITARY COMMISSIONS

Bush wanted to place those responsible for 9/11 and future terrorist plots on trial for war crimes. But incriminating information derived though the use of torture must be excluded from evidence in trials under American constitutional law. Lacking solid evidence, Bush sought show trials that could be conducted without customary safeguards. Accordingly, Bush authorized tribunals that would make up new rules, that is, would ignore American and international legal precedents. The new rules were designed without legislative or judicial approval, so the hastily improvised extrajudicial system was bound to offend Congress and the courts.

A series of unfavorable court rulings resulted. In 2004, the Supreme Court in *Rasul v Bush* said that Guantánamo was within its jurisdiction and that prisoners had the right of habeas corpus to appeal their detention. Bush authorized arraignments by military commissions through an executive order, and several pretrial hearings of prisoners were held, though procedures for the commissions were made up on the fly, therefore vulnerable to court challenge. In *Hamdan v Rumsfeld* (2006), the Supreme Court came close to calling Bush a war criminal for authorizing trials in military commissions without Congressional authorization.

Congress responded by passing the Military Commissions Act of 2006, which had several provisions limiting the rights of "alien enemy combatants": (1) They cannot invoke protections under the Geneva Conventions or other international legal standards. (2) They cannot obtain counsel of their own choosing. (3) They can be denied access to secret information used against them. (4) Proceedings can be kept secret. Moreover, they can be detained indefinitely until they either confess to a crime, are put on trial, or die in confinement.

The constitutionality of the Military Commissions Act was immediately challenged. Once again, the Supreme Court became the body to clarify the rights of prisoners before the newly authorized military commissions while the Bush administration was in denial about human rights violations at Guantánamo and elsewhere. Although the act originally banned habeas corpus challenges, some 200 of which had been filed after *Rasul*, the Supreme Court ruled that provision unconstitutional in *Boumediene v Bush* (2008), boilerplated from *Rasul*. As a result, the military had the choice of either charging all the Guantánamo prisoners or releasing them.

WAR CRIMES REGARDING TREATMENT OF PRISONERS

Having provided some background regarding the treatment of prisoners, the following discussion identifies specific war crimes violations organized into categories similar to those used in the Third Geneva Convention. Provisions in earlier and later international treaties, of course, also apply. The earliest provisions are listed first, and later treaties are quoted when they have new provisions or embellish upon earlier standards. When Alberto Gonzales argued that the Geneva Conventions were "outmoded," he did not make a similar determination of the Hague Conventions or many international agreements adopted after the Geneva Conventions.

The names of several prisoners are treated with some prominence in the present chapter because some have become celebrities. Alex Gibney's documentary *Taxi to the Dark Side* (2008) focuses on Dilawar, an Afghan taxi driver who is the second prisoner to die due to conditions of confinement. The rest have achieved fame from their experience at Guantánamo. David Hicks, an Australian, was the first prisoner to confess that he committed a "war crime" and the first to be sentenced; he is now free in Australia. Canadian Omar Khadr is the first juvenile ever accused of a "war crime." Afghan Mohammed Jawad, another juvenile charged for an alleged offense committed when he was 16 or 17, is the first alleged criminal to wear leg shackles in court. British nationals known as the Tipton Three (Ruhal Ahmed, Asif Iqbal, and Shafiq Rasul) were depicted in Michael Winterbottom's docudrama *The Road to Guantánamo* (2006). Salim Ahmed Hamdan is the Yemini who was the first to be tried at Guantánamo in 2008, but for violating American criminal law, not for "war crimes."

Others have become famous because their surnames have appeared in lawsuits filed pro bono by patriotic attorneys who have been attempting to rescue the rights of their clients as well as the reputation of the United States. The more anonymous inmates of Abu Ghraib in Baghdad and in orange jumpsuits at Guantánamo have also achieved fame because of strange photographs that have been displayed around the world. In his book *The Guantánamo Files*, historian Andy Worthington tracks down in what circumstances most of the detainees were apprehended and subsequently processed at Guantánamo.

Former Captain James Yee, the Muslim chaplain at Guantánamo from November 2002 to September 2003, has supplied some of the most detailed eyewitness observations on prison conditions. So has Erik

Saar, an Arabic-language translator at Guantánamo from December 2002 to June 2005. The reports of Lieutenant General Anthony Jones and Major General Antonio Taguba relied on sworn statements of soldiers at Abu Ghraib. A similar report by Lieutenant General Paul Mikolashek covered prisons in both Afghanistan and Iraq. Lieutenant General Randall Schmidt submitted a report on Guantánamo. More information has come to light as prisoners have been released.

War crimes about prisoners focus on how those in confinement have been mistreated. General standards of decency have been offended. Methods of interrogation have exceeded what is permissible. Living conditions have been substandard. Health and safety measures have been inadequate. Inmates have been overly restricted on what they can do. Transfers in and out of facilities have not met Geneva Convention requirements. Children, the elderly, ethnosectarian groups, and women have been treated improperly. And some detainees have disappeared as a result of extraordinary renditions. According to the Detainee Abuse and Accountability Project, at least 460 prisoners have suffered various forms of abuse, yet only 80 are scheduled for trial at Guantánamo.

I describe the inmates as "prisoners" because most have not been lawfully processed in accordance with Article 5 of the Third Geneva Convention to determine whether they are instead "security detainees." The following chapter deals in part with the procedures under which Afghans, Iraqis, and others have been rounded up for detention, whereas the present chapter deals with how they have been treated during confinement.

VIOLATING STANDARDS OF DECENCY

The treatment of civilian prisoners by Nazi Germany and military prisoners by Imperial Japan weighed heavily on the minds of those drafting the Third Geneva Convention. Those responsible for American-run prisons evidently forgot important lessons. Even in time of civil unrest and war, the International Covenant on Civil and Political Rights bans cruel and inhumane treatment (Article 7).

Hague II, 1899, Art. 4. Prisoners of war are in the power of the hostile Government, but not in that of the individuals or corps who captured them. They must be humanely treated. All their personal belongings, except arms, horses, and military papers remain their property.

War Crime #43. Inhumane Treatment. To be "inhumane" means to treat someone as less than human—as a lowly animal. Former Assistant Defense Secretary Lawrence Wilkerson has said that Bush in private conversation condoned the inhumane treatment. Captain Carolyn Wood, who designed her own unique set of weird procedures for mishandling prisoners in Afghanistan that were later applied to Abu Ghraib, was eventually awarded a Bronze Star for her efforts.

The degrading treatment began in Afghanistan, where one detainee described his quarters at Bagram Air Force Base as similar to a cage at the zoo in Karachi, Pakistan. Another prisoner at Bagram recalled being forced to fish for plastic bottle caps in a drum of excrement mixed with water. Ait Idr's face was forced into a toilet that was repeatedly flushed. After Martin Mubanga was refused the use of a toilet and then wet himself, a prison official used Mubanga's body as a mop to collect the liquid. The conditions in the prisons were so shocking that Canadian forces in Afghanistan stopped sending prisoners to the American-run prisons at the end of 2005, preferring to send them to facilities run by the Afghan government.

At Abu Ghraib, spitting on prisoners and hooding them for up to three days were some of the ways to treat prisoners as subhuman. Reports indicate that a guard rubbed fecal material onto one prisoner's body. Another had his face pushed into urine. Others were forced to drink urine.

Prisoners arriving at Guantánamo were first held in statuesque stress positions on the dirt for hours. Flies swarmed around those who passed out and fell onto the ground. They were then moved to wire-mesh open-air cages, exposed to the hot sun, rain, spiders, and snakes in twenty-three-hour isolation, deprived of human contact. One estimate is that one-fourth of the prisoners were subjected to isolation. For meals, they were not allowed table implements and had to eat "like an animal," according to Shafiq Rasul. (Forks were already used during the apogee of Arabic civilization, while Europeans were still eating with their hands.)

Guantánamo inmate Mohammed al-Qahtani, who was led around on a leash, was told that "he was less than human and that animals had more freedom and love than he does." He was then taken outside to see banana rats running free. When compared unfavorably to the rats, he began to cry. Later, he was called a pig and forced to do dog tricks.

A common dehumanizing and demasculinizing method has been to shave a person's head. Some had their eyebrows shaved off. Face and beard shaving, of course, are initiation rites in the armed services that are supposed to produce compliance and conformity, but they are contrary to the mores of many prisoners.

Upon assuming command at Guantánamo under the specific order of Defense Secretary Rumsfeld, Major General Geoffrey Miller urged subordinates to treat detainees "like dogs." Indeed, his subordinate Colonel Mike Baumgartner, who was in charge of the prison for a time, stated that every prisoner was in his opinion "nothing short of a damn animal." Prisoners were forced to crawl like animals. While crawling, their bodies were beaten, ridden, and spat and urinated upon.

War Crime #44. Depriving Prisoners of Their Property. On several occasions, clothes of prisoners were cut from their bodies upon capture or before being transferred to a place of detention. Some were chained naked to the ceiling, the cell doors, and the floor at Abu Ghraib, in Afghanistan, and at Guantánamo.

During the arrest of several Iraqis in 2004, American soldiers looted them of cash, according to their attorney, Talal al-Dawody. The Red Cross estimated that at least $36,000, several cars, wedding rings, and other property had been looted because receipts were not issued to Iraqi prisoners. One prisoner at Guantánamo complained that his briefcase, which contained an unspecified amount of cash, had been taken from him and never returned.

> **Hague IV, 1907, Art. 18.** Prisoners of war shall enjoy complete liberty in the exercise of their religion, including attendance at the services of whatever church they may belong to, on the sole condition that they comply with the measures of order and police issued by the military authorities.

War Crime #45. Religious Mistreatment. Perhaps the most serious verbal abuse has been to force prisoners to deny their faith. At Kandahar, prison guards dropped the Qur'an into toilet buckets, put obscene words on its pages, and even tore pages out to clean toilet buckets. Initially, prisoners at Abu Ghraib and Guantánamo were not allowed to have copies of the Qur'an, or possess prayer beads, caps, and oils. When prisoners substituted sheets for caps at Guantánamo, they were punished. When one Abu Ghraib inmate initially asked permission to pray, he was chained to the bars of his cell window for nearly five hours with his feet dangling off the floor.

Later, only cooperative inmates at Guantánamo were allowed to have beads, caps, and oils. Instead of prayer rugs, they were issued thin plastic sheets to place on the dirt floor in their cells. After being stripped naked for a few days, they were issued short pants so small that guards could see their genitals while they prayed on their knees. Calls to prayer were not always broadcast five times a day, and not with the correct Arabic words. Guards tried to disrupt prayers by making loud sounds, playing loud music, or bringing dogs into the cells. One prisoner's arm was broken by guards to stop him from praying. Some interrogations were deliberately held during prayer time.

After the Qur'an was supplied at Guanatánamo, prisoners were at first denied cloth to keep their Qur'ans clean and off the floor. Some guards have defaced, kicked, smashed, stomped on, or torn pages from the sacred book or have dropped the book on the floor. The Tipton Three recall that one guard threw a Qur'an into a toilet bucket. One pasted a picture of a prisoner whose knowledge of Islam was greatly respected among prisoners in a Qur'an with the label "hypocrite" in Arabic. A guard even allowed a dog to carry the Qur'an in its mouth. The most frequent cause of prison riots appears to be the guards' deliberate and repeated disrespect to the Qur'an.

Bush's frequent references to "Islamic extremists" or "Islamofascism" suggest that Islam is the problem. His subliminal message, which cannot fail to be heard down the chain of command, implies the demonization of a religion. Yet Muslims overwhelmingly oppose terrorism, some American allies in the Middle East could be said to run their governments in a fascist manner, and the Hamburg cell responsible for 9/11 consisted of Muslims alienated outside their homeland with little understanding of Islam.

> **POW Convention, 1929, Art. 2.** Prisoners of war are in the power of the hostile Power, but not of the individuals or corps who have captured them. They must at all times be humanely treated and protected, particularly against acts of violence, insults and public curiosity.... **Art. 3.** Prisoners of war have the right to have their person and their honor respected.

War Crime #46. Displaying Prisoners. In 2003, five American soldiers captured by Iraqi insurgents were displayed on Iraqi television. Rumsfeld then complained, "It is against the Geneva Convention to show photographs of prisoners of war in a manner that is humiliating for them." But the year before, when the first batch of Guantánamo prisoners were filmed kneeling in stress positions, he did not object.

Then in 2004 photographs of sexual abuse at Abu Ghraib amply documented violations of the privacy of prisoners. Specialist Sabrina

Harman, who took most of the snapshots, and her friend Charles Grainor were among the few punished for "embarrassing the military." Grainor had been ordered by an intelligence officer in one case to make a prisoner's "life a living hell for the next three days," leaving him to figure out what the order meant. Harman, who had ambitions of being a forensic police photographer, used her camera to record the appalling treatment on film.

> **POW Convention, 1929, Art. 76.** Belligerents shall see that prisoners of war dying in captivity are honorably buried and that the graves bear all due information, are respected and properly maintained.

War Crime #47. Denial of Decent Burial of Prisoners. In *Oath Betrayed*, Dr. Steven Miles presents considerable evidence of the failure to bury prisoners properly. In a particularly noteworthy case, a "ghost" prisoner had died during a CIA interrogation, whereupon his mutilated body was dumped at Abu Ghraib, packed into a body bag with ice for about twenty-four hours, and photographed. Later, his remains were transferred to the Baghdad morgue. He remained unclaimed because his family was not notified of his whereabouts, and his body was buried in an unmarked grave.

> **Geneva III, 1949, Art. 3.** In the case of armed conflict not of an international character occurring in the territory of one of the High Contracting Parties, each Party to the conflict shall be bound to apply, as a minimum, the following provisions: (1) Persons taking no active part in the hostilities, including members of armed forces who have laid down their arms and those placed hors de combat by sickness, wounds, detention, or any other cause, shall in all circumstances be treated humanely, without any adverse distinction founded on race, color, religion or faith, sex, birth or wealth, or any other similar criteria. To this end, the following acts are and shall remain prohibited at any time and in any place whatsoever with respect to the above-mentioned persons: (a) violence to life and person, in particular...cruel treatment and...(c) outrages upon personal dignity, in particular humiliating and degrading treatment...

War Crime #48. Cruel Treatment. "Cruelty" implies abuse undertaken for no purpose at all except to inflict suffering short of torture. Some at Abu Ghraib were immobilized by chains connected to the doors and bunk beds of their cells. Others were without food or sleep for up to forty-eight hours with their hands bound behind their backs, blindfolded. One member of the military police at Abu Ghraib has been quoted instructing a prison guard with a new prisoner, "I don't give a fuck what you do to him. Just don't kill him."

Exposure to the cold has been a common complaint. Salah Hassan, an Al-Jazeera photojournalist, was forced to stand naked for eleven hours in the cold autumn night. The next morning he was released for lack of evidence against him onto the streets of Baghdad in a jumpsuit covered with vomit.

More brutally, five Iraqi generals were beaten until blood covered their bodies. Others were doused with cold water while naked or shoved to the ground and stepped on. Some guards at Abu Ghraib removed mattresses from cells, dropped water on the floor, and ordered prisoners to sleep on their stomachs on the floor.

At Guantánamo, many were greeted with the words, "We can do anything we want." When prisoners were allowed to ambulate, the standard practice was to "frogmarch" them with chains on their legs in and out of their cells.

Sleep deprivation involved locking up prisoners in cells or interrogation rooms with continuous neon or strobe lights and loud music twenty-four hours a day for as long as forty-five days. Orders to do so came in the form of directives from Rumsfeld.

At Guantánamo, the cruelest procedure is EFRing (for Emergency Response Force), sometimes known as IRFing (for Immediate Response Force). The procedure involves a team of eight who don riot gear, pepper spray a prisoner, open the cell door, force him to the ground with fists or shields, then hold him down with their bodies and shields, tie up his ankles and wrists, and drag him out of the cell and down the hall. Rather than a distasteful assignment, on one occasion guards boasted of the brutality to Sergeant Heather Cerveny, an assistant to a military lawyer. Former prisoners Shafiq Rasul and Asif Iqbal describe the IRF in April 2002 of Jummah al-Dousari, who had become psychologically disturbed, in the following words:

> They stamped on his neck, kicked him in the stomach even though he had metal rods there as a result of an operation, and they picked up his head and smashed his face into the floor. One female officer was ordered to go into the cell and kick him and beat him, which she did, in his stomach.

In a practice run, platoon leader Specialist Sean Baker volunteered to be IRF'd. As a result, he sustained brain damage, had seizures, and said, "I don't want this to happen to anyone else." The Detainee Treatment Act of 2005 may prevent him from suing for damages. Some meting out the cruelty realized that most detainees had no information to disclose, but they were ordered to continue, knowing that the abuse served no purpose whatsoever.

War Crime #49. Outrages upon Personal Dignity. The term "outrage," when linked to "personal dignity," clearly refers to sexual abuse and related bizarre practices. For Middle Eastern Muslim men, nudity is an outrage, even when other men are present. Forcing prisoners to wear women's underwear or go naked have been common complaints in American penitentiaries from which some of the prison guards have been drawn, and those trained at Fort Lee were briefed on the utility of the techniques before being assigned to Abu Ghraib and elsewhere.

Many prisoners were stripped on arrival and left naked for up to three months in Abu Ghraib, Bagram, and Guantánamo. Prisoners have frequently been strip searched, including body cavities, even though there was no possible way for contraband to be in their possession. In addition, some prison personnel fondled, grabbed, or kicked genitals. Such words as "shithead" were inscribed on their blindfolds or foreheads. Naked pyramids and sodomy first occurred at Kandahar and later migrated to Abu Ghraib. Some men were photographed wearing women's undergarments on their heads, a practice subsequently held to be acceptable "standard operating procedure." David Hicks and others have complained of anal penetration by various objects, including enemas, a nightstick, and a phosphoric light, while blindfolded and shackled. Some prisoners have said that they would rather have electrodes placed on their private parts than have fingers placed up their anus to inspect them. One Abu Ghraib prisoner reported being forced to bend over, spreading his buttocks. Another was forced to masturbate or be whipped.

While interpreter Erik Saar was present, Mamdouh Habib was told that the fake blood being smeared on his body by a female interrogator was menstrual. One woman even stripped, pretended to masturbate, and forced an inmate to rub her breasts and genitalia. Rather than securing cooperation, prisoners have responded by reciting the Qur'an.

After the most sensational photographs of mistreatment emerged in 2004, President Bush apologized. Rumsfeld, who appeared graciously to accept responsibility, had been actually briefed nightly on the progress of the interrogations.

Nevertheless, on September 16, 2006, Bush expressed himself on the subject, as follows: "The Geneva Convention...says that there will be no outrages upon human dignity. It's very vague. What does that mean, 'outrages upon human dignity'? That's a statement that is wide open to interpretation." He recommended that Congress define the term more precisely.

But Congress had already done so in passing the Detainee Treatment Act in 2005, which Bush repudiated in his signing statement. Indeed, a careful reading of *The Terror Presidency* by Jack Goldsmith, the former head of the Department of Justice's Office of Legal Council, reveals very little dismay or shock over the indignities but instead a sense of chagrin, as Bush stated, over the inconvenience that "the Geneva Convention...standards are so vague that our professionals won't be able to carry forward the program, because they don't want to be tried as war criminals." But they can.

In 2008, Senator Don Wyden sought further clarification. He was informed by Deputy Assistant Attorney General Brian Benczkowski that some outrages would be permitted if the information to be extracted was thought to be considerable. Thus, there are no apparent limits to what self-proclaimed mindreaders might do.

INTERROGATION METHODS

One reason for the adoption of the Third Geneva Convention was a revulsion against German-run interrogation camps during World War II. President Bush's order to set up interrogation camps in Afghanistan, Iraq, Guantánamo, and other secret locations is a clear violation.

Detailed commentaries on interrogation methods have been written by Guantánamo inmates and their attorneys, but none match the details in former interrogator Tony Lagouramis' *Fear Up Harsh*. Videotapes, not yet fully accessible to the public, were made of some interrogation sessions. Initially, interrogators followed Geneva Convention restrictions in Afghanistan, but the brutal treatment within the prison cells was soon mirrored in the interrogation rooms for thousands of prisoners.

One military intelligence official boasted to journalists Dana Priest and Barton Gellman, "If you don't violate someone's human rights some of the time, you probably aren't doing your job." Prisoners with no useful information to provide had to undergo as many as two hundred interrogation sessions. One reason for excessive questioning is that several agencies were competing—the CIA, FBI, military intelligence, and a private contractor company. When a prisoner was suspected of having valuable information but did not divulge anything to an FBI interrogator, a rival agency sometimes took over, using different methods. For example, Salim Hamdan had been talking freely with an FBI interrogator for several days when he was suddenly transferred to solitary and went mute.

Erik Saar, military interpreter at Guantánamo, has noted that in one session a prisoner was asked the location of a Taliban "safe house" in Afghanistan, yet at the time the Taliban had been chased out of the country and the "safe house" would not have existed. The session seemed pointless to him. But that was only one of thousands of interrogations conducted by the United States after 9/11.

The entire range of unusual interrogation techniques at Guantánamo has been traced to the highest levels in Washington in *The Torture Team* by British attorney Philippe Sands. When prisoners at Guantánamo initially failed to provide useful intelligence, David Addington, Alberto Gonzales, and William Haynes went there, witnessed some interrogations, and returned to Washington to seek a legal justification for harsher techniques. As senior attorneys respectively for the Vice President, President, and Secretary of Defense, they prevailed on the Justice Department to issue what has become known as the "Torture Memo" and related legal statements. The Guantánamo interrogators, in short, were following orders from the White House based on Bush's executive order of February 7, 2002. Through executive orders, signing statements, and vetoes of Congressional legislation, Bush authorized torture and other harsh forms of interrogation throughout his presidency.

> **POW Convention, 1929, Art. 2.** Prisoners of war are in the power of the hostile Power, but not of the individuals or corps who have captured them.... Measures of reprisal against them are prohibited.

War Crime #50. Reprisals Against Prisoners. Even before interrogation, guards beat prisoners, most of whom were innocent, as a retaliation for the 9/11 attacks. During and following unproductive interrogations, various forms of reprisals were administered against prisoners, notably spitting, starving a prisoner for more than a week, severe beatings, or being shackled in extremely cold rooms. Deprivation of toilet facilities while handcuffed during interrogation, for example, resulted in soiling clothes that were not allowed to be changed for days. Reports indicate that more than half the prisoners have been beaten, even those who were cooperative.

According to Lieutenant General Sanchez, the naked pyramid, use of dogs, and other improper methods were reprisals against those who had engaged in a prison riot. The reason for the riot was that they had been confined for some time and had never been interrogated.

> **POW Convention, 1929, Art. 5.** Every prisoner of war is bound to give, if he is questioned on the subject, his true name and rank, or else his regimental number.... No coercion may be used on prisoners to secure information to the condition of their army or country. Prisoners who refuse to answer may not be threatened, insulted, or exposed to unpleasant or disadvantageous treatment of any kind whatever.

War Crime #51. Interrogation Beyond Name, Rank, and Serial Number. Extended and repeated interrogations are contrary to basic principles governing prisoner of war camps. When guidelines were formally approved, Category 1 procedures from Rumsfeld's playbook were tried first. When information was not forthcoming, Category 2 procedures were followed, with Category 3 in reserve. Whereas FBI agent Ali Soufan followed standard practice in informing prisoners that they had a right of non-self-incrimination and could remain silent at any American-controlled prison in the world, he was ordered not to do so at Guantánamo. Bush was fully aware that the interrogation methods went beyond normal questioning.

War Crime #52. Coercive Techniques. Law Professor Joseph Margulies interprets "coercive" to mean the exploiting of physical and psychological vulnerabilities, such as the "sleeping bag technique" in which claustrophobic fears are produced by stuffing a prisoner head-first into a sleeping bag. The "gloves are coming off" were the words disseminated from Rumsfeld's office to those interrogating prisoners in December 2001.

With Bush's approval, the techniques used in Afghanistan, Guantánamo, Iraq, and various secret prisons went far beyond those in the Army field manual, exploiting the fear of dogs showing their teeth and any phobias that could be determined. Wisam Ahmed recalls hearing the noise of an electric saw outside his cell in Afghanistan as a warning of what might happen to him. When Army interrogation techniques were revised in 2007, presumably to be in conformity with the Geneva Conventions, the CIA was still allowed to use more coercive measures than the military.

Guantánamo inmates report that before interrogation they were injected with an unknown substance that made them groggy, presumably a "truth serum." When they awakened, they began to talk, even agreeing to sign confessions that they did not fully understand. Although "confessions" emerged, without corroborating evidence they have no probative value.

War Crime #53. Threats and Unpleasant Treatment. Military intelligence, under orders from Rumsfeld, gave the codename Copper Green to a special unit preauthorized to engage in extraordinary techniques. The unit consisted of CIA and high-ranking officials from Delta Force and Navy Seals, but some CIA personnel soon withdrew from the unit when their lawyers realized that the harsh treatment went far beyond what they were allowed by their own manual. Bush gave the green light, according to journalist Seymour Hersh.

A frequent threat was to kill an uncooperative prisoner or to hold a mock execution. One of the most heinous was the threat to harm the seven-year-old son and nine-year-old daughter of Khalid Sheikh Mohammed, the admitted mastermind of the 9/11 plot. Nevertheless, he was not impressed, saying that they would join Allah in a better place. Moazzam Begg was falsely told that female screams were those of his wife.

At Guantánamo, threats to deprive prisoners of clothes, "comfort items," exercise, food, medicines, and showers have been common. Indeed, to gain cooperation from prisoners in Iraq, they were warned that they might be sent to Guantánamo.

Shafiq Rasul was told that failure to provide information would result in solitary confinement of up to one year. Others were threatened with dogs. Some interrogators threatened to rape a prisoner, male or female, or to rape members of their families in their homelands.

Regarding unpleasant treatment, in Afghanistan, Mohammed Ahmed Said Haidel was hit with his arms tied behind his back to the point that his head began to bleed. Ahmed Darabi was hung by his arms and repeatedly beaten, though he survived—unlike taxicab driver Dilawar, who died from the same treatment. Some prisoners at Abu Ghraib were shackled or forced to keep their arms suspended for hours. In perhaps the most famous of the photographs, Abdou Hussain Saad Faleh was told that he would be electrocuted if he moved while standing with arms outstretched.

The Schmidt Report identified many examples of unpleasant treatment at Guantánamo, where prisoners were shackled naked to the bottom of the interrogation room and defecated or urinated on themselves in sessions as long as twenty-four hours while the air conditioner was turned down to an uncomfortable temperature. Some were forced to kneel. Others had to squat—for hours at a time while chains cut into their flesh. Prisoners grew so weary of repeated questions in session after session that they became mute, silently praying.

War Crime #54. Systematic Insults. One technique has been to question a prisoner's masculinity after stripping him of all his clothes. One photograph suggests that a female prison official, Specialist Sabrina Harman, is making fun of a prisoner's penis. According to the Schmidt Report, a prisoner was accused of being gay and told that other inmates knew of his supposed sexual orientation. One internee was told that his mother and sisters had become whores. Namecalling has been common.

Geneva III, 1949, Art. 3. ... The following ... shall remain prohibited at any time and in any place whatsoever ...: (a) violence to life and person, in particular ... torture; (b) taking of hostages ...

War Crime #55. Torture. The concept of "torture" is defined in Article 1 of the Convention Against Torture and Other Cruel, Inhuman or Degrading Treatment or Punishment as "any act by which severe pain or suffering, whether physical or mental, is intentionally inflicted on a person [except for] pain and suffering arising only from, inherent in or incidental to lawful sanctions." The International Covenant on Civil and Political Rights also bans the use of torture, even in wartime (Article 7). Rather than following approved guidelines laid down for decades, many policymakers and field operatives were fascinating by the creativity employed in the television series *24*.

The so-called Torture Memo of August 1, 2002 (Appendix 1.1), defined physical "torture" as action intentionally resulting in "organ failure, impairment of bodily function, or even death" and mental torture as intentional only if continued for "months." What happened is that a program designed defensively to train combat soldiers to withstand torture was turned into an offensive program against suspected terrorists. The memo, written hastily after both forms of torture had already occurred, was designed to provide a legal basis for continuation of the same methods, but was withdrawn on December 30, 2004, with no apparent modification in prisoner treatment.

The most common form of torture used by American interrogators has consisted of beatings for several minutes, resulting in bleeding, broken bones, unconsciousness, or even death. In 2002, detainee Dilawar was struck more than 100 times in a twenty-four-hour period during his confinement in Afghanistan and eventually died. Another prisoner was hung from his handcuffs by a soldier who was referred to as the "King of Torture." Also at Bagram, Omar al-Faruq's hands and feet were bound for three months; while deprived of sleep, he was subjected to temperature extremes of 10 and 100 degrees. Qadir Khandan reports being forced to stand twenty-four hours for twenty days by American soldiers at a prison in Khost, Afghanistan.

A former FBI officer has reported that he derived considerable useful intelligence from Ibn Sheik al-Libi by using normal interrogation techniques. In January 2002, however, the CIA took control of him, torture was employed, and genuine cooperation ceased. Instead, he made up the story that interrogators wanted him to say—that Saddam Hussein was cozy with Osama Bin Laden. Later, in January 2004, al-Libi recanted. FBI Director J. Michael McConnell has certified that normal intelligence techniques are more effective than "enhanced" techniques, noting for example that valuable information was extracted from Saddam Hussein after he was captured. CIA Director George Tenet and FBI agent Dan Coleman agree that torture produced little if anything of value.

When Colonel Stuart Herrington (Retired) arrived at Abu Ghraib in December 2003, he found to his astonishment that it was "routine and acceptable to beat prisoners." That year, scorpions were reportedly placed on nude bodies of prisoners at Camp Bucca, Iraq. An FBI report in 2004 described torture during interrogations at Guantánamo as chaining detainees to the floor in fetal positions, first in a room so cold that the prisoners were shaking and then left in the unventilated room without air conditioning wherein the temperature exceeded 100 degrees.

According to the UN High Commissioner for Human Rights, lengthy interrogation that deprives a prisoner of sleep and is aimed at breaking the will of a prisoner "may in some cases constitute torture." The European Court of Human Rights came to a similar conclusion in *Ireland* v *United Kingdom* (1978). The State Department denounced sleep deprivation as an interrogation technique in its 2001 annual human rights report. Nevertheless, sleep deprivation has been used extensively, notably on Mohammed Jawad, who claims that he was shifted from one cell to another 112 times during two weeks in May 2004.

During the Tokyo War Crimes Trials, eight Japanese officers were convicted and executed for waterboarding. Rumors that the same procedure was used by the CIA after 9/11 prompted considerable controversy. Abu Zubaydah, the first high-level member of al-Qaeda to be captured, posed an early challenge. Field operatives were so nervous about how to interrogate him that they contacted CIA headquarters for authorization of specific techniques. CIA Director George Tenet then relayed their requests to the National Security Council, chaired by Condoleezza Rice, in the White House basement. In addition to Rice and Tenet, those micromanaging harsh treatment and torture then included Attorney General John Ashcroft, Vice President Dick Cheney, and Secretary of State Colin Powell. Bush was apprised of their meetings and admitted on April 11, 2008, that he approved. His Cabinet, according to former Admiral Alberto Mora, consented to the cruelty. John Kiriakou, a CIA officer present at Zubaydah's interrogation, has provided details about his waterboarding, which involved placing a plastic sheet over the subject's face, risking the possibility of asphyxiation. Zubaydah identified that Khalid Sheikh Mohammed was the mastermind behind 9/11, but evidently during normal rather than "enhanced" interrogation methods, according to *New York Times* journalist Scott Shane. In the Hamdan case, a physician attested that his "confession" came after more than fifty days of sleep deprivation, when he was promised that he would not be prosecuted for what he said.

CIA Director Michael Hayden admitted on February 5, 2008, that the CIA waterboarded three persons—Abd al-Rahim al-Nashiri, Khalid Sheik Mohammed, and Abu Zubaydah. The torture stopped when they articulated confessions about nonexistent and past plots and named names, some of whom were later cleared. Khalid Sheik Mohammed suffered a variety of "enhanced techniques" on 100 or so occasions during a two-week period at a secret prison in Poland, though he admitted his key role in 9/11 on Al-Jazeera television. The CIA was satisfied that waterboarding worked in thirty-five seconds, though the information was only obtained when Deuce Martinez, a "good cop" interrogator, was in charge. Although there are two sides to the debate on the effectiveness of torture techniques, there is no dispute that rapport-building interrogation has yielded more information.

Over a period of seventeen weeks, Mohammed al-Qahtani suffered a variety of enhanced interrogation techniques in Guantánamo. Cumulatively, they may be considered torture, according to an analysis of his interrogation log by Dr. Abigail Seltzer, a British National Health Service physician who deals with trauma patients. Susan Crawford, supervisor of the trials, evidently agreed on May 14, 2008, by dismissing charges against him, though her reasons were not made public.

Philippe Sands notes that the British use of torture during 1971–1972 on suspected members of the Irish Republic Army so infuriated Catholics in Northern Ireland that the conflict was extended fifteen to twenty years. Nazi Germany considered torture illegal against anyone but an "enemy of the state." A permanent exhibit of the torture inflicted by the United States after 9/11 will doubtless be called the George W. Bush Museum of Torture, given his persistent refusal to rule out cruel methods of interrogation.

War Crime #56. Taking Hostages. According to testimony before Congress by Army Specialist Samuel Provance, kidnapping was systematically used to coerce the confession or surrender of suspects who might have important information about the insurgency in Iraq. For example, a woman in Tarmiya, Iraq, was captured during a planned assault on a house on May 9, 2004, as a ploy to get her husband to surrender. The incident was reported as a war crime to a superior officer in a memorandum dated June 10 by a Defense Intelligence Agency officer who objected in advance to the plan.

Secretary Rumsfeld, according to his December 2002 memorandum, refused to rule out such tactics. Colonel David Hogg publicly defended the practice seven months later.

Torture Convention, 1985, Art. 2(1). Each State Party shall take effective legislative, administrative, judicial or other measures to prevent acts of torture in any territory under its jurisdiction.

War Crime #57. Failure to Prevent Torture. The record is replete with efforts to justify torture, beginning with the so-called Torture Memo of August 1, 2002. In 2002, key members of Congress were briefed on the harsh CIA techniques, but objections raised by Senator Jay Rockefeller and Representative Jane Harman were ignored. Khalid Sheikh Mohammed's "good cop" interrogator failed to report his fellow "bad cop" torturer associates for investigation.

Murat Kurnaz alleges that in 2005, while hung from a rack by ropes and cuffs with his arms above his head, Guantánamo physicians pulled him down every five to six hours. After checking his eyes and heart, they returned him to his position, thereby allowing his treatment to continue. Kurnaz's case is not unique.

> **Torture Convention, Art. 4.** Each State Party shall ensure that all acts of torture are offences under its criminal law. The same shall apply to an attempt to commit torture and to an act by any person which constitutes complicity or participation in torture.

War Crime #58. Complicity or Participation in Torture. FBI officials and medical personnel have been aware of CIA and military interrogators who have engaged in torture. They were complicit even if nonparticipants.

The extraordinary rendition program, as specifically authorized by Bush, was designed to outsource torture to other countries. As former Attorney General Alberto Gonzales conceded, "We can't fully control what that country might do." Sending a prisoner to a country that practices torture is complicity though not participation in torture, as contractors are liable for what subcontractors do. Bush's February 7, 2002, executive order, which authorizes torture, has never been revoked.

> **Geneva III, 1949, Art. 13.** Prisoners of war must at all times . . . be protected, particularly against acts of violence or intimidation . . .

War Crime #59. Failure to Protect Prisoners from Intimidation. Physical threats have been made during interrogation in order to force confessions. But there has been no effort to protect prisoners from coercive threats, and no personnel were authorized to stop ongoing abuse because the rulebook was thrown out when Bush said that the Geneva Conventions did not apply. Those with qualms of conscience have been told to shut up. Accordingly, Peter Jemley went AWOL in 2008 and applied for asylum in Canada.

In 2005, after the United States boasted that Libya had given up plans to develop weapons of mass destruction, a delegation from Tripoli arrived at Guantánamo to meet all prisoners of Libyan ancestry. One of the meetings was with British citizen Omar Deghayes, who had been cleared of involvement in terrorism. Nevertheless, the Libyans threatened to kill him if he chose to return to his country of origin. One inference is that American authorities brought the delegation to Guantánamo in order to intimidate prisoners of Libyan nationality.

> **Geneva III, 1949, Art. 42.** The use of weapons against prisoners of war, especially against those who are escaping or attempting to escape, shall constitute an extreme measure, which shall always be preceded by warnings appropriate to the circumstances. . . .

War Crime #60. Use of Weapons Against Prisoners. In Afghanistan, Moazzam Begg, David Hicks, and the Tipton Three had pistols pointed at their heads or even discharged next to their heads while being questioned on their knees in chains. Others have had rifle butts slammed into their bodies. One prisoner was forced to hold a smoke grenade after the pin had been removed. At Abu Ghraib, weapons were discharged excessively to control riots.

UNACCEPTABLE LIVING CONDITIONS

Among the sources of information about living conditions are the International Committee of the Red Cross and remarks made by prisoners during and after their confinement. According to military translator Erik Saar, Guantánamo was presented as a Potemkin village to most outsiders. But because of so many complaints, conditions improved over time for some, albeit not all, prisoners. Responsibility apparently rests with the generals assigned to maintain the prisons.

> **Hague II, 1899, Art. 7.** The Government into whose hands prisoners of war have fallen is bound to maintain them. Failing a special agreement between the belligerents, prisoners of war shall be treated as regards food, quarters, and clothing, on the same footing as the troops of the Government which has captured them.

War Crime #61. Inadequate Food. Food at the "dark prison" in Afghanistan, where prisoners have no access to light, has been regarded as rotten. According to Dr. Miles, the meal system at Abu Ghraib was chaotic and inadequate, hardly on a par with soldiers in the Green Zone. One prisoner reported consuming only a scrap of bread and a glass of milk three times daily.

Lieutenant General Sanchez allegedly authorized diet alteration at Abu Ghraib to increase the likelihood of obtaining useful information during interrogation. Contractors supplying food often provided inferior, even filthy, rations. One guard threw food rations into a toilet one day and said, "Go take it and eat it!"

At Guantánamo, food was withheld from prisoners on days when they were interrogated. Poor food quality has served as one reason for hunger strikes. Attorney Clive Stafford Smith once decided to consume some of the prisoner's lunches, and downed "slimy boiled tinned okra, dry undercooked rice and some rancid fish." For an encore he had "mashed tinned potatoes, tinned peas and kidney beans, washed down with iced tea." His comment, shared by prisoners, is that the meals were "revolting."

War Crime #62. Inadequate Clothing. Some prisoners have worn the same clothes for more than two months. At Guantánamo, they are furnished orange jumpsuits despite the fact that the color traditionally is associated with those on death row in Arabic-speaking countries. Prisoners have been forced to go naked for days or months.

War Crime #63. Inadequate Shelter. Tents have been pitched for prisoners at Abu Ghraib and Bagram. Many cells at American-run prisons in Afghanistan lack windows and adequate ventilation. When Guantánamo opened, open-air cages for prisoners originally had dirt floors or concrete with little protection from the 110° sun and intense humidity. Later, some cooperative prisoners were allowed air conditioning in their cells. While American soldiers live in relative luxury, many prisoners have been housed in pigsties.

> **POW Convention, 1929, Art. 10.** Prisoners of war shall be lodged in buildings or in barracks....With regard to dormitories the total surface, minimum cubic amount of air, arrangement and material of bedding—the conditions shall be the same as for the troops at base camps of the detaining Power.

War Crime #64. Cramped Housing. One of the reasons that so many prisoners were sent from Afghanistan to Guantánamo was overcrowding at the prisons. But even in mid-2008, some 630 prisoners were confined at Bagram, a number so far over capacity that a new facility was under construction. Some at Bagram live in wire-mesh pens surrounded by razor-wire coils with very little space for bathrooms.

Abu Ghraib was originally designed to hold far fewer prisoners than the 7,500 that were incarcerated in 2003. The main reason was that Iraqis were rounded up on flimsy pretexts, such as those who had cell phones.

Lieutenant General Raymond Odierno, in particular, authorized mass arrests based on minimal or no evidence. Although prison commander Brigadier General Janis Karpinski recommended the release of prisoners determined to have no intelligence value, chief intelligence officer Major General Barbara Fast insisted on keeping a surplus of prisoners.

At Guantánamo, the stench of body odor initially wafted through the cramped cages. As prisoners were released, conditions improved for some of those remaining.

> **Geneva III, 1949, Art. 21.** The Detaining Power may subject prisoners of war to internment. . . . Subject to the provisions of the present Convention relative to penal and disciplinary sanctions, prisoners of war may not be held in close confinement except where necessary to safeguard their health and then only during the continuation of the circumstances which make such confinement necessary.

War Crime #65. Close Confinement. "Close confinement" refers to the use of individual cells to accommodate single prisoners. According to the Geneva Conventions, cells can only be assigned when prisoners have committed a violation of prison rules. Thus, the initial use of individual cells is a prima facie violation of the Geneva Conventions, regardless of their size, as those who have watched the television series *Hogan's Heroes* will recall.

Prisoners at Guantánamo were first placed in 4′ by 6′ cages and later 6′ by 10′. They measured 6′ by 12′ at Mosul and 6′ by 9′ at Bagram. In quarters about the size of a king-sized bed, cots or sleeping pads were considerably smaller. Some cells in American-run prisons in Iraq have been so small that prisoners for months could neither lie down nor stand up. As of 2008, most prisoners at Bagram were still crammed eight to a cell, but some cages housed sixteen prisoners forbidden to look at and talk to one another.

> **Geneva III, 1949, Art. 22.** Prisoners of war may be interned only in premises located on land . . . and shall not be interned in penitentiaries.

War Crime #66. Internment on Ships at Sea. At least eight prisoners, including Martin Mubanda, have been held on the U.S.S. *Peleliu*, a warship. The amphibious assault ship U.S.S. *Bataan* housed Ibn Sheik al-Libi on January 8, 2002. The nongovernmental organization Reprieve is investigating a dozen other American vessels that may have been used as prisons.

After being held on board, prisoners have been flown to Guantánamo or to secret prisons. However, some may still be on board. Such internment and transfers would have to have been authorized at the highest levels.

War Crime #67. Internment in Penitentiaries. Abu Ghraib, used as a prison by Saddam Hussein, was utilized by the United States Army for internment and interrogation. The various "black sites" for extraordinary renditions in Poland and Romania were later revealed to have been former Soviet prisons. Guantánamo, in effect, serves as a penitentiary for those presumed guilty of offenses without trials.

> **Geneva III, 1949, Art. 25.** Prisoners of war shall be quartered under conditions as favorable as those for the forces of the Detaining Power who are billeted in the same area.... The premises provided for the use of prisoners of war individually or collectively, shall be entirely protected from dampness and adequately heated and lighted, in particular between dusk and lights out. All precautions must be taken against the danger of fire.

War Crime #68. Inadequate Heating. Lacking heat during cold weather in Afghanistan and Iraq, some prisoners have died. At Guantánamo, most prisoners have been allowed no relief from the high humidity and intense tropical heat. Guantánamo prisoners complain of being left for five hours or more in a severely chilled interrogation room but never questioned.

War Crime #69. Inadequate Lighting. Those at the "dark prison" in Afghanistan have been subjected to twenty-four-hour darkness. Guantánamo prisoners complain of constant lighting for up to twenty-four hours daily.

> **Geneva III, 1949, Art. 26.** ... Account shall ... be taken of the habitual diet of the prisoners.... Prisoners of war shall, as far as possible, be associated with the preparation of their meals; they may be employed for that purpose in the kitchens. Furthermore, they shall be given the means of preparing, themselves, the additional food in their possession. Adequate premises shall be provided for messing....

War Crime #70. Habitual Diet Ignored. Muslims have on occasion been served or forced to eat pork and drink liquor. Since one complaint was that the food was tasteless, Guantánamo later responded by supplying a minipacket of hot sauce with food, but that was a short-lived palliative.

War Crime #71. Prisoners Disallowed from Food Preparation. Although food preparation has been a bonanza for various private contractors, prisoners have not been allowed a role in preparing meals. Thanks to suggestions from attorney Clive Stafford Smith, Muslims from China at Guantánamo have planted seeds from the food that they consume. Of seven planter boxes allowed, one plant has thus far survived irrigation with the yellowish water that prisoners must drink.

War Crime #72. Solitary Confinement. Some have been held for years in solitary confinement in Afghanistan and Guantánamo. Salim Ahmed Hamdan was allowed to exchange messages with fellow prisoners for the first time on May 1, 2008, when the judge at his trial in Guantánamo accepted a motion from his defense attorney so that he could obtain corroboration for his contention that he was not guilty of charges filed against him. According to a Human Rights Watch report in 2008, 185 prisoners at Guantánamo are alone in small cells for twenty-two hours daily; the other two hours consist of solitary exercise in small cells. The Uighurs of China's East Turkestan, whom American authorities considered eligible for release in 2004, were not allowed to congregate together until 2008.

War Crime #73. Prisoners Not Allowed to Eat Together. Most Guantánamo prisoners have eaten alone rather than together. Although one camp at the facility was originally designed for common messing, the construction was later modified. Nevertheless, prisoners considered "cooperative" have been allowed to eat together.

Geneva III, 1949, Art. 28. Canteens shall be installed in all camps, where prisoners of war may procure foodstuffs, soap and tobacco and ordinary articles in daily use.

War Crime #74. Lack of Prison Canteens. No such facilities have existed. Soap is not sold by Bush's specific order, as explained in the White House fact sheet of February 7, 2002.

Geneva III, 1949, Art. 59. Cash which was taken from prisoners of war, in accordance with Article 18, at the time of their capture, and which is in the currency of the Detaining Power, shall be placed to their separate accounts. **Art. 60.** The Detaining Power shall grant all prisoners of war a monthly advance of pay. **Art. 63.** Prisoners of war shall be permitted to receive remittances of money addressed to them individually or collectively. . . . **Art. 64.** The Detaining Power shall hold an account for each prisoner of war. . . .

War Crime #75. Prisoners Not Allowed to Receive Funds to Purchase Personal Items. Despite generous payments to bounty hunters to collect prisoners, American-run prisons have followed none of the Geneva Convention guidelines regarding prisoner accounts. Instead, prisoners have paid in blood.

HEALTH ASPECTS

The Red Cross Convention of 1864 was devoted to ameliorating the health conditions of wounded soldiers on the battlefield. Later, the same concern was extended to prison conditions. Translator Erik Saar observed that physicians have often displayed little interest in the health of prisoners. Saifullah Paracha, asking a physician at Guantánamo whether he saw him more as a patient or as an enemy, was informed "enemy." Funding to maintain the health of prisoners must be requested by the president, so shortages can be traced to Bush. The shocking information for the following war crimes comes from Dr. Steven Miles, Physicians for Human Rights, and the Red Cross.

Red Cross Convention, 1864, Art. 6. Wounded or sick soldiers shall be entertained and taken care of, to whatever nation they may belong.

War Crime #76. Mistreatment of Wounded Prisoners. Photographs from Abu Ghraib include one in which a soldier is lying on the back of an inmate while blood is flowing from the latter's leg after a dogbite. In 2003, Ameen Sa'eed al-Sheik's wounded leg was beaten with a baton, yet the prison physician refused to show concern. Dr. Miles provides many other horrific examples of medical neglect of prisoners in American prisons from Afghanistan to Iraq to Guantánamo.

Hague II, 1899, Art. 23. Besides the prohibitions provided by special Conventions, it is especially prohibited:...[t]o kill or wound treacherously individuals belonging to the hostile nation or army...

War Crime #77. Killing and Wounding Prisoners Treacherously. To be "treacherous," a prisoner must be tricked into doing something or lied to. The extent of duplicity is difficult to document, since so many deaths and injuries have been inaccurately reported.

At Guantánamo, former Chaplain Yee reports that a guard once left a prison cell unlocked and dared the man to come out "if you're a man." When he did, he was beaten up so severely that his head was split open and he was hospitalized with blood still soaking up pieces of flesh in his cell. The Red Cross Report of 2004 provides more details of similar problems.

POW Convention, 1929, Art. 10. Prisoners of war shall be lodged in buildings or in barracks affording all possible guarantees of hygiene....The quarters must be fully protected from dampness...

War Crime #78. Unhygienic Housing. Outdoor tents have handled the overflow of prisoners at Abu Ghraib and Bagram. While at Kandahar, journalist Sami al-Hajj was not allowed to wash for about 100 days while his body was covered with lice, which can be a seedbed for typhus. Even today, prisoners at Bagram Air Force Base are exposed to asbestos and heavy metals from machinery for repairing aircraft. Prisoners in Afghanistan describe the water provided to them as "dirty." Instead of toilets, cells at Bagram and Guantánamo originally had buckets, seldom emptied.

Conditions at Abu Ghraib were described as "filthy." Some bleeding prisoners were forced to lie on the ground, naked. One of the scandalous photographs shows a prison guard appearing to urinate in a cell.

At Guantánamo, rats have roamed free in the cells. Prisoners have also observed guards spitting into their food.

POW Convention, 1929, Art. 11. ...Sufficiency of potable water shall be furnished....

War Crime #79. Water Deprivation. Denying water has been one technique used to extract information from prisoners. Cells in Afghanistan and at Abu Ghraib have lacked running water. Some Guantánamo prisoners, who abhor the sulphuric yellow-colored water made available to them, have even been denied that fluid from time to time.

One prisoner, desperately requesting water during an interrogation at Guantánamo, was presented with a water bottle after the bottom was punctured. As his fingers, numb from being suspended overhead, fumbled to open the top, all the water gushed out onto the floor.

> **POW Convention, 1929, Art. 13.** Belligerents shall be bound to take all sanitary measures necessary to assure the cleanliness and healthfulness of camps and to prevent epidemics. Prisoners of war shall have at their disposal, day and night, installations conforming to sanitary rules and constantly maintained in a state of cleanliness. Furthermore, and without prejudice to baths and showers of which the camp shall be as well provided as possible, prisoners shall be furnished a sufficient quantity of water for the care of their own bodily cleanliness. . . .

War Crime #80. Unhealthful Incarceration. Disease has spread easily, and mental health care has been largely unavailable. Showers in the sticky climate of Guantánamo and summertime heat in Baghdad have been permitted only twice weekly, if then. Karama Kahmisan reports being allowed only one use of the shower and toilet while kept in isolation naked for twenty-five days.

Shaker Aamer has made perhaps the most eloquent statement about the health of Guantánamo prisoners. He dictated the following to his attorney, Clive Stafford Smith, in 2005:

> I have got kidney problems from the filthy yellow water. I have lung problems from the chemicals they spread all over the floor. I am already arthritic at forty because I sleep on a steel bed and they use freezing air condition as part of the interrogation process. I have eyes that are ruined from the permanent, twenty-four-hours-a-day fluorescent lights. I have tinnitus in my ears from the perpetual noise. I have skin diseases from chemicals and never being allowed out to see the sun. I have ulcers and almost permanent constipation from the food.

Guantánamo prisoners are only allowed a toothbrush as a privilege at six-week intervals, though the length of the instrument appears insufficient to keep gums healthy. Toilet paper is yet another "privilege."

Red Cross visitors to Guantánamo have commented that prisoners have been extremely frightened about their situation. They correctly

predicted that mental health problems would emerge from the environment of trepidation that began when Major General Miller was in
charge. Translator Erik Saar, who observed one suicide attempt per
week during 2004, reports that many prisoners began hallucinating. As
of mid-2007, four detainees at Guantánamo had committed suicide.
There was a mass suicide protest on June 10, 2006.

Geneva III, 1949, Art. 3. . . . the following acts are and shall remain prohibited . . . (a) violence to life and person, in particular murder of all kinds,
mutilation, . . .

War Crime #81. Murder. At least 160 prisoners died in custody
from 2002 to 2007, of which at least 45 are confirmed homicides. Murat
Kurnaz reports that at least eight were tortured to death.

The first two confirmed homicides by American prison officials were
in Afghanistan, where two Afghans were beaten to death. Dilawar,
whose cries of agony prompted soldiers to silence him through repeated
beatings, died from the flogging. Mohammed Jawad, who was sent from
Afghanistan to Guantánamo in 2002, claims that he saw Americans
murdering inmates, something that even the Taliban never did.

Journalist Hersh reported that an Iraqi prisoner with mortal wounds
was left to die without medical treatment. Lieutenant General Sanchez
admitted to him that the neglect was an act of "execution."

In June 2003, a Marine reservist was accused of beating a prisoner to
death at a detention facility outside Nasiriyah. In 2007, Jermaine Nelson
and former Marine José Luis Nazario, Jr., were charged with killing
two bound prisoners in Falluja in November 2004 under orders from
their commanding officer. While on the phone, the commanding officer
asked Nazario if his prisoners were dead. When Nazario allegedly
answered in the negative, the order was "Make it happen." After he left
the army, Nazario was acquitted in federal court when the judge refused
to compel Nelson to testify, though charges against him had already
been dropped.

Four prisoners were shot dead during a prison riot at Abu Ghraib
involving stone throwing on February 5, 2005. Shortly thereafter, Iraqi
government officials protested the action.

War Crime #82. Mutilation. Some prisoners, according to Abu Ghraib
photographs and prison hospital records, have suffered facial lacerations
at the hands of American prison officials. The Schmidt Report documents

a case of lower lip edema and head laceration. The Taguba Report identifies an ear that was ripped. The penis of Binyam Mohamed was repeatedly cut while he was in detention in Morocco, where the CIA sent him, knowing that the authorities might engage in extreme forms of torture. Before he left Morocco, the mutilation was photographed, but his attorney has been refused a copy of the snapshots. Ha'il al-Maythali's testicles were permanently disfigured from torture. During 2008, acid was poured on some Afghan prisoners on the point of capture.

Geneva III, 1949, Art. 13. Prisoners of war must at all times be humanely treated. Any unlawful act or omission by the Detaining Power causing death or seriously endangering the health of a prisoner of war in its custody is prohibited.... In particular, no prisoner of war may be subjected to... medical or scientific experiments....

War Crime #83. Reckless Endangerment of Health in Prison. Several prisoners have suffered bleeding, blindness, broken bones, burns from boiling water or cigarettes or phosphoric liquid, hypothermia, permanent scars, or even have been left to die while in their cells or during interrogation. Beatings have resulted in unconsciousness or even death.

CIA Director George Tenet admitted flying a trauma physician to a secret prison during March 2002 in order to revive Abu Zubaydah, who had collapsed due to torture during interrogation. A "high-value" detainee thought to possess valuable information about al-Qaeda, Zubaydah's life was saved as physicians fiendishly treated him with the objective of returning him to more torment. No such extraordinary attention has been documented with any other prisoner, though medical personnel have been summoned on some occasions when prisoners have collapsed due to harsh interrogation measures.

After a beating of a prisoner at Bagram, a physician recommended a knee support, but security guards refused to allow tiny rods in an elastic band to protect him, so he was so wobbly that he later fell, and another tendon was severed. Now, he can hardly walk.

At Abu Ghraib, a man named Jamadi was brought into the prison by the CIA with blood over his face due to injuries, but hidden beneath a hood. During interrogation, he fell dead. His injuries and general health condition had been ignored.

Sadiq Zoman, who on July 21, 2003, entered American custody in full health, ended up in an Iraqi hospital in a coma one month later with burn marks on his skin, a broken thumb, electric burns on the soles of his feet and genitalia, whipmarks on his back, and marks of blunt instruments on the back of his head. The family commented that nothing had changed since the regime of Saddam Hussein.

Although Guantánamo authorities pride themselves on their medical team, short shackling has crippled at least one detainee for life. Shackles and rope have been so tight that skin has come off or bled. After guards broke two vertebrae of Sami al-Lithi, he was denied medical attention that would have saved him from permanent paralysis. Saifullah Paracha, denied proper cardiology treatment, suffered a double heart attack.

The Red Cross raised early concern over the reckless endangerment of mental health at Guantánamo. A common diagnosis has been post-traumatic stress disorder along with suicidal thoughts and behavior. Mohammed al-Qahtani, who entered in fit mental condition, was driven to a point where he began to hear voices in his isolation cell and to cower in the corner, covering himself with a sheet. Agoraphobia now disturbs the post-Guantánamo life of an Algerian. In 2008, the Center for Constitutional Rights sued the Pentagon over suicide deaths of two Guantánamo inmates to obtain compensation for their families.

War Crime #84. Involuntary Experimentation. Defense Secretary Rumsfeld authorized psychiatrists and psychologists to devise new forms of harsh interrogation in order to gain information. After consulting private medical records to find vulnerabilities, the prisoners' phobias and sensitivities were exploited to force prisoners to disclose information. The program, contrary to Hippocratic Oath and American Psychological Association standards, had never been tried before and therefore may be called an experiment—to see whether a prisoner will succumb and confess. The use of dogs to threaten prisoners was indeed based on a previous experimental trial. The Bush administration illogically credits the experiment to torture in innovative ways as a success, since no terrorist attacks have occurred in the United States since 9/11.

> **Geneva III, 1949, Art. 47.** Sick or wounded prisoners of war shall not be transferred as long as their recovery may be endangered by the journey, unless their safety imperatively demands it.

War Crime #85. Reckless Endangerment of Health During Transfers. Prisoners transported from one prison to another in Afghanistan were bound so tightly that one reported an inability to move his hands for six months and that shackles dug into his sides. Some were thrown to the ground from helicopters and badly injured. Others died while stuffed into sealed cargo containers.

Some prisoners arrived at Abu Ghraib after being tied to the hoods of military vehicles in the blazing hot sun. When they arrived, their bodies had serious burns.

Prisoners, shipped to Guantánamo on lengthy flights, suffered from lack of needed medical attention before and during their transfers to Guantánamo. They were denied food and water for about thirty-six hours, of which twenty hours was in the air, with shackles so tight on ankles that skin was torn. One prisoner suffocated and even died during transit. Shafiq Rasul, chained to the floor with no backrests, was in pain during the flight and lost feeling in his hands for the next six months. Hamdan's previous injury was inflamed by the cruel transfer methods.

> **Geneva III, 1949, Art. 15.** The Power detaining prisoners of war shall be bound to provide free of charge for their maintenance and for the medical attention required by their state of health.

War Crime #86. Denial of Medical Care. From December 2, 2002, to January 15, 2003, Secretary Rumsfeld even issued an order to deny prisoners the right to see a physician. Whereas American troops suffering serious injuries in Afghanistan and Iraq are flown to American military bases in Dubai or Germany for treatment, prisoners under their control are not.

Among the untreated noncommunicative maladies under American care are asthma, cancer, dermatitis, diabetes, headaches, heart conditions, hepatitis, leg wounds, and ulcers. Referral to physicians, at the discretion of nonphysicians at Guantánamo, has been withheld to induce cooperation. Prison guards have failed to call medics, cautioned by their superiors that the Red Cross would find entries in medical logbooks, and one at Abu Ghraib even stitched a wound for the camera. Omar Deghayes confessed to crimes that he did not commit because his American captors in Afghanistan refused to treat his leg wound and he feared amputation.

Medical facilities, medicines, staff, and supplies were inadequate for the large number of prisoners at Abu Ghraib, according to the Taguba Report. As of 2007, there were thirty-two physicians in Afghanistan and ninety-six physicians and twenty-seven surgeons in Iraq. Earlier, there were only four physicians for some 8,000 detainees at Abu Ghraib. Because no plastic surgeons are available for burn patients in Afghanistan, medical personnel ration treatment to Afghans with burns over more than half of their bodies.

The allocation of medical supplies and physicians from Congressional appropriations is determined by the president of the United States. He is thereby responsible when medical care is denied due to lack of resources.

From December 11, 2005, prisoners on hunger strikes at Guantánamo had feeding tubes jammed down their throats and into their stomachs, and then removed twice daily without anesthesia, producing sore throats. One attorney brought throat lozenges until they were banned. Yousef al-Shehri saw the feeding tube taken out of one prisoner and inserted into another without proper cleaning between administrations. Often, prisoners coughed up blood after tubes were withdrawn. A naval physician reportedly inserted a feeding tube into the stomach of a hunger striker and then moved the tube up and down until the man started violently throwing up blood.

According to the Tokyo Declaration of 1975, physicians are not allowed to interfere medically with those who want to stop eating. The authorities at Guantánamo were evidently ordered not to allow prisoners to die lest anti-American riots would break out around the world.

On December 30, 2007, Abdul Razzaq Hekmati died in Guantánamo at the age of sixty-nine of colorectal cancer. Colonoscopies of elderly prisoners only began in October 2007, when his cancer was first detected. Abdul Hamid al-Ghizzawi has been denied new reading glasses since his were broken in 2007.

Geneva III, 1949, Art. 17. . . . Prisoners of war who, owing to their physical or mental condition, are unable to state their identity, shall be handed over to the medical service.

War Crime #87. Failure to Provide Treatment for Mentally Incompetent Prisoners. Budgeted amounts for mental health treatment, including medicines, have been minimal in Afghanistan and Iraq. One elderly prisoner, observed with dementia, was eating his own feces. Rather than referring him and others for mental treatment, they were initially treated as zoo animals to be observed as curiosities.

The mental health unit at Guantánamo opened in March 2003, when many prisoners were engaging in such regressive behavior as repeatedly singing the same children's song to themselves. The Department of Defense has admitted that one-fifth of the prisoners are being treated for depression with Prozac, yet attorney requests for outside psychiatric evaluation have been denied. The one therapy that innocent prisoners need is to be released from confinement.

Geneva III, 1949, Art. 19. Prisoners of war shall be evacuated, as soon as possible after their capture, to camps situated in an area far enough from the combat zone for them to be out of danger. **Art. 23.** No prisoner of war may at any time be sent to or detained in areas where he may be exposed to the fire of the combat zone...Prisoners of war shall have shelters against air bombardment and other hazards of war...

War Crime #88. Locating a Prison in a Combat Zone. The decision to use Abu Ghraib as an American-run prison was over the objection of the officer in charge, Brigadier General Karpinski, who noted that there were daily bombardments of the site. The Red Cross also found three cluster bombings at Camp Bucca. Due to the shelling, at least thirty-eight persons have died and more than 100 have been wounded, mostly those housed in tents.

Geneva III, 1949, Art. 26. The basic daily food rations shall be sufficient in quantity, quality and variety to keep prisoners of war in good health and to prevent loss of weight or the development of nutritional deficiencies....

War Crime #89. Inadequate Nutrition. Dr. Miles has commented in detail on how food at Abu Ghraib was provided more at the convenience of private contractors than for prisoners. The result has been not just an inadequate amount but malnutrition. Lieutenant General Sanchez reportedly authorized diets of bread and water.

Geneva III, 1949, Art. 30. Every camp shall have an adequate infirmary where prisoners of war may have the attention they require....Prisoners of war suffering from serious disease, or whose condition necessitates special treatment, a surgical operation or hospital care, must be admitted

continued

> to any military or civilian medical unit where such treatment can be given, even if their repatriation is contemplated in the near future. Special facilities shall be afforded for the care to be given to the disabled.... The detaining authorities shall, upon request, issue to every prisoner who has undergone treatment, an official certificate indicating the nature of his illness or injury, and the duration and kind of treatment received. A duplicate of this certificate shall be forwarded to the Central Prisoners of War Agency.

War Crime #90. Inadequate Infirmary, Surgical, and Hospital Care. For those allowed medical care, the quality has been questionable due to underbudgeting. Medical evaluations, according to Dr. Miles, have been performed by untrained personnel.

Saifullah Paracha, on learning that facilities were "inadequate and risky" at Guantánamo, asked to be transferred to an up-to-date cardiac unit elsewhere. Abdul Hamid al-Ghizzawi, who is slowly dying of a liver disease and possibly AIDS, has also asked to go elsewhere for proper diagnosis and treatment. Their requests have been denied.

A prisoner who could not move a finger due to frostbite returned from surgery with all four fingers amputated. One prisoner at Guantánamo whose legs had been amputated after they froze while in prison in Afghanistan was not allowed to have a fresh change of bandages, so they were left full of blood and pus in his cell.

War Crime #91. Failure to Provide Care for the Disabled. No budgeted rehabilitation programs exist at any American-run prisons abroad. Some disabilities resulted from improper interrogation techniques, and disabled prisoners have been subjected to even further torture. One prisoner with amputated legs was beaten when he tried to sit on the toilet. Blinded in one eye, Omar Khadr has been denied sunglasses that he needs due to hypersensitivity to light in his remaining eye, which is deteriorating.

War Crime #92. Failure to Issue Proper Medical Records. Medical recordkeeping has been inadequate. In many cases, death certificates were not sent to next of kin because no person on the document was so listed because of hasty intake procedures.

Physicians at Guantánamo have reclassified suicides as "self-injurious behavior." Presumably, nonmedical superior officers sought to demonstrate a reduction in suicide attempts.

Federal District Judge John Bates ruled in April 2008 that Abdul Hamid al-Ghizzawi is not entitled to see his own medical records. His attorney presumed that either he is not being treated for AIDS or authorities told him in January 2008 that he has the disease in order to mortify him.

> **Geneva III, 1949, Art. 31.** Medical inspections of prisoners of war shall be held at least once a month. They shall include the checking and the recording of the weight of each prisoner of war. Their purpose shall be, in particular, to supervise the general state of health, nutrition and cleanliness of prisoners and to detect contagious diseases, especially tuberculosis, malaria and venereal disease. For this purpose the most efficient methods available shall be employed, e.g. periodic mass miniature radiography for the early detection of tuberculosis.

War Crime #93. Failure to Weigh Prisoners. Few prisoners, if any, have been weighed monthly to ensure that they were not losing weight. Malnutrition, thus, has occurred without an appropriate medical or nutritional response. The only time when prisoners were weighed appears to have been during hunger strikes at Guantánamo, as the authorities feared that secret hunger strikers would die, resulting in unfavorable publicity.

War Crime #94. Failure to Detect or Treat Contagious Diseases Properly. Some facilities have been determined to be death traps. Tuberculosis detection has not been part of the prisoner regimen at several prisons, and appropriate drugs have been in short supply in Afghanistan and Iraq. In one case, a prisoner in Iraq coughed up blood, whereupon he was treated for tuberculosis but then sent back without medications into the general population, where he could spread the highly contagious disease.

According to Guantánamo's chief medical doctor, Abdul Hamid al-Ghizzawi arrived at the naval base in perfect health. Subsequently, he was diagnosed with tuberculosis. His attorney suspects that he also acquired HIV during a blood transfusion in 2004 at the prison hospital.

> **Geneva III, 1949, Art. 68.** . . . The Detaining Power will, in all cases, provide the prisoner of war concerned with a statement showing the nature of the injury or disability, the circumstances in which it arose and particulars of medical or hospital treatment given for it. This statement will be signed by a responsible officer of the Detaining Power and the medical particulars certified by a medical officer.

War Crime #95. Failure to Provide Appropriate Medical Records upon Release. Some prisoners have sued, seeking compensation for maltreatment. Others would like to know what drugs were injected into them and which medicines they were forced to take. But documentation in support of their claims is often insufficient due to poor recordkeeping.

Geneva III, 1949, Art. 120.... Death certificates in the form annexed to the present Convention, or lists certified by a responsible officer, of all persons who die as prisoners of war shall be forwarded as rapidly as possible to the Prisoner of War Information Bureau established in accordance with... **Art. 122.** The death certificates or certified lists shall show particulars of identity... and also the date and place of death, the cause of death, the date and place of burial and all particulars necessary to identify the graves. The burial or cremation of a prisoner of war shall be preceded by a medical examination of the body with a view to confirming death and enabling a report to be made and, where necessary, establishing identity....

War Crime #96. Failure to Properly Annotate Death Certificates. Several death certificates have lacked the details required in one of the annexes to the Third Geneva Convention, according to Dr. Miles. The death of a young Afghan detainee who froze to death in 2002 was never recorded. Dilawar had three conflicting death certificates issued on his behalf. In November 2003, after beating Abed Hamed Mowhoush to death, military personnel stated that he died of natural causes on his death certificate.

Geneva III, 1949, Art. 121. Every death or serious injury of a prisoner of war caused or suspected to have been caused by a sentry, another prisoner of war, or any other person, as well as any death the cause of which is unknown, shall be immediately followed by an official enquiry by the Detaining Power....

War Crime #97. Failure to Properly Investigate Causes of Prisoner Deaths. Dr. Miles has faulted several homicide investigations. In some cases, investigation have not been conducted at all or have been delayed so long that adequate records have been compromised.

Protocol 1, 1977, Art. 16(2). Persons engaged in medical activities shall not be compelled to perform acts or to carry out work contrary to the rules of medical ethics or to other medical rules designed for the benefit of the

continued

wounded and sick or to the provisions of the Conventions or of this Protocol, or to refrain from performing acts or from carrying out work required by those rules and provisions. **(3)** No person engaged in medical activities shall be compelled to give to anyone belonging either to an adverse Party, or to his own Party except as required by the law of the latter Party, any information concerning the wounded and sick who are, or who have been, under his care, if such information would, in his opinion, prove harmful to the patients concerned or to their families. Regulations for the compulsory notification of communicable diseases shall, however, be respected.

War Crime #98. Violating Medical Ethics. Violations are amply documented in a 2005 issue of the *New England Journal of Medicine.* Denunciations of medical workers have come from the American Medical Association and the World Medical Association.

Dr. Steven Miles has accused physicians of betraying the Hippocratic Oath. Attorney Michael Ratner suggests that various breaches of medical ethics by physicians involve cooperating with "enhanced" interrogation techniques.

Physicians and other medical personnel are required to respect the confidentiality of medical records. However, nonmedical personnel at Guantánamo examined the medical files of patients to design methods of incarceration and interrogation that would frighten prisoners, such as exploiting fears of dogs and insects.

In addition, physicians under orders observed and assisted in interrogations that produced physical and psychological harm to prisoners. Rumsfeld rejected the Red Cross's determination that the use of psychiatrists and psychologists as resources in prisoner mistreatment is a war crime.

Torture Convention, 1985, Art. 14(1). Each State Party shall ensure in its legal system that the victim of an act of torture obtains redress and has an enforceable right to... the means for as full rehabilitation as possible....

War Crime #99. Failure to Rehabilitate Victims of Torture. The only documented example of a rehab program occurred after one Guantánamo prisoner came out of a coma induced by being IRF'd. Instead, Saudi Arabia and Yemen operate rehab programs for those returning from Guantánamo. The Saudi program includes religious reeducation, psychological counseling, furnished apartments, and even brides. Some 56 of 117 repatriated Saudis have been involved in the program. Although Washington might argue that the rehab program is merely outsourced, the Torture Convention assigns responsibility to the United States.

ACTIVITIES DISALLOWED

International standards require that inmates have opportunities for a variety of normal activities. Exercise and recreational opportunities are important aspects of humane treatment.

> **POW Convention, 1929, Art. 11.**. . . The use of tobacco shall be permitted. . . .

War Crime #100. Tobacco Deprivation. In 1929, the use of tobacco was considered to be one of several forms of harmless diversion. Bush's Executive Order of July 2, 2002, specifically denied Guantánamo prisoners the following: "access to a canteen to purchase food, soap, and tobacco."

American soldiers, however, have openly smoked tobacco. One Abu Ghraib guard was photographed pointing at a prisoner's genitals while a cigarette dangled from her mouth. There are reports of a guard who flicked lit cigarette butts at a naked prisoner, but those are mild compared to the bodies with actual cigarette burns. An FBI agent also reported that a lit cigarette was placed in the ear of a detainee during an interrogation in Iraq. At Abu Ghraib and Guantánamo, however, prisoners have sometimes been offered cigarettes in order to loosen their tongues.

> **POW Convention, 1929, Art. 13.**. . . Prisoners of war shall . . . take physical exercise.

War Crime #101. Exercise Deprivation. Exercise has been allowed, but reports vary on the duration. At Abu Ghraib, some detainees were forced to jump while nude.

When prisoners first arrived at Guantánamo, they were allowed no exercise. Later, David Hicks reported, skin came off prisoners wearing tight leg shackles during "jogging." One description of the early regimen at Guantánamo is as follows:

> [P]risoners would be strapped into heavy jackets, similar to straightjackets, with their arms locked behind them and their legs straddled by straps. Goggles were placed over their eyes and their heads were covered with a hood. The prisoner was then led at midday into what looked like a narrow fenced-in dog run…The restraints forced him to move, if he chose to move, on his knees, bent over at a forty-five degree angle. Most prisoners just sat and suffered in the heat.

More cooperative prisoners have more time for exercise, including time to play soccer together. The space for exercise initially measured $12'$ by $16'$. In March 2008, the exercise area was slightly enlarged for prisoners in isolation, though often the time allotted can be in the wee hours of the night. Exercise time, for those allowed, has varied from five minutes to the present minimum of two hours daily.

Geneva III, 1949, Art. 38. While respecting the individual preferences of every prisoner, the Detaining Power shall encourage the practice of intellectual, educational, and recreational pursuits, sports and games amongst prisoners, and shall take the measures necessary to ensure the exercise thereof by providing them with adequate premises and necessary equipment. Prisoners shall have opportunities for taking physical exercise, including sports and games, and for being out of doors. Sufficient open spaces shall be provided for this purpose in all camps.

War Crime #102. Inadequate Recreational Opportunities. Permanent or long-term solitary confinement can cause serious mental and physical deterioration, albeit slowly, especially when recreation is forbidden. Recreation, of course, is a broader concept than exercise.

Only cooperative prisoners have been allowed to read books or play chess. There is a library at Guantánamo for prisoners, but several books and magazines are banned, such as *Uncle Tom's Cabin*. Moazzam Begg was allowed to read novels by Brontë, Dickens, and Danielle Steele.

In January 2004, Jumah al-Dossari's attorney, Joshua Colangelo-Bryan, sent him three children's books in both Arabic and English, as he wanted to learn English. The authorities at Guantánamo returned them as "not cleared." He was thereby denied the dangerous opportunity to read *Beauty and the Beast*, *Cinderella*, and *Jack and the Beanstalk*.

Inmates have complained that they are denied information, either from newspapers or television, to keep up with world events. Their lawyers were forbidden from spreading news of the London bombing of July 7, 2005, though interrogators brought up the incident. In 2008, humanities courses began to be offered, though details have not been released.

TRANSFERS

From the point of capture, prisoners are usually transferred to an internment facility. Transportation has been unpleasant, even dangerous, as already noted (War Crime #85).

The program known as "extraordinary rendition" was instituted to send suspected terrorists to secret prisons. Several European countries cooperated at the time, but there was an outcry when the program was exposed. Movement of persons from one country to another requires approval at the highest levels of American government through diplomatic channels.

> **Geneva III, 1949, Art. 12.** Prisoners of war may only be transferred by the Detaining Power to a Power which is a party to the Convention and after the Detaining Power has satisfied itself of the willingness and ability of such transferee Power to apply the Convention.... Nevertheless, if that Power fails to carry out the provisions of the Convention in any important respect,... the Protecting Power... shall request the return of the prisoners of war. Such requests must be complied with.

War Crime #103. Prisoners Transferred to Countries Practicing Torture. Under direct orders from Bush, extraordinary renditions have removed at least fifty suspected terrorists seized in Afghanistan and elsewhere to Algeria, Egypt, Libya, Jordan, Morocco, Sudan, Syria, Thailand, Yemen, and elsewhere, where torture is very likely and heinously gruesome. One American official involved has admitted, "We don't kick the shit out of them. We send them to other countries so *they* can kick the shit out of them." Bush once mysteriously boasted that 200 persons were "no longer a problem" in his State of the Union address in 2003.

Alleged evidence of Saddam Hussein's connection to Osama Bin Laden was obtained through a phony confession following capture of Ibn Sheik al-Libi by the United States in Afghanistan and his transfer to a torture chamber in Egypt. His transfer was specifically authorized on September 17, 2001, by President Bush.

One of the most celebrated cases involves Maher Arar, a Canadian who was seized at JFK airport on September 26, 2002, en route from vacation in Tunisia to his home in Montréal. After a rushed hearing in which he was denied legal counsel, he was flown to Jordan and then Syria, where he was born, for interrogation including torture after Syrian authorities supplied ambiguous assurances of fair treatment. He went home in October 2003, when Damascus authorities were convinced that he had no links to terrorism.

Videotaped threats of torture were made by interrogators visiting from the home governments of prisoners at Guantánamo. Rather than using the taped statements as factors in refusing to send the prisoners to their homelands, the American authorities destroyed the tapes and thereby became complicit in several cases of torture when they were repatriated. In one case, a repatriated prisoner committed suicide after being threatened with waterboarding.

In June 2007, Abdullah Bin Omar was released from Guantánamo to Tunisia because he was deemed not to be a terrorist or war criminal. Upon his arrival in Tunis, where he had already been found guilty in a trial in absentia, he was arrested, slapped repeatedly, and threatened with rape, but evidently had nothing incriminating to confess. His wife and daughter were then seized and threatened with rape in his presence, whereupon he admitted that he was a terrorist and was punished accordingly.

Nevertheless, later in 2007 the Bush administration continued to order the release of Guantánamo internees to North Africa as if the coast were clear. In June, Congress successfully petitioned the State Department to stop the planned transfer of Abu Abdul Rauf Zalita to Libya. In August, Ahmed Relbacha asked the Supreme Court to halt his planned shipment to Algeria. And in December a Federal District Court stopped the impending transfer of Mohammed Abdul Rahman to Tunisia. All three feared torture or even death if they returned to their home countries.

Some in the Bush administration proposed moving all Guantánamo detainees to American-run facilities in Afghanistan or to prisons run by the Afghan government. However, the Canadian government stopped doing so in early 2008 on learning that Afghan authorities unacceptably beat their prisoners with wires and use electric shocks.

War Crime #104. Failure to Recall Prisoners Who Have Been Tortured After Their Transfer to Other Countries. At least twelve prisoners were tortured after their transfers. None have been recalled—deliberately, according to a Bush administration official interviewed for a *Washington Post* news story.

> **Geneva III, 1949, Art. 20.** The evacuation of prisoners of war shall always be effected humanely and in conditions similar to those for the forces of the Detaining Power in their changes of station. The Detaining Power shall supply prisoners of war who are being evacuated with sufficient food and potable water, and with the necessary clothing and medical attention. The Detaining Power shall take all suitable precautions to ensure their safety during evacuation, and shall establish as soon as possible a list of the prisoners of war who are evacuated.

War Crime #105. Inhumane Transfer of Prisoners. While some transfers have recklessly endangered the health of prisoners (War Crime #85), most have suffered from inhumane conditions. When some of the earliest prisoners were transported to an Army base in Afghanistan, they were beaten, kicked, and sat upon en route. Those transferred to Guantánamo as well as to secret prisons were often blindfolded and bound for trips of up to twenty-two hours while soiling themselves and being unable to move an inch. They were hit so that they were constantly kept awake. Adel Hassan Hamad, who was released from Guantánamo as an innocent person after years of abuse and torture, was even handcuffed and hooded on a military cargo flight back home to his native Sudan.

When Khalid el-Masri was released from a secret prison in Afghanistan after the CIA realized that he was not the man whom they sought, he was deposited on a desolate road in the wilderness of Albania on May 28, 2004, without funds to enable him to return home to his adopted country, Germany. Authority for the flight, as usual, came from the highest levels of the Bush administration.

> **Geneva III, 1949, Art. 48.** In the event of transfer, prisoners of war shall be officially advised of their departure and of their new postal address. Such notifications shall be given in time for them to pack their luggage and inform their next of kin.

War Crime #106. Failure to Notify Prisoners in Advance of Transfers. Guantánamo houses prisoners of forty or so nationalities. In almost every case, they have been captured and transferred without knowing their destination. The same has been true of victims of extraordinary rendition. As a result, their families have been angst-ridden about their whereabouts.

RELATIONS BETWEEN PRISONERS AND AMERICAN AUTHORITIES

Everyday conditions of confinement in American-run prisons have been unacceptable to most prisoners. Some have complained or wanted to complain. Others have reacted negatively and have been disciplined for various infractions of prison rules, though the punishment has been excessive. Still others have been fortunate enough to be represented by attorneys, who in turn have filed lawsuits on their behalf. Those in charge of prisons establish standard operating procedures for lower-ranking soldiers, so deviations from the Geneva Conventions are primarily the responsibility of the higher-ranking officers in charge.

Complaints, Representatives, and Discipline

The authority structure in American-run prisons abroad is extremely hierarchical. The reality is far from the paradigm case of the television comedy series *Hogan's Heroes*.

> **Geneva III, 1949, Art. 78.** Prisoners of war shall have the right to make known to the military authorities in whose power they are, their requests regarding the conditions of captivity to which they are subjected. They shall also have the unrestricted right to apply to the representatives of the Protecting Powers either through their prisoners' representative or, if they consider it necessary, direct, in order to draw their attention to any points on which they may have complaints to make regarding their conditions of captivity.... Even if they are recognized to be unfounded, they may not give rise to any punishment. Prisoners' representatives may send periodic reports on the situation in the camps and the needs of the prisoners of war to the representatives of the Protecting Powers.

War Crime #107. Failure to Allow Prisoners to Complain About Captivity Conditions. The main conduit for complaints has been indirect—from the prisoners to the Red Cross, which in turn has recommended systemic changes, mostly in vain. Direct complaints often have resulted in punishment.

At Guantánamo, translator Saar, Chaplain Yee, and the attorneys of the prisoners forwarded complaints, but prison guards usually ignored them. Guards lack identifying names or numbers sewn onto their uniforms, making difficult the possibility of complaints about specific persons.

By default, hunger strikes have been the main form of complaint. On July 6, 2005, a widespread hunger strike began at Guantánamo. The main complaint was that prisoners were being held without a proper trial. While the hunger strike was ongoing, detainee Shaker Aamer was suddenly approached by Colonel Mike Baumgartner, who had recently been appointed Commander of the Joint Detention Group that was in charge of the prison. After listening to several complaints serving as the basis for the strike, Baumgartner promised to make appropriate adjustments. When conditions improved somewhat, the strike ended on July 28. Suddenly, the "experiment" was called off on August 6. Nine days later, the hunger strike resumed. Aamer and others, who had set up an informal negotiation committee, were split up and reassigned to less favorable accommodations.

During 2006, President Bush pressured the government of Iran to release imprisoned journalist Akbar Ganji, who was on a hunger strike in an Iranian prison. Ganji was released in mid-March after a month of refusing food. Meanwhile, Guantánamo strikers were in the ninth month of their hunger strike with no sympathy from the White House. Ultimately, three committed suicide.

Torture Convention, 1985, Art. 13. Each State Party shall ensure that any individual who alleges he has been subjected to torture in any territory under its jurisdiction has the right to complain to and to have his case promptly and impartially examined by its competent authorities. Steps shall be taken to ensure that the complainant and witnesses are protected against all ill-treatment or intimidation as a consequence of his complaint or any evidence given.

War Crime #108. Failure to Respond to Complaints of Prisoners Alleging Torture. Although the Red Cross informed American authorities in Iraq about abuse at Abu Ghraib, their complaints were ignored until investigative media reporters released grotesque photographs. Attorneys representing tortured Guantánamo prisoners have tried to obtain the release of their clients due to their torture through lawsuits, but they have been opposed by the Bush administration.

> **Geneva III, 1949, Art. 79.** In all places where there are prisoners of war, except in those where there are officers, the prisoners shall freely elect by secret ballot, every six months, and also in case of vacancies, prisoners' representatives entrusted with representing them before the military authorities, the Protecting Powers, the International Committee of the Red Cross and any other organization which may assist them. These prisoners' representatives shall be eligible for re-election.

War Crime #109. Failure to Allow Prisoners to Elect Representatives. Prisoners have organized hunger strikes in part because the authorities at Guantánamo have not allowed them to elect representatives who might negotiate for better prison conditions. Conditions of confinement have been considered to be non-negotiable except during the Baumgartner "experiment." Shaker Aamer was not chosen in an election but because he was regarded as having leadership abilities.

> **Geneva III, 1949, Art. 86.** No prisoner of war may be punished more than once for the same act or on the same charge.

War Crime #110. Repeated Punishment. Beatings have been the most frequently repeated form of punishment for various infractions, such as talking. Guantánamo prisoners have complained of daily beatings and IRFings. Sami Laithi must hold the world's record, having been IRF'd three times in a single day.

> **Geneva III, 1949, Art. 87.** Prisoners of war may not be sentenced by the military authorities and courts of the Detaining Power to any penalties except those provided for in respect of members of the armed forces of the said Power who have committed the same acts.... Collective punishment for individual acts, corporal punishment, imprisonment in premises without daylight ... are forbidden.

War Crime #111. Punishment for Offenses Not Applied to American Soldiers. It is unimaginable that American soldiers would ever be chastised for writing "Have a nice day" on a polystyrene cup or for trying to use a toilet in private, but a double standard has been applied. The punishment at Guantánamo has been IRFing.

War Crime #112. Corporal Punishment. Beatings and IRFings can be triggered by nothing more than holding up a sheet so that a camera in a cell cannot see a prisoner defecate in private. Some beatings have been videotaped and presumably are available for viewing to members of Congress, according to attorney Michael Ratner. An interpreter, Erik Saar observed IRFing of prisoners several cells away from the one causing a disturbance, thereby warning prisoners that they might become unpopular with others for repeated "misconduct."

War Crime #113. Confinement Without Daylight. Many detainees have been assigned to windowless cells at the various American-run prisons. For example, Walid al-Qadasi was confined for three months in total darkness. At Guantánamo, Moazzam Begg waited nine months before seeing the sun.

Geneva III, 1949, Art. 88. . . . Prisoners of war who have served disciplinary or judicial sentences may not be treated differently from other prisoners of war.

War Crime #114. Unequal Treatment of Disciplined Prisoners. Detainees have been segregated on the basis of levels of "cooperation." At Guantánamo, the most cooperative wear white jumpsuits. The worst are clad in orange. Brown is the color for those in between the two categories. The various camps—Iguana, Romeo, X-Ray, and so forth—segregate prisoners on the basis of "privileges" allowed, such as whether a prisoner could escape from twenty-four-hour lighting in his cell. One of Shaker Aamer's complaints was to abolish the distinctions, but nothing was done.

Geneva III, 1949, Art. 90. The duration of any single punishment shall in no case exceed thirty days. . . .

War Crime #115. Punishment Exceeding Thirty Days. Solitary confinement in the various American-run prisons beyond thirty days has been administered to "high-profile" detainees as well as to the innocent Uighurs. Moazzam Begg was held incommunicado for eighteen months.

Because of his role in negotiating an end to the hunger strike at the invitation of Colonel Baumgartner, Shaker Aamer was placed in solitary confinement for a year.

> **Geneva III, 1949, Art. 96.**...Before any disciplinary award is pronounced, the accused shall be given precise information regarding the offenses of which he is accused, and given an opportunity of explaining his conduct and of defending himself...

War Crime #116. Discipline Without Following Procedures. No due process hearings are held before imposing punishment, which is often meted out to prepare prisoners for interrogation. At Guantánamo, the decision to IRF has been made on the spur of the moment, even in hospitals. Claims that those in solitary confinement have broken the rules are suspect, since there is no discipline proceeding, no regular review process, and no guidelines for punishment. Prisoners being punished profess ignorance, unaware of any rules that they may have violated.

Juridical Elements

Those captured as "enemy combatants," according to Bush, were exempt from international law as well as domestic criminal law. In other words, no law was applicable, so something had to be invented. At first, President Bush sought to try prisoners at Guantánamo by using ad hoc military commissions with few procedural guarantees, so he set them up by an executive order. In *Rasul v Bush* (2004), the Supreme Court scolded him, ruling that prisoners had a right to be represented in court by attorneys in order to challenge their charges before trial, so several habeas corpus petitions were filed.

Accordingly, Bush authorized a system of Combatant Status Review Tribunals (CSRTs) to determine charges to be filed before trials by Military Commissions. At the end of 2004, Bush also authorized an Administrative Review Board (ARB), similar to a parole board, with the power to determine annually whether prisoners should be released or held. In Afghanistan, a parallel body was set up, the Enemy Combatant Status Board (ECSB). In Iraq, the corresponding unit was the Combined Review and Release Board (CRRB). ARB decisions to authorize the release of a prisoner can be overruled by the Designated Civilian Official, an individual appointed by the president. In 2005, Congress passed the Detainee Treatment Act, which sought in part to quash pending habeas corpus petitions authorized by *Rasul*.

When prisoners were processed by CSRTs, attorneys immediately challenged their legality. In *Hamdam v Rumsfeld* the Supreme Court declared in 2006 that the CSRTs and military commissions violated Article 3, common to all four Geneva Conventions, which requires proceedings in regularly constituted courts. Both bodies were also unconstitutional because not authorized by Congress, which must approve new tribunals before they are constituted, as the American Constitution requires.

At the end of 2006, despite the opposition of the top lawyers (known as Judge Advocates General) of all four military services, Congress passed the Military Commissions Act to reconstitute and legalize CSRTs and Military Commissions. The law denied prisoners many rights that they would have enjoyed in a federal criminal court: (a) Someone involuntarily serving as a cook for al-Qaeda can fall within the definition of "illegal enemy combatant." (b) The prosecution can introduce unchallenged hearsay evidence. (c) No independent civilian defense lawyers are allowed to speak. (d) Coerced self-incriminating confessions, derived from torture, may be used. (e) Those charged are denied the right to examine or cross-examine secret evidence used against them. (f) The Geneva Conventions cannot be invoked in any proceeding. Although the law originally (g) banned habeas corpus appeals, that provision was struck down by the Supreme Court in *Boumediene v Bush* (2008).

Subsequently, every prisoner screened by a CSRT was found to be an "illegal enemy combatant." Military Commissions were again being challenged in court. UN High Commissioner for Human Rights Louise Arbour commented in 2008 that procedures still fell short of international standards.

In the first trial at Guantánamo, *U.S. v Hamdan*, two charges were made: Hamdan was accused of conspiracy and support for terrorism. Yet both offenses were based on American criminal laws, thus contradicting the original basis for a setting up trials outside federal courts. His seven-year ordeal, in short, was unnecessary, as he could have been convicted by a regularly constituted court six years earlier, and his conviction might even be overturned on appeal because of the well-recognized unfairness of the military commission process.

The procedures for Military Commissions are fivefold. First comes a *referral* from military prosecution attorneys to the Convening Authority, Judge Susan Crawford. Upon receipt of the charges, she reviews them and decides whether they warrant a trial and whether a death penalty is appropriate. Within thirty days, an *arraignment* is held in which defense attorneys are appointed by the military. Within 120 days, a *trial* is supposed to begin. A guilty *verdict* requires agreement among four of five or six jurors in a non-capital case and unanimity among all twelve jurors in a capital case. A three-fourths vote is required to impose sentences beyond ten years. Verdicts can be *appealed* to the Court of Military Commissions Review, then to the U.S. Court of Appeals for the District of Columbia, and even to the Supreme Court. Yet the legal maze has been unraveling as deviations from normal judicial process have been challenged both at proceedings of the Military Commissions and in federal courts.

Attorneys Joseph Margulies, Michael Ratner, Clive Stafford Smith, and others have provided authoritative accounts of the procedures involved, for which Bush is ultimately responsible. Their perspectives principally inform the discussion below.

Hague II, 1899, Art. 3. The armed forces of the belligerent parties may consist of combatants and non-combatants. In case of capture by the enemy both have a right to be treated as prisoners of war.

War Crime #117. Failure to Treat Captured Belligerents as Prisoners of War. Those captured on the battlefields in Afghanistan and Iraq were not treated as prisoners of war under provisions of the century-old Hague Convention or under Article 3 common to the Geneva Conventions of 1949. Similar misclassifications occurred at Guantánamo. CSRTs are now supposed to serve that function.

Hague II, 1899, Art. 14. A Bureau for information relative to prisoners of war is instituted, on the commencement of hostilities...to answer all inquiries about prisoners of war, and is furnished by the various services concerned with all the necessary information to enable it to keep an individual return for each prisoner of war. It is kept informed of internments and changes, as well as of admissions into hospital and deaths.

War Crime #118. Secret Detainees. Over the years, an estimated 53,000 prisoners have been secretly held at one time or another. "Ghost" detainees are in prisons with known locations but unregistered, incompletely registered on prisoner logs, or have been shifted around during Red Cross visits to elude discovery, as Rumsfeld desired. Others have been held in secret prisons, a practice criticized in the Taguba Report as contrary to international law.

The identities of prisoners at Guantánamo were not revealed until after a court order in 2006, but no list has ever been made public of those detained in Afghanistan or Iraq. When 2008 began, the whereabouts of nineteen were unknown.

In October 2003, CIA Director George Tenet asked Defense Secretary Donald Rumsfeld to have an Iraqi prisoner secretly detained at Camp Cropper so that the Red Cross would not know of his existence. His request for a "ghost" detainee was granted in November after approval by General Richard Myers, Chairman of the Joint Chiefs of Staff; then by General John Abizaid, Commander of American forces in the Middle East; and finally by Lieutenant General Ricardo Sanchez, the ground commander in Iraq. The stated reason for secrecy was to confuse al-Qaeda's command structure!

On September 6, 2007, at the suggestion of Secretary of State Condoleezza Rice and over the objections of Vice President Dick Cheney, President Bush made the extraordinary announcement that he had ordered the transfer of fourteen persons from secret prisons to confinement in Guantánamo. When they arrived, their specific whereabouts were unknown to nearly all prison officials. In March 2008, Muhammad Rahim was deposited in the same undisclosed compound at Guantánamo after being arrested in Pakistan and detained secretly for six months.

At least sixteen of those secretly imprisoned were later released. Khalid el-Masri, a German citizen interrogated in a secret location for five months, returned home to Germany.

Amnesty International reported that even in early 2007, when Abu Ghraib was formally under Iraqi control but with supervision by American military personnel, the practice of holding thousands of "ghost" detainees for as long as two years without disclosing their identities continued.

POW Convention, 1929, Art. 62. The prisoner of war shall be entitled to assistance by a qualified counsel of his choice, and, if necessary, to have recourse to the services of a competent interpreter. He shall be advised of his right by the detaining Power, in due time before the trial. In default

continued

of a choice by the prisoner, the protecting Power may obtain a counsel for him. The detaining Power shall deliver to the protecting Power, on its request, a list of persons qualified to present the defense. Representatives of the protecting Power shall be entitled to attend the trial of the case.

War Crime #119. Failure to Advise Prisoners of Their Right to Counsel. Upon arrival at Guantánamo and elsewhere, prisoners were told that they had no rights. To mortify them at Guantánamo, they were told that nobody cared about them, including their family and their government. When lawyers first arrived at Guantánamo in 2004, in response to *Rasul*, prisoners were initially incredulous.

War Crime #120. Denial of Right to Counsel. Prisoners at Guantánamo did not obtain the services of lawyers until 2004. Then the military selected attorneys for each defendant without consulting them, though none had prior experience in death penalty cases. Pro bono lawyers who arrived to assist specific prisoners were not initially allowed to function formally as legal representatives.

Since he had no choice in selecting his military-appointed attorney, Binyam Mohamed decided to represent himself. During his performance, he referred to the body as a "con-mission," that is, a con game with denial of justice as the clear mission.

By early 2008, half of prisoners at Guantánamo had not seen an attorney. The supply of defendants exceeds the number of assigned and pro bono attorneys. When preliminary hearings began that year, there were thirty-one prosecution attorneys and only nine military defense attorneys. American Bar Association rules require two attorneys for each military defendant in a capital case, so there were insufficient lawyers to handle the six rumored to be charged with the death penalty. However, the Military Commission senior staff quietly adopted a new rule, allowing pro bono attorneys to join the military defense attorneys, whereupon the American Civil Liberties Union and the National Association of Criminal Defense Lawyers raised $8.5 million to defray costs for some of the top lawyers in the United States, including former Attorney General Janet Reno, on behalf of the defense.

Legal representation has also been denied prisoners of American-run prisons in Afghanistan and Iraq. Nevertheless, Saddam Hussein was represented by attorneys on war crimes charges in an Iraqi court while confined in an American-run prison.

> **Geneva III, 1949, Art. 3.**. . . The following acts are and shall remain prohibited: . . . (d) the passing of sentences and the carrying out of executions without previous judgment pronounced by a regularly constituted court, affording all the judicial guarantees which are recognized as indispensable by civilized peoples.

War Crime #121. Failure to Try Accused Prisoners in a Regularly Constituted Court. In 1996, the United States complained when Perú used a military commission with limited rights to try American citizen Lori Berenson, who is still imprisoned there. Yet in 2002, Bush authorized military commissions by executive order. Disallowed by the Supreme Court in *Hamdan v Rumsfeld* (2006), Congress passed the Military Commissions Act of 2006 to provide a statutory basis for the tribunals.

In 2007, the United States offered to transfer prisoners held at Bagram or even Guantánamo to an Afghan government facility, provided that Afghanistan would duplicate the Guantánamo procedures. Rather than accepting the flawed system of commissions, President Hamid Karzai accepted the transferees for trial in Afghan courts, which have not been upgraded since the Soviet-era days before Taliban rule. Subsequently, thirty-two were flown back from Guantánamo and 220 were transferred from Bagram into an American-run wing of an Afghan prison. Although eighty-three have been tried, with a conviction rate of 80 percent, the rest have been held without charge or trial for months.

War Crime #122. Sentencing Without Having a Regularly Constituted Court. David Hicks, an Australian, was the first prisoner sentenced at Guantánamo. After pleading guilty of material support for terrorism, based on his admission under duress of training with al-Qaeda, he was returned to Australia in 2007. Whether his sentencing was by a "regularly constituted court" is moot, since his processing has ended, but the nongovernmental Australian Law Council has characterized the circumstances of Hicks's guilty plea as contrary to the rule of law. In January 2008, the Red Cross declared that Bush's military commissions were unacceptable under international law, a judgment that could inform an appeal of Hamdan's sentence.

> **Geneva III, 1949, Art. 5.**. . . Persons, having committed a belligerent act and having fallen into the hands of the enemy, . . . shall enjoy the
>
> *continued*

> protection of the present Convention until such time as their status has been determined by a competent tribunal.

War Crime #123. Failure to Use a Competent Tribunal to Determine Whether to Detain Prisoners. Article 5 of the Third Geneva Convention requires a timely hearing of those captured on the battlefield to determine whether they are indeed enemy personnel. In the early years, the Red Cross repeatedly complained that there was no such procedure in place at any of the American-run prisons overseas.

On August 24, 2004, Salim Ahmed Hamdan was among the first to have a hearing by a Military Commission. In *Hamdan v Rumsfeld* (2006) the Supreme Court declared that the commission procedure violated the Geneva Conventions. Thus, Rumsfeld, acting in accordance with an executive order by President Bush, was cited for several counts of a single war crime.

Several in Afghanistan were detained because they wore Casio watches, similar to the timepieces worn by the 9/11 hijackers. Abdul Razzaq Hekmati, the only prisoner to have died of natural causes while at Guantánamo, was turned in to the Americans by the governor of Helmand Province, whose corruption Hekmati had reported to the current government in Kabul.

Following passage of the Military Commissions Act of 2006, Bush reauthorized Combatant Status Review Tribunals at Guantánamo, superficially resembling Geneva Convention requirements. However, the procedures have many limitations and have not been applied to American-run prisons in Afghanistan or Iraq.

> **Geneva III, 1949, Art. 7.** Prisoners of war may in no circumstances renounce in part or in entirety the rights secured to them by the present Convention...

War Crime #124. Prisoners Have Been Forced to Renounce Their Rights. Before their release, some prisoners have been forced to sign statements saying that they have not been tortured or otherwise mistreated. The statements, of course, are designed to refute later claims of torture that might be lodged in court. Yaser Hamdi, an American citizen first sent to Guantánamo and later confined at the naval brig in Charleston, was forced to renounce his American citizenship before he could be released to his native Saudi Arabia.

Under the terms of the Military Commissions Act of 2006, prisoners at Guantánamo have been given a choice between pleading guilty and thereby having a military attorney represent them speedily before a military commission or pleading not guilty and being held indefinitely until or even after they face a trial. Accordingly, Australia's David Hicks entered a guilty plea in 2007, was sentenced to the five years when he already occupied a cell at Guantánamo, and returned to his home in Australia.

> **Geneva III, 1949, Art. 18.** At no time should prisoners of war be without identity documents.

War Crime #125. Depriving Prisoners of Identity Documents. By enforcing nudity, sometimes for days, prisoners clearly have been without identity documents. Binyam Mohamed, during his Military Commission hearing at Guantánamo in early 2006, pointed out that the military had no documentary proof that he was who they said he was.

Mistaken identity has indeed occurred. Chicken farmer Abdur *Sayed* Rahman, for example, was mistaken for Taliban Foreign Minister Abdur *Zahid* Rahman and abused before prison officials realized their error. Khalid *el*-Masri, who was also tortured, was assumed to be Khalid *al*-Masri. Omar Deghayes was held at Guantánamo on the basis of his resemblance to a Chechen terrorist whom his captors did not know was already dead. Ahmed Errachidi, a cook at the Westbury Hotel in London who was arrested while on vacation, was accused by Afghan bounty hunters of being at an al-Qaeda training camp. Deghayes and Errachidi returned home to England in December 2007 after five years in limbo.

> **Geneva III, 1949, Art. 39.** Every prisoner of war camp shall be put under the immediate authority of a responsible commissioned officer belonging to the regular armed forces of the Detaining Power. Such officer shall have in his possession a copy of the present Convention; he shall ensure that its provisions are known to the camp staff and the guard and shall be responsible, under the direction of his government, for its application.

War Crime #126. Failure to Disseminate Geneva Convention Provisions. Massive violations occurred in part because prison personnel from military reserve units were evidently not trained about the Geneva Conventions. Few, if any, copies of the Geneva Conventions were supplied to military personnel. After all, President Bush openly said that they were inapplicable.

> **Geneva III, 1949, Art. 41.** In every camp the text of the present Convention and its Annexes and the contents of any special agreement...shall be posted, in the prisoners' own language, at places where all may read them. Copies shall be supplied, on request, to the prisoners who cannot have access to the copy which has been posted. Regulations, orders, notices and publications of every kind relating to the conduct of prisoners of war shall be issued to them in a language which they understand. Such regulations, orders and publications shall be posted in the manner described above and copies shall be handed to the prisoners' representative. Every order and command addressed to prisoners of war individually must likewise be given in a language which they understand.

War Crime #127. Failure to Post the Geneva Conventions. A portion of the Geneva Conventions was originally posted by the Red Cross with the approval of Brigadier General Rick Baccus at Guantánamo, namely, the provision limiting interrogations to name, rank, and serial number. But signs were later removed, and Baccus was fired.

War Crime #128. Failure to Translate the Geneva Conventions for Prisoners. Translators, such as Erik Saar, are employed in the prisons. However, they have not translated Geneva Convention protections into the many languages for the benefit of the detainees.

> **Geneva III, 1949, Art. 69.** Immediately upon prisoners of war falling into its power, the Detaining Power shall inform them and the Powers on which they depend, through the Protecting Power, of the measures taken to carry out the provisions of the present Section. They shall likewise inform the parties concerned of any subsequent modifications of such measures.

War Crime #129. Failure to Publicly State How Prisoners Are to Be Handled. The Bush administration has kept a veil of secrecy over how prisoners have been treated, in part because regulations were designed on the fly. For example, Chaplain Yee was assigned to write some of the standard operating procedures shortly after his arrival at Guantánamo in mid-2003.

On September 16, 2005, Captain Ian Fishback wrote a letter to Senator John McCain, explaining that for seventeen months without success he had sought clarification on the standards of proper treatment for Guantánamo prisoners from all sorts of authorities, including his battalion commander and the Secretary of the Army. Heartbroken, as he put it, he concluded his letter, "I would rather die fighting than give up even the smallest part of the idea that is America." His letter is credited with the ultimate passage of the Detainee Treatment Act of 2005, which President Bush in his signing statement claimed would not apply if he believed that "national security" considerations were more important.

An unauthorized copy of the Guantánamo operating manual, dated March 2004, suddenly was leaked on the *wikileaks.org* website in November 2007. From February 14 to March 3, 2008, the document was not available on the Internet, as the website had been temporarily disabled under court order.

The Bush memo of July 20, 2007, on the subject of interrogation methods remains secret. The pretext for confidentiality is to avoid having al-Qaeda operatives learn which techniques they might have to endure after capture. National Intelligence Director Mike McConnell noted on July 22, 2007, "I would not want a U.S. citizen to go through the process."

Geneva III, 1949, Art. 77. The Detaining Powers shall provide all facilities for the transmission, through the Protecting Power or the Central Prisoners of War Agency . . . of instruments, papers or documents intended for prisoners of war or dispatched by them, especially powers of attorney and wills. In all cases they shall facilitate the preparation and execution of such documents on behalf of prisoners of war; in particular, they shall allow them to consult a lawyer and shall take what measures are necessary for the authentication of their signatures.

War Crime #130. Failure to Transmit Legal Documents to or from Prisoners. Detainees were entirely unaware of various motions filed on their behalf in court until lawyers were first allowed to fly to see them at Guantánamo in 2004. Most prisoners and their attorneys have been denied the right to examine evidence to be used against them due to "national security" considerations.

In 2007, a federal court required the Guantánamo court to turn over all prosecutorial evidence to the defense attorney in one case (*Bismullah v Gates*), but defense attorneys still are frustrated in seeking important evidence. In May 2008, a military commission judge who ordered the sharing of some prosecution documents with the defense was quickly replaced. In July, hundreds of pages of evidence relevant to the Hamdan case were suddenly produced one week before trial. Moreover, translations have lagged significantly behind the needs of defendants in court. Some prisoners have even been denied pencils and paper to write motions, and prison guards have refused to transmit motions to the court.

War Crime #131. Failure to Allow Visits Between Lawyers and Prisoners. In August 2004, soon after *Rasul v Bush*, Gitanjali Gutierrez was the first pro bono attorney to arrive at Guantánamo. Clive Stafford Smith, who waited fifteen months because the military twice claimed to have lost his application, made his first visit that November. Delays have been common as new lawyers are processed for security clearance. Attorneys were not allowed to speak to "high-value" detainees at Guantánamo until 2008. No lawyers have been allowed access to prisoners in Afghanistan, Iraq, or the various secret prisons.

Geneva III, 1949, Art. 84. . . . In no circumstances whatever shall a prisoner of war be tried by a court of any kind which does not offer the essential guarantees of independence and impartiality . . .

War Crime #132. Failure to Put Prisoners on Trial in Impartial Tribunals. President Bush torpedoed the presumption that Military Commissions could provide independent judgments on the prisoners at Guantánamo on July 3, 2003, when an unidentified "senior defense official" began an official press briefing with the words, "The President determined that there is reason to believe that each of these enemy combatants was a member of al-Qaeda or was otherwise involved in terrorism directed against the United States." Fourteen days later, Bush said, "The only thing I know for certain is that these are bad people." In 2006, he said, "Those held at Guantánamo include suspected bomb makers, terrorist trainers, recruiters and facilitators, and potential suicide bombers." In other words, the commander-in-chief proclaimed guilt before a trial. The officers serving on the Military Commissions, who are on the chain of command that begins with the president, could reasonably infer that they were ordered to agree with a guilty verdict before reviewing evidence. Such trials can only be shams.

Bush originally set up a process in which the executive branch at the highest level created the rules to be followed and appointed those who would interpret and carry out those rules, thereby leaving the legislative and judicial branches of government out of the loop despite the bedrock principle of checks and balances. Indeed, the development of procedures to try "enemy combatants" has been a work in progress from 2002. Bush's intent was to set up special military bodies with limited procedures. Accordingly, court challenges have been filed almost continuously. In 2005, William Haynes II, Defense Department General Counsel, who set up the legal process, allegedly ejaculated: "We can't have acquittals. If we've been holding these guys for so long, how can we explain letting them get off? We can't have acquittals. We've got to have convictions."

Thus far, eight military attorneys assigned to court duty in Guantánamo have resigned in protest. Attorney Stephen Abraham, during his six months as a government prosecutor at Guantánamo, discovered that many cases "lacked even the most fundamental earmarks of objectively credible evidence." Lieutenant Commander Charles Swift has called the tribunal a "kangaroo court." Captain John Carr characterized the proceedings as "rigged." Whereas no person could serve on a jury in a federal court who was affected by a criminal act in which defendants were charged with playing a role, Hamdan's jury consisted of at least two military officers who had been impacted by the war in Afghanistan.

Colonel Morris Davis, chief prosecutor from 2005 to 2007, accused the government of rushing to judgment in high-profile cases because "there's always been this mind-set that if we can knock a few of these [cases] off and just get the 9/11 suspects into the courtroom, whoever wins the election is not going to be able to stop it." Haynes, whose above-quoted sentences were reported in the press by Davis, resigned under fire in February 2008.

Davis also exposed an assertion about the "strategic political value" of the trials made by Air Force Brigadier General Thomas Hartmann, the chief adviser to Susan Crawford. Hartmann has denied making the statement, evidently referring to the 2008 election. Later, he was removed from his position. In March 2008, Navy Lieutenant Commander Brian Mizer filed a ninety-seven-page motion to dismiss the case against Salim Ahmed Hamdan, for whom he served as the defense attorney, on the grounds of prejudice. Those alleged to have made prejudicial statements are Crawford and Hartmann.

Among the major objections to military commission procedures are the use of classified evidence in closed sessions, destroyed documents, disappearing evidence, and hearsay reports. Another example of lack of basic rights is the case of six Algerians who were cleared of terrorism charges by judges in Bosnia, whereupon they were rounded up by American authorities for transfer to Guantánamo. When they arrived, they were declared enemy combatants and eligible for trials, thereby exposing them to double jeopardy.

In March 2008, military defense lawyers petitioned the U.S. Court of Military Commission Review to stop prosecuting attorneys from contacting detainees. It is a breach of legal ethics for prosecutors to speak directly with defendants without first obtaining permission from their defense lawyers.

Military prosecutors have a fundamental conflict of interest between obeying an order to find someone guilty without evidence and living up to the ethical standards of being an attorney. At Guantánamo, Bush is asking lawyers to act in a manner that may cause them to be disbarred in the states where they practice law.

> **Geneva III, 1949, Art. 99.**...No moral or physical coercion may be exerted on a prisoner of war in order to induce him to admit himself guilty of the act of which he is accused....

War Crime #133. Forced Self-Incrimination. Despite the *Miranda* right to remain silent during interrogation, which applies in the American legal system, many prisoners have been tortured to confess. Under duress, they have relinquished their non-incrimination right. Several Guantánamo prisoners are being held primarily because of admissions extracted under extreme duress by the CIA, which was seeking intelligence.

Agencies that taped interrogations and then destroyed the tapes, with or without making transcripts of the sessions, did so in violation of seventeen court orders. Without the tapes, defendants who were forced to make false confessions would not be able to defend themselves properly. Accordingly, defense attorneys believe that charges must be dismissed against twenty-one Guantánamo prisoners for prosecutorial obstruction of justice.

> **Geneva III, 1949, Art. 103.** Judicial investigations relating to a prisoner of war shall be conducted as rapidly as circumstances permit and so that his trial shall take place as soon as possible. A prisoner of war shall not
>
> *continued*

be confined while awaiting trial unless a member of the armed forces of the Detaining Power would be so confined if he were accused of a similar offence, or if it is essential to do so in the interests of national security. In no circumstances shall this confinement exceed three months.

War Crime #134. Failure to Provide Speedy Trials. The phrase "Justice delayed is justice denied" is a rewording often attributed to former British Prime Minister William Gladstone from one of the clauses in the Magna Carta. Although the first prisoners arrived at Guantánamo in 2002, none had been tried until mid-2008. Some 24,000 persons under American custody outside Guantánamo have neither been arraigned nor tried, many for more than five years.

In contrast, trials have already been held in Indonesia for the Bali hotel attacks during 2002, in Madrid for attacks on commuter trains during 2004, and in London for subway attacks during 2005. In 2008, Washington turned down requests from the Yemen government to return all their nationals from Guantánamo so that they may be given speedy trials.

Geneva III, 1949, Art. 105. The prisoner of war shall be entitled to assistance by one of his prisoner comrades, to defense by a qualified advocate or counsel of his own choice, to the calling of witnesses and, if he deems necessary, to the services of a competent interpreter. He shall be advised of these rights by the Detaining Power in due time before the trial. Failing a choice by the prisoner of war, the Protecting Power shall find him an advocate or counsel, and shall have at least one week at its disposal for the purpose. The Detaining Power shall deliver to the said Power, on request, a list of persons qualified to present the defense. Failing a choice of an advocate or counsel by the prisoner of war or the Protecting Power, the Detaining Power shall appoint a competent advocate or counsel to conduct the defense. The advocate or counsel conducting the defense on behalf of the prisoner of war shall have at his disposal a period of two weeks at least before the opening of the trial, as well as the necessary facilities to prepare the defense of the accused. He may, in particular, freely visit the accused and interview him in private. He may also confer with any witnesses for the defense, including prisoners of war. He shall have the benefit of these facilities until the term of appeal or petition has expired. Particulars of the charge or charges on which the prisoner of war is to be arraigned, as well as the documents which are generally

continued

communicated to the accused by virtue of the laws in force in the armed forces of the Detaining Power, shall be communicated to the accused prisoner of war in a language which he understands, and in good time before the opening of the trial. The same communication in the same circumstances shall be made to the advocate or counsel conducting the defense on behalf of the prisoner of war. The representatives of the Protecting Power shall be entitled to attend the trial of the case, unless, exceptionally, this is held in camera in the interest of State security. In such a case the Detaining Power shall advise the Protecting Power accordingly.

War Crime #135. Denial of the Right to Call Witnesses. Up to 2008, no witnesses had ever been called in Guantánamo proceedings. Some were scheduled to be flown in by the prosecution for the trial of Salim Hamdan. As originally proposed, Military Commissions would not even have allowed those accused to be witnesses at their own trials. The Department of Defense has claimed that defense attorneys have no authority to compel CIA or other personnel to testify whether they obtained evidence from torture. Guantánamo authorities have refused to make telephone calls in order to obtain information that might exonerate prisoners. Their attorneys have done so instead.

Abdul Razzaq Hekmati was an anti-Taliban war hero in Afghanistan. During his CSRT hearing, he requested witnesses, both from a fellow detainee and from two current Afghan government officials who pleaded in vain with the American ambassador in Kabul on Hekmati's behalf. His requests were denied, and he died in 2008 while still a prisoner.

Defendant Salim Ahmed Hamdan and other "high-value" detainees were refused the right to call witnesses at their CSRTs in 2007. However, in early 2008 Captain Keith Allred, the military commission judge in his trial, granted him the right to obtain written answers to questions put to some of the high-value detainees at Guantánamo with whom Hamdan is alleged to have been a co-conspirator, and defense witnesses flew to testify at his trial.

War Crime #136. Failure to Advise Prisoners of Geneva Convention Rights. Most prisoners were not told about their Geneva Convention rights until their attorneys appeared at Guantánamo in 2004. When Feroz Ali Abbusi tried to invoke Geneva Conventions protections at a hearing later that year, the tribunal president retorted as follows: "[I]nternational law does not matter here. Geneva Conventions does [*sic*] not matter here.... I don't care about international law. I don't want to hear the words 'international law' again. We are not concerned with international law."

War Crime #137. Failure to Facilitate Selection by Prisoners of Their Attorneys. In 2004, prisoners were first informed of their right to be represented by lawyers, thanks to *Rasul v Bush*. Lieutenant Commander Charles Swift, who vigorously defended Hamdan in military proceedings that the Supreme Court called unconstitutional, was denied a promotion and summarily replaced by another military lawyer.

To compromise the ability of lawyers to represent their clients, prison officials have masqueraded as lawyers at Guantánamo, providing phony information about themselves. To further discredit them, Muslim prisoners have been told that their lawyers are Jews.

Several prisoners called into the courtroom in 2008 have refused court-appointed attorneys, insisting that they will boycott the proceedings, which they regard as bogus. In 2005, Ali Hamza Ahmad Suliman al-Bahlul petitioned the Guantánamo commission to allow an attorney from his native Yemen. His request was denied. Only American lawyers can participate in proceedings.

War Crime #138. Failure to Allow the United Nations to Provide Attorneys for Prisoners. UN personnel have not been welcomed at American-run prisons. They have consistently objected to the proceedings.

War Crime #139. Failure to Provide Attorneys Free Access to Prisoners. Although some lawyers finally saw prisoners whom they represent at Guantánamo in 2004, conditions for their visits are at the discretion of and in accordance with rules established by those running the facility. Even when a lawyer arrives for an appointment, a visit could be capriciously denied or arbitrarily postponed for a day. Attorney Clive Stafford Smith's visits at Guantánamo have been limited to ten days every six weeks.

When lawyers take notes on their conversations with their clients, the notes cannot be taken out. They must be submitted for declassification (censorship) and must later be picked up in Washington, DC. The earliest pickup time is two weeks. Attorneys cannot discuss cases with one another and cannot discuss classified evidence with their clients.

War Crime #140. Failure to Provide Privacy During Visits Between Attorneys and Prisoners. Cameras and microphones have recorded everything said between detainees and their lawyers. Due to warrantless monitoring of all telephone calls in and out of the United States, eavesdropping has occurred. Moreover, there is no secure place to view and discuss secret intelligence documents. In *Al-Odah v United States* (2004), a court ordered that attorney-client privacy rights must be observed at Guantánamo, but the ruling has not affected all Guantánamo prisoners.

War Crime #141. Failure to Translate Legal Documents for Prisoners. Translations are not provided on a timely basis to facilitate discussions between lawyers and their clients. Defense attorneys must even bring and pay for their own translators to Guantánamo.

War Crime #142. No Right of Appeal. As originally established by Bush, Military Commissions would not have honored the right to appeal. ARBs and CSRTs, established later, do not allow appeals. After Congress passed the Military Commissions Act of 2006, the Court of Military Commission Review was set up as an appeal body. In a recent court case, a federal court judge ruled that he could review judgments from Military Commissions but not the procedures used. However, under the American system of checks and balances, courts ordinarily review decisions by the executive and legislative branches.

War Crime #143. Failure to Inform Prisoners Promptly of Charges Against Them. Thousands of prisoners have been held in American-run prisons worldwide without knowledge of charges against them, many for more than five years. What is being denied is the right of habeas corpus—the right of a prisoner to be represented in court in order to learn the reason for incarceration.

The right was first established by the Habeas Corpus Act of 1679 in response to the existence of secret prisons in various island locations within the British Isles. Indeed, the right of habeas corpus was not among the abuses of power delineated in the Declaration of Independence of 1776 because Britain recognized that right. The Supreme Court has insisted on the right of habeas corpus in *Rasul v Bush* (2004) and *Boumediene v Bush* (2008).

War Crime #144. Failure to Inform Prisoners' Attorneys of Charges Against Prisoners Whom They Represent. Paul Gardephe, who represents photographer Bilal Hussein, is one of several attorneys who sought the release of their clients without knowing why they were held. He even produced a forty-six-page exculpatory report on his client's behalf, but to no avail.

War Crime #145. Secrecy in Judicial Proceedings. Bush's original plan was for secret trials at Guantánamo. Lawsuits from 2004 have gradually opened various aspects of the proceedings to greater scrutiny, but defense lawyers in 2008 were still barred from accessing a classified database containing evidence to be presented against their clients because no declassification unit exists there.

ARBs, which decide whether inmates should continue to be held, are still conducted in secret—as are similar bodies in Afghanistan and Iraq. Only military detention officials, none of them lawyers, have been allowed at the CSRTs of high-value detainees. Sometimes rulings are not made public until a determination is made that their release would not harm national security.

In preparation for Omar Khadr's trial, the CSRT's decision whether to allow cross-examination of prosecution witnesses was made in camera. His civilian attorney, Joseph Margulies, remarked that "the government is trying to keep the secrecy of the proceeding a secret itself."

On January 31, 2005, District Court Joyce Hens Green ruled (*In re Guantánamo Detainee Cases*) that Guantánamo proceedings were illegal under American and international law. But the full text of her ruling was kept secret on the basis of the state secrets doctrine.

On February 23, 2006, a federal judge ordered the release of uncensored transcripts of all detainee hearings in *Associated Press v Department of Defense*. The ruling required submission of all evidence, without exception, to federal judges so that they could determine whether detainees were legitimately classified as illegal enemy combatants.

In 2007, after a three-judge panel headed by Colonel Morris Davis ruled that a Guantánamo inmate was not an enemy combatant, a second tribunal overruled the decision of the first. Davis, unaware of the existence of the second proceeding until the later decision was etched in stone, then resigned his position.

Some testimony in Hamdan's trial in 2008 was heard in secret. That is, the defendant lacked the rights both to confront his accuser and to hear those testifying on his behalf.

> **Geneva III, 1949, Art. 121.** Every death or serious injury of a prisoner of war caused or suspected to have been caused by a sentry, another prisoner of war, or any other person, as well as any death the cause of which is unknown, shall be immediately followed by an official enquiry by the Detaining Power.... Statements shall be taken from witnesses, especially from those who are prisoners of war.... If the enquiry indicates the guilt of one or more persons, the Detaining Power shall take all measures for the prosecution of the person or persons responsible.

War Crime #146. Failure to Prosecute Those Responsible for Prisoner Deaths. Detainee Habibulla, while in captivity in Afghanistan during 2002, died after being left for days with his arms shackled and tied to a ceiling beam. He was the first to die in American confinement abroad after 9/11. The following week, Afghan taxi driver Dilawar was the second to die; he was beaten and left to die in custody, also at Bagram.

Although investigations were conducted over the two deaths, no prosecutions resulted, though the methods used were then banned. Captain Wood, who was in command of the interrogator while both men were prisoners, was transferred to Abu Ghraib, where she instituted the same interrogation methods that were prohibited after her departure from Bagram.

Of at least forty-five detainee murders while in American custody, only twelve thus far have resulted in punishment of those involved. The highest-ranking soldier punished judicially for the death of a detainee is Major Clarke Paulus, who was dismissed from the service. Despite questionable shoot-to-kill methods of riot control at Iraqi prisons, commanding officers did not prosecute anyone.

> **Geneva III, 1949, Art. 130.** Grave breaches... shall be those involving any of the following acts, if committed against persons or property protected by the Convention:... torture or inhuman treatment... willfully causing great suffering or serious injury to body or health, [or] compelling a prisoner of war to serve in the forces of the hostile Power.... **Art. 131.** No High Contracting Party shall be allowed to absolve itself or any other High Contracting Party of any liability incurred by itself or by another High Contracting Party in respect of breaches referred to in the preceding Article.

War Crime #147. Absolving Liability for Redress. During the Gulf War of 1991, several Americans were captured when Iraq attacked Kuwait and then were tortured (beatings, electric shocks, starvation, threats of amputation and dismemberment and death) and forced to serve as human shields during combat. After survivors returned to the United States, they became aware that they were entitled to compensation for their suffering, and a judge in 2002 ruled that they were entitled to $959 million from the Iraqi government. While Saddam Hussein ruled the country, no such payments were forthcoming. When Iraq finances came under American control in 2003, seventeen claimants asked the Bush administration to effect the compensation. While American and Korean corporations were able to obtain billions in compensation for commercial debts, no such payments went to the seventeen, and in 2005 they were unable to persuade the Supreme Court in *Acree v Iraq* to order compensation payments from frozen Iraqi assets.

Meanwhile, the Bush administration barred compensation payments from the Iraqi government to American citizens on the pretext that Iraq needed the funds for reconstruction and no longer supported terrorism. Although President Bush was not responsible for the mistreatment in 1991, he was in violation of the Geneva Conventions for blocking payments while in office, yet another war crime.

In 2007, Congress required the compensation from Iraqi funds within the military appropriation act, but Bush vetoed the law because of that provision. In June 2008, Representative Bruce Braley proposed compromise legislation that would use American funds to pay claims at $415 million. There the matter rests.

> **Protocol 1, 1977, Art. 45(4)(g).** Anyone charged with an offence shall have the right to examine, or have examined, the witnesses against him and to obtain the attendance and examination of witnesses on his behalf under the same conditions as witnesses against him...

War Crime #148. Refusal to Allow Cross-Examinations. The Military Commissions Act of 2006 denies defendants the right of cross-examination, particularly secret testimony. Exculpatory documentary evidence has also been denied on "national security" grounds or because files have been "lost." The Military Commissions Act also allows the prosecution to introduce hearsay evidence, which cannot be challenged.

> **Protocol 1, 1977, Art. 82.** The High Contracting Parties at all times, and the Parties to the conflict in time of armed conflict, shall ensure that legal advisers are available, when necessary, to advise military commanders at the appropriate level on the application of the Conventions and this Protocol and on the appropriate instruction to be given to the armed forces on this subject.

War Crime #149. Failure to Provide Appropriate Legal Advice to Military Commanders Regarding Prisoners. Ordinarily, members of the Judge Advocate General Corps are present at places of detention and interrogation. That rule, however, has been violated. Lieutenant Colonel Thomas Berg, who investigated the deaths of Dilawar and Habibulla, noted that normal guidelines were inapplicable after Bush said that the Geneva Conventions did not apply. Lieutenant General Sanchez's request for a military attorney in Iraq was denied.

Protocol 1, 1977, Art. 86(1)...Parties to the conflict shall repress grave breaches, and take measures necessary to suppress all other breaches, of the Conventions or of this Protocol which result from a failure to act when under a duty to do so. **(2)** The fact that a breach of the Conventions or of this Protocol was committed by a subordinate does not absolve his superiors from penal or disciplinary responsibility, as the case may be, if they knew, or had information which should have enabled them to conclude in the circumstances at the time, that he was committing or was going to commit such a breach and if they did not take all feasible measures within their power to prevent or repress the breach.

War Crime #150. Failure to Prosecute Commanding Officers for Taking No Action to Stop Abuse against Prisoners. Prisoners at Bagram observed senior military officers touring the facility, observing prisoners chained to the ceiling and otherwise abused. But no orders were given to stop the offenses.

Thus far, military attorneys have failed to present the doctrine of command responsibility in a court-martial in order to find any superior officer responsible for the abuse and torture meted out to prisoners at Abu Ghraib or elsewhere. A Pentagon official has reported that Generals Abizaid and Sanchez kept the offenses at Abu Ghraib quiet until the lid blew off in the media. Bush has neither admitted nor denied that his secret executive order assigns him as ultimately culpable.

The Detainee Assessment Branch at Abu Ghraib received reports of detainee abuse long before sensational photographs were released. The branch then relayed the incidents to the top military intelligence officer in Iraq, Major General Barbara Fast, who was never prosecuted. Her immediate subordinate at Abu Ghraib, Lieutenant Colonel Steven Jordan, was cleared of any responsibility by a court-martial in 2007 despite the Fay/Jones Report assigning him culpability.

Seven subordinate military police were disciplined for the offenses at Abu Ghraib, based on the Uniform Code of Military Justice, which their superiors at the time told them was inapplicable. Only two lower-ranking intelligence officers who influenced the military police were convicted of any related offense. Most military intelligence officers instructed guards to humiliate prisoners sexually, according to Army Specialist Samuel Provance, who in turn was disciplined for whistleblowing. Indeed, Major General Taguba was prohibited from investigating upward in the chain of command.

The Schmidt Report resulted from complaints by FBI officials that military intelligence was using improper interrogation techniques at Guantánamo. After review of more than 24,000 interrogation logs for a period of more than three years, the only disciplinary action taken in response was a single reprimand (for pretending that red ink was menstrual blood) and a verbal admonishment (for using duct tape over a prisoner's mouth).

In February 2008, CIA Director Michael McConnell, admitting that waterboarding had been used in previous years, interpreted the Detainee Treatment Act of 2005 and the 2006 Supreme Court decision in *Hamdan v Rumsfeld* as banning waterboarding as well as "outrages upon personal dignity" and "humiliating and degrading treatment." However, during the same week Attorney General Michael Mukasey told Congress that he would not prosecute those who approved or previously engaged in waterboarding. Bush, who admitted approving torture on April 11, 2008, is the commanding officer who has not been prosecuted.

Protocol 1, 1977, Art. 87(1) ... Parties to the conflict shall require military commanders, with respect to members of the armed forces under their command and other persons under their control, to prevent and, where necessary, to suppress and to report to competent authorities breaches of the Conventions and of this Protocol.

War Crime #151. Failure of Commanding Officers to Report Offenses Against Prisoners to Superiors. Lieutenant General Sanchez was aware of abuses at Abu Ghraib, which had been reported to him by Retired Colonel Stuart Herrington, Brigadier General Janis Karpinski, and the Red Cross in 2003. His superior, General Abizaid, was also aware. There is no record that Abizaid reported the matter to his superiors in Washington until the matter became public, though Sanchez assumed they were reported to the Pentagon. Moreover, the FBI failed to instruct field agents in Iraq and elsewhere to make systematic, regular reports on abusive interrogations after closing a "War Crimes File" in 2002.

The Schmidt Report recommended that Major General Geoffrey Miller should be reprimanded for excesses at Guantánamo, in particular for the lengthy and intense interrogation of Mohammed al-Qahtani. But Miller's superior, General Bantz Craddock, disagreed with Schmidt, claiming that there was no violation of American policy.

> **Protocol 1, 1977, Art. 87(2).** In order to prevent and suppress breaches, ...Parties to the conflict shall require that, commensurate with their level of responsibility, commanders ensure that members of the armed forces under their command are aware of their obligations under the Conventions and this Protocol.

War Crime #152. Failure of Commanding Officers to Ensure That Subordinates Understand Geneva Convention Obligations Regarding Prisoners. Instead of relying on training guidelines that included Geneva Convention requirements, interrogators in Afghanistan and at Abu Ghraib were instructed to use Captain Wood's improvised set of techniques on prisoners. Later, Lieutenant General Sanchez issued ambiguous directives for Abu Ghraib.

In December 2002, military translator Erik Saar attended what he considered to be a surreal briefing at Guantánamo that explained the inapplicability of the Third and Fourth Geneva Conventions. The National Security Council is responsible for closing the FBI's file of war crimes abuses at Guantánamo. In 2005, when Captain Ian Fishback conscientiously tried to determine which Geneva Convention standards applied at Guantánamo in the treatment of prisoners, he was repeatedly told to "consider your career" instead. He considered his country instead by blowing the whistle.

In August 2007, Reserve Lieutenant Colonel Steven Jordan was acquitted of criminally failing to train Abu Ghraib jailers properly, but he was reprimanded for whistleblowing. Human Rights Watch, accordingly, assigns blame for the mistreatment of prisoners directly to the obfuscation of standards by President Bush and Secretary Rumsfeld that went down the chain of command as a puzzle to be solved at an individual level.

> **Protocol 1, 1977, Art. 87(3).** The High Contracting Parties and Parties to the conflict shall require any commander who is aware that subordinates or
>
> *continued*

> other persons under his control are going to commit or have committed a breach of the Conventions or of this Protocol, to initiate such steps as are necessary to prevent such violations of the Conventions or this Protocol, and, where appropriate, to initiate disciplinary or penal action against violators thereof.

War Crime #153. Failure of Commanding Officers to Prevent or Stop Subordinates from Mistreating Prisoners. The FBI was informed in 2002 at the highest level that CIA and military intelligence officers were mistreating prisoners, so the decision was made to stop participating when questionable techniques were used. However, no countervailing FBI action was taken to stop the abuse until the Abu Ghraib scandal of 2004.

Red Cross complaints about abuse at Abu Ghraib were presented to Lieutenant General Sanchez. Brigadier General Karpinski, who had independently reported the abuse to her superiors to little avail, was demoted to colonel and resigned in 2005, though she had no control over the secret unit sent by Rumsfeld to conduct abusive interrogations at the prison or the regular military intelligence unit commanded by Major General Fast. Indeed, Fast was evidently aware of abuses, which continued in 2004, when Karpinski was replaced by Major General Miller under whose command more of the abuses occurred. When Chief Warrant Officer Lewis Welshofer, Jr., was prosecuted for the murder of an Iraqi general at Abu Ghraib, he tried to defend himself by saying that his company commander and Lieutenant General Sanchez approved his action in stuffing the man into a sleeping bag, where he died from asphyxiation.

Although head slapping was banned by the Detainee Treatment Act of 2005, a secret memo written by Attorney General Gonzales authorized the technique on the basis of Bush's signing statement of that law in which the president claimed an exemption whenever warranted by national security considerations at his discretion. The Schmidt Report concluded that commanding officers were at fault for failing to monitor interrogations, but did not identify Bush as the principal commanding officer.

Admiral Alberto Mora objected strenuously to the harsh treatment at Guantánamo, particularly to the cruel interrogation of al-Qahtani, and said so. Rumsfeld then suspended the extraordinary procedures, but only temporarily. Thus, Rumsfeld assumed responsibility.

War Crime #154. Failure of Commanding Officers to Discipline or Prosecute Subordinates Who Mistreat Prisoners. Although more than 600 investigations of abuse have been conducted over the years, the Geneva Conventions have not been the basis for any prosecutions. Mistreatment has been prosecuted at Abu Ghraib and Bagram but not at Guantánamo. The usual discipline has been demotion in rank. Only fifty-four of 600 Americans accused of abuse have been convicted of any offense.

In one case, during 2004, a Defense Intelligence Agency official observed an interrogator unnecessarily slapping a prisoner who was providing useful information. When the official reported the incident as a "war crime," he was ignored.

Although FBI Director Robert Mueller and Attorney General John Ashcroft both knew about torture of prisoners, neither ordered prosecutions of the offenders. In 2007, Lieutenant Colonel Jordan was prosecuted for abuse at Abu Ghraib, but found not guilty. In 2008, the accusation against him was expunged. The remaining twenty-six military intelligence officers and soldiers identified by the Fay/Jones Report for misconduct at Abu Ghraib have escaped prosecution. Instead, the official line is that there were a few bad apples and isolated incidents— "Animal House on the night shift," according to the Schlesinger Report. But that description perhaps better fits the Situation Room at the White House during the early micromanaging of torture. The abuse in Afghanistan and Iraq has been systematic and widespread.

Karpinski, who reported sexual abuse at Abu Ghraib to her superiors, characterized the response as "light-hearted." Later, eleven persons were officially disciplined for the abuses, receiving only reprimands, but none for torture. Journalist Thomas Ricks reports that Major General Raymond Odierno, instead of prosecuting a soldier in Iraq for shooting a handcuffed prisoner, merely had him discharged from service.

Colonel Thomas Pappas, who admitted that he authorized the use of dogs at Abu Ghraib, was granted immunity of prosecution so that he could testify against those who handled the dogs. According to several sworn statements, Major General Miller initially recommended the use of dogs, but he was allowed to refuse to testify against himself and quietly retired in 2006. Never disciplined, Miller was later awarded the Distinguished Service Medal.

Torture Convention, 1985, Art. 2(1). Each State Party shall take effective legislative, administrative, judicial or other measures to prevent acts

continued

of torture in any territory under its jurisdiction. **(2)** No exceptional circumstances whatsoever, whether a state of war or a threat of war, internal political instability or any other public emergency, may be invoked as a justification of torture. **(3)** An order from a superior officer or a public authority may not be invoked as a justification of torture.

War Crime #155. Attempting to Justify Torture. Bush's statement accompanying his signature on the Detainee Treatment Act of 2005 says,

> The executive branch shall construe ... the Act, relating to detainees, in a manner consistent with the constitutional authority of the President to supervise the unitary executive branch and as Commander in Chief and consistent with the constitutional limitations on the judicial power ...

In short, Bush reserved the right to justify torture in an emergency situation. Interrogators, in turn, have been led to believe that the Detainee Treatment Act immunizes them from possible prosecution. The text of the "Torture Memo" was accepted by Bush until rescinded by the Department of Justice nine months later, but the spirit of the memo continued to guide interrogators who were given "immunity in advance" in accordance with Rumsfeld's memo of December 2, 2002. Douglas Feith, who testified before Congress in July 2008, even attributed to Attorney General Ashcroft the view that useful intelligence could not be derived by following Geneva Convention guidelines. One Kafkaesque defense articulated by an interrogator is that torture is justified as self-defense, that is, defense of the United States!

During the first half of 2008, the White House began a public campaign to argue that some waterboarding was torture but some was not. Attorney Philippe Sands, who interviewed top lawyers in the Bush administration, reveals that none expressed any contrition or regrets about the mistreatment of prisoners. Nevertheless, the CIA claims to have last used the practice in 2003 and officially removed torture from its toolkit in 2005, but the agency could waterboard anytime in the future after a new legal review.

Torture Convention, 1985, Art. 6(1). The State Party in territory under whose jurisdiction a person alleged to have committed any offence referred to in article 4 [namely, "an attempt to commit torture and to an act by any

continued

person which constitutes complicity or participation in torture"]... shall take him into custody... to enable any criminal or extradition proceedings to be instituted. (2) Such State shall immediately make a preliminary inquiry into the facts.

War Crime #156. Failure to Arrest and Prosecute Torturers. To date, only one soldier, Sergeant Joshua Claus, has been arrested, prosecuted, sentenced, and imprisoned (for five months) because he was involved in waterboarding. David Passaro is the only civilian official implicated for torture, also at Bagram.

While Abu Zubaydah was undergoing interrogation in 2002, FBI personnel left the room when the CIA began waterboarding. FBI officials informed the CIA that the procedures were illegal and "didn't even want to be in the room" as participants. Later, the FBI indicated that no reliable information was derived from the torture, but they did not proceed to arrest those involved in torture for possible prosecution.

Although journalist Seymour Hersh learned that orders went out from Washington not to investigate the role of civilian authorities or high-ranking military personnel in the abuse, the Defense Department and FBI referred to the Department of Justice thirty-one cases of abuse, possibly including torture, by civilian contractors in Iraq. But only two were pursued. After Major General Taguba reported "numerous incidents of sadistic, blatant, and wanton criminal abuses," he was forced to resign on orders emanating from Defense Secretary Rumsfeld for not being "part of the team."

War Crime #157. Failure to Investigate Allegations of Torture. Whereas the Taguba Report investigated Abu Ghraib, and the Schmidt Report covered Guantánamo, no systematic report exists about torture in Afghanistan. FBI personnel were aware that torture was occurring, but there was no investigation.

Despite the existence of videotapes of Zubaydah's torture from 2002, which must have been known to FBI personnel, the CIA videotapes were not subpoenaed by the FBI but instead remained in CIA possession until they were destroyed in 2005. The tapes might have provided definitive evidence to sue those responsible for torture or to provide exculpatory evidence for defendants' confessions. Some persons involved in torture were investigated, but most were merely charged with dereliction of duty.

Prisoners secretly shipped to third countries have complained about torture, a crime that has universal jurisdiction. However, the Bush administration never instituted legal proceedings against those practicing torture abroad, thereby becoming complicit.

> **Torture Convention, 1985, Art. 9(1).** States Parties shall afford one another the greatest measure of assistance in connection with civil proceedings brought in respect of any of the offences referred to in article 4 [engaging in torture, complicity in or participation in torture], including the supply of all evidence at their disposal necessary for the proceedings.

War Crime #158. Refusal to Cooperate in Investigations and Prosecutions of Torturers. The CIA deliberately destroyed hours of secret videotapes made during Abu Zubaydah's secret interrogation, including waterboarding, which were subsequently sought by Congress, a federal court, and other investigative bodies in November 2005. Similar videotaped evidence of interrogations has been routinely destroyed at Guantánamo despite the court order.

In 2007, the "state secrets" doctrine was invoked successfully by the Attorney General's office to dismiss *El-Masri v Tenet*, in which Kalid el-Masri sought to sue the United States for his torture in Egypt. Other courts cases have similarly been unable to proceed when the state secrets doctrine has been cited as the basis for failing to divulge information, including cases filed outside the United States. Only one third of reported cases of abuse have been investigated.

> **Torture Convention, 1985, Art. 14(1).** Each State Party shall ensure in its legal system that the victim of an act of torture obtains redress and has an enforceable right to fair and adequate compensation including the means for as full rehabilitation as possible....

War Crime #159. Failure to Compensate Victims of Torture. After returning home to Montréal in 2003 from nearly one year of torture in Syria, Maher Arar filed suit in federal court for compensation. Although he had been cleared of terrorism charges, the American government refused to remove his name from the terrorism watch list, thereby ensuring that the lawsuit would be quashed under the state secrets doctrine. Instead, in 2007, he received from the Canadian government an official apology and C$11.5 million in compensation. Congress apologized to Arar during his testimony before a joint session by satellite television later that year. In June 2008, subcommittee chair Jerrold Nadler called for an independent prosecutor to charge those involved in "a deliberate plot to abuse the procedures so they could railroad Arar to Syria, where they knew he would be tortured." In addition, lawyers representing ten Iraqis brutalized by British soldiers sued under provisions of the European Convention for the Protection of Human Rights and Fundamental Freedoms. They obtained £2.83 for their clients in 2008.

Although some of those wrongly detained in Iraq have left prison with as much as $1,500 in compensation, Salim Mahmud Adam and Adel Hassan Hamad, Sudanese released from Guantánamo in December 2007, are among the many who have not been compensated. Their attorney has filed suit in an American court. While in confinement, Hamad's family was so impoverished that his only daughter became sick and died, relevant factors in assessing damages.

At least thirty-eight former prisoners at Guantánamo have been repatriated because they were judged not to be enemy combatants, yet none have been compensated for their mistreatment during confinement. A provision of the Military Commissions Act of 2006 blocks any such action. But, of course, Bush has refused to allow compensation to American victims of torture by Saddam Hussein (War Crime #147).

Torture Convention, 1985, Art. 15. Each State Party shall ensure that any statement which is established to have been made as a result of torture shall not be invoked as evidence in any proceedings, except against a person accused of torture as evidence that the statement was made.

War Crime #160. Admission of Statements Resulting from Torture into Evidence. Several detainees at Guantánamo have been held for prosecution based on "confessions" extracted by torture or the threat of torture. Procedures disallow defense attorneys from raising the question whether confessions were derived from torture, and tapes of the interrogations were destroyed despite court orders.

Morris Davis, chief prosecutor at Guantánamo from 2005 to 2007, refused to use tainted evidence. When he was overruled, he resigned in protest. In 2008, nevertheless, all charges were dropped without explanation against Mohammed al-Qahtani, who clearly had been tortured. Similarly, an al-Qaeda member convicted in Spain for the Madrid bombing during 2004 was set free by an appeals court in 2008 because the evidence against him had been obtained at Guantánamo, a judgment that will apply elsewhere in Europe, thereby impeding counterterrorism efforts. However, the judge in Hamdan's trial at Guantánamo ruled that any statements made under "high coercive" conditions would be excluded.

During 2005, the FBI began to reinvestigate alleged war crimes offenses of fifteen Guantánamo detainees, hoping that they might obtain the same confessions without torture. One aim was to derive evidence for cases that might ultimately be tried by the Military Commissions or in federal courts on the American mainland. Defense attorneys have argued that any later uncoerced admissions to the FBI in an environment where torture might be expected to occur would be "fruit of a poisonous tree" and therefore inadmissible and unlawful.

RELATIONS BETWEEN PRISONERS AND OUTSIDERS

The Geneva Conventions give prisoners the right to be visited by the Red Cross and to be contacted by members of their family. When war ends or the reasons for their confinement prove false, they should be repatriated as soon as feasible.

Outside Organizations

The International Committee of the Red Cross and the Red Crescent Society have been empowered by various international treaties with the right to visit prisoners in order to verify whether their detentions accord with international standards. They generally avoid public comments in order to enhance their effectiveness in encouraging remedies to problems. When their quiet approach is unproductive, they can make their observations public.

In addition, various United Nations agencies can initiate or receive complaints, whereupon they usually request responses in writing and sometimes request site visits. In 2006, UN Secretary-General Kofi Annan recommended the immediate closure of Guantánamo due to documented reports of human rights violations.

Hague II, 1899, Art. 15. Relief Societies for prisoners of war, which are regularly constituted in accordance with the law of the country with the object of serving as the intermediary for charity, shall receive from the

continued

belligerents for themselves and their duly accredited agents every facility, within the bounds of military requirements and Administrative Regulations, for the effective accomplishment of their humane task.

War Crime #161. Refusal to Allow the Red Cross Access to Prisoners. One way to keep the identity of prisoners secret is to deny access to the Red Cross. The orders to do so in the earlier years came from Secretary of Defense Rumsfeld after a request by CIA Director Tenet.

Lieutenant General Sanchez specifically denied access to eight detainees. After the Abu Ghraib scandal broke, the Red Cross was denied access to the parts of the prison where the misconduct had occurred. Although the Red Cross was later allowed to check on the medical and social needs of the prisoners at various locations, some prisoners are still unknown to them.

The CIA refuses to allow the Red Cross access to those held in secret locations, including Diego Garcia. The military will not permit the Red Cross to visit one of the prison compounds on Guantánamo. Whenever the Red Cross has been allowed to visit prisoners, access has not been granted immediately but must await the interrogation and processing of prisoners. In 2008, President Bush vetoed the intelligence budget, which contained a provision requiring all American-run prisons to allow Red Cross access to all prisoners.

POW Convention, 1929, Art. 79. A central information agency for prisoners of war shall be created in a neutral country. The International Committee of the Red Cross shall propose the organization of such an agency to the interested Powers, if it considers it necessary. The function of that agency shall be to centralize all information respecting prisoners, which it may obtain through official or private channels; it shall transmit it as quickly as possible to the country of origin of the prisoners or to the Power which they have served. These provisions must not be interpreted as restricting the humanitarian activity of the International Committee of the Red Cross.

War Crime #162. Failure to Establish a Central Prisoner of War Agency. In addition to an initial failure to cooperate with the Red Cross and Red Crescent, the United States failed to establish a neutral international agency to keep track of prisoners. UN agencies could have played that role.

Geneva III, 1949, Art. 10. When prisoners of war do not benefit or cease to benefit, no matter for what reason, by the activities of a Protecting Power or of an organization..., the Detaining Power shall request...or shall accept, subject to the provisions of this Article, the offer of the services of a humanitarian organization, such as the International Committee of the Red Cross, to assume the humanitarian functions performed by Protecting Powers under the present Convention.

War Crime #163. Failure to Request Assistance from a Humanitarian Organization. American forces in Afghanistan were overloaded with prisoners after achieving military supremacy. Similarly, Abu Ghraib was overcrowded when American troops began to arrest hundreds as possible insurgent sympathizers. To assist, the United States as Detaining Power was supposed to request services of a Protecting Power or a humanitarian organization, such as the Red Cross or the Red Crescent. The Bush administration failed to do so initially despite criticisms from Amnesty International, Human Rights Watch, and other organizations. Later, the Red Cross and Red Crescent were admitted, but restricted.

Geneva III, 1949, Art. 70. Immediately upon capture, or not more than one week after arrival at a camp, even if it is a transit camp, likewise in case of sickness or transfer to hospital or another camp, every prisoner of war shall be enabled to write direct to...the Central Prisoners of War Agency...a card...informing...of his capture, address and state of health. The said cards shall be forwarded as rapidly as possible and may not be delayed in any manner. **Art. 71.** Prisoners of war shall be allowed to send and receive letters and cards. If the Detaining Power deems it necessary to limit the number of letters and cards sent by each prisoner of war, the said number shall not be less than two letters and four cards monthly, exclusive of the capture cards provided for in Article 70, and conforming as closely as possible to the models annexed to the present Convention. Further limitations may be imposed only if the Protecting Power is satisfied that it would be in the interests of the prisoners of war concerned to do so owing to difficulties of translation caused by the Detaining Power's inability to find sufficient qualified linguists to carry out the necessary censorship. If limitations must be placed on the correspondence addressed to prisoners of war, they may be ordered only by the Power on which the prisoners depend, possibly at the request of the Detaining Power. Such letters and cards must be conveyed by the most

continued

rapid method at the disposal of the Detaining Power; they may not be delayed or retained for disciplinary reasons.

War Crime #164. Prisoners Prevented from Contacting the Red Cross and the Red Crescent Society. Those in secret American-controlled prisons have been cut off from the Red Cross and Red Crescent. When the two organizations visit nonsecret prisons, they are not always allowed face-to-face interviews with prisoners.

Geneva III, 1949, Art. 72. Prisoners of war shall be allowed to receive by post or by any other means individual parcels or collective shipments containing, in particular, foodstuffs, clothing, medical supplies and articles of a religious, educational or recreational character which may meet their needs, including books, devotional articles, scientific equipment, examination papers, musical instruments, sports outfits and materials allowing prisoners of war to pursue their studies or their cultural activities.

War Crime #165. Parcels to Prisoners Disallowed. Shipments from the Red Cross were denied to those in American-run prisons outside the United States in the early years. Locations of the various secret prisons around the world were not disclosed. Currently, the Iraqi Red Crescent Society drops off food for prisoners at American-run prisons.

Geneva III, 1949, Art. 78. Prisoners of war shall have the right to make known to the military authorities in whose power they are, their requests regarding the conditions of captivity to which they are subjected. They shall also have the unrestricted right to apply to the representatives of the Protecting Powers either through their prisoners' representative or, if they consider it necessary, direct, in order to draw their attention to any points on which they may have complaints to make regarding their conditions of captivity. These requests and complaints shall not be limited...They must be transmitted immediately. Even if they are recognized to be unfounded, they may not give rise to any punishment. Prisoners' representatives may send periodic reports on the situation in the camps and the needs of the prisoners of war to the representatives of the Protecting Powers.

War Crime #166. Failure to Allow Prisoners to Complain to UN Bodies. Some prisoners have voiced complaints directly to Red Cross visitors. But the United Nations, established as the Protecting Power by Security Council resolutions, has repeatedly been denied access to all American-run prisons on the pretext that the United States is "not subject to international human rights law because of the armed conflict."

> **Geneva III, 1949, Art. 121.** Every death or serious injury of a prisoner of war caused or suspected to have been caused by a sentry, another prisoner of war, or any other person, as well as any death the cause of which is unknown, shall be immediately followed by an official enquiry by the Detaining Power. A communication on this subject shall be sent immediately to the Protecting Power. Statements shall be taken from witnesses, especially from those who are prisoners of war, and a report including such statements shall be forwarded to the Protecting Power....

War Crime #167. Failure to Share Inquest Investigations with the UN. United Nations offices in Baghdad, Kabul, and elsewhere have not been consulted after deaths in American-run prisons. According to Dr. Miles, records have been improperly kept (War Crime #92).

> **Geneva III 1949, Art. 125.** Subject to the measures which the Detaining Powers may consider essential to ensure their security or to meet any other reasonable need, the representatives of religious organizations, relief societies, or any other organization assisting prisoners of war, shall receive from the said Powers, for themselves and their duly accredited agents, all necessary facilities for visiting the prisoners, distributing relief supplies and material, from any source, intended for religious, educational or recreative purposes, and for assisting them in organizing their leisure time within the camps. Such societies or organizations may be constituted in the territory of the Detaining Power or in any other country, or they may have an international character.

War Crime #168. Failure to Provide Opportunities for Non-governmental Organizations to Assist the Religious and Other Needs of Prisoners. The only international organizations allowed inside prisons are the Red Cross and the Red Crescent. A representative of the Human Rights Commission of Pakistan, an independent organization, has specifically been refused access to Pakistani prisoners at Guantánamo.

Geneva III, 1949, Art. 126. Representatives or delegates of the Protecting Powers shall have permission to go to all places where prisoners of war may be, particularly to places of internment, imprisonment and labor, and shall have access to all premises occupied by prisoners of war; they shall also be allowed to go to the places of departure, passage and arrival of prisoners who are being transferred. They shall be able to interview the prisoners, and in particular the prisoners' representatives, without witnesses, either personally or through an interpreter. Representatives and delegates of the Protecting Powers shall have full liberty to select the places they wish to visit. The duration and frequency of these visits shall not be restricted. Visits may not be prohibited except for reasons of imperative military necessity, and then only as an exceptional and temporary measure. . . .

War Crime #169. Denial of Access of UN Agencies to Places of Departure, Passage, Arrival, and Incarceration. Requests for visits from other UN agencies have been unsuccessful. The UN Special Rapporteur on Torture was denied access to prisoners at Guantánamo during 2005 and cancelled a planned visit. The request of the UN Special Representative for Children in Armed Conflict, to attend proceedings related to the planned trial of Omar Khadr for alleged acts committed while he was 15, was denied in January 2008.

Protocol 1, 1977, Art. 45(2). If a person who has fallen into the power of an adverse Party is not held as a prisoner of war and is to be tried by that Party for an offence arising out of the hostilities, he shall have the right to assert his entitlement to prisoner-of-war status before a judicial tribunal and to have that question adjudicated. . . . The representatives of the Protecting Power shall be entitled to attend the proceedings in which that question is adjudicated, unless, exceptionally, the proceedings are held in camera in the interest of State security. In such a case the detaining Power shall advise the Protecting Power accordingly.

War Crime #170. Failure to Allow UN Officials to Attend Arraignments. Until December 13, 2007, no UN official was allowed to attend pre-trial hearings at Guantánamo. On that day, a United Nations official finally arrived for that purpose. Washington had finally given permission.

Repatriation

About two dozen prisoners at Guantánamo may be found guilty of crimes, if their convictions are not thrown out because of tainted evidence. But thousands, innocent of any crimes and with no useful intelligence to provide, have been held for months or even years without being repatriated. Those repatriated appear to have been sent home primarily due to diplomatic pressure by friendly governments.

Hague II, 1899, Art. 20. After the conclusion of peace, the repatriation of prisoners of war shall take place as speedily as possible.

War Crime #171. Failure to Repatriate Prisoners Promptly. The Afghan War wound down during summer 2002. The "mission accomplished" sign concerning the Iraq War was posted on the U.S.S. *Lincoln* on May 1, 2003. But more prisoners were then collected, not released.

One element of the Bush Doctrine is that a state of war exists as long as terrorist groups are hatching plots against the United States. Prisoners, according to Bush, may be held until the end of that war—that is, indefinitely or until Bush's successor says that the war is over. However, in *Hamdi v Rumsfeld* (2004), the Supreme Court accepted the policy of indefinite detention so long as armed combat continues.

Many prisoners have been detained though not accused of any crimes. Indeed, the initial Guantánamo commandant went to Afghanistan to complain that too many "Mickey Mouse" prisoners were being sent. Interrogators in Afghanistan agreed, but still kept questioning prisoners whom they knew had no intelligence information. Even though the CIA informed the White House that most prisoners at Guantánamo were innocent of any crime, Bush would not order their release or stop their abuse.

At Abu Ghraib, Major General Walter Wodjakowski reportedly told Brigadier General Janis Karpinski in 2003, "I don't care if we're holding 15,000 innocent civilians." Several who were determined to be innocent were kept in prison on the order of Major General Barbara Fast, even after an order had been given for their release.

Despite Defense Secretary Rumsfeld's statement that those at Guantánamo were the "worst of the worst," about half of those held at Guantánamo have been released, and a quarter are still being held despite the assessment that they never were combatants and have no intelligence to offer.

In response to complaints that no procedures were in place, Bush in 2004 authorized the establishment of Administrative Review Boards, which were tasked to examine each Guantánamo inmate annually in order to determine whether he should be held or released. Even when some prisoners were deemed not to be enemy combatants, however, the Boards have not always released them. For example, none of the 110 prisoners eligible for release in 2006 were repatriated.

President Bush indicated on June 14, 2006, that he wanted to close Guantánamo at some point, and indeed about 150 were eligible for release when 2008 began. However, reasons for retaining innocent prisoners have varied from "releaseaphobia" (fear that prisoners would become terrorists if allowed their freedom), probable mistreatment on arrival in countries that torture (especially in North Africa), failure of host countries to accept conditions required by the United States after their release (initial incarceration, interrogation, and subsequent surveillance), or caution among host countries over accepting former detainees. Another reason for not repatriating more prisoners earlier is that there would be a public relations disaster if a large number were released at the same time; they were "trickled out" to avoid headlines.

The Bush administration claims that thirty-six former Guantánamo detainees have acted as terrorists after their release, although that figure includes former prisoners who have merely talked to the press or written books. Some have clearly been radicalized by their mistreatment. Abdullah Saleh al-Ajmi, for example, was tortured into making a false confession, detained without charges from 2001 to 2005, sent to Kuwait, put on trial and acquitted there, but then participated in a suicide bombing on April 26, 2008. In his martyrdom audio recording before his death, he referred to his detention at Guantánamo as "deplorable." His attorney indicated that he was deeply affected by his suffering under American confinement. Since he did not have the option of suing Bush, he found another way to vent his protest.

A Pakistani police investigation found that al-Qaeda and Taliban leaders organized the prisoners during exercise time or in lower-security blocks to engage in hunger strikes or suicides. Thus, by failing to release those mistakenly captured promptly, Bush's policies allowed a few hardened terrorists to brainwash and train many of the innocent to join their cause after experiencing unjustifiably harsh treatment.

Pressure from home countries has resulted in several releases of prisoners from Guantánamo to the following countries: Afghanistan, Australia, Belgium, Britain, Denmark, France, Germany, Pakistan, Russia, Spain, and Sweden. Diplomatic pressure has been unsuccessful for some remaining from Afghanistan (all those remaining), Britain (Binyam Mohammed), Canada (Omar Khadr), and Yemen (eighty-five). Family members of several dozen Yemenis submitted a petition for their release while engaging in a sit-in in front of their country's parliament on February 10, 2008.

Alas, the Uighurs (Turkestanis) would doubtless be mistreated if returned to China. Five have been accepted by Albania despite Chinese protests. Albania has also agreed to receive an Algerian, an Egyptian, and a Russian.

After seven years at Guantánamo, Uighur Huzaifa Parhat was ordered released, transferred, or given a new hearing by an Appeals Court decision. *Parhat v Gates*, rendered on June 23, is the first such habeas corpus case to be reviewed favorably. On October 7, al Uighurs were ordered released in *Kiyemba v Bush*. Some 269 similar cases are expected to be consolidated into a single ruling.

Even were a prisoner acquitted in a trial at Guantánamo, he could be held indefinitely. Detainees remain at the discretion of the American government despite Geneva Convention requirements. One solution is to grant them asylum.

POW Convention, 1929, Art. 68. Belligerents shall be required to send back to their own country, without regard to rank or numbers, after rendering them in a fit condition for transport, prisoners of war who are seriously ill or seriously wounded.

War Crime #172. Failure to Repatriate Seriously Ill or Wounded Prisoners. Some persons were incarcerated despite medical problems. Dilawar, whose legs were so badly beaten by interrogators that they looked as if they had been run over by a truck, was kept in confinement in Afghanistan even after his guards noticed that he was dying.

After they have become seriously ill, many prisoners have not been sent home. Abdul Razzaq Hekmati, a Guantánamo prisoner with terminal colorectal cancer, died in December 2007. Fellow inmates Abdul Hamid al-Ghizzawi and Saifulla Paracha remain despite serious illnesses.

Journalist Sami al-Hajj was flown home to Sudan on May 1, 2008, for hospitalization due to the effects of a sixteen-month hunger strike. Since the hunger strike ended three years earlier, the question remains why the American government did not negotiate an earlier release with Sudan.

Contact with Families

When a member of a family is missing, the rest of the family agonizes, wondering whether that person is alive or dead. Yet Bush's authorized roundups of thousands of persons have ignored the human suffering to those whose cultures are more family-oriented than is the case with the individualistic culture prevalent in much of the United States.

> **POW Convention, 1929, Art. 8.** As soon as possible, every prisoner must be enabled to correspond with his family himself.... **Art. 36.** Within a period of not more than one week after his arrival at the camp, and likewise in case of sickness, every prisoner shall be enabled to write his family a postal card informing it of his capture and of the state of his health. The said postal cards shall be forwarded as rapidly as possible and may not be delayed in any manner.

War Crime #173. Denial and Delay of Correspondence Between Prisoners and Their Families. Although the Red Cross operates a mail delivery system on behalf of prisoners, at least 30,000 persons have been detained for months or even years without being permitted to inform members of the families, who have had reason to believe that they were dead.

At Guantánamo, prisoners were at first denied even paper and pens. Later, outgoing mail was withheld to force prisoners to confess. Hamdan was not allowed to contact his wife for six months.

Khalid el-Masri's wife indeed thought he had abandoned her when he did not return home from a vacation in Macedonia in 2003, so she returned to her native Lebanon. When he was released from secret confinement, he was shocked that she was not in their home at Neu Ulm, Baden-Württemberg.

Letters in English, even when redacted, reach their destinations sooner than those written in other languages. Interpreters are backlogged at least four months due to censorship involving security considerations.

> **Geneva III, 1949, Art. 71.**...Prisoners of war who have been without news for a long period, or who are unable to receive news from their next of kin or to give them news by the ordinary postal route, as well as those
>
> *continued*

> who are at a great distance from their homes, shall be permitted to send telegrams, the fees being charged against the prisoners of war's accounts with the Detaining Power or paid in the currency at their disposal. They shall likewise benefit by this measure in cases of urgency. As a general rule, the correspondence of prisoners of war shall be written in their native language. The Parties to the conflict may allow correspondence in other languages. . . .

War Crime #174. Prisoners Have Not Been Allowed to Send Telegrams. In 1949, when the Geneva Conventions were adopted, telegrams provided the most immediate form of written person-to-person contact; telephones were still a luxury for most persons around the world. Nowadays, when e-mails and faxes are equivalent forms of rapid transfer of information, they are not available to prisoners.

Thanks to Red Cross pressure, inmates at Bagram were first allowed videoconferences with their families in January 2008. Two months later, Guantánamo inmates were permitted to telephone their relatives for hour-long conversations, privileges that are allowed once or twice yearly or when there has been a death in the family.

> **Torture Convention, 1985, Art. 11(1)** . . . In the event of death of the victim as a result of an act of torture, the dependents shall be entitled to compensation.

War Crime #175. Failure to Compensate Dependents of Fatal Victims of Torture. Some Abu Ghraib victims of torture, including the man packed in ice, were never registered as inmates. He was obviously tortured to death, but relatives did not know of his demise and remain uncompensated. Although the military has paid some compensation to Iraqis for misconduct by American soldiers, none of those abused in prison have received compensation for mistreatment by prison officials, suggesting that the denial has been made in Washington, not in the field.

Regarding Guantánamo inmates who have been released from Guantánamo, none have been compensated by the United States even after court action. Instead, lawsuits are being pursued in foreign courts. In 2008, London compensated heirs of Baha Mousa, who died from beatings while held prisoner at a British facility near Basra. Americans tortured by Iraq during the Gulf War (War Crime #147) await action by a new president.

DISCRIMINATION

Although prisoners are supposed to be treated equally, some provisions allow for more delicate handling of certain types of prisoners. The wounded, for example, are especially to be protected. The present section deals with women, nationality, race, religion, the elderly, and children.

Treatment of Women

Some Muslim women were incarcerated at Abu Ghraib. Rather than respecting their rights, some were very badly handled. In mid-2008, twelve women were confined in the American-run prisons in Iraq. However, one woman, Aafia Siddiqui, suddenly appeared in federal court in New York on August 5, 2008, after a five-year disappearance. She was charged with the same offense under American criminal law as Salim Hamdan—aiding a terrorist organization. The inference is that if Hamdan had been a woman, he would never have been sent to Guantánamo. Sex discrimination can cut both ways in the topsy-turvy brave new world of George W. Bush.

> **POW Convention, 1929, Art. 3.** Women shall be treated with all the regard due to their sex.

War Crime #176. Sexual Abuse of Females. On October 6, 2003, a female Abu Ghraib detainee was tortured and ordered to take off her clothes before interrogators. One woman at Abu Ghraib was forced to strip in front of her nephew. A girl was sexually abused by two interrogators. A videotape even shows a uniformed American soldier sodomizing a female prisoner. Other women have alleged rape and sexual abuse.

> **Geneva III, 1949, Art. 25.** . . . In any camps in which women prisoners of war, as well as men, are accommodated, separate dormitories shall be provided for them.

War Crime #177. Women Confined in the Same Prison Facility as Men. At Abu Ghraib, women and men were in the same compound, though not in the same cells. No women have been held at Guantánamo.

> **Geneva IV, 1949, Art. 97.** A woman internee shall not be searched except by a woman.

War Crime #178. Women Prisoners Searched by Men. In Abu Ghraib, women have been forced to disrobe and be searched by men. Photographs were taken of one such woman, an alleged prostitute.

Nationality, Race, and Religion

Among those rounded up in Afghanistan and Pakistan, those from Arabic-speaking countries were considered ipso facto to be likely members of al-Qaeda. Bush's antipathy toward extremist Muslims has been loud and clear. Abusive ethnic and religious epithets have been used.

> **Geneva III, 1949, Art. 16.** . . . All prisoners of war shall be treated alike by the Detaining Power, without any adverse distinction based on race, nationality, religious belief or political opinions, or any other distinction founded on similar criteria.

War Crime #179. Discrimination Based on Nationality, Race, or Religion. American citizens accused of terrorism have been tried in federal courts. Noncitizens are discriminatorily slated for trial under different procedural standards in military tribunals at Guantánamo.

The first English word that fifteen-year-old Mohammed el-Gharani heard was the word "nigger" from prison guards at Guantánamo. The same word was shouted at two prisoners in Afghanistan. Although that utterance of prejudice may not be indicative of any overt discrimination, Ibrahim Ahmed Mahmoud Qosi believes that his Sudanese nationality explains why he is still detained.

The CIA specifically encouraged authorities in Afghanistan and Pakistan to detain suspicious persons from Arabic-speaking countries. As a result, Guantánamo was filled with many persons who had nothing to do with al-Qaeda but happened to be businesspeople, charity workers, teachers, and other visitors from Arabic-speaking countries. Later, those from Afghanistan, Australia, Belgium, Britain, Denmark, France, Germany, Pakistan, Russia, Spain, and Sweden were repatriated, leaving primarily Arabic-speaking nationalities incarcerated.

Regarding discrimination based on religion, former Captain James Yee experienced much hostility at Guantánamo toward Muslim employees of the United States compared with Christian employees. He believes that excessive brutality was meted out to prisoners because of their religion. In any case, Bush's repeated references to "Islamofascism" and apparently exclusive roundup of Muslims for detention give unmistakable prima facie evidence of discrimination based on religion.

Treatment of the Elderly

There is no exact count of the total number of elderly persons who have been locked up in all American-run facilities overseas, though about two hundred detainees over 60 were held in American-run prisons in Iraq during mid-2008. Most of those captured have been young men who have survived abusive and harsh treatment.

> **Geneva III, 1949, Art. 45.** Prisoners of war other than officers and prisoners of equivalent status shall be treated with the regard due to their . . . age.

War Crime #180. Elder Abuse. The Red Cross found a prisoner in Iraq aged 61 requiring skin grafts and finger amputations due to rough handling in prison. Regardless of the fact that one prisoner was senile, drinking, eating, and lying in his own excrement, and another walked with a cane, they were held nearly a year at Guantánamo in misery. A prisoner in his 70s with a heart condition was refused an EKG on the pretext that he was malingering about chest pains. One incontinent prisoner over 90 was observed using a walker while shackled, a sight that apparently evoked no sympathy from his captors. Mohamed Sadiq, perhaps the oldest prisoner at Guantánamo, finally went home to Afghanistan at the age of 93 after several years of confinement.

Treatment of Children

The Convention on the Rights of the Child (CRC) defines a "child" as someone under 18 who needs special protection. The American government considers a person aged 16 as an adult. Because of a dispute over which persons in American custody are children, the numbers cited below differ from those accepted by the Bush administration. In 2008, the United States reported to the UN-assisted Committee on the Rights of the Child that the United States from 2002 had detained 2,400 children in Iraq and 100 in Afghanistan, though another source claims that the figure for Afghanistan is 800. As of May 2008, there were 21 at Guantánamo. That month, the Committee upbraided the United States for charging minors with war crimes instead of treating underage persons as victims of war.

> **Protocol 1, 1977, Art. 78(1).** No Party to the conflict shall arrange for the evacuation of children, other than its own nationals, to a foreign country except for a temporary evacuation where compelling reasons of the health or medical treatment of the children or, except in occupied territory, their safety, so require. Where the parents or legal guardians can be found, their written consent to such evacuation is required. If these persons cannot be found, the written consent to such evacuation of the persons who by law or custom are primarily responsible for the care of the children is required. Any such evacuation shall be supervised by the Protecting Power in agreement with the Parties concerned, namely, the Party arranging for the evacuation, the Party receiving the children and any Parties whose nationals are being evacuated. In each case, all Parties to the conflict shall take all feasible precautions to avoid endangering the evacuation.

War Crime #181. Transfer of Children from Their Home Countries. At least 800 boys, aged 10 to 15, were captured in Afghanistan during 2002, from whom as many as sixty-four children have been sent to Guantánamo, some long enough to have reached adulthood. Khalid Sheikh Mohammed's two children, aged 7 and 9, were separately detained to force him to confess.

War Crime #182. Failure to Obtain Permission from Parents or Guardians for Transfer of Their Children. Transfers have occurred without consulting or even informing parents. For example, family members knew nothing of Hassin Bin Attash's extraordinary rendition experience in Jordan or Ahmad Bashir's disappearance for two years in a secret prison. Khalid Sheikh Mohammed, however, was painfully aware that Americans were threatening to harm his children.

> **Protocol 1, 1977, Art. 77(4).** If arrested, detained or interned for reasons related to the armed conflict, children shall be held in quarters separate from the quarters of adults, except where families are accommodated as family units...

War Crime #183. Incarceration of Children in the Same Quarters as Adults. Children were placed in the same prison alongside adults at Abu Ghraib, where rapes were reported of both male and female children. Teenagers were placed in the same camp at Guantánamo with the other detainees, some initially in solitary confinement.

> **Protocol 1, 1977, Art. 78(2).** Whenever an evacuation occurs...each child's education, including his religious and moral education as his parents desire, shall be provided while he is away with the greatest possible continuity.

War Crime #184. Failure to Provide Education for Imprisoned Children. Captain James Yee left Guantánamo on September 10, 2003. No Muslim chaplain has ever replaced him. Since then, the boys have not been provided appropriate religious education. From March 2003, some boys have learned English and other subjects appropriate to their age. American officials claim that children currently detained in Afghanistan and Iraq are allowed age-appropriate education.

> **CRC, 1989, Art. 9(3).** States Parties shall respect the right of the child who is separated from one or both parents to maintain personal relations and direct contact with both parents on a regular basis...

War Crime #185. Withholding Parental Contact from Child Detainees. Contrary to the Convention on the Rights of the Child (CRC), Omar Khadr was first allowed contact with his mother by means of a telephone conversation in mid-2007, some five years after his arrest in Afghanistan, when he was no longer a child. Mohammed Ismail Agha, aged 12 or 13, was first allowed to write his dad after ten months of confinement at Guantánamo, but his letter did not reach home in Afghanistan until one year later. Letters to parents of three young prisoners were sent in 2003, two years after their imprisonment, but only after they learned how to read and write.

> **CRC, 1989, Art. 9(4).** Where such separation results from any action initiated by a State Party, such as the detention... of the child, that State Party shall, upon request, provide the parents, the child or, if appropriate, another member of the family with the essential information concerning the whereabouts of the absent member(s) of the family...

War Crime #186. Failure to Inform Parents of the Whereabouts of Detained Children. In most cases, weeks or even years elapsed before parents were informed of the imprisonment of their children. Khalid Sheikh Mohammed never learned where his children were held. Mohammed el-Gharani's family learned three years after his capture when they were contacted by his attorney, Clive Stafford Smith.

> **CRC, 1989, Art. 13(1).** The child shall have the right to freedom to... seek, receive and impart information and ideas of all kinds, regardless of frontiers, either orally, in writing or in print...

War Crime #187. Refusal to Allow Child Detainees to Receive Information. Most children were held incommunicado at Guantánamo until April 2003. Mohammed Jawad remains in solitary confinement. Omar Khadr's attorney has been forbidden to supply him Internet articles.

> **CRC, 1989, Art. 19(1).** States Parties shall take all appropriate... measures to protect the child from all forms of physical or mental violence, injury or abuse, neglect or negligent treatment, [or] maltreatment...

War Crime #188. Failure to Protect Child Detainees from Abuse. Mistreatment occurred initially at Bagram and continued at Abu Ghraib and Guantánamo until at least 2004. American guards videotaped Iraqi male prisoners raping young boys but took no action to stop the offenses. Children in Abu Ghraib were deliberately frightened by dogs. At Guantánamo, adult prisoners protested that juveniles were kept in solitary confinement, but their complaints were ignored. Omar Khadr and Mohammed Jawad attest that they were treated brutally.

> **CRC, 1989, Art. 19(2).** Such protective measures should... include... social programs to provide necessary support for the child... as well as for
>
> *continued*

other forms of prevention and for identification, reporting, referral, investigation, treatment and follow-up of instances of child maltreatment...and, as appropriate, for judicial involvement.

War Crime #189. Failure to Provide Social Programs for Child Detainees to Deal with Prison Abuse. Although three children at Guantánamo were given opportunities for education and recreation, the rest were not. Omar Khadr has been released from solitary confinement but not Mohammed Jawad.

War Crime #190. Failure to Establish Programs to Prevent Prison Abuse of Child Detainees. The only "program" to stop mistreatment of the boys has been the termination of solitary confinement, which remains as a matter of policy to be employed under circumstances determined by American officials.

War Crime #191. Failure to Investigate Abuse of Child Prisoners. Army Specialist Samuel Provance testified about abuse of children at Abu Ghraib before Congress in February 2006. In a videotape of Omar Khadr's interrogation by Canadian authorities, he blurted out "I was tortured," and he cried "Mommy!" Yet there have been no systematic investigations of reported incidents of child abuse by the Bush administration at any American detainment venues.

War Crime #192. Failure to Prosecute Prison Personnel Who Abuse Child Detainees. Provance, who abused a child under orders, was demoted, not prosecuted. The officer who ordered him to engage in abuse was not court-martialed.

Although Omar Khadr has accused Sergeant Joshua Claus of his torture, Claus has not been charged with mistreatment. Indeed, the military tried to keep Claus's identity secret until a Guantánamo judge ordered the information to come out.

CRC, 1989, Art. 31(1). States Parties recognize the right of the child to rest and leisure, to engage in play and recreational activities appropriate to the age of the child...

War Crime #193. Failure to Provide Recreational Activities for Child Prisoners. There is no record of recreation for the hundreds of children detained at Bagram or at Abu Ghraib. Recreational opportunities at Guantánamo were minimal until April 2003, when three of the very youngest were housed together in a minimum security camp and permitted recreation. Nevertheless, in April 2008 guards confiscated a copy of the screenplay of *Lord of the Rings* from Omar Khadr that had been supplied by his military attorney, who was also ordered not to play chess and dominoes with his client. Mohammed Jawad has received promises of books to study that have not been kept.

> **CRC, 1989, Art. 37(1).** No child shall be subjected to torture or other cruel, inhuman or degrading treatment or punishment. Neither capital punishment nor life imprisonment without possibility of release shall be imposed for offences committed by persons below eighteen years of age.

War Crime #194. Inhumane Treatment of Child Detainees. Perhaps the worst incident at Abu Ghraib involved a girl aged 12 or 13 who was stripped naked and beaten. She screamed for help to her brother in an upper cell.

Iraqi journalist Suhaib Badr-Addin al-Baz, who heard the girl's screams, witnessed an ill 15-year-old who was forced to run up and down Abu Ghraib with two heavy cans of water. When he stopped, he was beaten. When he collapsed, guards stripped him and poured cold water on him. Finally, a hooded man was brought in. When unhooded, the boy realized that the man was his father, who doubtless was being intimidated into confessing something.

While General Hamid Zabar was being questioned in Iraq, his interrogators decided to arrest his frail 16-year-old son in order to produce a confession. After soldiers found the boy, he was stripped, drenched with mud and water, and exposed to the cold January night while driven about in the open back of a truck. When presented naked to his father, he was shivering due to hypothermia, clearly needing medical attention.

Considerable abuse was meted out to Mohammed Jawad and Omar Khadr in Afghanistan. While still wounded from battle, Omar was interrogated many times, sometimes while hooded with dogs barking near him, so he confessed to stop the pain. After arriving at Guantánamo, Omar was shackled to the floor in stress positions until he soiled himself. His bound body was twice used as a mop to wipe his own urine mixed with pine oil after which he was refused a shower and a change of clothing. He was also administered a brutal beating while on a hunger strike, threatened with rape, and denied pain medication.

War Crime #195. Indefinite Detainment of Children. Executive orders authorized the indefinite detainment of at least 800 boys in Afghanistan. Of those sent to Guantánamo, nine have remained on an indefinite basis.

> **CRC, 1989, Art. 37(3).** Every child deprived of liberty...shall have the right to maintain contact with his or her family through correspondence and visits, save in exceptional circumstances...

War Crime #196. Failure to Allow Parents to Visit Child Detainees. No parents have visited their sons in Guantánamo. Such travel is neither approved nor budgeted. Those confined in Afghanistan and Iraq are currently allowed family visits.

> **CRC, 1989, Art. 37(4).** Every child deprived of his or her liberty shall have the right to prompt access to legal and other appropriate assistance, as well as the right to challenge the legality of the deprivation of his or her liberty before a court or other competent, independent and impartial authority, and to a prompt decision on any such action.

War Crime #197. Failure to Allow Child Prisoners to Have Legal Counsel. Omar Khadr, detained in 2002, was first visited by a military defense lawyer, Lieutenant Commander William Kuebler, in 2004. By then, Khadr was an adult. Air Force Major David Frakt was first allowed to see his client, Mohammed Jawad, in 2008. The youngest children at Guantánamo were repatriated without seeing an attorney.

War Crime #198. Failure to Provide an Impartial Tribunal for Child Prisoners. Colonel Peter Brownback, judge at the pretrial hearing for Omar Khadr, ruled on May 8, 2008, that the prosecution must produce all relevant documents or the case will be suspended indefinitely, whereupon he was replaced by another judge. Among the missing documents is the initial report by Sergeant First Class Christopher Speer, which did not accuse him of any wrongdoing, as well as a videotape of his interrogation, possibly while he was being tortured. After Speer died, his commanding officer changed the report to accuse Khadr of Speer's death. Khadr's military attorney has been refused an interview with that superior officer. Nevertheless, Canada's Supreme Court has ruled that Canadian officials violated the law by interrogating him at Guantánamo in 2003–2004, and a lower court in 2008 ordered the release of a taped interrogation in which Khadr displayed apparent evidence of torture on his body.

During the arraignment of Mohammad Jawad in 2008, the judge asked him if he accepted the assigned military defense attorney as his lawyer. When he replied in the negative, the judge asked whether he knew another lawyer. His reply was "Since I don't know any lawyer, how can I have them represent me? ... I should be given freedom so that I can find a lawyer." His request to hunt for a lawyer was then denied. Lacking an accepted defense attorney, proceedings in his case were postponed in view of the shortage of available military attorneys at Guantánamo.

War Crime #199. Failure to Provide Speedy Trials for Child Prisoners. The first tribunal to assess Omar Khadr's status met in 2007 and decided that he was an "illegal enemy combatant." By then he was an adult. Mohammed Jawad was a child when first imprisoned in 2002. Their trials are pending.

CRC, 1989, Art. 39. States Parties shall take all appropriate measures to promote physical and psychological recovery and social reintegration of a child victim of: any form of neglect, exploitation, or abuse; torture or any other form of cruel, inhuman or degrading treatment or punishment; or armed conflicts. Such recovery and reintegration shall take place in an environment which fosters the health, self-respect and dignity of the child.

War Crime #200. Failure to Provide Post-Confinement Social Programs for Abused Child Prisoners. In 2003, Secretary of Labor Elaine Chao gave a speech on behalf of the need to rehabilitate child soldiers from Burundi, Colombia, El Salvador, Sierra Leone, Sri Lanka, and Uganda. While she spoke, Mohammed Jawad and Omar Khadr were being abused at Guantánamo.

From 2001, the United States has provided more than $34 million for the program of the UN Children's Fund to rehabilitate and reintegrate child combatants in Afghanistan, possibly some of those returning from Guantánamo. Not a penny has been spent on Mohammed Jawad and Omar Khadr, who were captured in Afghanistan and have languished in Guantánamo, abused but not rehabilitated and not provided an opportunity to live normal lives.

CRC, 1989, Art. 40(2)(b). Every child alleged as or accused of having infringed the penal law has at least the following guarantees: (i) To be presumed innocent until proven guilty according to law; (ii) To be informed promptly and directly of the charges against him or her, and, if appropriate,

continued

through his or her parents or legal guardians, and to have legal or other appropriate assistance in the preparation and presentation of his or her defense; (iii) To have the matter determined without delay... in the presence of legal or other appropriate assistance and, unless it is considered not to be in the best interest of the child, in particular, taking into account his or her age or situation, his or her parents or legal guardians; (iv) Not to be compelled to give testimony or to confess guilt; to examine or have examined adverse witnesses and to obtain the participation and examination of witnesses on his or her behalf under conditions of equality; (v) If considered to have infringed the penal law, to have this decision and any measures imposed in consequence thereof reviewed by a higher competent, independent and impartial authority or judicial body according to law...

War Crime #201. Presumption of the Guilt of Child Prisoners Before Trials. According to Omar Khadr's attorney, Lieutenant Commander Kuebler, the legal proceedings at Guantánamo are "a process that's not designed to be fair; it's designed to produce convictions.... Instead of a presumption of innocence and of a public trial... we start with a presumption of guilt and a secret trial." From information revealed thus far, Khadr is to be charged with attacking an American soldier, though he claims that his action was in self-defense while injured and under imminent attack.

War Crime #202. Failure to Promptly Inform Child Prisoners of Charges Against Them. None of the boys transferred from Afghanistan to Guantánamo knew what crimes they might have committed. Omar Khadr and Mohammed Jawal, though first interrogated in Afghanistan, waited five years before being officially designated "illegal enemy combatants."

War Crime #203. Forcing a Child Prisoner to Incriminate Himself. The basis for Omar Khadr's imprisonment is in part what he said during an interrogation. However, he claims that he was under duress.

War Crime #204. Failure to Allow Witnesses to Testify on Behalf of Child Prisoners. On November 8, 2007, just thirty-six hours before Omar Khadr's arraignment, his defense attorney learned of an American witness to his alleged offense who had submitted a report in 2002 with potentially exculpatory testimony. But the witness was never summoned in part because his name was never revealed, and the report was not allowed to be introduced into evidence by the military panel even though the report was accidentally seen by the press.

War Crime #205. Failure to Allow Appeals from Legal Proceedings of Child Prisoners. Prior to passage of the Detainee Treatment

Act of 2005, no right of appeal existed. There are no appeals from the Administrative Review Board at Guantánamo and similar boards in Afghanistan and Iraq.

DISAPPEARANCES

The International Convention for the Protection of All Persons from Enforced Disappearance was adopted in 2005 after decades of a practice, particularly in South America, of having governments arrest someone in the middle of the night and then dispatch that person to a secret location, including the depths of the Atlantic Ocean, whereupon relatives assumed that they were dead.

President Bill Clinton authorized a similar program, known as "extraordinary rendition," on the basis of Presidential Decision Directive 39, dated June 21, 1995. He approved fourteen individual cases.

After 9/11, the program was continued. What was formerly a retail operation, however, became a wholesale roundup of suspected terrorists in several dozen countries around the world. The treaty is relevant to war crimes because those who disappeared have been identified as violent international criminals active in the "war on terror."

There are two types of disappearance. Some became "ghost" detainees, that is, persons whose names were not listed on the rosters of well-known prisons. Others were secret detainees in the extraordinary rendition program, held at locations known only by CIA personnel and others most directly involved. President Bush specifically ordered some of the earliest detainees to be rendered. Others were rounded up in a worldwide manhunt without much executive supervision. Either way, hundreds have disappeared without a trace.

Enforced Disappearances Convention, 2005, Art. 1(1). No one shall be subjected to enforced disappearance. **(2).** No exceptional circumstances whatsoever, whether a state of war or a threat of war, internal political instability or any other public emergency, may be invoked as a justification for enforced disappearance.... **Art. 6(2).** No order or instruction from any public authority, civilian, military or other, may be invoked to justify an offence of enforced disappearance.

War Crime #206. Extraordinary Renditions. The existence of enforced disappearances is beyond dispute. Many airplanes transporting secret detainees flew from airports in Europe. When that fact was leaked by civilian ground personnel, the Council of Europe launched an investigation. Jeppesen Dataplan of San Jose, California, has been sued in federal court for providing logistics for some of the flights. Attorneys testifying before Congress on June 5, 2008, agreed that criminal prosecutions are warranted for the rendition of Canadian citizen Maher Arar.

About 100 "ghost" detainees were being held in Iraq according to General Paul Kern's testimony before Congress in 2004. Most at Guantánamo were "ghost detainees" until 2006, when their names were released due to a court-enforced Freedom of Information Act request. Those presumed dead had a second life. Nevertheless, Mustafa Naser's whereabouts remain a mystery today. Indicted in Spain for the Madrid bombing in 2004, Washington has refused to disclose where he is under lock and key.

War Crime #207. Issuance of Executive Orders Authorizing Enforced Disappearances. In January 2002, Bush specifically ordered the transfer of Ibn Sheik al-Libi from Afghanistan to Egypt, where he was tortured. On September 6, 2006, Bush announced that fourteen victims of extraordinary rendition were being shipped from previously undisclosed locations to Guantánamo, where they were housed in a secret compound at the naval base.

> **Enforced Disappearances Convention, 2005, Art. 6(1).** Each State Party shall take the necessary measures to hold criminally responsible at least: (a) Any person who commits, orders, solicits or induces the commission of, attempts to commit, is an accomplice to or participates in an enforced disappearance; (b) A superior who: (i) Knew, or consciously disregarded information which clearly indicated, that subordinates under his or her effective authority and control were committing or about to commit a crime of enforced disappearance; (ii) Exercised effective responsibility for and control over activities which were concerned with the crime of enforced disappearance; and (iii) Failed to take all necessary and reasonable measures within his or her power to prevent or repress the commission of an enforced disappearance or to submit the matter to the competent authorities for investigation and prosecution; (c) Subparagraph (b) above is without prejudice to the higher standards of responsibility applicable under relevant international law to a military commander or to a person effectively acting as a military commander.

War Crime #208. Failure to Prosecute Those Responsible for Enforced Disappearances. Bush is primarily responsible but exempt under international law from prosecution so long as he remains in

office. The names of the operatives involved in extraordinary renditions have not been disclosed. In 2005, the Italian government issued
arrest warrants for the CIA agents who removed Abu Omar, an Italian
citizen, from a street in Milan and flew him to a secret prison in
Egypt in 2003. However, nobody has been apprehended in connection
with the extraordinary rendition of Canadian engineer Maher Arar,
who was detained at JFK airport in 2002 and flown to Syria to be
tortured.

> **Enforced Disappearances Convention, 2005, Art. 16(1).** No State
> Party shall expel, return ("refouler"), surrender or extradite a person to
> another State where there are substantial grounds for believing that he or
> she would be in danger of being subjected to enforced disappearance.

**War Crime #209. Sending Prisoners to Countries Where
Enforced Disappearance Is Likely.** Some 150 prisoners were secretly
handed over to Egypt in January 2002. Along with several other countries, they kept the names of the rendered captives a secret. Two Algerians released from Guantánamo were reported missing in 2008.

> **Enforced Disappearances Convention, 2005, Art. 17(3).** Each State
> Party shall assure the compilation and maintenance of one or more up-to-
> date official registers and/or records of persons deprived of liberty, which
> shall be made promptly available, upon request, to any judicial or other
> competent authority or institution authorized for that purpose by the law of
> the State Party concerned or any relevant international legal instrument to
> which the State concerned is a party. The information contained therein
> shall include, as a minimum: (a) The identity of the person deprived of lib-
> erty; (b) The date, time and place where the person was deprived of lib-
> erty and the identity of the authority that deprived the person of liberty; (c)
> The authority that ordered the deprivation of liberty and the grounds for
> the deprivation of liberty; (d) The authority responsible for supervising the
> deprivation of liberty; (e) The place of deprivation of liberty, the date and
> time of admission to the place of deprivation of liberty and the authority
> responsible for the place of deprivation of liberty; (f) Elements relating to
> the state of health of the person deprived of liberty; (g) In the event of
> death during the deprivation of liberty, the circumstances and cause of
> death and the destination of the remains; (h) The date and time of release
> or transfer to another place of detention, the destination and the authority
> responsible for the transfer.

War Crime #210. Failure to Disclose Basic Information about Victims of Enforced Disappearance to Appropriate Authorities. Governments have been kept in the dark regarding their nationals who are secret detainees. When hundreds were transported from Afghanistan to Guantánamo in 2002, the current Afghan government had not yet been established.

> **Enforced Disappearances Convention, 2005, Art. 18(1).** ... Each State Party shall guarantee to any person with a legitimate interest in this information, such as relatives of the person deprived of liberty, their representatives or their counsel, access to at least the following information: (a) The authority that ordered the deprivation of liberty; (b) The date, time and place where the person was deprived of liberty and admitted to the place of deprivation of liberty; (c) The authority responsible for supervising the deprivation of liberty; (d) The whereabouts of the person deprived of liberty, including, in the event of a transfer to another place of deprivation of liberty, the destination and the authority responsible for the transfer; (e) The date, time and place of release; (f) Elements relating to the state of health of the person deprived of liberty; (g) In the event of death during the deprivation of liberty, the circumstances and cause of death and the destination of the remains.

War Crime #211. Failure to Disclose Basic Information about Victims of Enforced Disappearance to Family and Legal Representatives. Families of those who disappeared knew as little as their governments. Relatives of a young Afghan who died of hypothermia while chained to the floor during 2002, for example, were never informed where he was detained.

> **Enforced Disappearances Convention, 2005, Art. 21.** Each State Party shall take the necessary measures to ensure that persons deprived of liberty are released in a manner permitting reliable verification that they have actually been released. Each State Party shall also take the necessary measures to assure the physical integrity of such persons and their ability to exercise fully their rights at the time of release, without prejudice to any obligations to which such persons may be subject under national law.

War Crime #212. Failure to Provide Verification of Release of Disappeared Detainees. When Khalid el-Masri was transferred from a secret prison in Egypt to the Albanian wilderness, nobody was informed, including his government or his spouse. When Bush disclosed that fourteen previous secret detainees would be transferred to Guantánamo in 2007, any remaining secret detainees remained in limbo. One secret prisoner was revealed six months later, another in August 2008.

Enforced Disappearances Convention, 2005, Art. 24(1). For the purposes of this Convention, "victim" means the disappeared person and any individual who has suffered harm as the direct result of an enforced disappearance. (2). Each victim has the right to know the truth regarding the circumstances of the enforced disappearance, the progress and results of the investigation and the fate of the disappeared person. Each State Party shall take appropriate measures in this regard.

War Crime #213. Failure to Inform Rendered Persons of the Reasons for Their Disappearance, Investigation of Their Case, and Plans for Their Future. When Shafiq Rasul arrived at Guantánamo in 2002, he was informed, "You are now the property of the U.S. Marine Corps." He and the rest of the inmates did not realize that they might be there indefinitely. They soon learned that they had no rights and no clear future.

Enforced Disappearances Convention, 2005, Art. 24(3). Each State Party shall take all appropriate measures to search for, locate and release disappeared persons and, in the event of death, to locate, respect and return their remains.

War Crime #214. Failure to Release Disappeared Persons. Luckily, Maher Arar and Khalid el-Masri went home. Others have remained in secret confinement.

War Crime #215. Failure to Return the Bodies of Those Who Die While Disappeared to Next of Kin. Some secret detainees appear to have died before their identities have been either discovered or revealed to the families. For example, the body of Jamadi was left unclaimed in the Baghdad morgue after he died at Abu Ghraib.

Enforced Disappearances Convention, 2005, Art. 24(4). Each State Party shall ensure in its legal system that the victims of enforced disappearance have the right to obtain reparation and prompt, fair and

continued

adequate compensation. **(5).** The right to obtain reparation referred to in paragraph 4 of this article covers material and moral damages and, where appropriate, other forms of reparation such as: (a) Restitution; (b) Rehabilitation; (c) Satisfaction, including restoration of dignity and reputation; (d) Guarantees of non-repetition.

War Crime #216. Failure to Provide Reparation and Compensation to Victims of Enforced Disappearance. Professor Janessa Gans describes the steps required to apply for compensation after confinement as "a difficult and bureaucratic process." Some prisoners have sued after leaving confinement. Some cases are pending, but others have been dismissed in federal courts on the basis of the state secrets doctrine.

Enforced Disappearances Convention, 2005, Art. 24(7). Each State Party shall guarantee the right to form and participate freely in organizations and associations concerned with attempting to establish the circumstances of enforced disappearances and the fate of disappeared persons, and to assist victims of enforced disappearance.

War Crime #217. Failure to Cooperate with NGOs Seeking to Rescue Victims of Enforced Disappearance. Human Rights First and other nongovernmental organizations (NGOs) have strongly protested the extraordinary rendition program. Bush has recalcitrantly refused to allow any intervention in the program.

CONCLUSION

Clearly, one would not want to be a prisoner under American control outside the United States after 9/11. The wholesale violations of international law are a disgrace for which President Bush has yet to apologize. Indeed, he has consistently refused to answer specific questions about how prisoners are treated. Yet many commentators have had a lot to say in condemnation. Possibly the most severe was a statement by attorney Theodore Sorensen that the torture that has been authorized "is evidence of a sick mind and an uncivilized chain of command."

Both interpreter Saar and Chaplain Yee note that those imprisoned at Guantánamo, some of whom were not religious before confinement, drew strength from their religious beliefs in the face of capricious, vicious treatment. Evidence exists that the experience of being brutally treated in an American-run prison outside the United States has served to recruit many more terrorists.

Many countries have decided to emulate the well-known practices at Abu Ghraib, Bagram, and Guantánamo, as documented in annual human rights reports of the Department of State. When Washington criticized Malaysia for indefinite detention of alleged terrorists in 2003, the response from Kuala Lumpur was that the practice was "just like the process in Guantánamo," whereupon the criticism was withdrawn. Egypt, Sudan, and Zimbabwe have also sought to justify their own practices by explicitly referring to Guantánamo.

On January 17, 2008, a training manual of the Canadian Foreign Ministry was reported in the press to have added the United States to its watchlist of countries practicing torture along with Afghanistan, China, Egypt, Iran, Israel, México, Saudi Arabia, and Syria. The interrogation techniques cited were "forced nudity, isolation, and sleep deprivation." When the report created a backlash in Washington, the Foreign Ministry pusillanimously announced that the training manual would be revised.

Although some conditions have improved a bit due to international and legal pressure, most war crimes involving the treatment of prisoners remain unaddressed. Although both presidential candidates proposed to close Guantánamo, they were silent during the campaign on American-run prisons elsewhere. The next president will have to cope with the fact that more than two centuries of American moral leadership in the world have been dumped into an Orwellian memory hole by George W. Bush.

Chapter 5

CRIMES COMMITTED IN THE POSTWAR OCCUPATIONS

Although victorious armies throughout history have often treated vanquished people unjustly, benevolent occupation was considered desirable in the laws of warfare of ancient India, which insisted that conquerors should respect the immovable assets of the country, comfort the sick and distressed, and respect the customs and laws of the people. The prophet Mohammed urged his warriors to treated conquered peoples mercifully. Similar to Moses's only clear prohibition in warfare, Mohammed insisted that armies should respect fruit trees.

Legal theorist Hugo Grotius stated that civilians who have been liberated from oppression should have their full rights restored. The earliest codification of the law of occupation was penned in the Lieber Code, which insisted that military rule should be guided by principles of "justice, honor, and humanity." The Code, issued by President Abraham Lincoln in 1863, authorized American officers to punish soldiers for cruelty, plunder, and reprisals meted out to an enemy.

According to Article 42 of the Hague Convention on the Laws and Customs of War on Land of 1899 (Hague II), foreign occupation exists as long as foreign troops have control in a country. Article 6 of the Geneva Convention Relative to the Protection of Civilian Persons in Time of War (Geneva IV) clarifies that occupation exists as long as military operations continue.

American military forces have remained in Afghanistan and Iraq, so both countries have remained under military occupation. For the occupations to end, all foreign forces must either leave or stay on the basis of a treaty with the sovereign states of Afghanistan and Iraq.

Whereas international law regarding aggression, the conduct of war, and treatment of prisoners is relatively straightforward, war crimes related to occupation lack clarity. Eyal Benvenisti's *The International Law of Occupation*, published in 1993 and updated to 2003, provides the most coherent explanation of the subject.

THE OCCUPATION IN AFGHANISTAN

On October 7, 2001, the United States and allies entered Afghanistan under the banner Operation Enduring Freedom (OEF), a global effort that also has components in the Caucasus, the Horn of Africa, the Sahara, and the Philippines. Most Afghans, lacking newspapers or radios, knew nothing about the war until American or Northern Alliance forces suddenly appeared. After Kabul fell, OEF-Afghanistan forces remained in the country, but Washington decided to rely on warlords so that troops could be withdrawn for the war in Iraq.

The occupation of Afghanistan was at first quite orderly (Table 5.1). Hamid Karzai, the current president of the country, was chosen to head the Afghan Interim Administration at a conference in Bonn, Germany, attended by thirty exiled Afghan leaders in December 2001. That same month, when most fighting in Afghanistan subsided, UN Security Council Resolution 1386 authorized the multinational International Security Assistance Force (ISAF) for Afghanistan alongside OEF-Afghanistan. ISAF was initially given responsibility for providing security so that the new Kabul government could establish civilian rule, which emerged when a new constitution was adopted and elections were held.

The United States is not the lead country of ISAF, as responsibility rotates semiannually among the contributing countries involved. The American military is supposed to train the new Afghan army, Germany the police force. Italy is advising Kabul on legal matters. Japanese forces are assigned the task of disarming warlord militias. Britain has responsibility for eradicating the narcotics industry. But there has been little success in fulfilling the mandate. Afghanistan has become a narco-state, wherein both governmental and antigovernmental forces finance operations through the opium trade. The Taliban, in particular, offers soldiers twice as much as they would receive from the Kabul government.

In response to a resurgence of Taliban resistance, troops from the North Atlantic Treaty Organization (NATO), to which the United States contributes, assumed command of ISAF in August 2003. UN Security Council Resolution 1510 of October 13, 2003, extended ISAF's

Table 5.1
Milestones in the Occupation of Afghanistan

Date	Event
10/7/2001	Beginning of the war
12/5/2001	Bonn Agreement reinstates the 1964 constitution, calls for Emergency Loya Jirga
12/20/2001	UN Security Council Resolution 1386 authorizes International Security Assistance Force
12/22/2001	Afghan Interim Authority established; Hamid Karzai selected as Chairman of its Afghan Interim Administration
5/23/2002	Security Council Resolution 1413 extends ISAF until 12/20/2002
6/10/2002	Emergency Loya Jirga convenes
6/13/2002	Hamid Karzai selected president of the Transitional Islamic State of Afghanistan
11/14/2002	UN Security Council Resolution 1444 extends ISAF until 12/20/2003
10/13/2003	UN Security Council Resolution 1510 extends ISAF until 10/13/2004 beyond Kabul
1/4/2004	Constitution adopted for the Islamic Republic of Afghanistan
9/17/2004	UN Security Council Resolution 1563 extends ISAF until 10/13/2005
10/9/2004	Hamid Karzai elected president of the Islamic Republic of Afghanistan
12/8/2004	Hamid Karzai sworn in as president
9/13/2005	UN Security Council Resolution 1623 extends ISAF until 10/13/2006
9/12/2006	UN Security Council Resolution 1707 extends ISAF until 10/13/2007
9/17/2007	UN Security Council Resolution 1776 extends ISAF until 10/13/2008

mandate outside Kabul to provide "security and law and order throughout the country." ISAF's mandate has been continued, most recently in Resolution 1776, to October 13, 2008, again in cooperation with OEF-Afghanistan and operated by NATO forces.

After taking office, President Karzai offered an amnesty to members of the Taliban and their sympathizers. But ISAF pursued the Taliban, provoking objections from Karzai in April 2008. Members of the American-led coalition suspect that Karzai's criticism is campaign rhetoric, as he seeks another term in office in 2009. Meanwhile, Karzai has reportedly branded some of this opponents as Taliban for NATO action when in fact they are merely his political opponents.

Mistakes in the ongoing conflict with the Taliban have already been noted in chapter 3. The mistreatment of prisoners at American-run prisons, which continues to the present, has been described in Chapter 4.

THE OCCUPATION OF IRAQ

After Congress passed the Joint Resolution to Authorize Military Force in Iraq on October 2, 2002, the United States and allies attacked Iraq on March 20, 2003. Bush unilaterally declared "mission accomplished" on May 1. There was no attempt to obtain a surrender agreement with Saddam Hussein or his government, which went into hiding when it became clear that there would be no negotiated peace.

With the end of the Cold War, the United Nations took charge of at least four countries that were in turmoil after negotiated ends of violence—Angola, Bosnia, Cambodia, and Kosovo. But Washington had no intention of allowing the UN to play such an exclusive role in Iraq after American troops entered Baghdad on April 5, 2003. Defense Secretary Donald Rumsfeld had a vague hope that countries in the multi-country coalition would send large numbers of volunteer personnel to assist as peacekeepers, and then most American forces would leave when a new government was quickly installed. But the relatively short and uncomplicated civilian occupation in Afghanistan stands in contrast with the longer and more controversial occupation of Iraq.

Because American forces occupying Baghdad were not instructed to negotiate with a defeated government, the Iraqi state expired without an immediate replacement. Nevertheless, Iraqis quickly reorganized political authority at local levels, and a self-appointed Leadership Council of seven exile leaders convened to agree upon a provisional government that they expected would soon be blessed by the American military authorities. The seven did not select a nominal head, and none had a military force of any consequence that might constitute a power base.

The Leadership Council was composed of representatives from three main Islamic traditions. The Kurds, who speak a non-Arabic language, live in the northern part of Iraq. In the south are Shi'ites, who speak Arabic and follow a more hierarchical Islamic tradition in which ayatollahs are leaders. Arabic-speaking Sunnis, who live in the central part of Iraq, have governed the country for hundreds of years. Their latest leader was Saddam Hussein.

One member of the Leadership Council, Ahmed Chalabi, was in the Kurdish region of Iraq before the war ended. He had impressed Rumsfeld's advisers as the new potential head of the country to whom the United States could quickly entrust authority.

When Chalabi flew to southern Iraq on order of Defense Secretary Rumsfeld in early April 2003, he tried to proclaim himself the head of the new Iraqi government. Although a Shi'ite, he was rebuffed in a speech to an assembly of Iraqis in the streets. Other members of the Leadership Council also did not trust him, in part because of his alleged past business irregularities. To further confuse matters, Lieutenant General David McKiernan entered Baghdad and declared himself governor of the city. The reestablishment of Iraqi sovereignty thereafter followed a curious path (Table 5.2).

Before victory in Baghdad, Rumsfeld appointed Retired Lieutenant General Jay Garner to head the Office of Reconstruction and Humanitarian Assistance (ORHA). Garner was not issued a formal mandate, but after his arrival in Baghdad on April 21 he accepted the Leadership Council of seven returning exiles and sought to reconstitute the bureaucracy of the previous government in order to return the country to normalcy. He also began to plan for elections within ninety days in the belief that Rumsfeld had placed him in charge as temporary occupation administrator, that is, as custodian of Iraqi sovereignty.

When Chalabi proved unacceptable to the Iraqis, he tried to undermine Garner, claiming that the general was empowering members of the former ruling Ba'ath Party. Instead of installing an interim government, President George W. Bush came up with a new plan, agreeing to send J. Paul Bremer III to head an occupying government known as the Coalition Provisional Authority (CPA), which would be the temporary sovereign authority for Iraq. However, Bush provided no written mandate for the CPA, which was to be under American and nominal British control. Accordingly, American and British UN representatives asked the Security Council to provide a legal basis for the occupation.

Bremer, who arrived in Baghdad on May 12, claimed to have direct authority from President Bush to establish transitional arrangements for the return of sovereignty from the CPA to an Iraqi government while bringing about civilian reconstruction. The CPA then absorbed Garner's ORHA.

Hundreds of civilians flew from the United States to work for the CPA on three-month assignments. Well-connected to leaders in the Republican Party, few had professional qualifications for the various

Table 5.2
Milestones in the Occupation of Iraq

Date	Event
3/20/03	Beginning of the war
4/21/2003	Retired General Jay Garner arrives in Baghdad as head of the Office of Reconstruction and Humanitarian Assistance
5/12/2003	L. Paul Bremer III arrives in Baghdad as Coalition Provisional Administrator, recognizes the Iraqi Leadership Council
5/22/2003	UN Security Council Resolution 1483 recognizes Anglo-American occupation
5/31/2003	Garner resigns, leaves Iraq
6/2/2003	Sergio de Mello arrives as UN Special Representative for Iraq
7/13/2003	Bremer replaces the Leadership Council with the Governing Council
8/19/2003	De Mello is killed in an insurgent attack
10/16/2003	UN Security Council Resolution 1511 recognizes the Coalition Provisional Authority, Governing Council, and Multinational Force-Iraq
3/8/2004	Bremer proclaims a Transitional Administrative Law for Iraq
6/1/2004	Iraqi Governing Council dissolves, naming Iyad Allawi as Prime Minister of the Iraqi Interim Government to replace the CPA
6/8/2004	UN Security Council Resolution 1546 accepts June 30 as CPA's final day
6/28/2004	Bremer leaves Baghdad, CPA is dissolved, Interim Government begins
1/30/2005	Elections held for a temporary National Assembly
4/28/2005	Ibrahim al-Ja'afari selected as interim Prime Minister
8/11/2005	UN Security Council Resolution 1637 extends MNF-I until 12/31/2006
10/15/2005	New constitution for the Republic of Iraq adopted by referendum, replacing Transitional Administrative Law
12/15/2005	Elections held for the Council of Representatives
5/20/2006	Nuri al-Maliki selected as Prime Minister
11/28/2006	UN Security Council Resolution 1723 extends MNF-I until 12/31/2007
12/18/2007	UN Security Council Resolution 1790 extends MNF-I until 12/31/2008

tasks of civilian reconstruction. Garner left in disgust on May 31, although his assignment was supposed to expire in September.

Congress's Joint Resolution of October 2002 authorized military force to eliminate Iraq's supposed military threat and to force the country to comply with UN resolutions. Both were accomplished by May 1, 2003. Accordingly, American military force no longer fulfilled the requirements of Congressional authorization. The anomaly, which persists to the present, resulted in action by the UN Security Council to legitimize the continuing presence of non-Iraqi troops in the country.

On May 22, 2003, UN Security Council Resolution 1483 confirmed Britain and the United States as official occupying powers. The resolution explicitly referred to responsibilities under the Hague and Geneva Conventions but asserted an additional requirement that the occupation must benefit the people of Iraq. The resolution permitted the replacement of former Iraqi laws, provided that the new laws would permit the Iraqi people "to determine their own political future and control their own natural resources... to form a representative government based on the rule of law that affords equal rights and justice to all Iraqi citizens without regard to ethnicity, religion, or gender." Subliminally, the occupation was mandated to implement provisions of the International Covenant on Political and Civil Rights as well as the International Covenant on Economic, Social, and Cultural Rights. In effect, the United States and Britain were to operate an informal trusteeship until sovereignty could be returned to an Iraqi government. Britain assumed control over the southern area around Basra, leaving control of the rest to the United States.

Resolution 1483 also set up the Development Fund for Iraq, which pooled about $1 billion from the former UN oil-for-food program and another $1 billion from previously frozen Iraqi assets. The Fund was made available to CPA for humanitarian needs, subject to audits by the International Advisory and Monitoring Board, also set up by the resolution. Controversies emerged from the CPA's use of the funds, however.

On June 2, 2003, Sergio de Mello arrived in Baghdad as UN Secretary-General Kofi Annan's Special Representative for Iraq. His assignment was to assist the CPA's efforts to establish a transitional Iraqi government while promoting humanitarian assistance, including the resumption of the UN food rationing scheme that began when sanctions were imposed on the regime of Saddam Hussein after the Gulf War of 1991. On August 19, de Mello died from an insurgent bomb outside his headquarters. Most of the UN staff left Iraq shortly thereafter, leaving Bremer with full authority as the civilian occupying viceroy.

With or without obtaining approval from Washington, Bremer proclaimed rules of various sorts to govern the country while American military commanders exercised independent control, sometimes at odds with Bremer. CPA Order 1 (May 16, 2003) disallowed most members of the Ba'ath Party from working for the government, the country's largest employer. CPA Order 2 (May 23, 2003) disbanded the entire Iraq army, a decision that Bremer hoped would serve in part to allay Shi'ite fears that Sunni death squads might continue to haunt them. Whereas the Americans and British felt reasonably safe throughout the country in the earliest days, journalists and scholars agree that the first two CPA decisions gradually brought about an insurgency by putting hundreds of thousands of Iraqis out of work, who therefore became enraged by the occupation. Limited insurgent attacks then began.

On July 13, 2003, dissatisfied with the Leadership Council, Bremer appointed members of a Governing Council, whose twenty-five members were somewhat more broadly representative of ethnosectarian and other interests than the Leadership Council. Instead of selecting technocrats who could handle matters competently, his selection of politicians served to exacerbate rivalries between Shi'ites and Sunnis as well as between returning exiles and those who had remained in Iraq during the rule of Saddam Hussein. When Bremer soon judged the larger body to be ineffectual, he proposed a three-year transition to involve an interim constitution and elections. But Iraqis then took exception to his plan for a lengthy occupation, and the insurgency became increasingly unrelenting.

In October 2003, when the insurgency was clearly out of control, UN Security Council Resolution 1511 recognized the legitimacy of the CPA and the Iraqi Governing Council. The White House agreed with the Security Council that June 30, 2004, would be a deadline for the end of CPA operations, thereby countermanding Bremer's lengthy timetable.

Military forces of Britain, the United States, and a few allies formed what 1511 recognized as the Multinational Force-Iraq (MNF-I), which has remained since the mid-2004 transfer of civilian authority. The UN assigned the MNF-I responsibility "to contribute to the maintenance of security and stability ... including by preventing and deterring terrorism" as an occupying military force after the end of the CPA in accordance with an exchange of letters between the American and Iraqi governments, as later noted in Resolution 1546 on June 8. One of the letters, written by Secretary of State Colin Powell, indicated that American forces would abide by "the law of armed conflict, including the Geneva Conventions." But Rumsfeld, not Powell, gave orders to MNF-I.

In March 2004, Bremer proclaimed a Transitional Administrative Law to provide a temporary legal framework until adoption of a constitution. On June 1, the Governing Council dissolved itself, having chosen Iyad Allawi as Prime Minister of the Interim Government. In Resolution 1546 of June 8, the UN Security Council recognized the transfer of sovereignty to take place at the end of June. On June 28, when Bremer departed and the CPA was abolished, the American Embassy in Baghdad absorbed most of CPA's operations and staff. The Interim Government immediately took over all government functions except those involving the MNF-I, which has continued to control American reconstruction funds and therefore has served as the liaison between policymakers in Washington and personnel in the Iraqi ministries.

Due to mortal threats from insurgents, many Sunnis boycotted elections held by the Interim Government at the end of January 2005 to select members of a temporary National Assembly. The newly elected legislature selected Ibrahim al-Ja'afari as interim Prime Minister in April 2005 and then drafted a constitution for the Republic of Iraq, which in turn was approved in a referendum on October 15. Following elections for a permanent Council of Representatives at the end of 2005, the current Prime Minister, Nuri al-Maliki, was chosen on May 20, 2006.

The Security Council extended the MNF-I mandate each year, most recently in Resolution 1790 of December 18, 2007, with the understanding that the occupation would end on December 31, 2008, unless Iraq's government wanted an earlier termination. Until then, MNF-I could still act without the permission of the Baghdad government.

In mid-2008, negotiations for a status-of-forces agreement were under way, based on terms of reference in an exchange of letters between President Bush and Prime Minister al-Maliki during December 2007. One effect of the agreement might be to exempt American troops not only from Iraqi national law but also from being subject to the International Criminal Court if Iraq were later to join that body. MNF-I, principally commanded by American forces, is expected to leave Iraq's cities in mid-2009 and fully leave the country by 2011. Until then, ISAF-I presumably would retain law and order functions, but under the authority of the Iraqi government and subject to international legal requirements.

EVIDENCE OF WAR CRIMES

Self-serving accounts of the occupation of Iraq by Americans directly involved provide some information about the various events. However, three of the most eloquent and comprehensive statements appear in journalist Rajiv Chandrasekaran's *Imperial Life in the Emerald City: Inside Iraq's Green Zone* (2006), the scholarly *Iraq in Fragments: The Occupation and Its Legacy* (2006) by Professors Eric Herring and Glen Rangwala, and *The Occupation of Iraq: Winning the War, Losing the Peace* (2007) by Ali A. Allawi, onetime Minister of Finance in the Transitional Government whose brother was Prime Minister of the Transitional Government. In addition, interview material for Charles Ferguson's documentary *No End in Sight* (2007) was released in book form in 2008. No authoritative accounts have yet been published on the occupation in Afghanistan. However, United Nations agencies and other organizations have issued human rights reports for both countries.

To evaluate war crimes in the American occupations of Afghanistan and Iraq, the main sources are two of the Hague Conventions and the Fourth Geneva Convention of 1949 (Appendix 5.1). In addition, Protocol 1 to the Geneva Conventions, as adopted in 1977, covers situations where an occupied people are resisting the occupying power.

War crimes of the multinational military forces have been identified in Chapters 3 and 4. In an interview with Charles Ferguson, Gerald Burke, onetime senior adviser to the Baghdad police chief, characterized the American occupation as engaging in "military operations," not "police operations."

The present chapter identifies several problem areas—public and political order, criminal justice, the economy, problems of discrimination, social and cultural issues, public health, and relations with outside organizations. Fifty-two war crimes are delineated below.

RE-ESTABLISHING PUBLIC ORDER

The primary responsibility of an occupying power is to stop all hostilities so that a country can return to normal. Although a semblance of normality existed in the early months, both in Afghanistan and Iraq, violence returned. Occupation authorities have had to cope with criminal elements, ethnosectarian and tribal rivalries, and insurgents determined to drive out the occupiers.

Hague II, 1899, Art. 43. The authority of the legitimate power having actually passed into the hands of the occupant, the latter shall take all steps in his power to re-establish and insure, as far as possible, public order and safety . . .

War Crime #218. Failure to Re-Establish Public Order and Safety. In Afghanistan, Kabul was seized relatively quickly, and the Taliban and al-Qaeda fled toward Pakistan. But American forces largely left much of the country under the control of the warlords, some of whom were not entirely prepared to accept rule from Kabul and whose harsh methods apparently provoked sympathy for the return of the Taliban. Some 100,000 troops commanded by warlords to maintain their fiefdoms are three times the total number of American forces in Afghanistan and more than twelve times the number of ISAF troops.

Although warlords have received at least $70 million in cash payments from the United States, some have collected road tolls, kidnapped, raped, and robbed those under their control. Warlord Hazrat Ali, for example, reportedly forced Karzai's representative in Nangrahar Province to leave and declared himself governor. Warlord Mohammed Atta placed Karzai's police chief in Balkh Province under house arrest.

After Bush reassigned many American forces to Iraq in 2003, the Taliban was able to regroup. They regained strength at a time when ISAF was unprepared. Blaming Washington for the resurgence of the Taliban, President Karzai points to the failure to create a trained police force and to seal the border with Pakistan. He also believes that American soldiers who have killed innocent civilians and mistreated prisoners are partly responsible for the re-emergence of the Taliban.

In Iraq, Defense Secretary Rumsfeld wanted the military to seize control of Baghdad as soon as possible, but he approved sending a small contingent and refused to allow the First Cavalry Division to enter the city despite contrary advice from military commanders. Although Saddam Hussein had maintained order in Baghdad with 250,000 troops, only 7,000 soldiers marched into Baghdad. Local firefighters and police were not on duty when looting began one hour later.

Lieutenant General David McKiernan, who arrived later in Baghdad, issued an order to the population to stop the chaos, including children dropping grenades from building tops, but his order was never posted on the streets or enforced because of fundamental disagreements in the field and in Washington over who was in charge of the city. Bush preferred a smaller footprint than the generals who were fighting the enemy every day. The Oil Ministry, already being looted when troops first appeared, was then the only place secured by force from the looting.

Initially, the U.S. military asked Iraqi armed forces to guard the Iranian border. After L. Paul Bremer III arrived to head the CPA and

Lieutenant General Ricardo Sanchez was assigned as the top commander over the operation in early May 2003, proposals for border control were turned down. Since borders of Iraq were left unguarded, new militias entered, and looted goods were smuggled out.

Before Saddam Hussein went into hiding, he formulated a plan to launch an insurgency against whatever authority sought to assert sovereignty. Taking note of the small number of troops in the occupation army, the insurgency soon emerged. However, there was no immediate plan in Washington to deal with the unrest. American forces instead secured themselves in base compounds, under orders to withdraw by the end of June, while a search for hidden weapons of mass destruction drained intelligence officers away from gathering information about the insurgency.

The Iraqi population was expecting Americans to stabilize the situation. The Iraqi army went home from the barracks and never surrendered. Flyers during the war promised fair treatment for those who did so. Indeed, Garner's assistant, Colonel Paul Hughes, had by May 9 obtained the cooperation of 100,000 Iraqi military personnel to be paid to assist in order maintenance and postwar reconstruction, and more were continuing to sign up every day.

The Iraqi police disappeared when the Americans entered Baghdad. Many of their facilities were looted and burned, unavailable for occupancy. Nevertheless, 40 percent of them reported for work soon after the war ended. Then came CPA Order 1 (May 16, 2003), which stripped them of leadership, leaving only the lower ranks, notorious for brutality and corruption. Mostly untrained, they were accustomed to sitting in their compounds until residents requested assistance. Although Garner proposed reconstituting the police force, National Security Adviser Condoleezza Rice turned down his request to do so. Bremer decided to build a new police force, but Bush gave that task little priority in terms of funding and training personnel.

CPA Order 2 (May 23) disbanded the Iraqi military despite vehement objections from Garner and others. The order had been drafted before Bremer arrived in Baghdad. He was unaware that nominal members and nonmembers of the Ba'ath Party in the Iraqi army, many of whom hated the Saddam Hussein regime, were awaiting an order from Sanchez to stop the disorder. As a result of the CPA Orders 1 and 2, 400,000 persons were thrown out of work, and the insurgency mounted attacks within three days. Bremer's plan was to organize a new Iraqi army, but those assigned to the task then estimated that a new military force would not be completed until 2006 or 2008.

After street protests by members of the former Iraqi armed forces, Bremer relented and agreed in June to pay stipends to those fired, monthly for 50,000 officers and onetime measly $50 payments for 200,000 conscripts. But that did not restore public order, as payments were not made until July 2003 or later, if at all. Those same men needed remunerative work, so as paid insurgents they were able to use the weapons that they had taken home before the invasion.

When American troops tried to deal with the insurgency and other forms of unrest, they lacked the personnel to restore order, a task that was not fully achieved until 2008. Over the years, more than 250 Iraqi interpreters on the American military payroll have been killed, further frustrating the effectiveness of the CPA and the MNF. From 2003 to 2005, only 6 percent of the "pacification operations" were designed to create a secure environment for Iraq. The main objective was instead to prevent American casualties.

When Bremer left at the end of June 2003, only 30 percent of the new police force had received CPA-funded training. Infiltrated by members of criminal elements and rival militias, some were already engaged in extortion, kidnapping, murder, and other crimes. There were no investigations of the crimes in most cases. When more affluent Iraqis pleaded for help from the Americans to stop family members from being kidnapped for ransom, they were told that Iraqi-on-Iraqi issues were not an American responsibility.

Meanwhile, Bremer constituted a Governing Council on the basis of ethnosectarian, gender, and other divisions, a dramatic change in how Iraq had been governed for centuries. As a result, there was an enhanced struggle for power among elite elements, and militias loyal to some of the elites emerged. Bremer even refused to provide security to members of the Governing Council, one of whose members was assassinated on September 2, 2003.

Soon, Iraqi government officials moved into the Green Zone with the CPA to gain greater security. That left the rest of the country in the Red Zone. The CPA, in short, operated without daily contact with the increasing chaos outside while basking in six cocktail lounges, a discotheque, a shopping arcade, a large garden, two Chinese restaurants, a fancy café, and a twenty-four-hour cafeteria.

After the CPA dissolved on June 28, 2003, the American military remained but was unable to find a formula to stop criminal activities, insurgents, ethnic cleansing, and terrorists. The Americans largely ignored complaints about the lawlessness of military contractors until several Iraqi civilians were murdered on September 16, 2007.

In 2007, after years of preemptive killings of innocent Iraqi drivers by American soldiers at checkpoints, the military decided to pay local groups up to $300 per month in order to maintain checkpoints. They also hired Sunni warlords to fight al-Qaeda. Tens of thousands were placed on the payroll. While the checkpoints were often operated by local militias with their own agenda, sometimes engaging in extortion and gangland murders, al-Qaeda troublemakers went elsewhere in the country to cause unrest.

Scholar Thomas Smith has made a convincing case that Americans did not use their troops to full benefit. To minimize G.I. casualties, half the troops were assigned to force protection roles rather than combat. In other words, resources for Iraqi security were equal to those deployed for the security of American soldiers. But MNF-I's main assignment was Iraqi security.

Although an escalation in American troops in early 2007, known as the "surge," arrested mini–civil wars in Baghdad, Basra, and Kirkuk, General David Petraeus admitted in mid-2008 that civil wars could easily heat up again, especially when American troops were reduced in number. Violent incidents declined, but Iraqis continued to be killed on a daily basis and Iraqi merchants have been forced to submit to shakedowns by Iraqi militias as well as corrupt police. In sum, Bush pursued a military policy rather than brokering a diplomatic solution to conflicts that were fundamentally rooted in political disagreements.

> **Hague II, 1899, Art. 47.** Pillage is formally prohibited.

War Crime #219. Complicity with Pillage. Failure to stop the initial looting in Baghdad made the United States complicit in the massive theft of artifacts, computers, desks, food, gold, silver, weapons, and other marketable goods. Some American soldiers even cheered on the looters; others watched, lacking orders to react.

Even after the initial looting of property by criminal elements, some former government workers entered unimpeded to destroy government documents and records. Baghdad's zoo was unguarded, so residents killed animals for dinner. Such weapons as AK-47s, lying unattended in the zoo and other public places, were hauled away gratis, sometimes under the noses of the American military to be used against them later.

According to several sources, CPA officials and contractors were corrupt and mismanaged funds. Some of the Iraqis hired were criminals whom Saddam Hussein had released from prisons before the invasion. For example, the MNF looked the other way while Iraqi Defense Ministry officials purchased shoddy equipment for the Iraqi army and then fled the country, depositing at least $1 billion in offshore banks. Later, some of the funds apparently leaked back to the insurgent and ethnosectarian violence.

> **Hague II, 1899, Art. 56.** The property of the communes, that of religious, charitable, and educational institutions, and those of arts and science, even when State property, shall be treated as private property. All seizure of, and destruction, or intentional damage done to such institutions, to historical monuments, works of art or science, is prohibited, and should be made the subject of proceedings.

War Crime #220. Failure to Apprehend and Prosecute Looters. In December 2002, Saddam Hussein released 100,000 criminals from custody, so some started looting as the Americans entered the country. Since commanders gave the order not to intervene, the pillage continued in each city as the American military marched north to Baghdad. The initial commander in charge of Baghdad, Lieutenant General James Conway, did not request or exercise authority to stop the looting, which continued for more than a month, even involving industrial cranes to haul away parts of power plants. Among the items looted were nuclear materials that might be used for radiological weapons.

When looting arose, Rumsfeld dismissively remarked, "Stuff happens," and the MNF never cracked down even though stolen goods were for sale at open markets in Baghdad. Bremer briefly considered giving a shoot-to-kill order to stop looters, but there was an insufficient number of American troops in Baghdad to round up the lawbreakers. Among the places from which property was absconded were electric plants, food depots, hospitals, industrial plants, libraries, museums, schools, and universities.

> **Geneva IV, 1949, Art. 20.** Persons regularly and solely engaged in the operation and administration of civilian hospitals, including the personnel engaged in the search for, removal and transporting of and caring for wounded and sick civilians, the infirm and maternity cases, shall be respected and protected.

War Crime #221. Failure to Provide Security for Hospitals. Looters in Baghdad hauled away beds, medical equipment, and medicines. Only one of the forty hospitals for the five million residents was open after the bombing and looting. As a result, sick Iraqis were often denied access to treatment. An investigation of public health by a Belgian nongovernmental organization reported that hospital personnel feared reprisals if they answered questions about conditions.

> **Geneva IV, 1949, Art. 33.** No protected person may be punished for an offence he or she has not personally committed.... [L]ikewise all measures of intimidation or of terrorism are prohibited.

War Crime #222. Intimidation of Civilians from Living Ordinary Lives. On April 28, 2003, American troops opened fire and killed about a dozen teenage demonstrators at a school in Falluja. That single act turned the city into the first hotbed of the insurgency.

Iraqis were intimidated not just in Falluja but in general. Civilian homes were destroyed only to demonstrate the power of the soldiers. Journalist Michael Massing reports an incident in which a squad of soldiers entered a schoolyard unannounced: When a student hit one with a stone, three in the squad displayed their guns, kicked the child for a few minutes, and threatened next time to use their weapons.

More indignities occurred on the highways. While Iraqis traveled along a road, they were often stopped by American soldiers, who pointed their guns at them and yelled in a language they could not understand, making ordinary life seem perilous. American contractors frequently ran Iraqis off the roads while going 100 miles per hour. In 2006, Prime Minister al-Maliki complained that such tactics had been a "daily occurrence" by troops who "do not respect the Iraqi people."

During 2007, a plan was formulated to establish walled communities inside Baghdad to restrict the flow of firearms and explosive materials. Entry and exit from the walled communities, necessary to maintain security, then restricted residents from enjoying their formerly free if dangerous city.

In April 2008, President Karzai complained that American forces had produced fear in the population by arresting too many civilians and mistreating them while confined. He also criticized the Americans for killing too many civilians in the ground campaign against the Taliban.

> **Cultural Property Convention, 1954, Art. 4(3).** Each High Contracting Party undertakes to prevent the exportation, from a territory occupied by it during an armed conflict, of cultural property... **Art. 19(1).** In the event of an armed conflict not of an international character occurring within the territory of one of the High Contracting Parties, each party to the conflict shall be bound to apply, as a minimum, the provisions of the present Convention which relate to respect for cultural property.

War Crime #223. Failure to Stop the Theft of Cultural Property. The National Museum was looted while American soldiers witnessed from their Humvees. Ambassador Barbara Bodine asked the military to protect world heritage sites, but they refused, particularly after Defense Secretary Rumsfeld pooh-poohed concern over the loss of vases on April 11, 2003. Richard Armitage, in an interview with journalist Charles Ferguson, implied that the decision not to intervene came from Bush.

The pillage occurred not just at the National Museum but in the Modern Art Museum and the provincial museums of Babylon, Kufa, Mosul, Nasiriya, and Tikrit. The National Theater was looted and burned three weeks after Baghdad was under American control. Later, the military was ordered to protect the National Museum.

However, looting at 12,000 unprotected sites continued into 2008, possibly resulting in the loss of more artifacts than those taken from the National Museum and smuggled out of the country. Of 15,000 ancient artifacts stolen from the National Museum and archaeological sites in 2003, some 8,500 have been thus far recovered.

> **Protocol 1, 1977, Art. 79.** Journalists engaged in dangerous professional missions in areas of armed conflict... shall be protected as such under the Conventions and this Protocol, provided that they take no action adversely affecting their status as civilians...

War Crime #223. Failure to Protect Journalists. News media tend to highlight sensational events, much to the chagrin of policymakers. Al-Jazeera, a television network in Arabic-speaking countries, has provided information about the excesses of the American occupation, though balanced with news favorable to the White House. Its offices in Afghanistan and Iraq have been bombed by American warplanes, as noted in Chapter 3. Indeed, on April 16, 2004, Bush shared his quixotic craving to wipe out the Arab-language network's headquarters with Prime Minister Tony Blair, who reportedly talked him out of the plan. Nevertheless, the Al-Jazeera office in Baghdad has been wiretapped, and the Al-Jazeera website has been hacked.

In Afghanistan, individual journalists have been either harassed or insufficiently protected from the wars. In December 2001, Sami al-Hajj, an Al-Jazeera journalist, was arrested in Afghanistan and sent to Bagram and later to Kandahar and Guantánamo. Although he was at first determined to be an enemy combatant, he was never prosecuted, and he was released to go home to Sudan on May 1, 2008. Jawed Ahmad, an employee of a Canadian television network, was arrested in Afghanistan on October 26, 2008, was beaten, and had his teeth broken, but he was not accused of any crime.

Iraq has the worst record of unsolved murders of journalists in the world, with a total of seventy-nine compared to eight for Afghanistan as of early 2008. Among the journalists killed in Iraq since the beginning of the American occupation, Tareq Ayyoub died because of the bombing of the Al-Jazeera office in Baghdad. Wisam Ali Udah was gunned down by an American sniper as he walked home in Baghdad at the end of May 2008.

An international incident involving Italy resulted on March 4, 2005, when infantry personnel opened fire on the car of Italian journalist Giuliana Sgrena, who died. She had encountered a roadblock that had no warning signs or lights. Eleven shots were fired three seconds after soldiers gave arm signals in the dark.

Several journalists have been arrested in Iraq. From 2005 to 2007, writer Kamal Said Qadir was detained by Kurdish security forces. Pulitzer Price winner Bilal Huseein was arrested on April 12, 2006, as a "terrorist media operative" because he appeared quickly at scenes of insurgent attacks, but he was released two years and four days later.

The American military also planted about a thousand news stories in Arabic-language and Iraqi news media, paying from $40 to $2,000 for each article. While the CPA media tried to spread favorable news, Bremer ordered the shutdown of Al-Hawza, the press of Muqtada al-Sadr, for sixty days from March 28, 2004. CPA Order 14 (June 10, 2003) banned unfavorable news and Order 19 (July 10) restricted the right to protest. Two other newspapers were also shut down as well as Radio Baghdad and the Baghdad office of Al-Jazeera.

CIVIL AND POLITICAL CONDITIONS

The Geneva Conventions assume that occupations will be short and self-rule will quickly return to the defeated country. Yet occupation armies remain in Afghanistan and in Iraq after more than five years, limiting the ability of both governments to act autonomously.

Hague II, 1899, Art. 43. The authority of the legitimate power having actually passed into the hands of the occupant, the latter shall take all steps in his power to . . . respect . . . unless absolutely prevented, the laws in force in the country.

War Crime #225. Failure to Respect the Legal Framework. On taking office, President Hamid Karzai sought to bring peace as soon as possible by offering amnesty to former Taliban government workers, but the Bush administration refused to allow him to exercise the right of pardon. During 2008, ISAF and the government were also at odds regarding tactics, with Karzai objecting that Afghans were being arrested unnecessarily.

The United States has continued to collect prisoners through warrantless house searches, sending some of those captured to a prison system inside the country but outside Afghan government control. For example, two persons seized at their homes without a warrant during February 2003, Abdul Ghafour and Mohibullah, opened their doors after American helicopters made a menacing show of force. Similar searches and arrests without legal warrants occurred to thousands of Iraqis who were detained at Abu Ghraib.

The Iraqi legal framework was technically in place as American troops asserted control over Baghdad. But the civilian justice system was immediately overridden by martial law. After his arrival in Baghdad, Bremer issued 100 orders and innumerable decisions, many of which had the effect of canceling previous laws. Order 10 (June 5, 2003) transferred all prisons to CPA control.

UN Security Council Resolution 1483 allowed Bremer to supersede undemocratic laws, having directed him to pave the way for representative government. But he ignored legal arrangements unrelated to that goal. For example, CPA Order 39(3) of December 20, 2003, asserts, "This order replaces all existing foreign investment law," a clear violation.

Perhaps the most insidious was CPA Order 17 (September 18, 2003), which immunized MNF-I as well as civilian and military contractor personnel from Iraqi law; in other words, they could not be sued by Iraqis for war crimes. Contractor personnel, drawn as they have been from many countries, were also immune at the time from prosecution under American civil, military, and penal law. On June 26, 2004, Bremer revised Order 17 to extend the immunity beyond the end of the CPA as a condition of transfer of sovereignty, evidently asserting that the occupation recognized by Resolution 1483 would continue to trump Iraqi law so long as MNF-I remained in Iraq.

When top ranks of the Saddam Hussein regime were arrested, they were held in American-run prisons. Under Security Council Resolution 1546, some 14,000 prisoners were supposed to have been turned over to the Ministry of Justice when the CPA expired. But they were not.

UN Charter, 1945, Art. 1. The purposes of the United Nations are: (1) To maintain international peace and security...(2) To develop friendly relations among nations based on respect for the principle of equal rights and self-determination of peoples...

War Crime #226. Failure to Allow Self-Government. Sovereignty was quickly restored in Kabul, Afghanistan, though the United States has supported warlords in the provinces who prevent the Kabul government from extending control beyond the capital. Financial contributions from Washington went to elect President Hamid Karzai but not to his fifteen opponents, while gun-toting thugs forced voters to support him.

When Iraqi communities began to organize politically as the American army marched toward Baghdad, Washington did not take notice. Moreover, Garner arrested Mohammed Mohsen al-Zubaidi, who proclaimed himself major of Baghdad.

Rumsfeld arranged to fly Ahmed Chalabi to Iraq to take over, but he was rejected by the people, leaving Washington stunned, without an immediate backup plan. Soon, Ayatollah Muhammad Baqir al-Hakim, who had entered Iraq from Iran with a contingent of 10,000 supporters, called on May 12 for an end to the military occupation and rapid transfer of power to the Iraqis.

Instead of transferring sovereignty, the United States requested Security Council authorization to legalize Bremer's occupation government. When Resolution 1483 was adopted on May 22, Bremer gained control of the UN oil-for-food fund and was able to claim legitimacy for American military bases throughout the country without Iraqi approval.

Former Finance Minister Ali Allawi and others have made a strong case that there was an alternative to the CPA—rapid reestablishment of an Iraqi government. But the idea of a provisional government had been rejected in the White House as early as December 14, 2002.

When a Leadership Council of seven exile leaders met with Bremer, requesting a provisional government, he turned down their proposal. Instead, he created a twenty-five-member Governing Council, again mostly of returning exiles, in order to marginalize the seven.

Bremer famously said, "I am the law." Tribal leaders whom he appointed at the local level clashed with better-known Iraqis who were planning elections for councils in several cities. The effect was to weaken opposition to the CPA from those with national stature, including leaders of political parties. Rebuffed and lacking funds for the elections, local administrative structures then disbanded.

Bremer appointed "advisers," many of whom were entirely unqualified, to run the various ministries alongside Iraqi technocrats. Since he allocated funds to his advisers, they were in fact running government functions, including hospitals, schools, and utilities, while many Iraqi ministry officials thought that they had been reduced to errand boys.

When the UN asked the Governing Council to take the Iraq seat in the General Assembly, the Iraqis thus had no sovereign control of their own government. Bremer refused to sign some decisions by the Governing Council, would not allow Iraqi input into key economic decisions, and disallowed Iraq ministry officials from seeking independent funds to restore the infrastructure. Bremer demanded a transition plan from the Governing Council, which in turn insisted that he transfer sovereignty to them as the interim government.

When Bremer intimated that he alone would be in charge of the process of writing the new constitution, Grand Ayatollah Ali al-Sistani had had enough: He issued a fatwa on July 1, 2003, demanding elections before a constitution. Although Bremer appeared to back down, he nevertheless issued the Transitional Administrative Law after imposing some clauses to a provisional draft approved by the Governing Council, which wanted more time to hammer out differences in the wording.

Bremer issued various CPA orders with little or no input from the Governing Council or the government ministers. For example, the newspaper Al-Hawza was shut down without consulting the Minister of Communications.

Because the CPA frustrated Iraqi efforts to achieve self-government, Muqtada al-Sadr revealed the existence of his Mahdi Army on July 2003 and declared on October 11, 2003, that he headed an "independent government." He continued to operate on that basis until 2008.

In the selection of an interim prime minister to serve when the CPA's term was to expire on June 30, 2004, several nominees were proposed by UN Special Representative Lakhdar Brahimi. Rather than agreeing to a list containing two popular politicians, Washington vetoed them and chose Iyad Allawi as Prime Minister, who then filled the Interim Government cabinet. On April 8, 2004, Bremer fired Interior Minister Nuri al-Badram and vetoed Prime Minister Allawi's choice for national security adviser, Qassim Da'ud. Journalists report that Washington eventually dumped Allawi and later his successor, Ibrahim al-Ja'afari.

Partial sovereignty returned to an Iraqi government when Bremer left Baghdad on June 28, 2004. Government buildings were then returned from the CPA to the provisional Iraqi government. When Allawi proposed an amnesty for insurgents after Bremer left town, however, Washington nixed his proposal.

One year later, when the Allawi government was deliberating over the text of a new constitution, Bush imposed an artificial deadline for completion of August 15, 2005, thereby ensuring that many loose ends would remain, as they have to the present. Most Sunnis then boycotted the referendum on the constitution.

In June 2007, Iraq's parliament demanded the right to vote on any further extension of the American occupation. At the end of the year, however, President Bush exchanged letters with Prime Minister al-Maliki that established principles for the continuation of American troops in Iraq beyond January 1, 2009. The Pentagon reportedly hoped to establish fifty-eight long-term military bases in Iraq. In June 2008, after widespread demonstrations in Iraq on the pending negotiations, a majority of the parliament petitioned Congress to have all American forces leave as soon as possible—and before any security agreement would be signed between the two countries. Although al-Maliki agreed to submit the text to parliament, the weak government of Iraq is in no position to stand up to the United States.

Geneva IV, 1949, Art. 3. . . . The following acts are and shall remain prohibited at any time and in any place whatsoever: . . . (d) The passing of sentences and the carrying out of executions without previous judgment pronounced by a regularly constituted court, affording all the judicial guarantees which are recognized as indispensable by civilized peoples.

War Crime #227. Failure to Recognize Local Courts. Although there was a functioning judiciary under Saddam Hussein, CPA Order 1 devastated the personnel running the courts; in particular, the Council of Judges was abolished. CPA Order 3 (June 18, 2003), which was to have imported sixty-four judges in ninety days, was never implemented, though Order 13 (June 18) created the Central Criminal Court and Order 35 (September 18) reinstated the Council of Judges. At the local level, Bremer authorized tribal leaders to fill in the void through Order 58 (February 10, 2004).

In April 2003, an Iraqi judge ordered the arrest of Shi'ite cleric Muqtada al-Sadr and eight cohorts for the murder of a pro-Western cleric, Sayyid Abdul Majid al-Khoei. The American military, presumably under orders that came from Rumsfeld, ignored the order and later regretted the decision.

The Iraqi criminal justice system was also ignored when the MNF shoehorned thousands of Iraqis suspected of having information about insurgents into Abu Ghraib, the facility once used to hold those imprisoned in accordance with sentences established by Iraqi courts. Once at Abu Ghraib, Iraqis were denied access to their own courts.

Whereas CPA Order 7 (June 9, 2003) immunized American troops from prosecution in Iraqi courts for violations of the Geneva Conventions, including those committed at Abu Ghraib, Bush's Executive Order 13303 of May 22, 2003, immunized American contractors in Iraq from prosecution in American courts. In 2006, an amendment to the Defense Authorization Act placed defense contractors under the Uniform Code of Military Justice. When Blackwater was charged with responsibility for the deaths of about a dozen Iraq civilians in September 2007, however, the Department of Defense refused to court-martial those responsible, especially since the State Department offered them immunity before recording their statements for the record.

Saddam Hussein and several cohorts were tried in the Special Court, established by Order 48 (December 10, 2003), not the regular court. In the eyes of some Iraqis and others, the proceedings were illegitimate. After his conviction, he was retained inside an American-controlled prison until the day of his execution.

Others have been held in confinement by American authorities without processing by Iraqi courts. In June 2004, after Iyad Akmush Kanum was acquitted in an Iraqi court of attempted murder of American soldiers, he was sent to Abu Ghraib rather than being released. In March 2008, two prominent Iraqis were acquitted by the Supreme Judicial Council, but they were not released from American military confinement in accordance with the court's judgment. American officials claimed that the UN mandate allowed them to detain anyone they thought was a "security risk," even when an Iraqi judicial body believed otherwise, while refusing to hand over Sons of Iraq members accused of murder in Iraqi courts.

The American military has also been reluctant to turn prisoners over to a special court in Afghanistan that might place them on trial for terrorist-related offenses. The reported reason is a fear that they are dangerous and might be released.

CRIMINAL JUSTICE PROBLEMS

The International Covenant on Civil and Political Rights recognizes that the maintenance of law and order trumps most civil and political rights. However, the following rights cannot be denied, even in time of disorder: right to life, right to executive pardon, and freedom of conscience, religion, and thought. The Covenant also bans under all circumstances cruel and inhuman punishment, involuntary human experimentation, and slavery or forced labor.

Occupation armies have remained in Afghanistan and Iraq because of continuing violence. Much of the conflict, however, has required a police response. Whereas improper treatment while in prison has been identified in Chapter 4, the present section deals with misconduct by military or police before imprisonment as well as juridical aspects after confinement.

Hague IV, 1907, Art. 44. A belligerent is forbidden to force the inhabitants of territory occupied by it to furnish information about the army of the other belligerent, or about its means of defense.

War Crime #228. Unwarranted Interrogation of Civilians. Due to the insurgency in Iraq, the American military arrested some 43,000 Iraqis to obtain intelligence information. Prisoners of war are only allowed to provide names, ranks, and serial numbers in accordance with the Third Geneva Convention, and civilians are similarly protected under the Fourth Geneva Convention. But their rights were ignored when they were questioned about the insurgency by the American military, often on insubstantial pretexts. Many abuses have been reported.

Hague IV, 1907, Art. 50. No general penalty, pecuniary or otherwise, shall be inflicted upon the population on account of the acts of individuals for which they cannot be regarded as jointly and severally responsible.

War Crime #229. Collective Punishment. The initial mass roundup of those in Afghanistan who had committed no anti-American acts may be regarded as a form of collective retaliation for the 9/11 attacks, as authorized by Bush. The mass firings of members of the Iraqi armed forces by CPA Order 2 (May 23, 2003) may be considered collective punishment of the vanquished by the victors. To counter the Iraq insurgency, American military engaged in mass arrests and nighttime raids, often smashing in doors—that is, other forms of collective punishment. For example, in November 2003, after an attack on American troops, the entire town of Abu Hishma, Iraq, was surrounded with razor wire, and residents were required to have American-issued identification cards to enter and leave.

> **Geneva IV. 1949, Art. 3.** . . . The following acts are and shall remain prohibited at any time and in any place whatsoever . . . : (a) violence to life and person, in particular murder of all kinds, mutilation, cruel treatment and torture; (b) taking of hostages; (c) outrages upon personal dignity, in particular humiliating and degrading treatment . . .

War Crime #230. Cruel Treatment of Civilians. Afghan warlords backed by the United States have captured innocent people and tortured them to obtain ransom money. Various forms of abuse occur "right under the mustaches of the Americans," according to a resident of a province under the control of warlord Ismail Khan.

One evening during the early Iraqi occupation, military police arrested two Baghdad residents for violating a curfew. Rather than taking them to a place of detention, they pushed them into the Tigris River. One, who could not swim, drowned.

At checkpoints, American military personnel have been abusive and crass when Iraqis have been unable to understand their commands in English. Soldiers have repeatedly entered homes peremptorily, without giving residents a chance to evacuate before searches, and then zip-cuffed the men and shocked the women. The Governing Council condemned occupation forces for "cruelty and violence used against citizens whose homes were being searched."

> **Geneva IV, 1949, Art. 24.** The Parties to the conflict shall take the necessary measures to ensure that children under fifteen, who are orphaned or are separated from their families as a result of the war, are not left to their own resources . . .

War Crime #231. Unjustified Arrest of Children. Mass arrests of Afghans and Iraqis to obtain intelligence have yielded children as young as twelve years old. More recently, troops of warlord Hazrat Ali, who is supported by the United States, have been accused of seizing teenage boys to serve as sex slaves.

> **Geneva IV, 1949, Art. 42.** The internment or placing in assigned residence of protected persons may be ordered only if the security of the Detaining Power makes it absolutely necessary....

War Crime #232. Unjustified Internment. Both in Afghanistan and Iraq, large numbers of persons were arrested and incarcerated in American-run prisons based on a mere suspicion that they were enemies of the United States. In fact, bounty hunters in Afghanistan, Iraq, and Pakistan were paid sums of money to collect as many as they could, few of whom were immediate security threats. At least three persons picked up in Afghanistan had actually been fighting alongside American forces.

> **Geneva IV, 1949, Art. 45.** Protected persons shall not be transferred to a Power which is not a party to the Convention. Protected persons may be transferred by the Detaining Power only to a Power which is a party to the present Convention and after the Detaining Power has satisfied itself of the willingness and ability of such transferee Power to apply the present Convention.... In no circumstances shall a protected person be transferred to a country where he or she may have reason to fear persecution for his or her political opinions or religious beliefs.

War Crime #233. Transfer to Countries That Persecute Political Opinions. More than 100 persons have been shipped from occupied Afghanistan to secret prisons on the pretext that they shared the political opinions of al-Qaeda. In 2003, suspected terrorist Hiwa Abdul Rahman Rashul was shipped from Iraq to Afghanistan then back to Iraq, where his presence was hidden from the Red Cross on orders from Rumsfeld. The form of persecution was torture.

> **Geneva IV, 1949, Art. 64.** The penal laws of the occupied territory shall remain in force, with the exception that they may be repealed or suspended by the Occupying Power in cases where they constitute a threat to its security or an obstacle to the application of the present Convention....

War Crime #234. Failure to Observe Existing Penal Laws. CPA Order 31 (September 10, 2003) revised Iraq's Penal Code by increasing penalties for certain crimes. Even minutiae of Baghdad traffic laws were revised in Order 86 (May 26, 2004), but enforcement of the traffic code was lax. For example, Blackwater escort vehicles violated the law with impunity by driving in the following manner: "careen around corners, jump road dividers, reach speeds in excess of 100 mph and often cross over to the wrong side of the road [while]... honking at, cutting off, pelting with water bottles (a favorite tactic) and menacing with weapons anyone in their way." In one situation described by former American official Janessa Gans, "The lead Suburban in our convoy loomed up behind an old, petering sedan driven by an older man with a young woman and three children [and]... smashed heedlessly into the car, pushing it into the barrier."

> **Geneva IV, 1949, Art. 64.** The penal provisions enacted by the Occupying Power...shall not be retroactive.

War Crime #235. Penalties Imposed for Past Acts. CPA Order 1 banned the top echelons of Ba'ath Party members from future government employment without a hearing or trial. Many physicians, schoolteachers, university professors, and others were declared to have committed a punishable offense by being members of the Ba'ath Party, which was legal before the occupation. They lost their jobs due to Bremer's ex post facto order.

> **Geneva IV, 1949, Art. 68.** Protected persons who commit an offence which is solely intended to harm the Occupying Power, but which does not constitute an attempt on the life or limb of members of the occupying forces or administration, nor a grave collective danger, nor seriously damage the property of the occupying forces or administration or the installations used by them, shall be liable to internment or simple imprisonment, provided the duration of such internment or imprisonment is proportionate to the offence committed....

War Crime #236. Disproportionate Penal Servitude. Many persons have been confined in American-run prisons in Afghanistan and Iraq without committing any offenses. Lengthy detainment before interrogation is, as at Abu Ghraib, a form of disproportionate penal servitude.

> **Geneva IV, 1949, Art. 84.** Internees shall be accommodated and administered separately from prisoners of war and from persons deprived of liberty for any other reason.

War Crime #237. Interned Persons, Prisoners of War, and Common Criminals Accommodated and Administered Together. American-run prisons in Afghanistan and Iraq, notably Abu Ghraib, have mixed different types of prisoners together without first properly sorting them out. In Iraq, criminals (looters) were housed along with persons merely suspected of withholding information about the insurgency.

> **Protocol 1, 1977, Art. 33(1).** As soon as circumstances permit, and at the latest from the end of active hostilities, each Party to the conflict shall search for the persons who have been reported missing by an adverse Party. Such adverse Party shall transmit all relevant information concerning such persons in order to facilitate such searches.

War Crime #238. Failure to Account for Missing Persons. In research for his book *The Guantánamo Files*, historian Andy Worthington took extraordinary measures to account for every prisoner arrested in Afghanistan and later imprisoned at the American naval base on Cuban soil. Nevertheless, some remain unaccounted for—deliberately so. The American government has not filled in the gaps for him.

> **Protocol 1, 1977, Art. 75(4).** No sentence may be passed and no penalty may be executed on a person found guilty of a penal offence related to the armed conflict except pursuant to a conviction pronounced by an impartial and regularly constituted court respecting the generally recognized principles of regular judicial procedure . . .

War Crime #239. Failure to Ensure Fair Trials of Repatriated Prisoners. For several years, the United States held Afghans accused of war crimes at Bagram Air Force Base, from which some were sent to Guantánamo. In 2008, about two hundred of those detained at Bagram were turned over to the Afghan government for trials based on "terse summaries of allegations ... by the United States military." Although seventeen had been acquitted by early April, sixty-five were convicted.

By providing such skimpy evidence, the United States is violating its fiduciary responsibility to ensure that repatriated prisoners of war have fair trials.

ECONOMIC AND FINANCIAL CONDITIONS

Wars wreak economic disaster. The occupying power is not supposed to add to the economic and financial problems of the defeated country. In Afghanistan, where poppy fields have reemerged, they have been herbicided by American airplanes without a program for alternative agricultural production. In Iraq, the CPA tried to transform a socialist economy into a market economy, thereby administering an additional shock treatment.

Accounting records for billions of dollars of CPA spending as well as for contracts signed by the CPA are incomplete. Some $12 billion derived from Iraqi assets that were shipped to the CPA in hundred dollar bills have never been accounted for. The BBC claims to have tracked down $23 billion that was lost or stolen, but the Bush administration has prevented courts from releasing relevant records. Expenses of American contractors were inflated far beyond the amounts needed or spent for specific purposes, and some contractors even billed the Iraqi government for overhead costs. The United States officially sought to rebuild Iraq after the war, spending $118 billion by mid–2008, of which private contractors account for $100 billion. Iraqis expected a lot more.

Hague II, 1899, Art. 46. . . . Private property . . . must be respected.

War Crime #240. Confiscation of Private Property. In Afghanistan, American-supported members of the government in Kabul as well as the police seized some of the choice real estate in the city for their homes after achieving military victory alongside the American troops. Those living in the properties were summarily evicted.

Bush's Executive Order 13290 of March 20, 2003, confiscated Iraqi property in the United States and Iraqi funds in American banks. The money was later forwarded to the CPA.

CPA Order 1 confiscated all Ba'ath Party assets and took over its businesses. Houses and villas of former senior officials were taken over by the American military shortly after the fall of Baghdad. Ba'ath Party buildings were seized in accordance with CPA Order 4 (June 27, 2003). According to journalist Thomas Ricks, American military at checkpoints in Baghdad stole thousands of dollars from Iraqis, including their vehicles.

The $1.3 billion American embassy, located on choice riverfront real estate, consists of 104 acres that were sequestered by the CPA for a staff of 4,000, mostly military personnel. The plan for the compound includes apartments, a cinema, a clubhouse, office buildings, a power station, schools, sewage and water treatment facilities, and swimming pools. American military bases have squatted on Iraqi land.

> **Hague II, 1899, Art. 48.** If, in the territory occupied, the occupant collects the taxes, dues, and tolls imposed for the benefit of the State, he shall do it, as far as possible, in accordance with the rules in existence and the assessment in force, and will in consequence be bound to defray the expenses of the administration of the occupied territory on the same scale as that by which the legitimate Government was bound.

War Crime #241. Lowering Tax Revenues. CPA Order 37 (September 19, 2003) suspended all tax payments for the rest of the year while instituting a flat tax rate of 15 percent on individuals and corporations, effective 2004, thereby reducing state revenues on the wealthiest businesses and individuals. Exempt from taxes (and tariffs, according to Order 38 on September 19) were the CPA, MNF-I, contractors, and subcontractors. CPA Order 39 (September 19) permitted all capital in the country to be transferred out tax free. In reaping huge profits, Bechtel, Halliburton, and their subcontractors decapitalized the Iraq government.

War Crime #242. Secret Contract Awards. Rather than allowing Iraqi businesses to bid on contracts, Halliburton and other American corporations were awarded large reconstruction contracts without competitive bidding. In some cases, the contracts were awarded in principle even before the war began. Exact amounts were unavailable for auditing when the CPA was abolished. In 2004, a civilian Pentagon official balked at releasing funds to Halliburton subsidiary KBR because of a lack of documented expenses. As a result, he was fired.

> **Hague II, 1899, Art. 53.** An army of occupation can only take possession of the cash, funds, and property liable to requisition belonging strictly to the State, depots of arms, means of transport, stores and supplies, and, generally, all movable property of the State which may be used for military operations.

War Crime #243. Diversion of State Property for Nonmilitary Operations. When Bremer first arrived, the presidential palaces had been state property. Soon, the CPA appropriated the Republican Palace as its headquarters and cordoned off a section of the city as the Green Zone.

During the first year of occupation, $20 billion in oil sales went into the Development Fund for Iraq, which the CPA then used to pay private contractors (some of which contributed $500,000 to Bush's 2004 campaign for re-election). Halliburton, for example, was awarded $1.6 billion.

When Bremer left Iraq, account books were incomplete. The audit completed on July 15, 2004, revealed many violations of Security Council Resolution 1483 because of major gaps in reporting. For example, the audit established that Development Fund for Iraq expenditures were mostly siphoned off to food rations, fuel subsidies, wages, and other costs of government, but comparatively little to development. Eric Herring and Glen Rangwala in *Iraq in Fragments* characterize what happened as follows: "fraud, theft, cost mischarging, product substitution, bribery, kickbacks, gratuities, bid rigging, conflicts of interest, public corruption, computer crime, embezzlement, and false claims."

Hague II, 1899, Art. 55. The occupying State shall only be regarded as administrator and usufructuary of the public buildings, real property, forests, and agricultural works belonging to the hostile State, and situated in the occupied country. It must protect the capital of these properties, and administer it according to the rules of usufruct.

War Crime #244. Privatizing State Assets. The CPA seized all government assets during the initial occupation and utilized oil revenues to defray administrative costs. Firing of Ba'ath Party members left buildings and ministries almost unattended, so many were restaffed by American civilian personnel.

CPA Order 20 (July 17, 2003) set up the Trade Bank of Iraq, giving Bremer the power to monitor all capital going in and out of the country. Although CPA Order 39 (September 19, 2003) declared all state enterprises but the oil industry privatized, privatization proved impractical. Order 40 (September 19, 2003) gave JP Morgan considerable control of some of the banking sector, which was previously run by the state. Only six foreign banks were allowed initially, but Order 94 (June 9, 2004) abolished that limit.

When the Governing Council condemned the privatization decrees as contrary to the Geneva Conventions, one of Bremer's staff said, "I don't give a shit about international law. I made a commitment to the president that I'd privatize Iraq's businesses."

Shortly before Bremer left Baghdad, six international oil companies reportedly signed forty-year agreements to develop, rehabilitate, produce, and market the oil from the State Oil Marketing Organization. Herring and Rangwala characterize the lengthy contracts as "back door privatization." Since CPA Order 39 allowed 100 percent repatriation of profits by foreign-owned businesses, the effect of mortgaging the oil industry to foreign corporations would be to further decapitalize Iraq. The Oil Ministry estimated in 2008 that foreign companies controlled 87 percent of Iraqi oil. Since the oil industry is the chief source of income for Iraq, the effect is to hamstring Iraq's state finances for the next four decades. Similar arrangements were made in Afghanistan.

War Crime #245. Failure to Maintain Material Conditions of State Property. After the looting, many government buildings were set on fire. Indeed, the destruction from looting in Baghdad exceeded that from bombing.

Vital services, from electricity to transportation to water, were not available to the population at prewar levels while the CPA was in charge. CPA's response lagged behind need while many unqualified Americans in charge of ministries negotiated contracts with American firms, which in turn often failed to restore services or delayed doing so. Instead of repairing existing facilities at a reasonable cost, the American contractors were awarded $5 billion but spent little on the ground. In 2008, for example, power lines downed during the siege of the city in 2004 still awaited attention. Because much of Baghdad had only two hours of electricity per day, street lamps did not work. The National Council of Churches and related organizations in nearly two dozen countries have called for billions of dollars in reparations to the Iraq government.

Geneva IV, 1949, Art. 51. Every such person shall, so far as possible, be kept in his usual place of employment. Workers shall be paid a fair wage and the work shall be proportionate to their physical and intellectual capacities. The legislation in force in the occupied country concerning working conditions, and safeguards as regards, in particular, such matters

continued

as wages, hours of work, equipment, preliminary training and compensation for occupational accidents and diseases, shall be applicable ... **Art. 52.** All measures aiming at creating unemployment or at restricting the opportunities offered to workers in an occupied territory, in order to induce them to work for the Occupying Power, are prohibited.

War Crime #246. Mass Unemployment. CPA Orders 1 and 2 fired more than half the workforce. Technocrats who initially showed up for work in the ministries to keep government functioning were suddenly fired with no prospect of re-employment. Under Bremer, subsidies of fertilizers and pesticides were eliminated, resulting in unemployment in the agricultural sector as well. The CPA estimated that unemployment in Iraq one year after the war fell only to 35 percent. Meanwhile, unemployment in Afghanistan remains high because of a lack of reconstruction of the infrastructure damaged during the war.

Geneva IV, 1949, Art. 39. Protected persons who, as a result of the war, have lost their gainful employment, shall be granted the opportunity to find paid employment.

War Crime #247. Failure to Provide Re-Employment Opportunities. After CPA Orders 1 and 2 served to fire an estimated 400,000 Iraqi government employees, Bremer not only failed to set up an agency to re-employ them but also dissolved the Union of the Unemployed, arrested their leaders, and enforced the pre-CPA law banning trade unions. Although funds were available to create jobs for Iraqis, Bremer's assistants failed to do so on a timely basis.

Civilian contractors brought personnel from outside Iraq. Only 77,000 Iraqis were hired for reconstruction work during Bremer's management; many qualified engineers and technocrats who applied outside the gates of the Green Zone were turned away without ever having their applications considered. The insurgency, meanwhile, found jobs for unemployed Iraqis who were willing to take up arms.

Geneva IV, 1949, Art. 53. Any destruction by the Occupying Power of real or personal property belonging individually or collectively to private persons, or to the State, or to other public authorities, or to social or cooperative organizations, is prohibited, except where such destruction is rendered absolutely necessary by military operations.

War Crime #248. Unnecessary Destruction of Private Property. Based on CPA Order 4 (May 25, 2003), Ba'ath Party buildings were destroyed. During the high point of the insurgency, a brigade commander blew up a house that an Iraqi was building as a "demonstration of force," even though the man building the house had been helping a military police battalion. During military raids to arrest possible insurgents, property inside houses was sometimes broken or destroyed.

War Crime #249. Unnecessary Destruction of State Property. Defense Department contractor Halliburton lost one-third ($18.6 million) of its assigned government property in Iraq, including trucks, computers, and office furniture. Auditors failed to account for 6,975 of 20,531 items on the ledgers of Halliburton's KBR unit, according to Stuart Bowen, Jr., Special Inspector General for Iraqi Reconstruction. For example, trucks with flat tires were destroyed rather than repaired.

Protocol 1, 1977, Art. 69(1). . . . The Occupying Power shall, to the fullest extent of the means available to it and without any adverse distinction, also ensure the provision of clothing, bedding, means of shelter, other supplies essential to the survival of the civilian population of the occupied territory and objects necessary for religious worship.

War Crime #250. Failure to Provide Necessities of Daily Living. After the Afghan War, there was little reconstruction outside Kabul, since warlords reasserted control in the provinces. The failure to rebuild the damaged infrastructure was not immediately noticed amid the new freedom of movement, especially the sound of music, and the return to normality after repressive Taliban rule. Although the United States contributed $1 billion monthly for its military forces, and about the same amount from 2001 to 2003 for reconstruction, only $110 million in projects were completed to serve as examples of American support for Afghan development. Some 70 percent of the aid went to Kabul, whereas most of the country is rural. That the postwar period was corrupt and Kabul-oriented meant that the poppy fields blossomed due to a neglect of Afghan agricultural aid despite fertile soil and a hardworking farming tradition. The Taliban eventually saw that neglect as an opportunity to regain strength.

Food, fuel, power, telephones, and water were in short supply after the invasion of Iraq. Efforts to restore them to prewar levels were insufficient, though they were soon in abundance in the Green Zone.

From 2003, Congress appropriated about $42 billion for reconstruction in Iraq. During March 2008, nearly 900 contracts out of 47,321 were terminated due to poor performance and other considerations. However, from 2003 to 2008 the United States used more of Iraqi money ($50.6 billion) than American money ($47.5 billion) in the country. From the viewpoint of ordinary Iraqis, necessities of daily living were ignored amid the accounting fiasco and contractor bonanza.

Contractors, hired for repairs on a no-bid basis so that their arrival would not be delayed by paperwork requirements, did not show up until July and August, two to three months after the shortage was acute. By then, insurgents had targeted some of the infrastructure and proceeded to intimidate repair personnel. Of approximately $18 billion appropriated for initial civilian reconstruction, the CPA allocated only $1 billion, much of which was never spent or was incompetently managed. Funds for public works restoration from Iraqi oil revenues were also diverted to security needs, resulting in the cancellation of projects for electricity, sanitation, and water. Electric generation of 4,400 megawatts before the war compared with only 3,900 by October 2003. New power plants required natural gas, which had to be imported.

As ethnic cleansing proceeded in 2006, some one million Sunni refugees fled internally within Iraq and two million to neighboring countries. However, the United States refused to provide refugee assistance. Because UN and American agencies have provided so little aid to Iraqis, and the Iraq government is extraordinarily corrupt and inefficient, the Mahdi Army of Muqtada al-Sadr moved into the breach as a reliable source of economic assistance to the less affluent Shi'ite population.

Electricity and water remained scarce commodities even by 2008. A tank of gas cost $80 on the black market for those who could not endure long lines at government pumps. Because of curfews and the building of walls associated with the "surge" of 2007–2008, traffic was banned in and out of Baghdad enclaves, so food and medicines were in increasingly short supply. Travel bans have been imposed in other cities as well.

DISCRIMINATION

An occupying power will, of course, try to root out remnants of the political leaders and armies of the vanquished power. Otherwise, the Geneva Conventions require occupation authorities to be evenhanded to all. Discrimination on the basis of ethnicity, gender, political opinions, religion, and other conditions can only serve to delegitimize the occupying power.

> **Hague II, 1899, Art. 46.** . . . Religious convictions and liberty . . . must be respected.

War Crime #251. Failure to Respect Religious Convictions. The CPA purged school textbooks of references to Islam and quotations from the Qur'an.

> **Geneva IV. 1949, Art. 3(1).** Persons taking no active part in the hostilities, including members of armed forces who have laid down their arms and those placed hors de combat by sickness, wounds, detention, or any other cause, shall in all circumstances be treated humanely, without any adverse distinction founded on race, color, religion or faith, sex, birth or wealth, or any other similar criteria.

War Crime #252. Ethnosectarian Discrimination. Bremer made efforts to include Kurds, Shi'ites, Sunnis, and other categories of Iraqis in advisory roles. CPA resources were allocated on the basis of those very divisions. The result was resentment, particularly among Sunnis. The Kurds, meanwhile, enjoyed favorable treatment, as they were allowed to maintain their own militias while the Americans sought to dismantle Shi'ite and Sunni militias.

Along with the "surge" in American military forces that began in 2007, walls were built around ethnically pure neighborhoods in Baghdad, a city that had already changed from a 50:50 division between Shi'ites and Sunnis to a 80:20 division favoring Shi'ites. In effect, U.S. policy ratified ethnosectarian segregation of the city and the country, perhaps the most fundamental social transformation of Iraq wrought by the American occupation.

War Crime #253. Discrimination in Awarding Contracts. After the war, Iraqi companies were on the scene and knowledgeable about how to fix many infrastructure problems. Instead of paying them for the work or allowing former German and Italian contractors to resume operations, initial restoration primarily awaited negotiation with American contractors. Countries that did not contribute troops for the invasion and occupation were excluded from bidding until June 2004.

During 2004, forty-eight of the fifty-nine prime contracts were awarded to American corporations, for which the Defense Department later found inadequate accounting in the millions. Rather than providing funds directly to upgrade Iraqis universities, which had to rebuild libraries after the looting, some $25 million was awarded to American university personnel to provide technical assistance.

Despite the CPA goal of turning the socialist economy of Iraq into free-market capitalism, seeds from patented genetically modified organisms had been introduced into the country. Order 81 (April 26, 2004) banned selling the seeds or using the seeds in the following year, thus locking Iraqi agriculture into dependence on American agricultural corporations that market the seeds.

War Crime #254. Gender Discrimination. American-backed warlords in Afghanistan have neglected women's rights. Warlord Ismail Khan, a favorite of Rumsfeld, reportedly has forced girls to study in sex-segregated schools. Mujahideen leader Abdul Rabb al-Rasul Sayyaf allegedly requires women to stay at home. Dr. Masouda Jalal received no funds from Washington when she ran for parliament, whereas millions from the United States were contributed to the presidential campaign of Hamid Karzai. Mandatory headscarf wearing has resumed.

Although women had some freedom in the secular society of Saddam Hussein, the rise of ayatollah-centered Shi'ite power in Iraq has meant pressure for women to manifest various signs of subordination. Bremer's Transitional Administrative Law provided protections for women, but enforcement machinery was not established. Today, Iraqi militias require the wearing of headscarves.

> **Geneva IV, 1949, Art. 27.** Protected persons are entitled, in all circumstances, to respect for their persons, their honor, their family rights, their religious convictions and practices, and their manners and customs. They shall at all times be humanely treated, and shall be protected especially against all acts of violence or threats thereof and against insults and public curiosity. Women shall be especially protected against any attack on their honor, in particular against rape, enforced prostitution, or any form of indecent assault. Without prejudice to the provisions relating to their state of health, age and sex, all protected persons shall be treated with the same consideration by the Party to the conflict in whose power they are, without any adverse distinction based, in particular, on race, religion or political opinion.

War Crime #255. Dishonoring Women. Beyond merely discriminating against women, Afghan warlord Ismail Khan apparently subjects females to virginity tests. Warlord Hazrat Ali's troops have allegedly engaged in sexual violence against women. Troops of warlord Abdul

Rabb al-Rasul Sayyaf reportedly enter homes at night to rape women. American commanders, who support the warlords, have not openly raised objections.

Although Bremer was eager to provide greater freedom for women, the society slipped from a secular to a more sectarian façade during his watch. Iraqi gangsters, meanwhile, forced women into the sex industry and shipped them out of the country. The MNF, responsible for maintenance of security, has not stopped the flow.

The United States has paid Iraqis to operate checkpoints at various locations throughout the country. Women, however, have been hassled on some occasions. Suhair Shakir reports that, in spring 2007, a young man at a checkpoint, spinning his pistol on his finger, asked her the whereabouts of her headscarf. A few months later, he told her that she could not drive unescorted after 5 P.M.

Geneva IV, 1949, Art. 13. The provisions... cover the whole of the populations of the countries in conflict, without any adverse distinction based, in particular, on race, nationality, religion or political opinion, and are intended to alleviate the sufferings caused by war.

War Crime #256. Discrimination Against Nominal Members of a Political Party. CPA's Order 1 dissolved the Ba'ath political party. As a result at least 50,000 from the top layers of the party, including 300 academics and 5,000 high school teachers, were unemployed. Workers had been paid extra amounts if they joined the Ba'ath Party, so many did, including museum workers, schoolteachers, and university professors, though they did not subscribe to the policies of the government. Order 1 was designed by Douglas Feith, Undersecretary of Defense for Policy, and presented to Bremer before he flew to Iraq.

After Bremer arrived, he appointed various officials at local levels, excluding members of political parties that expressed opposition to his rule. As a result, local government was disconnected from national government.

Geneva IV, 1949, Art. 70. Protected persons shall not be arrested, prosecuted or convicted by the Occupying Power for acts committed or for opinions expressed before the occupation, or during a temporary interruption thereof, with the exception of breaches of the laws and customs of war.

War Crime #257. Arrest of Persons for Pre-Occupation Political Opinions. Whereas President Karzai offered an amnesty to members of the Taliban who laid down their arms, ISAF under NATO command has pursued a different course. For example, a former member of the Taliban who accepted amnesty was arrested and released three times by American security personnel while trying to run a printshop in Kabul. Similarly, Bremer ordered the arrest of members of the Ba'ath Party, including technocrats.

SOCIAL AND CULTURAL PROBLEMS

The cultures and societies of Afghanistan and Iraq are quite different from American culture and society. Many artifacts from their cultural heritage date back thousands of years. Whereas the Taliban destroyed important cultural artifacts, the treasure trove in Iraq was well preserved under Saddam Hussein. The American occupation, however, miscalculated regarding tribal and ethnosectarian loyalties and has been insensitive to the severe loss of cultural property.

Hague II, 1899, Art. 46. Family honors and rights . . . must be respected.

War Crime #258. Failure to Respect Family Honors. When soldiers have approached homes to question residents in order to obtain information about insurgents, Afghan and Iraqi family customs have been ignored. Women have been interrogated, and house searches have been conducted without the presence of male heads of households. The elderly have been publicly humiliated. Abusive language has been used.

Geneva IV, 1949, Art. 25. All persons in the territory of a Party to the conflict, or in a territory occupied by it, shall be enabled to give news of a strictly personal nature to members of their families, wherever they may be, and to receive news from them. This correspondence shall be forwarded speedily and without undue delay. **Art. 26.** Each Party to the conflict shall facilitate enquiries made by members of families dispersed owing to the war, with the object of renewing contact with one another and of meeting, if possible. It shall encourage, in particular, the work of organizations engaged on this task provided they are acceptable to it and conform to its security regulations.

War Crime #259. Withholding News from Family Members. There are many accounts of family members seeking those suddenly missing from their homes in Baghdad when suspected insurgents were arrested. Officials at Abu Ghraib and the Green Zone refused to disclose their whereabouts.

> **Geneva IV, 1949, Art. 47.** Protected persons who are in occupied territory shall not be deprived, in any case or in any manner whatsoever, of the benefits of the present Convention by any change introduced, as the result of the occupation of a territory, into the institutions or government of the said territory . . .

War Crime #260. Charging for Formerly Free Government Services. One service provided by the regime of Saddam Hussein was free medical care. When James Haveman, Jr., arrived in Baghdad to run the health ministry, he immediately imposed co-pays for physician visits.

> **Geneva IV, 1949, Art. 50.** The Occupying Power shall, with the cooperation of the national and local authorities, facilitate the proper working of all institutions devoted to the care and education of children.

War Crime #261. Failure to Reopen Schools. Because the CPA prohibited members of the Ba'ath Party from working for the government, many teachers were thrown out of work, and some schools closed. Other schools had been bombed, but reconstruction was slow. Before its departure, nevertheless, the CPA repaired 100 out of 270 schools in Sadr City. Muqtada al-Sadr's organization repaired some of the rest.

> **Cultural Property Convention, 1954, Art. 5(2).** Should it prove necessary to take measures to preserve cultural property situated in occupied territory and damaged by military operations, and should the competent national authorities be unable to take such measures, the Occupying Power shall, as far as possible, and in close co-operation with such authorities, take the most necessary measures of preservation.

War Crime #262. Failure to Restore Cultural Property Damaged by Military Operations. Instead of providing finances to restore militarily damaged and criminally looted cultural property, an international conference was convened to raise needed funds. The American contribution was only part of the pledged amount.

HEALTH CONDITIONS

Disease often spreads due to the dislocations produced by war, so occupation powers are responsible to restore public health. In Iraq, medicines were already in short supply before the war. The desire to privatize all sectors of the economy, including the health industry, complicated the return to normality.

Geneva IV, 1949, Art. 55. To the fullest extent of the means available to it the Occupying Power has the duty of ensuring the food and medical supplies of the population; it should, in particular, bring in the necessary foodstuffs, medical stores and other articles if the resources of the occupied territory are inadequate. **Art. 60.** Relief consignments shall in no way relieve the Occupying Power of any of its responsibilities under Articles 55, 56 and 59. The Occupying Power shall in no way whatsoever divert relief consignments from the purpose for which they are intended, except in cases of urgent necessity, in the interests of the population of the occupied territory and with the consent of the Protecting Power.

War Crime #263. Providing Insufficient Food. CPA Order 1 fired the Iraqi administrator of the UN oil-for-food program and food distribution program at a time when there was an urgent food shortage. Although the UN oil-for-food program was transferred to CPA control, its funds were diverted to other uses. Rice, for example, was unavailable in March 2004. The CPA refused to import food from Iran to relieve the crisis. Meanwhile, there was more than enough food for Americans in the Green Zone.

War Crime #264. Providing Insufficient Medical Supplies. After looters stripped hospitals bare, there was a shortage of drugs, gauze, gloves, medicines, oxygen, syringes, and other medical supplies. Just before the war, contracts for some $500 million in medical supplies had been signed, to be drawn from the UN's oil-for-food account. After the war, American and British vetoes in the Security Council blocked the release of funds. Instead, the money was diverted to the CPA, which failed to purchase needed supplies. Bremer's medical administrator, James K. Haveman, Jr., reportedly reduced the number of prescription drugs for use in the country. Tylenol, for example, is unavailable today.

> **Geneva IV, 1949, Art. 56.** To the fullest extent of the means available to it, the Occupying Power has the duty of ensuring and maintaining, with the cooperation of national and local authorities, the medical and hospital establishments and services, public health and hygiene in the occupied territory, with particular reference to the adoption and application of the prophylactic and preventive measures necessary to combat the spread of contagious diseases and epidemics. Medical personnel of all categories shall be allowed to carry out their duties. If new hospitals are set up in occupied territory and if the competent organs of the occupied State are not operating there, the occupying authorities shall, if necessary, grant them the recognition provided for in Article 18. In similar circumstances, the occupying authorities shall also grant recognition to hospital personnel and transport vehicles under the provisions of Articles 20 and 21. In adopting measures of health and hygiene and in their implementation, the Occupying Power shall take into consideration the moral and ethical susceptibilities of the population of the occupied territory.

War Crime #265. Reduction in the Quality of Medical Care. On May 23, 2003, the CPA fired top-level employees of the Iraqi government, including medical personnel, many of whom left the country for employment elsewhere. The best hospital in Baghdad was converted into an American military hospital. Yarmouk Maternity Hospital, meanwhile, lacked basic sanitation, equipment, and supplies.

Although the U.S. Agency for International Development sent Dr. Frederick Burkle, a well-qualified health administrator, immediately after the war, he was fired one week later because he lacked political connections. Haveman, his replacement, reportedly failed to authorize funds for emergency rooms to treat victims of the insurgency, the most important medical problem at the time.

Hospitals operated without meeting minimum standards of sanitation. A report by a Belgian physician in April 2004, after visiting twenty-five clinics, hospitals, and pharmacies, is particularly stark:

Nowhere had any new medical material arrived since the end of the war. The medical material, already outdated, broken down or malfunctioning after twelve years of embargo, had further deteriorated over the past year. In places where looting had taken place, there is now less material than before, as in Baghdad's rehabilitation centre, which is supposed to provide the entire country with prostheses. Or as in the burns section of the Al Nour Hospital, where there is no possibility of sterile treatment, as a result of which all patients with major burns are doomed to die. Or as in the intensive care unit of the Kadhemya Hospital—which has 8 of the 16 high intensive care beds for Baghdad—where only three respiration machines are functioning.

Subsequently, due to insurgent attacks on educated Iraqis, more physicians fled the country to avoid being assassinated, as some already had been. The insurgency operated in a manner similar to the Khmer Rouge in Cambodia, seeking to eliminate those with college degrees who might provide leadership for post-Saddam Iraq.

War Crime #266. Reduction in the Quality of Public Health. In Iraq, the World Health Organization reported a tripling in cases of severe diarrhea. Other waterborne diseases, notably cholera and hepatitis, became endemic. Infant mortality increased as did the incidence of contagious disease, such as tuberculosis.

The population, particularly children, suffered from chronic malnutrition. The main reason, according to UN Special Rapporteur on Right to Food Jean Ziegler, was the food shortage. A similar problem plagues Afghanistan.

Clean drinking water was unavailable to one-third of Baghdadians as late as one year after the war. Although chlorine is used to make drinking water safe, the American military refused to allow chlorine shipments, as the chemical can be used in bombmaking. Dirty water collected in the streets, a breeding ground for the insects that forced Green Zone residents to use mosquito netting until they obtained air conditioning.

The Rustamiya sewage treatment plant for Baghdad was broken. Bechtel Corporation, which had a contract to fix the problem, did not do so. Some 1.5 tons of raw sewage were dumped daily into the Tigris River. Streets with raw sewage in Sadr City were not cleared until April 4, 2004, when Muqtada al-Sadr took credit for the effort. Yet in 2008, as the American military footprint increased in Sadr City and elsewhere, garbage and raw sewage was spotted on the streets.

During the war, some of the ammunition contained depleted uranium, a carcinogen. Some Iraqi military equipment was destroyed with the use of depleted uranium, but the American military refused to cordon off those areas, where children frequently played, vegetables were planted, and citizens went to obtain metals for recycling. Radioactive materials at Iraq's nuclear facilities were also looted, including containers later used for milk and water. As a result, several children developed leukemia.

Looters attacked an important public health facility, stealing live HIV viruses and black fever bacteria. Marines observed the looting but were not ordered to stop the potential for later bioterrorism.

The flight of physicians due to lack of security is a major factor in the decline of public health. The Baghdad psychiatric hospital uses old equipment and has only two psychiatrists on its staff.

OUTSIDE ORGANIZATIONS

Opponents of the American occupations in Afghanistan and Iraq could easily persuade residents that they were suffering from brazen attempts by Crusaders to take over their countries. Accordingly, the United States asked the United Nations Security Council for official approval. Nevertheless, American officials have often been uncooperative with UN and nongovernmental agencies that have sought to assist the peoples of the two countries.

> **Geneva IV, 1949, Art. 12.** . . . In cases of disagreement between the Parties to the conflict as to the application or interpretation of the provisions of the present Convention, the Protecting Powers shall lend their good offices with a view to settling the disagreement. For this purpose, each of the Protecting Powers may, either at the invitation of one Party or on its own initiative, propose to the Parties to the conflict a meeting of their representatives, and in particular of the authorities responsible for protected persons, possibly on neutral territory suitably chosen. The Parties to the conflict shall be bound to give effect to the proposals made to them for this purpose.

War Crime #267. Flouting UN Recommendations. In fall 2003, some members of the Iraq insurgency asked the UN to mediate in setting up negotiations with Bremer, but he refused any contact. Instead, the UN was the place where Iraqis brought complaints about the occupation, which in turn were relayed to the CPA.

Bremer repeatedly refused to listen to UN Secretary-General Kofi Annan as well as his representatives in Iraq, Sergio de Mello and Lakhdar Brahimi. The most important disagreement was over how soon to transfer sovereignty and to whom.

As the Protecting Power, the United Nations issued regular reports on human rights abuses that the United States was responsible to correct. Washington for the most ignored the recommendations. For example, rather than listening to requests from the World Health Organization for improvements in public health, Bremer fired UN personnel who were trying to restore clean water and instead awarded a contract for the work to Bechtel, which reportedly did nothing. The World Health Organization, a UN Specialized Agency, asked the CPA and American military for a map of locations where ammunition with uranium traces was stored or used, but the request was denied.

> **Geneva IV, 1949, Art. 59.** If the whole or part of the population of an occupied territory is inadequately supplied, the Occupying Power shall agree to relief schemes on behalf of the said population, and shall facilitate them by all the means at its disposal. Such schemes, which may be undertaken either by States or by impartial humanitarian organizations such as the International Committee of the Red Cross, shall consist, in particular, of the provision of consignments of foodstuffs, medical supplies and clothing.

War Crime #268. Failure to Accept Relief Organizations. Whenever there is an inadequate supply of food and medicines, the occupying power is supposed to seek assistance from other agencies. The United States failed to do so on a timely basis and even held up the arrival of UN and international aid agencies.

> **Geneva IV, 1949, Art. 144.** The High Contracting Parties undertake, in time of peace as in time of war, to disseminate the text of the present Convention as widely as possible in their respective countries, and, in particular, to include the study thereof in their programs of military and, if possible, civil instruction, so that the principles thereof may become known to the entire population. Any civilian, military, police or other authorities, who in time of war assume responsibilities in respect of protected persons, must possess the text of the Convention and be specially instructed as to its provisions.

War Crime #269. Failure to Disseminate the Fourth Geneva Convention Text to Occupation Personnel. The official debunking of the Geneva Conventions by President Bush and others in his administration is a matter of record. Given the extraordinary number of violations, a reasonable inference is that occupation personnel were not apprised of their responsibilities under international law.

Nevertheless, CPA Order 48 (December 10, 2003) cited thirty-five war crimes offenses drawn from the Geneva Conventions to instruct the Iraqi Special Court that tried Saddam Hussein and high-ranking members of his government. CPA Order 100 (June 28, 2004), issued on the day Bremer departed from Baghdad, asked the successor government to consider what Iraqi leaders had long requested—abiding by the International Covenant on Civil and Political Rights.

CONCLUSION

President Bush's goal of turning totalitarian Afghanistan and Iraq almost overnight into exemplary capitalist democracies was, in retrospect, rather naïve, conceived in geopolitical rather than humanitarian priorities. After many years, both Afghanistan and Iraq still have occupation armies that are trying to establish order. Both have had elections but are illiberal democracies, that is, they have an outward appearance of elections and parliaments but lack procedural guarantees of civil liberties and vibrant civil societies. Their economies appear capitalist but retain large government and black market sectors.

The Iraq situation was worsened by a conundrum identified by scholars Eric Herring and Glen Rangwala—that Iraq could not achieve security without development, whereas without security there could be no development. The same applies to Afghanistan. Similarly, many Afghans and Iraqis want the occupation to end, but they fear that violence will skyrocket into chaos after the Americans leave. In Afghanistan, General Dan McNeill lamented in 2008 that 400,000 troops were needed to cope with the rise of al-Qaeda and the Taliban, yet NATO had only about 50,000 troops under his command. However, insofar as the aim of entering Afghanistan in 2001 was to ensure that the country would no longer harbor al-Qaeda, that goal has long since been achieved. Now that Osama Bin Laden's base of operations is in Pakistan, the original rationale for an American role has evaporated. Thus, ISAF is interfering in a civil war, and the American occupation has lost legitimacy in the eyes of many Afghans. In the opinion of former Finance Minister Ali Allawi, the Americans brought about the worst social calamity upon Iraq since the Mongol invasion of 1258, having descended on the country like a "plague of locusts." One cannot minimize the extent of national humiliation felt in Afghanistan and Iraq due to foreign occupation.

In a foreword to a report on war crimes by Physicians for Human Rights, former retired Major General Antonio Taguba asserted, "There is no longer any doubt as to whether the current administration has committed war crimes. The only question that remains to be answered is whether [they] will be held to account." That question is taken up in Part III of the present volume.

Part III

PROSECUTION OF WAR CRIMES

Any trial of members of George W. Bush's administration for war crimes will impose a grave responsibility. Some of the wrongs to be condemned and punished have been calculated, some inadvertent. But they have been so devastating to those affected that civilization cannot tolerate their being ignored, because civilization cannot survive their being repeated over and over again. That George W. Bush may submit to the judgment of the law would be one of the most significant tributes that power could pay to reason.

What makes such a trial significant is that the defendants have been living symbols of the arrogance and cruelty of power. They are symbols of fierce nationalisms and of militarism, of intrigue and war-making that have embroiled the people of Afghanistan and Iraq, crushing their manhood, destroying their homes, and impoverishing their lives. They have so identified themselves with the policies in which they believe and with the forces they directed that any tenderness to them is a victory and an encouragement to all the injustices that are attached to their names. Civilization can afford no compromise with the political forces that would gain renewed strength if we deal ambiguously or indecisively.

The real complaining party is Civilization. International law, a struggling and imperfect force, points to the sequence of aggressions and war crimes and to the greater potentialities for destruction elsewhere in the days to come. It is not necessary to argue the proposition that to start or wage an aggressive war has the moral qualities of the worst of crimes. The refuge of the defendants can be only their hope that international law will lag so far behind the moral sense of mankind that conduct that is crime in the moral sense must be regarded as innocent in law.

Civilization asks whether law is so laggard as to be utterly helpless to deal with crimes by criminals of this order of importance. It does not expect that war can be made impossible. It does expect that juridical action will put the forces of international law, its precepts, its prohibitions, and, most of all, its sanctions, on the side of peace, so that men and women of good will, in all countries, may have "leave to live by no one's leave, underneath the law."

Civilization itself is on trial when major war criminals go about their business with impunity. That was the sentiment expressed by Justice Robert Jackson at Nuremberg, and that is the thesis of the current volume. The final chapters identify where and why lawsuits may be filed against members of the Bush administration and against George W. Bush himself.

Chapter 6

TRIBUNALS FOR WAR CRIMES PROSECUTION

Prosecutions at the Nuremberg War Crimes Trials after World War II would be different from those that might be pursued against the Bush administration. At Nuremberg, the offenses involved millions of victims. George W. Bush is charged with engaging in retail, not wholesale, violations of war crimes.

The Nuremberg trials were a form of justice imposed on those who lost in war, whereas Bush and his cohorts are not under arrest pending trial. However, the potential for allowing a superpower to perpetrate war crimes with impunity would not only bury the concept of war crimes and trivialize Nuremberg but might usher in a new era of international barbarism wherein a lone superpower could operate unchecked as a world tyrant. In that sense, prosecution of the war crimes of Bush and others may compare with the historical significance of Nuremberg.

Before World War II, the international law of war crimes was primarily about state behavior. During the Nuremberg and Tokyo war crimes trials, the defendants were considered as individuals who gave improper orders to subordinates. The law of warfare, thus, became transformed into international criminal law.

Defenders may claim that some of the 269 war crimes were committed without George W. Bush's approval or even knowledge. The principle of command responsibility, in which the commander-in-chief is responsible for all actions of those who follow his orders, is one effective way to determine culpability. The Nuremberg Charter is extremely clear in stating that principle:

Nuremberg Charter, 1945, Art. 6.... Leaders, organizers, instigators and accomplices participating in the formulation or execution of a common plan or conspiracy to commit any of the foregoing crimes [namely, Crimes Against Peace, War Crimes, and Crimes Against Humanity] are responsible for all acts performed by any persons in execution of such plan. **Art. 7.** The official position of defendants, whether as Heads of State or responsible officials in Government Departments, shall not be considered as freeing them from responsibility or mitigating punishment.

Insofar as the Bush administration has engaged in war crimes, justice requires that those responsible be brought before a tribunal to answer for their deeds. Indeed, Bush has already been a defendant in several lawsuits, and he has repeatedly lost on procedural grounds (Table 1.2). American courts, international courts, European courts, and people's courts are possible venues for trial. Legislative institutions may also play a role. Internet bloggers and journalists are the primary sources for information below, as cited in the appended References, because few relevant prosecutions have emerged thus far.

AMERICAN TRIBUNALS

Congress, of course, could have impeached Bush and his cohorts and removed them from office because of war crimes, but time ran out in 2008. Instead, Congress held hearings, placing the administration of George W. Bush on the defensive. Constrained by executive privilege and the state secrets doctrine, Congressional hearings have yielded few facts. Congress could have voted to censure Bush, a procedure followed only once—in the case of President Andrew Jackson. But that would have served to exonerate other members of the Bush administration.

Congress could decide to establish a "truth commission" modeled on such bodies as the Argentine or South African truth commissions to determine the facts and recommend prosecutions based on sworn evidence. In 2008, Congress set up a similar body, the bipartisan Wartime Contracting Commission, to investigate improprieties of corporations doing business in Afghanistan and Iraq in order to recommend criminal prosecutions. Some 900 whistleblower cases alleging contractor fraud were proceeding at a snail's pace at the Justice Department in mid-2008. In June 2008, sixty members of Congress called for a special prosecutor to handle investigations and prosecutions regarding the sole issue of interrogation policies.

Alternatively, the matter of war crimes could be handled entirely by courts on a case-by-case basis. Relevant causes of judicial action are found in the Constitution, congressional laws, and various international agreements ratified by the Senate. Some planks in the Bush Doctrine have already been rejected by the courts on the basis of domestic law (Table 1.2), though in *Demore v Kim* (2003), the Supreme Court has allowed him to establish different rules for aliens than for citizens.

Those in the armed forces can be prosecuted for war crimes in military tribunals. Indeed, some courts-martial already have been held. The highest-ranking officer held liable thus far, Brigadier General Janis Karpinski, appears to have been a scapegoat for interrogation techniques used at Abu Ghraib, since as prison administrator she had no authority over questioning by the CIA, FBI, and military police. Those in the Bush administration who objected to war crimes have been reassigned or forced to resign.

Several high-profile review panels have exonerated the military top brass. A civilian panel, whose members were selected by Secretary of Defense Donald Rumsfeld and chaired by James Schlesinger, replicated findings of the military panels.

First Lieutenant Ehren Watada, the first U.S. commissioned officer to refuse to serve in Iraq, cited the UN Charter as a principal reason for his action. Hoping to test his belief, he remained in the service so that he would be court-martialed. The tribunal, however, refused to accept his "war crime" defense and declared a mistrial on procedural grounds.

Civilians, such as Bush after January 20, 2009, can be tried in federal district courts. Penalties either are provided in the text of the laws or are at the discretion of federal judges.

The Senate has ratified most of the international agreements listed in previous chapters. Not ratified are the conventions on children's rights, cultural property protection, enforced disappearances, incendiary weapons, and Protocol 1 to the Geneva Conventions of 1949, though various administrations have indicated a desire to observe the provisions. Several laws have sought either to implement the treaties or to establish war crimes without reference to treaties (Table 6.1).

The Neutrality Act of 1794, which has been amended over time, bans individual Americans from participating in wars in which the United States is not a party. Those found guilty can be assessed a $10,000 fine, two-year imprisonment, or both. The bombings of supposed terrorists in Somalia, engulfed as it is in civil war, might be grounds to prosecute those who commanded the airplanes.

Table 6.1
American Laws Banning War Crimes

Name	Passed	Issue Addressed
Neutrality Act	1794	American residents cannot take part militarily in a foreign war unless the United States is a party
Alien Tort Claims Act	1798	Aliens can sue torturers
Genocide Convention Implementation Act	1988	Criminalizes those who commit or incite genocide
Torture Victim Protection Act	1992	Enables a victim of torture to sue a torturer
Anti-Terrorism and Effective Death Penalty Act	1996	Authorizes civil damages against foreign states complicit in injury due to torture, extrajudicial execution, aircraft hijacking, and hostage taking
War Crimes Act	1996	Criminalizes major Hague Convention and Geneva Convention war crimes
Expanded War Crimes Act	1997	Criminalizes violations of common Article 3 to the Geneva Conventions
Civil Liability for State Sponsors of Terrorism Act (Flatlow Amendment)	1997	Authorizes civil damages against personal acts of officials, employees, or agents of terrorist states
Foreign Affairs Reform and Restructuring Act[a]	1998	Bans extradition to countries that practice torture
Torture Victims Relief Act	1998	Provides compensation to torture victims
Military Extraterritorial Jurisdiction Act	2000	Authorizes trials in the United States of defense personnel committing felonies outside the United States
Victims of Trafficking and Violence Protection Act	2000	Authorizes freezing foreign state assets to compensate victims of terrorism
USA Patriot Act[b]	2001	Criminalizes terrorism and permits prosecution of contractors for federal crimes on bases abroad
Terrorism Risk Insurance Act	2002	Authorizes freezing private assets of terrorists to compensate victims
Detainee Treatment Act	2005	Criminalizes torturers of detainees but exempts those who believe legal opinions that their acts did not constitute torture
Military Commissions Act	2006	Establishes procedures for trials of terrorists

[a] The full title is United States Policy with Respect to the Involuntary Return of Persons in Danger of Subjection to Torture, which is a provision in the Foreign Affairs Reform and Restructuring Act.

[b] The full name is the Uniting and Strengthening America by Providing Appropriate Tools Required to Intercept and Obstruct Terrorism Act.

The Alien Tort Claims Act of 1798 permits aliens residing in the United States to sue for injuries inflicted on them abroad. Thus far, relevant cases have been filed, but they have been dismissed. *Al-Odah v United States* (2003) and *Ali v Rumsfeld* (2007) were filed on behalf of several persons who claimed that they were mistreated in Afghanistan, Guantánamo, or Iraq, but the cases were dismissed at the district court level under the sovereign immunity doctrine, that is, because the defendants were then in office. Once out of office, the cases could be revived. Other defendants in *Ali* were Colonel Thomas Pappas, Brigadier General Janis Karpinski, and Lieutenant General Ricardo Sanchez.

In *Arar v Ashcroft* (2006) and *El-Masri v Tenet* (2006), foreign nationals sued under the Alien Tort Claims Act because they were tortured after being subjected to extraordinary rendition. Similar cases have been filed by several former Guantánamo prisoners, including Salim Mahmud Adam and Adel Hassan Hamad. The cases of the Tipton Three, who sued for $10 million each in damages, have also been unsuccessful. The cases have been dismissed primarily because judges have accepted the state secrets doctrine, which allows the government to claim immunity from prosecution whenever national security considerations prevent introduction of vital evidence in court. A new administration in Washington might waive the state secrets doctrine to allow prosecutions to go forward, as presidential candidate Barack Obama hinted in 2008. Others have told reporters that they plan to sue in the future.

Implementing legislation for the Convention Against Torture, the Torture Victim Protection Act, passed in 1992. The law, later supplemented with funds for compensation of victims, applies to any public official who tortures or attempts to torture someone outside the United States. The maximum penalty is life imprisonment if death results; otherwise, the maximum penalty is twenty years. The statute applies to the treatment of prisoners in Afghanistan, Iraq, and in the various secret prisons. (Those at Guantánamo have a cause of action in the War Crimes Act of 1996, as explained below.) In early 2008, more than 250 Iraqis filed suit in federal court against CACI, a federal contractor, for its role in their torture at Abu Ghraib. The door to sue Bush appears to have opened when he admitted his approval of torture techniques on April 11, 2008.

President Bush realized that his orders to torture prisoners in Afghanistan, Guantánamo, Iraq, or in secret prisons might implicate him or members of his administration. Accordingly, a compliant Congress gave him a lollipop within a provision of the Detainee Treatment Act of 2005 that immunizes those who have tortured but at the time believed legal opinions that assured them that their actions were lawful. The Military Commissions Act of 2006 also excludes claims arising from collateral (unintended) damage. The ex post facto provision of the Detainee Treatment Act, which has not been tested in court, in effect gives license to bad legal advice.

An interesting legal test was filed in January 2008 by José Padilla, the American citizen who was held at the Navy Brig in Charleston as an "enemy combatant" and later found guilty of lesser offenses. The defendant is former Justice Department official John Yoo. Padilla alleges that Yoo's memo, later adopted by Rumsfeld and Bush, led to his mistreatment as a prisoner, including some of the same cruelties inflicted upon prisoners at Guantánamo.

Under the Religious Freedom Restoration Act of 1993, the pending case, *Rasul v. Myers,* sues for the defiling of religious beliefs at Guantanamo. Plantiffs also claim that their torture while confined is contrary to the constitutional ban on "cruel and unusual punishment." In late October 2008, the Supreme Court was expected to decide whether to hear the case.

The War Crimes Act of 1996 criminalizes key provisions of the Fourth Geneva Convention, including illegal seizure and wanton property destruction. The death penalty may apply if a war crime results in death. Otherwise, fines and prison terms may be imposed by judges against offenders. Knowledge of a pattern of abuse without efforts to stop the abuse is considered a crime under the law.

One provision of the War Crimes Act of 1996 criminalizes "grave breaches" of the Geneva Conventions. Among the "grave breaches" are willful killing, torture, cruel and inhumane treatment, biological experiments, deliberately causing great suffering or serious injury to body or health, outrages upon personal dignity, taking hostages, unlawful deportation, unlawful detention, and denial of the rights of fair and regular trial to prisoners of war. In 1997, the law was broadened to cover any offense contained in Article 3 common to the four Geneva Conventions, the very provision that the Supreme Court ruled had been violated in *Hamdan v Rumsfeld* (2006).

On procedural grounds, Bush and Rumsfeld have already lost several but not all relevant cases, though courts have backed them up in other instances. When appellate judges find procedural errors at trial, they usually order retrials, but in *Hamdan* the error was a denial of "the rights of fair and regular trial" at Guantánamo, thus a violation of the War Crimes Act of 1996. But no plaintiff then sought to enforce the law on Rumsfeld for carrying out Bush's executive order, as both Bush and Rumsfeld were still in office and therefore temporarily immune from prosecution.

In *Rasul v Bush* (2004) and *Boumediene v Bush* (2008), the Supreme Court ruled that Guantánamo is within the jurisdiction of federal courts and that prisoners there can challenge grounds for being held indefinitely without being charged with an offense. A lower court in *Bismullah v Gates* (2007) gave an attorney representing a Guantánamo client the right to inspect all the prosecutor's evidence, but the ruling has not been faithfully observed in other cases.

The Foreign Affairs Reform and Restructuring Act of 1998 prohibits extradition of an alien in the United States to a country that might torture that person on arrival. Maher Arar, who was sent from JFK airport to Syria, presumably has a cause of action based on the law.

At his trial in 2007, civilian contractor David Passaro sought to call as witnesses Vice President Cheney, Attorney General Gonzales, and former CIA Director Tenet to verify that the interrogation methods that he used in Afghanistan were formally approved. He also tried to introduce statements by President Bush into the record. The federal judge denied his requests. He was found in violation of a provision of the USA Patriot Act of 2001 for assaulting a prisoner who later died, and he was sentenced to eight years and four months in prison.

Some provisions of the Detainee Treatment Act of 2005 and the Military Commissions Act of 2006 diluted the War Crimes Act. The Article 3 prohibition was reinterpreted to consist only of specified grave breaches, from which several provisions were deleted—outrages upon personal dignity, unlawful deportation, unlawful detention, wanton property damage, and illegal seizure. The 1996 provision that suffering had to be serious was diluted to "severe" harm. A provision deleting unlawful deportation as an offense repealed a key provision of the Foreign Affairs Reform and Restructuring Act of 1998, which banned transferring prisoners to countries that might torture them.

The Military Commissions Act of 2006 prohibits the use of any other Geneva Convention provisions as causes of action in American courts. Congress also infringed on the independence of courts by instructing judges not to accept interpretations of the law based on legal reasoning used abroad.

American citizen Cyrus Kar and longtime American resident Numan Adnan Al-Kaby, who were held at Abu Ghraib, sued Bush to obtain their release. Rather than defending the decisions in court to hold them arbitrarily, they were released in 2005 just before trials were scheduled. Subsequently, Kar sued for the torture that he received while in confinement, a case that cannot go forward until Bush leaves office, since sitting presidents are immune from criminal prosecution.

There has been much quibbling over what constitutes "torture." Nevertheless, there is ample legal precedent to disallow a variety of techniques (Appendix 6.1). International lawyer Philippe Sands has suggested that those who collaborated to raise the bar on acceptable torture (Table 1.1) might be charged with conspiracy to promote war crimes. If so, the Racketeer Influenced and Corrupt Organizations Act of 1990 would apply with regard to such offenses as kidnapping, murder, torture, and threats to commit violence. Depending on the severity of the crimes, penalties can range from a fine, three or more years' imprisonment, or capital punishment.

In *The Prosecution of George W. Bush for Murder* (2008), Los Angeles attorney Vincent Bugliosi makes a strong case for prosecution of Bush for murder. His argument, based on the legal theories of aiding and abetting as well as vicarious liability, is that the stated reasons for going to war in Iraq were lies. He devotes much attention to the fact that Bush ignored an explicit CIA judgment that Saddam Hussein's Iraq did not constitute an imminent threat to the security of the United States—and yet he asserted just the opposite one week after receiving that assessment. As a consequence of his order for military action, more than 4,000 young American soldiers went to battlefields under false pretences and died, so Bugliosi argues that under the law Bush is culpable. Accordingly, he asserts, Bush can be prosecuted for conspiring to commit murder by the Attorney-General of the United States or by state attorneys-general or county district attorneys for the murder of any soldier from their jurisdiction who died while fighting Bush's war in Iraq. Since there is no statute of limitations for murder, Bush may thus live out his life under a Damoclean sword.

Bugliosi persuasively suggests a line of questioning that would trap Bush on the witness stand into infuriating a hypothetical normal jury. If Bush were convicted of murder, it would be up to the jury to determine the proper punishment, including the death penalty. Vermont senatorial candidate Charlotte Dennett promised to retain Bugliosi as Special Prosecutor to sue Bush if she were elected.

Bush's subordinates might also be implicated. Those involved might welcome a plea bargain for immunity to testify against Bush, provided that a prosecutor made such an offer, though they might receive presidential pardons, though acceptance of a pardon is conditional on admission of guilt. Bugliosi also points out that Congress is not guilty of the murders of American soldiers in Iraq because its consent to military action in Iraq was premised on the fraudulent case presented by Bush.

A lesser offense under the law, though not suggested by Bugliosi, might involve prosecution for reckless endangerment of all soldiers, living or otherwise, due to Bush's anemic response to requests for body armor and vehicles that could survive bomb attacks as a proximate cause of thousands of American casualties. In civil actions, cases might be filed to obtain monetary compensation on behalf of Americans who have died or been injured in Bush's wars.

A basic principle of international law is that international courts cannot act until domestic remedies have been exhausted. If there are no war crimes prosecutions, or American courts dismiss war crimes lawsuits, then international courts and the courts of other countries can assume jurisdiction after Bush leaves office.

INTERNATIONAL TRIBUNALS

The United Nations was founded on the basis of the need to stop illegal warmaking. The UN Charter expects the Security Council alone to have the power to approve the use of force. Indeed, the Security Council authorized international troops in Korea in 1950 and the Congo in 1960. Specific war crimes offenses are monitored by various UN-assisted committees, which issue reports.

General Assembly Resolution 57/219 (2002) and Security Council Resolution 1456 (2003) by implication condemned the American failure to follow international law in combating terrorism. According to Secretary-General Kofi Annan in 2004, the Iraq War was illegal, but that was his personal opinion.

The International Court of Justice (ICJ) at The Hague, a Specialized Agency of the UN, can accept war crimes complaints, but enforcement of the court's rulings are left to the Security Council. In 1999, Serbia filed an ICJ case that accused the American-led campaign of North Atlantic Treaty Organization (NATO) countries of committing genocide through indiscriminate bombing of Serbia. The case was dismissed because the United States had filed reservations to the Convention on the Prevention and Punishment of the Crime of Genocide. Later, the International Court for the Former Yugoslavia contemplated handling the indiscriminate aerial bombing of Serbia by the United States on behalf of NATO during the Kosovo War but eventually demurred.

ICJ accepts complaints by states against states and does not handle cases involving individuals. Countries that might file cases against the

United States at some time in the future are Afghanistan, Iran, Iraq, Pakistan, Somalia, and Turkey.

Protocol 1 to the Geneva Conventions of 1949 provides for a permanent body known as the International Humanitarian Fact-Finding Commission. Located in Berne, the body is responsible for investigating and reporting on grave breaches of the Geneva Conventions when so asked by countries ratifying the protocol. However, the body has not received a petition from any state. Its first petition, filed April 1, 2003, by the organization Reporters Without Borders, related to attacks during the Iraq War on press centers and television studios, but no action was taken.

On viewing a documentary about the disappearance of up to 3,000 Taliban prisoners at the hands of American captors during 2008, European Parliamentarian André Brie called for an international commission to investigate. The European Parliament did investigate the use of European airports for extraordinary renditions by the United States, and the practice apparently stopped. Anne-Marie Lizin, the Organization for Security and Cooperation in Europe's special envoy on Guantánamo, has called for a deadline for closing the prison.

Britain originally recommended making the Nuremberg tribunal a permanent court. The proposal came to fruition in 1998, when the International Criminal Court (ICC) was established specifically to handle major international crimes, particularly war crimes. Although provisions of its statute are much leaner than those in the Hague and Geneva Conventions, the United States does not accept the court's jurisdiction and has been trying to undermine its existence. Nevertheless, the Athens Bar Association filed a complaint in July 2003 with the ICC against Bush in connection with the Iraq War, though the court has no jurisdiction over nonmembers. Luis Moreno-Ocampo, ICC Chief Prosecutor, predicts that Iraq may one day file war crimes claims against Tony Blair and George W. Bush before the court, which is located at The Hague.

Because Guantánamo is located on the island of Cuba, Inter-American regional organizations may act. In 2002, the New York–based Center for Constitutional Rights testified at a proceeding of the Inter-American Commission on Human Rights. The commission in 2005 condemned procedures at Guantánamo and called for an end to extraordinary renditions, torture, and using torture-derived evidence. The body also recommended the establishment of a competent tribunal that would respect the rights of those accused.

In 2008, Guantánamo detainee Djamel Ameziane filed a complaint against the United States over his imprisonment with the Inter-American

Commission on Human Rights. The complaint alleges solitary confinement for more than six years, arbitrary detainment, torture, denial of medical care, and denial of his right to practice his religion without insult.

The Inter-American Court of Human Rights, a regional ICJ equivalent, might also become involved. An injured person or a member state must first request action from the Commission before the case can be referred to the Court. If a state fails to respond to the Commission's judgment, such as the Commission's condemnation of the treatment of prisoners at Guantánamo in 2005, the Commission can ask the Court to proceed. Since the United States does not accept the applicability of the American Convention on Human Rights, the Court would have to apply principles from the American Declaration of the Rights and Duties of Man, which has provisions similar to those of the Geneva Conventions without mentioning the context of war. Economic sanctions are the only enforcement tool.

Guantánamo has also held prisoners from Ethiopia, North Africa, and Sudan, so the African Court on Human and Peoples' Rights might be approached to assume jurisdiction. The procedure is similar to that followed in the Inter-American system.

The European Court of Human Rights, which can serve as an appeals court for the national courts of members of the Council of Europe, might become involved, since nationals of several European countries have been held at Guantánamo. They or their home countries could file complaints based on provisions in the European Convention for the Protection of Human Rights and Fundamental Freedoms that are similar to the Geneva Conventions.

According to Article 89 of Protocol 1 to the Geneva Conventions, serious violations of the Conventions or the Protocol are supposed to prompt ratifying states to act individually or collectively in conformity with the UN Charter. Although the United States has not ratified the Protocol, other states have pledged to take appropriate action. Any country in the world could convene a special war crimes court or initiate a trial in its own domestic courts.

NATIONAL TRIBUNALS OUTSIDE THE UNITED STATES

Within Europe and elsewhere, increasing approbation has been given to the concept of "universal jurisdiction," that is, the legal principle that some crimes are so outrageous that every court in the world has the authority to prosecute the offenders. From 1980, when the Vienna Convention on the Law of Treaties went into effect, a consensus based on international custom has recognized that about a dozen crimes have universal jurisdiction in the contemporary world, where criminals can easily cross borders to seek refuge from liability.

Perhaps at the top of the list of crimes with universal jurisdiction are those identified at the Nuremberg War Crimes Trials. Piracy (terrorism), slavery and the slave trade, and suppression of the right of self-determination of peoples have been well-established international or universal crimes for a century or more.

Crimes against humanity, an innovation at Nuremberg, are now understood to cover widespread attacks inside a country that include murder, extermination, sexual or nonsexual enslavement, mass deportations or population transfers, mass arrests, torture, rape, enforced pregnancy or sterilization, group persecution, enforced disappearances, and apartheid. Genocide, a related offense, was not identified until after Nuremberg.

Two newly recognized universal crimes are the conduct of the drug trade and the conduct of the sex trade. A current candidate for the status of a universal crime is arbitrary, prolonged detention. Collectively, crimes with universal jurisdiction are known by the Latin term *jus cogens* (compelling law).

The significance of *jus cogens* is that legislation about universal crimes trumps all domestic and international laws throughout the world. Countries that pass "universal jurisdiction" laws can proceed to try individuals for offenses committed on their own citizens or perhaps even on the citizens of other countries. There is no possible refuge in the world for those who conspire to commit universal crimes except to be the head of a government, who necessarily will be vilified for perpetrating those offenses.

In 1998, when Chile's Augusto Pinochet was served a warrant in England from a Spanish judge for offenses committed while he was president of Chile from 1973 to 1990, the world suddenly awoke to the principle of universal crimes. Although Pinochet eventually returned to Chile for trial and died before he was convicted, the case alerted the world to a new era in world justice.

Former Secretary of State Henry Kissinger rarely travels out of the United States nowadays, as authorities in France and elsewhere want him for questioning in regard to the coups that brought Pinochet and other dictators to power in Latin America. Baltazar Garzón, the judge

Table 6.2
Lawsuits Filed against the Bush Administration Abroad

Venue	Date	Defendants	Offenses
Belgium*	2003	Bush, Franks, Powell, Rumsfeld	Afghan and Iraq wars
Belgium*	2003	Franks	Injuries from cluster bombs in Iraq
Belgium*	2003	Ashcroft, Bush, Rice, Rumsfeld, Wolfowitz	Crimes against humanity in Afghanistan and Iraq
Germany*	2004	Rumsfeld, Tenet	Torture in Iraq
Britain	2004	Dunlavey, Miller, Myers, Rumsfeld	Torture in Guantánamo
Germany*	2006	Addington, Bybee, Cambone, Gonzales, Haynes, Miller, Pappas, Rumsfeld, Sanchez, Wojdakowski, Yoo	Torture in Guantánamo and Iraq
France	2007	Rumsfeld	Torture in Iraq and Guantánamo

*Cases dismissed

who asked Britain to extradite Pinochet to Spain, now publicly accuses Bush of war crimes and apparently is preparing such a case.

Today, the domestic courts of some European countries have already entertained war crimes prosecutions of members of the Bush administration, based on the principle of universal jurisdiction (Table 6.2). Although most cases have been dismissed, evidently because Bush is still in office, more lawsuits are expected after January 20, 2009. Mass arrests, transfers of suspected terrorists to secret prisons, and mistreatment of prisoners have risen to the level of universal crimes from the perspective of judges in European countries. Some of those returning from American detention facilities to countries of their citizenship and residence have filed lawsuits against Bush, Rumsfeld, and others.

In Belgium, where the identity of complainants can be kept confidential, three lawsuits were filed in 2003 against members of the Bush administration. One accused Bush, Secretary of State Colin Powell, Defense Secretary Donald Rumsfeld, and General Tommy Franks of crimes regarding the Afghan and Iraq wars. The second lawsuit also cited Franks; seventeen Iraqis and two Jordanians accused him of injuries resulting from cluster bombs that he authorized for use in the Iraq war. The third case was against Bush, Rumsfeld, Attorney General John Ashcroft, National Security Adviser Condoleezza Rice, and Deputy Defense Secretary Paul Wolfowitz for crimes committed in Afghanistan and Iraq.

Furious over the filings, Rumsfeld blustered that NATO headquarters could be moved from Belgium. The government in Brussels then amended the law to provide that only lawsuits involving Belgian nationals or residents could be entertained in court, and the Court of Cassation dismissed the complaints. However, copies of the lawsuits were dispatched to Washington.

Four German residents filed suit against Defense Secretary Rumsfeld and CIA Director George Tenet in 2004 for their torture while in American confinement. Since Rumsfeld was about to attend a NATO meeting in Germany, he pressured the government to drop the complaint. In 2006, the court dismissed the lawsuit because the complaint had not first been handled by the United States, which of course has original jurisdiction over its own citizens. Rumsfeld then attended the conference.

Rumsfeld, cited by the Supreme Court in June 2006 for violating common Article 3 of the Geneva Conventions, resigned in November. The complaint was then filed again in Germany, since an American court had indeed exercised its responsibility to process the complaint. In addition to twelve plaintiffs who were tortured, including Mohammed al-Qahtani, co-plaintiffs included nongovernmental organizations located in Argentina, Bahrain, Canada, Chad, Colombia, Congo, Egypt, France, Germany, Jordan, México, Nicaragua, Sénégal, and the United States. However, the case was dismissed in 2007.

Those involved in extraordinary renditions have also been sued. In 2005, Italy issued arrest warrants for CIA agents who abducted Abu Omar and flew him to Egypt. In 2007, German prosecutors issued arrest warrants for CIA agents involved in the rendition of Khalid el-Masri in 2004.

Former Defense Secretary Rumsfeld received a shock while giving a talk in Paris during October 2007. As soon as he arrived on French soil, a complaint was filed on the basis of the Convention Against Torture. The complaint noted that the French government was obligated to pursue the case because neither the American government nor the International Criminal Court had taken up the matter despite a well-documented paper trail and testimony from former Brigadier General Janis Karpinski implicating Rumsfeld with command responsibility for torture. Rumsfeld reportedly sneaked out after his talk to avoid arrest and returned to the United States.

Jean-Pierre Dubois, president of La Fédération Internationale des Ligues des Droits de l'Homme, filed the complaint, possibly on behalf of Brahim Yadel, a former Guantánamo prisoner who is a French citizen. Dubois asserted, "Because the USA is the super power of the beginning of this century and, above all, because it is a democracy, the impunity of Donald Rumsfeld is even more insufferable than that of a Hissène Habré or a Radovan Karadžić." Wolfgang Kaleck, head of the European Court of Human Rights who filed the case in Germany earlier during 2007, issued a statement approving the French action. The irony is that judicial action against Rumsfeld had occurred in Europe before any of the prisoners once under his control had been put on trial at Guantánamo.

The British government is also liable for war crimes lawsuits. In 2007, the House of Lords ruled that the government was liable for the death of Baha Mousa in 2003 from torture during his detention by British military officials in Basra. The Tipton Three and five other former British detainees at Guantánamo sued their own government in April 2008, though three weeks earlier the House of Lords refused to rule on the legality of British entry into the Iraq War. A lawsuit filed on behalf of Binyam Mohamed demanded in 2008 that London turn over documents that might serve to exonerate him in pending proceedings at Guantánamo.

In 2008, the Supreme Court of Canada referred to the operation of Guantánamo as "illegal under both U.S. and international law." Later, Canadian Prime Minister Stephen Harper was sued for failing to secure the release of Omar Khadr, a Canadian citizen held at Guantánamo.

Courts in Afghanistan and Iraq have already been busy processing defendants supplied to them by the United States. Were American military personnel to leave both countries, residents might no longer be intimidated from pressing cases against Bush before their own courts. Thousands of innocent Afghans and Iraqis have been killed, wounded, and subjected to false arrest, and most property damage remains uncompensated. Nevertheless, Washington may bully both countries in order to stop future legal action.

PEOPLE'S TRIBUNALS

Many citizens around the world want the offenses of the Bush administration to stop as soon as possible. Apart from efforts of Amnesty

International, the Center for Constitutional Rights, Human Rights First, Human Rights Watch, and other nongovernmental organizations that now plan to set up a truth commission, more than twenty ad hoc people's tribunals have emerged on four continents (Table 6.3). Most have focused on Iraq, primarily on the legality of the war.

The silent tribunals are the public opinion polls. The court of public opinion in the United States is profoundly ambivalent. According to *Who Speaks for Islam?* (2008), 24 percent of Americans in a Gallup

Table 6.3
People's Tribunals

Title	Venue	Date
International Criminal Tribunal for Afghanistan	Tokyo	12/2002
World Tribunal on Iraq	Barcelona	5/2003
(unknown)	Costa Rica	9/2003
World Tribunal on Iraq	London	11/2003
World Court of Women on US War Crimes	Mumbai	1/2004
Peoples' Inquiry	London	2/2004
World Tribunal on Iraq	Copenhagen	3/2004
Brussels Tribunal	Brussels	4/2004
World Tribunal on Iraq	New York	5/2005
World Tribunal on Iraq	Istanbul	6/2004, 3/2005, 6/2005
World Tribunal on Iraq	Germany	6/2004
International Criminal Tribunal on Iraq	Japan	7/2004, 12/2004
World Tribunal on Iraq	New York	8/2004
Iraq War Crimes Tribunal	New York	9/2004
International War Crimes Tribunal	Hiroshima	10/2004
World Tribunal on Iraq	Lisbon	Fall 2004
World Tribunal on Iraq	Stockholm	11/2004
Arab Court on Iraq	Beirut	12/2004
World Tribunal on Iraq	Rome	12/2004
Session on Media and Disinformation	Genoa	1/2005
Session on Media Wrongs Against Truth and Humanity	Rome	2/2005
International Commission of Inquiry on Crimes Against Humanity Committed by the Bush Administration	New York	9/2006
People's Anti-War Tribunal	Los Angeles	10/2008

Poll accept American killing of innocent civilians in the "war on terror" as often or sometimes justified and 6 percent believe such killings are completely justifiable. Although some of the propaganda from the Bush administration may account for the support for such an obvious war crime, most of the remaining 76 percent are opposed. Support for the Iraq War, similarly, was less than a majority in the United States in 2006, when voters elected a Democratic Party majority to Congress.

A Pew Research Center survey of ten countries in 2001 found that 58 percent of the people viewed America favorably. By 2007, that number had slipped to 39 percent. Only 15 percent in Pakistan and 9 percent in Turkey, respectively, had a positive view of the United States.

CONCLUSION

George W. Bush probably expects to be prosecuted for war crimes. The long list of Justice Department memoranda and executive orders were written because he suspected that he may have violated the most palpable interpretations of the law. He sought clever legal opinions that would release him from obvious legal constraints, but not from the best legal minds. He has heard condemnations of war crime violations by many Americans and Europeans as well as by the Red Cross and UN officials. On leaving office, he doubtless expects that various legal opinions will have their say in court, and he may seek to issue blanket pardons for hundreds of persons involved in the skulduggery.

One thread runs through what has been presented thus far. Components of the Bush Doctrine (aggression without UN authorization, flouting the law regarding the conduct of war, disdain for the Geneva Conventions, and the arbitrary actions of the Coalition Provisional Authority without any legal basis) have one thing in common. They typify the concept of a government run by men, not laws. But when Bush leaves office, he will no longer be immune from prosecution.

Should Bush and his administration be held accountable under domestic or international law? The final chapter poses that question.

Chapter 7

THE BUSH ADMINISTRATION'S WAR CRIMES LIABILITY

Aware that many of his decisions may violate the Geneva Conventions, George W. Bush has been playing a game of chicken regarding war crimes. Congress has held hearings about war crimes, but stopped short of impeaching him. At the international level, no world court has exercised jurisdiction. Some national courts have admitted cases for consideration. Thousands of private citizens have branded him a war criminal. But he is not the first head of state to be so accused.

FAMOUS WAR CRIMINALS

The first person tried as a war criminal was Scottish national hero Sir William Wallace. He was executed in London during 1304 or 1305 for the murder of civilians in war, having allegedly spared "neither age nor sex, monk nor nun," including the burning of the town of Lanark in 1297 and the murder of its sheriff. He had been fighting for Scotland's independence from England, which also accused him of treason. The film *Braveheart* (1995) is very loosely based on his life.

The first war crimes trial, which convened in 1474, sentenced Peter von Hagenbach to death. The Duke of Burgundy, who aspired to become the king of France, had placed von Hagenbach as the ruler of the fortified city of Breisach on the Upper Rhine, whereupon he confiscated private property and imposed new taxes and his troops murdered and raped those in town and the surrounding communities. He also interfered with merchants going past Breisach on the route from Switzerland to Frankfurt. After a coalition of countries successfully laid siege to the city, capturing von Hagenbach, the Archduke of Austria assembled a court of twenty-eight judges from each of the countries in the coalition. To defend himself against the charges of murder, rape, and killing residents in houses where his soldiers were quartered, von Hagenbach invoked the headquarters doctrine—that he was following orders from the Duke of Burgundy. The court did not accept his argument, thereby affirming the principle of command responsibility.

Napoléon Bonaparte, following his capture in 1814, was accused at the Congress of Vienna by the victorious allies that defeated him of violating a customary law of warfare. His crime was to violate the terms of a treaty of peace, the Treaty of Tilsit, when he attacked Russia. Although he was not put on trial, he was exiled, the first time that a head of state or government had been punished for an identifiable war crime.

Based on the Lieber Code, Captain Henry Wirz, who commanded a Confederate prison camp, was tried for "conspiracy to destroy prisoners' lives in violation of the laws and customs of war" and "murder in violation of the laws and customs of war." He was convicted in a court-martial at Washington during 1865.

Kaiser Wilhelm of Germany was accused in 1919 under the terms of the Treaty of Versailles of violating the laws of warfare by launching the aggression that started World War I. A special tribunal, with one judge to be appointed by each of the principal Allied and Associated Powers, was authorized to try him for a "supreme offense against international morality and the sanctity of treaties." However, he fled to the Netherlands, which refused to surrender him.

During World War II, the Allied Powers agreed that individuals should be held accountable for war crimes. Meanwhile, Nazi Germany treated many American, British, and other Allied prisoners of war according to the terms of the Geneva Convention in order to ensure that Allied forces would treat captured German soldiers in an equivalent manner. Japan, however, observed no such scruples.

In 1945, the Charter of the International Military Tribunal was drafted for trials at Nuremberg, Germany. Adolf Hitler was dead, but his immediate subordinates, ministers in the Nazi government, were among those charged before four judges, one appointed by each of the Allied powers, in November 1945. Guilty verdicts for some but not all were rendered. Death sentences were carried out for ten defendants two weeks later, Reichsmarschall Hermann Göring having committed suicide just before. Many others, including Nazi judicial officials and physicians, were also tried and convicted, some at trials outside

Nuremberg. Benjamin Ferencz was Chief Prosecutor at the trial in which leaders of mobile SS *Einsatzgruppen* units were found guilty of murdering in cold blood at least one million Jews and others resisting Nazi occupation as well as causing the deaths of about three million Russian POWs.

Even before the trials of the Nazis, General Tomoyuki Yamashita was hastily placed on trial by an American Military Commission at Manila in 1945 for violations of the law of warfare. Charged with offenses of soldiers under his command, who murdered, plundered, raped, mistreated prisoners of war, and engaged in summary executions in the Philippines, he was executed in February 1946, a verdict upheld by the Supreme Court of the United States.

The first heads of government placed on trial were Kiichirō Hiranuma, Kōki Hirota, Kuniaki Koiso, and Hideki Tojo, who served as prime ministers of Japan during World War II. Their trials began in May 1946, and they were found guilty and executed during 1948 in Tokyo under terms of an agreement similar to that governing the Nuremberg trials. Their offenses were mistreating POWs of war and civilian internees, plundering and destroying public and private property of foreign countries, and "other barbaric cruelties upon the helpless civilian population." Some subordinates were subsequently tried, both in Tokyo and in the liberated countries. The Tokyo court consisted of judges drawn from the victorious powers.

Slobodan Milosovič was the next head of government put on trial for war crimes. He was indicted during 1999 while still President of Yugoslavia by a special international court set up by the UN Security Council. Turned over to the court in 2001, he faced sixty-six counts of war crimes while president of Serbia, notably complicity in the genocide of Bosnian Muslims from 1992 to 1995. However, he died in 2006 just before his trial was to conclude.

In November 2006, the judge of a French court issued an arrest warrant for Paul Kagame for conspiracy to shoot down the airplane on which Rwandan President Juvénal Habyarimana was flying. That act provoked genocide in Rwanda during 1994. As current president of Rwanda, however, Kagame is immune from prosecution under international law. When he leaves office, the court may prosecute the case. In May 2008, a Spanish court issued arrest warrants for forty Rwandan military officers for participation in the genocide.

In immediate response to action by the French magistrate to indict President Kagame of Rwanda, his government set up an independent commission of inquiry during 2006 regarding France's role in the genocide. On August 6, 2008, a 500-page report identified France's Operation Turquoise of abetting hate, ethnic killings, and other related genocide crimes perpetrated by the extremist Interahamwe Hutu militia in June and August 1994. Specifically identified in the report as culpable for the operation are the late French president François Mitterrand, former Prime Minister Edouard Balladur, thirteen other French politicians, and more than twenty senior military officers for their active involvement in the massacre. Indictments seem likely.

On December 30, 2006, Saddam Hussein became the latest head of state to be tried, convicted, and executed for crimes against humanity. The specific charge in the trial, which began one year after his capture in 2003, was the murder of 148 Shi'ites and torture of women and children in Dujail, a town where assassins allegedly plotted to kill him during 1982—an instance of retaliation against innocent civilians. The court, an Iraqi tribunal designed specifically for war crimes, has placed some of his associates on trial. Those convicted await execution.

Charles Taylor, former president of Liberia, is currently on trial for war crimes. Originally indicted on war crimes charges in 2003 by the Special Court for Sierra Leone, the case was transferred to the International Criminal Court at The Hague in 2006. The trial on eleven counts began in January 2007.

In July 2008, Radovan Karadžič, onetime President of Republika Srpska, was arrested in Serbia for the Srebrenica Massacre of 1995. He was transferred to The Hague for trial before the International Criminal Court for the Former Yugoslavia.

Also in July 2008, ICC Prosecutor Luis Moreno-Ocampo recommended the indictment of Sudan's President Omar Hassan al-Bashir for ongoing genocide and war crimes in Darfur. The latter case, involving a sitting head of state, may cause Bush to wonder whether he will be held to account before or after leaving office.

Reflecting on the fact that heads of government and heads of state have been tried on a variety of charges over the years, one fact is obvious: Only those defeated have been prosecuted for war crimes. However, the types of offenses for which they have been tried are not significantly different from those committed by George W. Bush and his subordinates in the "war on terror." And the Supreme Court has already found Bush and Rumsfeld to have flouted procedural rules clearly established by the Geneva Conventions.

BUSH'S LIABILITY

Although some of the evidence against Bush is found in documents that he signed, most of the incriminating facts are hearsay, that is, reported second- or third-hand, and would have to be presented and corroborated in a court where sworn witnesses could be challenged. Based on what has been identified in the pages above, the assignment of culpability may be placed in five categories within the table in Appendix 7.1, which is admittedly impressionist, relying mainly as it does on secondary and incomplete information.

First of all, Bush (coded GWB in Appendix 7.1) has been linked to specific war crimes. When Bush's policies were understood by subordinates, those in the other four categories might fall in line, but they may have been blameless by not consciously implementing his directives. Cabinet-level officials (coded CL), mostly former Defense Secretary Donald Rumsfeld, have translated policies into verbal or written instructions. L. Paul Bremer III, Coalition Provisional Administrator in Iraq, operated as if he were a Cabinet-level official and is so classified.

At the apex of the military chain of command are the admirals and generals with command responsibility. Sometimes the top brass (coded TB) received direct orders from the Secretary of Defense, but on other occasions they exercised their own judgment. In the former case, they are part of a conspiracy to commit war crimes. They are individually liable when they act independently of civilian authority. They will undoubtedly be faulted for decisions by Machiavellian politicians.

Field personnel (coded FP) are those at the bottom of the chain of command. Most have been trained to abide by the Geneva Conventions yet were told by some immediate field commanders (coded FC) not to do so. Although some low-ranking soldiers have been called "rotten apples in the barrel," and have been appropriately prosecuted for various offenses, others merely obeyed orders coming from those above them in the chain of command.

Appendix 7.1, in sum, finds fault at several levels. Bush is associated with 103 of the 269 war crimes. Bremer, Rumsfeld, and perhaps other Cabinet-level officials account for 144 war crimes. Bush repeatedly said that he had "full confidence" in Rumsfeld, who appears to have acted on his own in making several important decisions.

Top military officials may lack exculpatory evidence for 177 war crimes that might be lodged against them. Poor judgment by field commanders is associated with 107 war crimes. Very little information about both levels has come to light, so the ratings are mostly inferences.

The so-called rotten apples among field personnel appear to be responsible for at most 56 types of war crimes. But most received unlawful orders, tried to navigate conflicting guidelines, or were left in the lurch with no clear standard operating procedures to follow.

Were the culpability of senior officials to eviscerate responsibility from those down the chain of command, the count would remain at 103 for Bush, but the burden would be lifted from others. Bremer and Rumsfeld, who consulted with Bush on important decisions, would be left holding the bag for perhaps 49 crimes. Top brass would be relieved of all but 87 war crimes. Field commanders would be charged with 26 offenses. That leaves field personnel, many of whom have been court-martialed or otherwise disciplined, with responsibility for only five unique types of war crimes. But, of course, the judgments are based on a variety of sources, some of which may not hold up in court provided that prosecutions ever occur.

WHY BUSH AND COMPANY SHOULD NOT BE PROSECUTED

Although there is little doubt that Bush has committed war crimes, many observers feel that his misconduct should not be brought before the bar of justice. The reasoning, much of which has been presented on talk-show programs, deserves serious consideration:

1. Bush's main argument appears to be that the "war on terror" is a special case, unprecedented in international law. His attorneys persuaded him that the Geneva Conventions were outmoded.

2. A similar view is based on the presumption that a war is ongoing and Bush was acting as a war president. In other words, actions by a head of state in the self-defense of a country may be claimed to trump all other considerations, including domestic and international law.

3. Although the Supreme Court has chastised Bush on procedures, he has responded by conforming to legal rulings. Given his good faith in compliance, it may be difficult to prove that he acted maliciously.

4. Bush accepts history as the proper court. Even if he mistakenly went outside the framework of international law, posterity may judge that he did his best to protect the American people by rooting out terrorists. He may not finish the job, but he expects one day to be credited with embarking on the path to eventual success.

5. Some dispute the authority of international law, which tends to be obeyed by countries only when in their self-interest. National laws and policies prevail over vague provisions of international law. Law is meaningless without enforcement, so in a world with only one superpower and a toothless United Nations, there is no objective enforcement mechanism. In a world of sovereign states, other countries have no right to impose international rules on American citizens. Military commanders need flexibility rather than being lawyer'd to death with restrictions on their ability to do their jobs.

6. Some members of the judiciary, including Justices of the Supreme Court, do not allow international law principles to guide their judgment unless they have been explicitly incorporated into Congressional laws. Even when the United States has ratified treaties, reservations have been attached to limit their scope under American law. Accordingly, members of the Bush administration may never be convicted of war crimes, particularly by judges whom Bush has appointed to the bench.

7. Trials of Bremer, Bush, Rumsfeld, and others conducted outside the United States would raise an outcry in the United States as forms of mischief that might unite the American public in calling for retaliation. Defendants from the former White House and Cabinet would never submit to judgments abroad and would not accept rulings made in their absence.

8. Some believe that prosecution of Bush and his cohorts will air dirty linen that will serve to recruit more terrorists. The assumption is that few in the world know about international law and war crimes, so putting Bush on trial would open a Pandora's box.

9. Members of Bush's political party, aware that the Republican Party may have reached a nadir in public popularity, fear that trials might serve the interests of the Democratic Party. Bob Barr, a former Republican member of Congress, has indeed joined the Libertarian Party, which might grow as the Republican Party wanes. Therefore, Republicans will try to block trials of members of the Bush administration by legislative maneuvers, such as ceasing cooperation with Democrats, thereby paralyzing lawmaking.

10. If prosecutions were to emerge in the United States during 2009, the agency to do so would ordinarily be the Department of Justice, which is headed by an attorney general. If that person is a Republican, no cases will be allowed. Prosecution by an attorney general appointed by a Democratic president will be seen as a divisive "witch hunt."

11. Objectivity is impossible. The dispute, after all, is over a matter of policy. Rather than a serious war crimes investigation, a hatchet job will emerge. Bitterness will result, and recriminations will last for decades.

12. Prosecutions might drag on for years. Public opinion, some may argue, will not abide lengthy prosecutions of Bush and his associates. Accordingly, voters may defeat moralistic, sanctimonious officeholders who agree to prosecute.

13. Courts handle legal questions, not political questions. According to the political question doctrine, courts do not interfere with the executive branch in such matters.

14. Prosecution may accomplish nothing. Documents and evidence may be lost, as has already occurred. Some witnesses may have lapses of memory. Plaintiffs may lack the means or credibility to sue. Future presidents might pardon those who are convicted.

WHY BUSH AND COMPANY SHOULD BE PROSECUTED

Although the case against prosecuting Bush as a war criminal is eloquent, the fact is that he has been sued and he already has lost in court on procedural matters. Several parallel arguments may serve to refute the considerations advanced by those who prefer to give a pass to the Bush administration:

1. The "terrorism is a special case" argument is incorrect in legal terms. Some 9/11 conspirators were tried and convicted in Spain under existing national and international laws. If Bush did not believe that existing international treaties cover the subject, he should have convened an international conference to rewrite international law when world public opinion was on his side after 9/11.

2. The view that wartime presidents have unchecked powers has already lost in the Supreme Court, which told him that he does not have a "blank check" or impunity from prosecution. In *Marbury v Madison* (1803), the Supreme Court established the principle that courts can review the legality of executive actions. As columnist Maureen Dowd suggests, the time has come to take Bush's "black hood" off the Constitution.

3. Bush has acted maliciously, not in good faith. Improvements in Guantánamo have not gone far enough, particularly in regard to what at least one former prosecutor has called "kangaroo court" procedures.

After Bush tried to authorize torture secretly, Congress found out and sought to ban torture. Yet Bush's signing statement attached to the Detainee Treatment Act of 2005 indicated that he would ignore the law if he so chose, and a secret Justice Department ruling backed him up. In 2008, he vetoed a Congressional law that explicitly banned waterboarding.

4. The "history will vindicate me" argument is perhaps the most absurd. The effect of Abu Ghraib, Guantánamo, public statements denouncing "Islamists," and killing of innocents has made Bush the world's best recruiter for al-Qaeda. Terrorists, which have increased in number, have cited Bush's war crimes as the reason for their sacrifices.

5. The belief that international law is passé is perhaps the most danger- ous and even un-American argument. If international law has ques- tionable norms, they can be clarified in court as is the case with domestic law. The danger is that without international standards countries are free to violate human rights with impunity and cannot be morally constrained. Some countries have already cited the Bush Doctrine to justify conduct that has been condemned by the Depart- ment of State as violations of human rights. From the text of the Constitution to the formation of the United Nations, the United States has been the principal advocate of international law. For Bush to turn his back on the heritage of the country borders on treason. Making up his own rules in the name of flexibility to achieve widely shared goals should be called what it is—tyranny.

6. The expectation that Bush-appointed judges will exonerate him from war crimes out of skepticism about international law is a prediction and therefore not easy to refute. Nevertheless, the Supreme Court has already informed Bush that he has exceeded his authority. In the case of *Kar v Bush,* where the Bush administration was likely to lose, the American authorities in Iraq released Cyrus Kar from Abu Ghraib in 2007 rather than trying in court to justify the incarceration of an American citizen because his taxi driver was carrying materials for explosives. The case was then moot.

7. Bush and associates may not submit to the judgment of foreign courts that convict them of war crimes. But that is not really an argu- ment against their prosecution. They can just shred their passports and live the rest of their lives in infamy.

8. The Pandora's box argument is articulated by those who believe that the rest of the world is unaware of Bush's war crimes. The opposite is true. Bush's actions, known throughout the world as blatant war crimes, have served to increase support for anti-American attacks as evidenced in part by the establishment of safe havens for al-Qaeda

in Pakistan. Americans who blindly trust Bush are the ones who are uninformed.

9. If Republicans want to lift the cloud that already hangs over their party, they could best do so by weeding out the "rotten apples" who allowed such disgraceful behavior to proceed.

10. The expectation that war crimes prosecutions will divide Republicans from Democrats to the point of disrupting normal legislation has merit. Current deep partisan divisions can be traced in part to the unsuccessful impeachment of President Bill Clinton. The country needs a transformative leader who can bring the nation together to turn over a new leaf. An end to partisan bickering is a noble goal. Accordingly, both parties should unite by drawing the line at Bush's barbarism.

11. Courts uphold standards of objectivity. Those who object to unfavorable rulings can always appeal. High-profile lawbreakers often experience redemptive contrition when they lose.

12. The spectacle of a long trial of former leaders can indeed have an adverse impact on public opinion. When the public no longer respects its leaders, voters may either stop voting or vote for leaders of new, untainted political parties. It is difficult to advocate placing an entire political system in turmoil for the sake of catching a few notorious criminals. Nevertheless, such trials will doubtless take place in other countries. Under the principle of exhaustion of local remedies, lawsuits elsewhere can only be stopped by bringing Bush to justice in Washington.

13. The political question doctrine applies to policy judgments when there is ambiguity in the law. The law of warfare is clear. Prosecution will clarify the meaning of what is prohibited to those who are uninformed.

14. Sufficient documents and other evidence exist for prosecutions. Congressional hearings have already obtained relevant sworn testimony. Credible and responsible witnesses and plaintiffs have already filed suit. Even if future presidents might pardon those who are convicted, what is most important is the education of the leaders and the public about war crimes. When more persons are aware of prohibitions against improper conduct of war, fewer future offenses will occur.

Although the arguments for and against prosecution may cancel out one another, there are other possible reasons for desiring prosecution. Whether war crimes trials occur in the United States or elsewhere, larger issues are at stake. In the arguments below, rebuttals follow each of the additional reasons for prosecution:

15. The United States cathartically needs to exorcise the specter of war crimes in order to regain world leadership and respect. BUT if there is

no broad consensus within the United States on a desire to prosecute, trials inside the country will project a fluctuating, politicized foreign policy.

16. The world will be in chaos if the United States decides to abandon international law. Convictions in American courts on specific war crimes, such as indefinite detention and torture, are more likely to end that practice worldwide by showing that the lone superpower will no longer play the role of bully, maintaining an international double standard. Currently, the world is at a crossroads between rule by law or rule by the United States. BUT some will argue that the stakes are exaggerated.

17. The effort of a president of the United States to violate American law, both secretly and openly, has dire consequences for the future of the republic. Future presidents may cite precedents from the Bush administration and go beyond them in tearing up constitutional checks and balances that are at the core of American democracy. If one president is not accountable for war crimes, then another will feel free to operate an imperial presidency wherein the role of Congress is reduced to rubberstamping proposals from the White House, thereby informing the American people that the Constitution is a mere piece of paper. BUT opponents may respond that impeachment is the proper response, and thus Congressional Democrats are to blame if they have not acted constitutionally.

18. Deep within American culture today there is what the French call *incivisme*, that is, disrespect for government and the law. The Watergate, Iran-Contra, Enron, and Abu Ghraib scandals communicate to the public that the rich and well connected can break laws with impunity while ordinary Americans have to put up with arrogant bureaucrats, shyster lawyers, and crooked businesses. The public has revolted quietly by nonvoting, running red lights, computer mendacity, steroid use in sports, running up unsupportable credit card debts, and other examples of a breakdown of civility and sagacity. Indeed, a recent Gallup Poll report by John Esposito and Dalia Mogahed revealed that 30 percent of Americans today believe that it is justifiable to kill innocent civilians in the "war on terror." BUT the contrary argument was articulated by Democratic Representative Howard Berman, who opposed President Bill Clinton's impeachment. Quoting former First Lady Barbara Bush, Berman said that the American people are too wise to be fooled by politicians.

19. If notorious lawbreakers in the Bush administration go unpunished for horrendous offenses, those very offenses may be replicated by the police, by parents and spouses, and by schoolyard bullies in a society that will become increasingly nasty and brutish. As Louis Brandeis said in *Olmstead v United States* (1928), "If the government

becomes a lawbreaker, it breeds contempt for law; it invites every man to become a law unto himself; it invites anarchy." The integrity of the law demands that lawbreakers must be brought to justice. BUT the rebuttal is that the American legal system will doubtless survive without hysterical war crimes prosecution.

20. Fighting terror by using terrorist tactics, from indiscriminate bombing to torture in secret prisons, makes no sense and justifies more anti-American terrorism. American soldiers and tourists abroad are imperiled as a result. The best way to end the belief that Washington condones terror tactics is to have a court declare those tactics illegal. BUT case-by-case adjudication, opponents will argue, is better than overdramatic war crimes prosecution, and military courts-martial have indeed already punished some of those who misbehaved.

21. Terrorists have reasons for their actions, most of which are misguided. On policy matters, they differ fundamentally from American views of the world in an ideological struggle that is unlikely to end in a decade or two. The Cold War, a recent era when there was an ideological conflict in the world, was won in part by emphasizing human rights. Terrorists will continue indefinitely to attract support as long as the United States decides to violate human rights and assume the moral low ground. According to the National Intelligence Estimate for 2006, the American conduct of war in Iraq is an important reason for the increase in terrorism. BUT a new leader elected in 2008 may provide moral and sensible leadership and embark upon a more successful path through positive action from which war crimes trials would detract.

22. Much more difficult to rebut is the argument, presented by former Admiral Alberto Mora to Congress on June 17, 2008, that Bush has impeded the campaign to end terrorism. Expanding on his thesis, the following considerations should be kept in mind: (a) Bush's excesses have lost the struggle for "hearts and minds." (b) Leaders of countries that cooperated with the United States have been discredited or voted out of office. (c) Many of the same allied countries have withdrawn their troops from Iraq and are reluctant to send military support to Afghanistan. (d) Moderates throughout the Islamic world have been marginalized as radical elements, portraying Bush's "war" as anti-Islamic, have sold a more compelling anti-American case to ordinary Muslims. (e) Some persons formerly held at American-run prisons recall bitter experiences that serve to recruit anti-American volunteers. (f) Innocent persons who were frivolously captured and transferred to and mistreated at Abu Ghraib, Guantánamo, and elsewhere have come under the influence of hardened terrorists. When they are released, they may join terrorist networks with new

determination. (g) Nonaligned countries have been reluctant to cooperate in the worldwide crackdown on terrorists. (h) Because of the use of torture, British intelligence has ceased cooperation with the United States in the "war on terror." (i) According to the April 2006 National Intelligence Estimate, "jihadists" have increased numerically and have been dispersed globally.

CONCLUSION

The reasons for prosecuting Bush and top members of his administration are questionable or compelling, depending on one's point of view. More extensive debate on each point could occupy an entire book. Nevertheless, the facts and issues presented in this volume are indisputably important.

Although some lawyers in the Bush administration criticized the relevance of the Geneva Conventions during 2001–2003, the highly publicized abuses at Abu Ghraib and Guantánamo have served to swing the pendulum back to increased respect for the international law of warfare. As John McCain once said, the measures used to combat terrorists are more "about us" than "about them." The belief that war crimes have been committed will never fade way.

There are two concepts of the defense of the country called the United States of America. The one that the Bush administration has had in mind consists of some 300 million–plus persons within fifty states, several territories, various land and sea borders, the ground below, and the airspace above. The second concept is of a country founded on the basis of democratic ideals embedded in the Declaration of Independence, the Constitution, the Bill of Rights, the Gettysburg Address, and the "I Have a Dream" speech.

Perhaps Langston Hughes said it most eloquently seventy years ago:

Let America be the dream the dreamers dreamed—
Let it be that great strong land of love
Where never kings connive nor tyrants scheme
That any man be crushed by one above.

The Bush administration lost sight of the latter conception and thereby endangered the American way of life. Discrediting the Bush Doctrine may thus be a precondition for successful counterterrorism.

Some may pigeonhole the present volume into a "blame America first" category of leftist academics. On the contrary, my *International*

Human Rights: A Comprehensive Introduction (2008), identifies human rights issues around the world, including those of Saddam Hussein and the Taliban. Those who equate criticism of the Bush administration with criticism of America obviously confuse the part for the whole. The criticism herein is leveled in light of America's long tradition of human rights leadership, which has sadly been flushed down a Potomac toilet.

The United States, from the beginning, has been in the forefront of efforts to promote civilized rules of conduct by forging international law. Bush has repudiated a long line of leadership that began when George Washington ordered humane treatment of the Hessians. The Lieber Code, as promulgated by Abraham Lincoln during the Civil War, established the very foundation of the modern law of warfare. Instead, the Bush administration, without remorse, trashed fundamental documents of American government and major international initiatives championed by presidents George Washington, Thomas Jefferson, James Madison, Abraham Lincoln, William McKinley, Theodore Roosevelt, Calvin Coolidge, Herbert Hoover, Harry Truman, Lyndon Johnson, Gerald Ford, and Ronald Reagan. Surely these distinguished presidents have been turning in their graves as Bush has spat upon their legacies.

For far too long, the world has lived at the mercy of the Faustian pact between George W. Bush and Osama Bin Laden. Bush's outrageous actions have aided Osama Bin Laden by providing fertile grounds for attracting anti-Western recruits from around the world. Osama Bin Laden's surreal statements, in turn, have been seized upon by Bush and others to support an ill-conceived militarized "war on terror" that has ignored the struggle for hearts and minds. Instead, that "war" has been fought by hearts hardened to the cruelty and, in the words of Ted Sorensen, has been waged by minds that are sick. When Bush leaves office, the pact will be passed on to Bush's successor.

However, Bush need not suffer punishment for war crimes. After all, Bush's policies have rid the world of Saddam Hussein and, temporarily, Taliban rule over Afghanistan. The "surge" did quiet violence in Iraq. And there have been no terrorist attacks in the United States since 9/11. Nevertheless, a fair hearing appears necessary to determine the facts. The minimum goal should be to stop more war crimes by exposing and confronting them, not to exact revenge.

A sustained campaign to embark on war crimes trials has yet to be launched. Sadly, there is no Eleanor Roosevelt with the political courage and energy for that effort today. Nevertheless, a large number of dedicated attorneys have already come forward to defend those in Guantánamo whose rights have been unmercifully trashed. Among the most prominent are Northwestern University Professor of Law Joseph Margulies; Michael Ratner, President of the New York–based Center for Constitutional Rights; and Clive Stafford Smith, Legal Director of the British organization Reprieve.

As a scholar, not a political leader or crusading lawyer, I can only say that the purpose of this book is to inform that campaign of the enormity of injustices that need to be addressed. If the very concept of "war crimes" has any meaning, they must be identified now so that a line can be drawn that no American president will ever cross again. At the top of the list of my recommendations is that Congress should organize a "truth commission" to gather sworn evidence in order to corroborate statements by investigative reporters and others cited herein. Consistent with several proposals before Congress in 2007–2008, elements of the Bush Doctrine should be criminalized so that the Constitution will once again be the revered basis for American law and presidential action. Something must be done to deter future presidents from trying to hijack the Constitution, stack the courts, ignore Congress, cow the media, and manufacture public consent for unwise policies.

Bush has accomplished what Osama Bin Laden never thought possible—a transformed United States where leaders have abandoned democratic principles and loyal citizens are profoundly ashamed of how the ideals of the country they love so much have been abandoned. Something must be done or Americans will believe that whatever Bush has done was right. Bringing George W. Bush and his administration to justice for war crimes is the most compelling way in which to dispel the fiction that what has been done was necessary and proper. Otherwise, the specter of war crimes will continue to haunt the world, and civilization itself will unravel helplessly.

APPENDICES

Appendix 1.1
Legal Opinions and Executive Orders of Questionable Legality

Date	Author	Title or Document	Conduct Authorized
9/17/2001	George W. Bush	Secret presidential findings	CIA can arrest, capture, detain secretly, torture, and kill any member of al-Qaeda
9/25/2001*	John Yoo	*The President's Constitutional Authority to Conduct Military Operations Against Terrorists and Nations Supporting Them*	"Any means, anywhere, against any enemy" regardless of the War Powers Resolution
9/25/2001	Alberto Gonzales	*Decision re: Application of the Geneva Convention on Prisoners of War to the Conflict with Al Qaeda and the Taliban*	Geneva Conventions are "obsolete" and "quaint"

(*continued*)

Appendix 1.1 (*continued*)

Date	Author	Title or Document	Conduct Authorized
9/28/2001*	Patrick Philbin and John Yoo	*Possible Habeas Corpus Jurisdiction over Aliens Held in Guantánamo Bay, Cuba* [the Jurisdiction Memo]	Denial of habeas corpus to Guantánamo detainees
11/13/2001*	George W. Bush	*Detention, Treatment, and Trial of Certain Non-Citizens in the War Against Terrorism*	Detention procedures
1/9/2002*	John Yoo and Robert Delahunty	*Application of Treaties and Laws to Al Qaeda and Taliban Detainees* [the Geneva Memo]	CIA free to ignore Geneva Conventions
1/18/2002	George W. Bush	Directive (classified)	OK'd the 1/9/2002 memo
1/19/2002*	Donald Rumsfeld	*Memorandum for Chairman of the Joint Chiefs of Staff, re: Status of Taliban and Al Qaeda*	OK'd 1/9/2002 memo
1/22/2002*	Jay S. Bybee	*Application of Treaties and Laws to al Qaeda and Taliban Detainees*	Armed forces may ignore Geneva Conventions
1/25/2002*	Alberto Gonzales	*Decision re: Application of the Geneva Convention on Prisoners of War to the Conflict with Al Qaeda and the Taliban*	OK'd 1/22/2002 memo
2/7/2002*	George W. Bush	*Humane Treatment of al Qaeda and Taliban Detainees*	OK'd Bybee memo

(*continued*)

Appendix 1.1 (*continued*)

Date	Author	Title or Document	Conduct Authorized
2/7/2002*	Jay S. Bybee	*Status of Taliban Forces Under Article IV of the Third Geneva Convention of 1949*	Taliban militia not protected by Geneva Convention
2/26/2002*	Jay S. Bybee	*Potential Legal Constraints Applicable to Interrogations of Persons Captured by U.S. Armed Forces in Afghanistan*	Detainees lack legal protections (*Miranda* warning, attorney-client privilege, etc.)
8/1/2002*	Jay S. Bybee	*Standards of Conduct for Interrogation Under 18USC §§2340-2340A* [the Torture Memo]	Torture OK unless intended to cause organ failure/death
8/1/2002*	John Yoo	*The Views of Our Office Concerning the Legality, Under International Law, of Interrogation Methods to Be Used on Captured Al Qaeda Operatives*	Torture OK unless intended to cause organ failure/death
10/1/2002	Lieutenant Colonel Diane Beaver	*Legal Review of Aggressive Interrogation Techniques*	18 forms of abuse OK
10/11/2002	Lieutenant Colonel Jerald Phifer	*Memorandum for Commander, Joint Task Force 150*	Categories I–IV proposed
10/25/2002*	General James T. Hill	*Counter-Resistance Strategies*	Categories I and II OK
11/27/2002*	William J. Haynes II	*Counter-Resistance Strategies*	Categories I and II OK
12/2/2002	Donald Rumsfeld	*Detainee Interrogations*	Categories I and II OK

(*continued*)

Appendix 1.1 (*continued*)

Date	Author	Title or Document	Conduct Authorized
1/15/2003*	Donald Rumsfeld	*Counter-Resistance Techniques*	Rescinded 12/2 memo
3/27/2003	Major General Geoffrey D. Miller	*Approval of Camp Delta Operating Procedures* (revised in 2004)	OK'd use of extreme psychological distress and avoiding Red Cross visits
4/4/2003*	Donald Rumsfeld	*Working Group Report on Detainee Interrogations in the Global War on Terrorism*	OK'd 35 interrogation techniques
4/16/2003*	Donald Rumsfeld	*Counter-Resistance Techniques in the War on Terrorism*	OK'd 35 interrogation techniques
9/14/2003	Lieutenant General Ricardo Sanchez	*Interrogation and Counter-Resistance Policy*	OK'd 29 interrogation techniques
3/28/2004	Major General Geoffrey Miller	*Standard Operating Procedures* (manual to guide interrogation of prisoners)	OK'd interrogation techniques outside the Army field manual
10/12/2004	Lieutenant General Ricardo Sanchez	*Interrogation and Counter-Resistance Policy*	OK'd 17 interrogation techniques
3/19/2004*	Jack Goldsmith III	*Draft of an Opinion Concerning the Meaning of Article 49 of the Fourth Geneva Convention as It Applies in Occupied Iraq*	OK to transfer persons from Iraq to Guantánamo
5/11/2004	Paul Wolfowitz	*Administrative Review Procedures for Enemy Combatants in the Control of the Department of Defense at Guantánamo Naval Base, Cuba*	Article 3 of Geneva III may be violated

(*continued*)

Appendix 1.1 (*continued*)

Date	Author	Title or Document	Conduct Authorized
7/7/2004	Paul Wolfowitz	*Order Establishing Combatant Status Review Tribunal*	Article 5 of Geneva III may be violated
12/30/2004	Daniel Levin	*Legal Standards Applicable Under 18USC§§2340-2340A*	Slightly revised Torture Memo
2/5/2005	Alberto Gonzales	(secret)	Torture OK
5/10/2005	Alberto Gonzales	(secret)	Torture OK
5/30/2005	Alberto Gonzales	(secret)	Torture OK
12/30/2005	George W. Bush	Signing statement accompanying the Detainee Treatment Act of 2005	Torture OK if required by national security considerations
July 2006	George W. Bush	(secret)	Enhanced interrogation techniques OK
9/6/2006	George W. Bush	*President Discusses Creation of Military Commissions to Try Suspected Terrorists*	Immunity from prosecution for those committing acts construed as torture
7/20/2007	George W. Bush	*Interpretation of the Geneva Conventions Common Article 3 as Applied to a Program of Detention and Interrogation Operated by the Central Intelligence Agency*	Requires adequate food, clothing, shelter, water, medical care; bans religious and sexual abuse
7/20/2007	George W. Bush	(secret)	OK'd various interrogation techniques
3/5/2008	Deputy Assistant Attorney General Brian Benczkowski	Letter to Senator Ron Wyden	Nonintentional outrages upon personal dignity

*Reprinted in Greenberg and Dratel (eds.), *The Torture Papers*

Appendix 2.1
International Agreements Outlawing Aggressive War

International Agreement	Adopted
Final Act of the Congress of Vienna	1815
Convention for the Pacific Settlement of International Disputes (Hague II)	1899
Convention for the Pacific Settlement of International Disputes (Hague IV)	1907
General Act for the Renunciation of War	1928
Convention on Duties and Rights of States in the Event of Civil Strife	1928
Charter of the United Nations	1945
Charter of the International Military Tribunal (Nuremberg)	1945
Charter of the International Military Tribunal for the Far East	1946
Rome Statute of the International Criminal Court	1998

Appendix 3.1
International Agreements Governing the Conduct of War

International Agreement	Adopted
Strasbourg Declaration	1675
Declaration of Paris	1856
Convention on the Amelioration of the Conditions of the Wounded on the Field of Battle (Red Cross Convention)	1864
Additional Articles Relating to the Condition of the Wounded in War	1868
St. Petersburg Declaration	1868
Brussels Declaration	1874
Convention with Respect to the Laws and Customs of War on Land (Hague II)	1899
Convention for the Adaptation to Maritime Warfare of the Principles of the Geneva Convention of 1864 (Hague III)	1899
Convention Relative to the Opening of Hostilities (Hague III)	1907
Convention Respecting the Laws and Customs of War on Land (Hague IV)	1907
Convention Respecting the Rights and Duties of Neutral Powers and Persons in Case of War on Land (Hague V)	1907
Convention Relating to the Status of Enemy Merchant Ships at the Outbreak of Hostilities (Hague VI)	1907
Convention Relating to the Conversion of Merchant Ships into War-Ships (Hague VII)	1907
Convention Relative to the Laying of Automatic Submarine Contact Mines (Hague VIII)	1907
Convention Concerning Bombardment by Naval Forces in Time of War (Hague IX)	1907
Convention for the Adaptation to Maritime War of the Principles of the Geneva Convention (Hague X)	1907
Convention Relative to Certain Restrictions with Regard to the Exercise of the Right of Capture in Naval War (Hague XI)	1907
Convention Concerning the Rights and Duties of Neutral Powers in Naval War (Hague XII)	1907
Protocol for the Prohibition of the Use in War of Asphyxiating, Poisonous or Other Gases, and of Bacteriological Methods of Warfare	1925
Convention on Duties and Rights of States in the Event of Civil Strife	1928
Convention on Maritime Neutrality	1928

(continued)

Appendix 3.1 (*continued*)

International Agreement	Adopted
Convention for the Amelioration of the Condition of the Wounded and Sick in Armies in the Field	1929
Charter of the International Military Tribunal (Nuremberg Charter)	1945
Charter of the International Military Tribunal for the Far East	1946
Convention for the Amelioration of the Condition of the Wounded in Armies in the Field (Geneva I)	1949
Convention for the Amelioration of the Condition of Wounded, Sick and Shipwrecked Members of Armed Forces at Sea (Geneva II)	1949
Convention for the Protection of Cultural Property in the Event of Armed Conflict	1954
Protocol to the Convention for the Protection of Cultural Property in the Event of Armed Conflict	1954
Convention on the Prohibition of Military or Any Hostile Use of Environmental Modification Techniques	1976
Protocol Additional to the Geneva Conventions of 12 August 1949, and Relating to the Protection of Victims of International Armed Conflicts (Protocol 1)	1977
Protocol Additional to the Geneva Conventions of 12 August 1949, and Relating to the Protection of Victims of Non-International Armed Conflicts (Protocol 2)	1977
Convention on Prohibitions or Restrictions on the Use of Certain Conventional Weapons Which May Be Deemed to Be Excessively Injurious or to Have Indiscriminate Effects	1977
• Protocol on Non-Detectable Fragments (Protocol I)	1980
• Protocol on Prohibitions or Restrictions on the Use of Mines, Booby-Traps and Other Devices (Protocol II)	1980
• Protocol on Prohibitions or Restrictions on the Use of Incendiary Weapons (Protocol III)	1980
• Protocol on Blinding Laser Weapons (Protocol IV)	1989
International Convention Against the Recruitment, Use, Financing and Training of Mercenaries	1990
Protocol on Prohibitions or Restrictions on the Use of Mines, Booby-Traps and Other Devices, as Amended	1996
Joint Convention on the Safety of Spent Fuel Management and on the Safety of Radioactive Waste Management	1997

(*continued*)

Appendix 3.1 (*continued*)

International Agreement	Adopted
Convention on the Prohibition of the Development, Production, Stockpiling and Use of Chemical Weapons and on Their Destruction	1997
Convention on the Prohibition of the Use, Stockpiling, Production and Transfer of Anti-Personnel Mines and on Their Destruction	1997
Rome Statute of the International Criminal Court	1998
Second Protocol to the Hague Convention of 1954 for the Protection of Cultural Property in the Event of Armed Conflict	1999
Optional Protocol to the Convention on the Rights of the Child on the Involvement of Children in Armed Conflict	2000

Appendix 4.1
International Agreements Concerning Treatment of Prisoners

International Agreement	Adopted
Convention for the Amelioration of the Condition of the Wounded in Armies in the Field (Red Cross Convention)	1864
Convention with Respect to the Laws and Customs of War on Land (Hague II)	1899
Convention Respecting the Laws and Customs of War on Land (Hague IV)	1907
Geneva Convention of 27 July 1929 Relative to the Treatment of Prisoners of War	1929
Geneva Convention Relative to the Treatment of Prisoners of War (Geneva III)	1949
International Covenant on Civil and Political Rights	1967
Protocol Additional to the Geneva Conventions of 12 August 1949, and Relating to the Protection of Victims of International Armed Conflicts (Protocol 1)	1977
Protocol Additional to the Geneva Conventions of 12 August 1949, and Relating to the Protection of Victims of Non-International Armed Conflicts (Protocol 2)	1977
Convention Against Torture and Other Cruel, Inhuman or Degrading Treatment or Punishment	1985
Convention on the Rights of the Child	1989
International Convention for the Protection of All Persons from Enforced Disappearance	2005

Appendix 4.2
Interrogation Techniques Permitted by the Army Field Manual

Abbreviation	Interrogation Technique
Direct	Asking straightforward questions
Incentive/Removal of Incentive	Providing a reward or removing a privilege, above and beyond those that are required by the Geneva Convention, from detainees
Emotional Love	Playing on the love a detainee has for an individual or group
Emotional Hate	Playing on the hatred a detainee has for an individual or group

(*continued*)

Appendix 4.2 (*continued*)

Abbreviation	Interrogation Technique
Fear Up Harsh	Significantly increasing the fear level in a detainee
Fear Up Mild	Moderately increasing the fear level in a detainee
Reduced Fear	Reducing the fear level in a detainee
Pride and Ego Up	Boosting the ego of a detainee
Pride and Ego Down	Attacking or insulting the ego of a detainee, not beyond the limits that would apply to a POW
Futility	Invoking the feeling of futility of a detainee
We Know All	Convincing the detainee that the interrogator knows the answer to questions he asks the detainee
Establish Your Identity	Convincing the detainee that the interrogator has mistaken the detainee for someone else
Repetition Approach	Continuously repeating the same question to the detainee within interrogation periods of normal duration
File & Dossier	Convincing the detainee that the interrogator has a damning and inaccurate file, which must be fixed
Mutt & Jeff	A team consisting of a friendly and harsh interrogator; the harsh interrogator might employ the Pride and Ego Down technique
Rapid Fire	Questioning in rapid succession without allowing detainee to answer
Silence	Staring at the detainee to encourage discomfort
Change of Scenery Up	Removing the detainee from the standard interrogation setting (generally to a more pleasant location, but no worse)
Change of Scenery Down	Removing the detainee from the standard interrogation setting and placing him in a setting that may be less comfortable; would not constitute a substantial change in environmental quality
Hooding	Questioning the detainee with a blindfold in place; for interrogation purposes, the blindfold is not on other than during interrogation
Mild Physical Contact	Lightly touching a detainee or lightly poking the detainee in a completely non-injurious manner; includes softly grabbing of shoulders to get the detainee's attention or to comfort the detainee

(*continued*)

Appendix 4.2 (*continued*)

Abbreviation	Interrogation Technique
Dietary Manipulation	Changing the diet of a detainee; no intended deprivation of food or water; no adverse medical or cultural effect and without intent to deprive subject of food or water, e.g., hot rations to MREs
Environmental Manipulation	Altering the environment to create moderate discomfort (e.g., adjusting temperature or introducing an unpleasant smell), conditions would not be such that they would injure the detainee; detainee would be accompanied by interrogator at all times
Sleep Adjustment	Adjusting the sleeping times of the detainee (e.g., reversing sleep cycles from night to day), this technique is NOT sleep deprivation
False Flag	Convincing the detainee that individuals from a country other than the United States are interrogating him
Threat of Transfer	Threatening to transfer the subject to a third country that subject is likely to fear would subject him to torture or death; the threat would not be acted upon, nor would the threat include any information beyond the naming of the receiving country
Isolation	Isolating the detainee from other detainees while still complying with basic standards of treatment
Use of Prolonged Interrogations	The continued use of a series of approaches that extend over a long period of time (e.g., 20 hours per day per interrogation)
Forced Grooming	Forcing a detainee to shave hair or beard; force applied with intention to avoid injury; Would not use force that would cause serious injury
Prolonged Standing	Lengthy standing in a "normal" position (non-stress); this has been successful, but should never make the detainee exhausted to the point of weakness or collapse; not enforced by physical restraints; not to exceed four hours in a 24-hour period

(*continued*)

Appendix 4.2 (*continued*)

Abbreviation	Interrogation Technique
Sleep Deprivation	Keeping the detainee awake for an extended period of time; allowing individual to rest briefly and then awakening him, repeatedly; not to exceed four days in succession
Physical Training	Requiring detainees to exercise (perform ordinary physical exercises actions, e.g., running, jumping jacks); not to exceed 15 minutes in a two-hour period; not more than two cycles per 24-hour period; assists in generating compliance and fatiguing the detainees; no enforced compliance
Face Slap/Stomach Slap	A quick glancing slap to the fleshy part of the cheek or stomach; these techniques are used strictly as shock measures and do not cause pain or injury; they are only effective if used once or twice together; after the second time on a detainee, it will lose the shock effect; limited to two slaps per application; no more than two applications per interrogation
Removal of Clothing	Potential removal of all clothing; removal to be done by military police if not agreed to by the subject; creating a feeling of helplessness and dependence; this technique must be monitored to ensure the environmental conditions are such that this technique does not injure the detainee
Increasing Anxiety by Use of Aversions	Introducing factors that of themselves create anxiety but do not create terror or mental trauma (e.g., simple presence of dog without directly threatening action); this technique requires the commander to develop specific and detailed safeguards to insure detainee's safety

Source: Working Group Report, *Detainee Interrogations in the Global War on Terrorism: Assessment of Legal, Historical, Policy, and Operational Considerations* (April 4, 2004)

Appendix 4.3
Forms of Abuse at American-Run Prisons Outside the United States

Type	Example
Death	Excesses associated with interrogation
	Homicides from beatings; punishment for disobeying an order resulting in death
Deprivation: Property	Cutting off clothes from body[b]
	Nude confinement
	Stealing possessions
Deprivation: Health-Related	Denial of medical care, denial of medicines
	Denial of toilet access
	Food and water deprivation[a,b]
	Sleep deprivation (four hours maximum per day)[a,b]
Deprivation: Sensory	Auditory (72 hours)
	Blindfolding and hooding (up to 16 days)[b]
	Lengthy isolation (longer than 30 days)[a,b]
	Months without seeing the sun
	Packing a detainee naked, bound with duct tape, in a shipping container
	Sleeping bag technique (place prisoner in sleeping bag with movement impossible)
Deprivation: Shaving	"Accidental" eyebrow shaving
	Forced shaving of head, including beard[b]
Deprivation: Shelter	Caging
	Exposure to excessive cold (placed in icy room)[b], heat, and humidity
	Overcrowding in cells
Overexposure	"Bitch in a box" (confining prisoner to car trunk on hot day)
	Excessive cold (air conditioning, dousing with cold water, exposure to freezing temperatures without protection)
	Excessive heat (under blazing hot sun for hours)[b]
	Placing scorpions on body
	Spraying mace in eyes
	Spraying with fire extinguisher
Pain: Asphyxiation	Chest compression
	Choking and gagging
	Pouring water down nose or throat (inc. waterboarding)

(*continued*)

Appendix 4.3 (*continued*)

Type	Example
Pain: Beating and Excessive Physical Pressure	Beating with a baton, broom handle, chair[c]
	Bending back thumbs
	Breaking limbs and ribs
	Emergency Response Force (EFR), that is, forced cell extraction
	Forced stress positions for hours
	Kicking, punching (with fist to chest, etc.), slamming (against wall, etc.), stomping on body
	Lying on top of a prone prisoner with a knee pressed to prisoner's back
	Shaking, slapping more than twice in an interrogation
	Standing on prisoner's body, including neck
	Tight handcuffing and shackling (causing numbness or bleeding)
	Whipping
Pain: Bondage	Chaining (to a harness, the floor, the ceiling)
	Handcuffing (to bed, door of cell, etc.)
	Short shackling (hands and feet bound together, bolted to the floor, resulting in a fetal or squat position for up to eight hours at a time)
	Spreadeagling, inc. while handcuffed
	Straightjacketing of arms and legs
	Tied to the top of a vehicle as if a slain deer
Pain: Burning	Chemical (pouring phosphoric liquid on bodies)[c]
	Electric burns
	Thermal (strapping bound prisoners to hoods of vehicles, causing severe burns)[c]
Pain: Electrical	Electric shocks to genitals and other sensitive external body parts[c]
Pain: Exhaustion	Forced exercises beyond point of exhaustion (on stomach, jumping up and down)[b]
	Forced standing for more than four hours (until hypothermia sets in)[b]
	Stress positions for long periods of time[a,b]
Pain: Medical Procedure	Denial of access to painkillers
	Forced administration of drugs
	Forced administration of enemas and suppositories

(*continued*)

Appendix 4.3 (*continued*)

Type	Example
Pain: Mutilation	Biting by dogs and humans
	Cutting into flesh
Psychological: Degradation	Displaying a nude person who has been strapped to a board
	Eating without table implements
	Forced to crawl on stomach
	Forced crossdressing (wearing female underclothes, sometimes on the head)
	Forced nudity for days at a time
	Forced nudity in front of opposite sex, including relatives
	Forced to find objects in excrement
	Forced to wear vomit-covered jumpsuit
	Placing a dog on a naked body
	Questioning a man's masculinity or sexual orientation
	Smearing excrement on prisoner's body or prison garment
	Smearing fake menstrual blood on prisoner
	Spitting, urination on prisoner
	Wiping hair and clothes in feces and urine
	Writing on forehead or other body parts
Psychological: Disorientation	Administering mind-altering drugs, such as "truth serums"[b]
	Aversion therapy (exposing prisoner to sources of phobias, such as cockroaches)[b]
	False flag (pretending that the interrogator is from another country)
Psychological: Religious	Abuse of Qur'an
	Disrupting prayer
	Forced renunciation of faith
Psychological: Self-Degradation	Forced accusation or confession (in response to pain or threat)
	Forced to bark like a dog and do dog tricks
	Forced masturbation, including simulated fellatio
	Forced self-urination (denial of access to toilet)
	Left lying in feces

(*continued*)

Appendix 4.3 (*continued*)

Type	Example
Psychological: Threatened Actions	Death threat[c], mock execution[c]
	Forced presence during torture of others[c]
	Threatened electrocution (standing hooded on a box with wires to fingers, penis, toes and a sandbag on the head)
	Threat to inflict pain[b]
	Threat to the person's family, including rape
	Threat to rape or other sexual acts[c]
	Use of unmuzzled dogs to threaten[a]
Psychological: Perceptual Monopolization	Blindfolding (hooding for three days)[b]
	Bombardment by loud music and meowing of a cat food commercial
	Confinement (in small windowless cell)
	Exposure to excessively bright lights
	Immobilization
	Interrogation up to 20 hours without stopping, on 48 of 54 consecutive days
Psychological: Verbal Abuse	Denigration of the person's religion
	Insults (calling the person "gay," etc.)
Sexual	Anus insertions and inspections
	"Dominatrix" posing with chained male
	Female straddling prisoner on floor and gyrating above
	Fondling of the genitals of bound prisoners
	Forced sexual acts, including masturbation
	Kicking groin
	Naked pyramid of bodies with top guy's penis touching bottom guy's butt
	Penis bondage, including attaching wires
	Photographing/videotaping chained detainees, nude bodies, and sexual acts
	Raping women[c]
	Sodomizing, including children, using broomstick, dildo, or chemical[c]

[a]Permitted by Abu Ghraib poster
[b]Permitted by the CIA
[c]Disallowed by the Torture Memo dated August 1, 2002
Principal sources: Hersh, *Chain of Command*; Red Cross Report; Margulies, *Guantánamo and the Abuse of Presidential Power*; Miles, *Oath Betrayed*; Physicians for Human Rights, *Break Them Down: Systematic Use of Psychological Torture by U.S. Forces*; Schmidt Report; Taguba Report

Appendix 5.1
International Agreements Concerning Postwar Occupation

International Agreement	Adopted
Convention with Respect to the Laws and Customs of War on Land (Hague II)	1899
Convention with Respect to the Laws and Customs of War on Land (Hague IV)	1907
Charter of the United Nations	1945
Convention Relative to the Protection of Civilian Persons in Time of War (Geneva IV)	1949
Convention for the Protection of Cultural Property in the Event of Armed Conflict	1954
Protocol Additional to the Geneva Conventions of 12 August 1949, and Relating to the Protection of Victims of International Armed Conflicts (Protocol 1)	1977

Appendix 6.1
Guidelines for Defining "Torture" Under American Law

Legal Basis	Prohibited Conduct
Constitution, Article 8, 1791	"Cruel and unusual punishments"
Brown v Mississippi (287 US 278), 1936	Mock execution Severe whipping
Watts v Indiana (338 US 49), 1949	6 days of repeated questioning in solitary confinement without advice of counsel or friends
Rochin v California (342 US 165), 1953	Pumping a stomach
Trop v Dulls (356 US 86), 1958	Bathroom deprivation
Spano v New York (360 US 315), 1959	8 hours of continuous questioning
Wright v McMann (387 F.2d 519), 1967	Prolonged nude solitary confinement in bitter cold without soap and toilet paper
Knecht v Gillman (488 F.2d 1136), 1973	Involuntary injection that produces vomiting for 15 minutes
United States v Toscanino (500 F.2d 267), 1974	Police kidnapping involving beating, sleep and food deprivation, alcohol flushed into eyes and nose, forced enemas, electric shocks (to earlobes, genitals, toes)
Estelle v Gamble (429 US 97), 1976	Failure to provide medical attention to an injured prisoner
Hutto v Finner (437 US 678), 1978	Solitary confinement beyond 30 days
Maxwell v Mason (668 F.2d 361), 1981	Lack of bedding and clothing
Youngberg v Romeo (457 US 678), 1982	Bodily restraints
United States v Lee (744 F.2d 1124), 1984	Waterboarding
Burton v Livingston (791 F.2d 97), 1986	Baiting to justify shooting
Tillery v Owens (907 F.2d 418), 1990	Overcrowded, unsanitary conditions
Torture Victim Protection Act, 1992	Severe pain or suffering, mental or physical/mental torture (prolonged mental harm caused or resulting from (1) intentional infliction or threatened infliction of severe physical pain and suffering;

(*continued*)

Appendix 6.1 (*continued*)

Legal Basis	Prohibited Conduct
	(2) administration of mind-altering substances or procedures to disrupt the victim's senses; (3) threat of imminent death; or (4) severe physical suffering, or application of mind-altering substances to another
Congressional discussion during the debate to ratify the Convention Against Torture, 1994	Electric shocks to sensitive parts of the body
	Sustained systematic beating
	Tying up or hanging in positions that cause extreme pain
Eason v Thaler (14 F.3d 8), 1996	26 days of confinement in cell except for occasional showers
War Crimes Act, 1996	Willfully causing serious injury to persons
Hilao v. Estate of Marcos (103 F.3d 789), 1996	7 months of confinement in a "suffocatingly hot" and cramped cell
	8 years of solitary or near-solitary confinement
	Extended shackling to a cot
	Repeated threats of death and electric shock
	Severe beatings
	Sleep deprivation
	Waterboarding
Lucien v Peters (107 F.3d 873), 1997	Noise bombardment
Foreign Affairs Reform and Restructuring Act, 1998	Expelling or extraditing a foreign national to a country where torture is highly likely
Torture Victims Relief Act, 1998	Deliberate mental and physical damage caused by governments to individuals to destroy individual personality
	Rape and sexual assault
	Threat to torture
JAMA v INS (22F.2d 353), 1998	24 hours of bright light in cell
	Filthy conditions (smell of human excrement)
	Verbal humiliation
Cicippio v Islamic Republic of Iran (18 F. Supp. 2d 62), 1998	Electric shocks
	Frequent beatings

(*continued*)

Appendix 6.1 (*continued*)

Legal Basis	Prohibited Conduct
	Pistol whipping
	Russian roulette
	Threats of imminent death
Tachiona v Mugabe (2234 F.2d 401), 2002	Beating with bars, rocks, rods
	Electric shocks
	Whipping
Daliberti v Republic of Iraq (146 F. Supp. 2d 91), 2001	Threats of physical torture, such as cutting off fingers or pulling out fingernails
	Electric shock to testicles
Mehinovic v Vuckovic (198 F. Supp. 2d 1322), 2002	Severe beatings to the genitals, head, and other parts of the body with metal pipes, brass knuckles, batons, a baseball bat, and various other items
	Removal of teeth with pliers
	Kicking in the face and ribs
	Breaking of bones and ribs
	Dislocation of fingers
	Drawing on the victim's forehead
	Hanging the victim and beating him
	Extreme limitations of food and water
	Russian roulette
	Prolonged mental harm caused by or resulting from intentional infliction or threatened infliction of severe physical pain or suffering and the threat of imminent death
Sackie v Ashcroft (270 F. Supp. 2d 596), 2003	Forced drug use
	Threats of imminent death over 3 to 4 years
	Kidnapping and forcing a child to be a soldier
Hawkins v Holloway (316 F.3d 777), 2003	Threat of deadly force
Lhanzom v Gonzales (430 F.3d 833), 2005	Excessive cold

Appendix 7.1
War Crimes Culpability of the Bush Administration

TYPE OF WAR CRIME	GWB	CL	TB	FC	FP
Legality of the War					
#1 Waging Aggressive War	X	X	X		
#2 Aiding Rebels in a Civil War	X				
#3 Threatening Aggressive War	X				
#4 Planning and Preparing for a War of Aggression	X	X	X		
#5 Conspiracy to Wage War	X	X			
#6 Propaganda for War	X	X			
Conduct of War: Prohibited Targets					
#7 Failure to Observe the Neutrality of a Hospital				X	X
#8 Destruction of Undefended Targets			X		
#9 Bombing of Edifices Devoted to Art, Charity, Religion, and Science		X		X	X
#10 Failure to Compensate	X				
#11 Naval Bombardment of Undefended Buildings, Dwellings, Towns, and Villages	X	X	X		
#12 Bombing of Neutral Countries	X	X	X		
#13 Failure to Observe the Neutrality of Hospital Employees			X	X	X
#14 Failure to Respect the Neutrality of a Voluntary Aid Society				X	X
#15 Hostile Acts on the Ground Directed at a Museum				X	X
#16 Indiscriminate Attacks against Civilians	X	X	X	X	X
#17 Failure to Protect Cultural Property		X	X	X	X

(continued)

TYPE OF WAR CRIME	GWB	CL	TB	FC	FP
Conduct of War: Prohibited Weapons					
#18 Use of Arms and Projectiles to Cause Superfluous Injury			X		X
#19 Use of Napalm			X		
#20 Use of White Phosphorous			X		X
#21 Use of Depleted Uranium Weapons			X		X
Conduct of War: Misconduct by Soldiers					
#22 Killing or Wounding Civilians Treacherously	X				X
#23 Failure to Accept the Surrender of Combatants		X	X	X	
#24 Pillage			X	X	X
#25 Failure to Attend to the Wounded				X	X
#26 Failure to Provide Proper Burials to Enemy Soldiers Killed in Combat				X	X
#27 Excessive Targeting of Civilians	X	X	X	X	X
Conduct of War: Misconduct by Commanders					
#28 Failure to Notify Authorities of Bombardments	X		X		
#29 Indiscriminate Naval Bombardments		X	X		
#30 Naval Bombardments Without Warning			X	X	
#31 Extrajudicial Executions	X	X	X	X	X
#32 Reprisals against Innocent Civilians	X	X	X	X	X
#33 Depriving Civilians of Food and Drinking Water				X	
#34 Excessive Military Force	X	X	X	X	X

(continued)

277

Appendix 7.1 (*continued*)

TYPE OF WAR CRIME	GWB	CL	TB	FC	FP
#35 Failure to Provide Battlefield Officers with Appropriate Legal Advice	X	X			
#36 Failure to Prosecute Commanding Officers for Failure to Stop Battlefield Offenses			X		
#37 Failure of Commanding Officers to Report Battlefield Offenses to Their Superiors				X	
#38 Failure of Commanding Officers to Ensure That Subordinates Understand Geneva Convention Obligations Regarding the Conduct of Warfare	X	X	X	X	
#39 Failure of Commanding Officers to Prevent Subordinates from Plotting War Crimes on the Battlefield				X	
#40 Failure of Commanding Officers to Discipline or Prosecute Subordinates Who Commit War Crimes on the Battlefield			X	X	
Conduct of War: Prohibited Combatants					
#41 Funding War Mercenaries	X	X			
#42 Mercenaries Have Engaged in Combat		X			
Treatment of Prisoners: Violating Standards of Decency					
#43 Inhumane Treatment		X	X	X	X
#44 Depriving Prisoners of Their Property				X	X
#45 Religious Mistreatment				X	X
#46 Displaying Prisoners			X	X	X

(*continued*)

TYPE OF WAR CRIME	GWB	CL	TB	FC	FP
#47 Denial of Decent Burial of Prisoners				X	X
#48 Cruel Treatment		X	X	X	X
#49 Outrages upon Personal Dignity	X	X	X	X	X
Treatment of Prisoners: Interrogation Methods					
#50 Reprisals Against Prisoners	X	X	X	X	X
#51 Interrogation Beyond Name, Rank, and Serial Number	X	X	X	X	
#52 Coercive Techniques	X	X	X	X	X
#53 Threats and Unpleasant Treatment	X	X	X	X	X
#54 Systematic Insults					X
#55 Torture	X	X	X	X	X
#56 Taking Hostages				X	X
#57 Failure to Prevent Torture	X	X	X	X	
#58 Complicity or Participation in Torture	X	X	X	X	X
#59 Failure to Protect Prisoners from Intimidation	X	X	X	X	
#60 Use of Weapons Against Prisoners	X				X
Treatment of Prisoners: Unacceptable Living Conditions					
#61 Inadequate Food			X	X	X
#62 Inadequate Clothing			X	X	
#63 Inadequate Shelter			X		
#64 Cramped Housing			X		
#65 Close Confinement			X		

(continued)

TYPE OF WAR CRIME	GWB	CL	TB	FC	FP
#66 Internment on Ships at Sea	X	X	X		
#67 Internment in Penitentiaries		X			
#68 Inadequate Heating			X		
#69 Inadequate Lighting			X		
#70 Habitual Diet Ignored			X		
#71 Prisoners Disallowed from Food Preparation			X		
#72 Solitary Confinement			X	X	
#73 Prisoners Not Allowed to Eat Together			X	X	
#74 Lack of Prison Canteens	X	X	X		
#75 Prisoners Not Allowed to Receive Funds to Purchase Personal Items	X	X	X		
Treatment of Prisoners: Health Aspects					
#76 Mistreatment of Wounded Prisoners	X			X	X
#77 Killing and Wounding Prisoners Treacherously				X	X
#78 Unhygienic Housing			X		
#79 Water Deprivation		X		X	X
#80 Unhealthful Incarceration			X		
#81 Murder	X	X	X	X	X
#82 Mutilation					X
#83 Reckless Endangerment of Health in Prison			X	X	X
#84 Involuntary Experimentation	X	X	X	X	X
#85 Reckless Endangerment of Health during Transfers			X	X	X

(*continued*)

TYPE OF WAR CRIME	GWB	CL	TB	FC	FP
#86 Denial of Medical Care		X	X	X	X
#87 Failure to Provide Treatment for Medically Incompetent Prisoners		X	X	X	
#88 Locating a Prison in a Combat Zone			X		
#89 Inadequate Nutrition			X		
#90 Inadequate Infirmary, Surgical, and Hospital Care	X	X	X		
#91 Failure to Provide Care for the Disabled		X	X		
#92 Failure to Keep Proper Medical Records			X	X	
#93 Failure to Weigh Prisoners				X	
#94 Failure to Detect or Treat Contagious Diseases Properly			X	X	
#95 Failure to Provide Appropriate Medical Records upon Release			X	X	
#96 Failure to Properly Annotate Death Certificates				X	
#97 Failure to Properly Investigate Causes of Prisoner Deaths		X	X	X	
#98 Violating Medical Ethics		X	X	X	
#99 Failure to Rehabilitate Victims of Torture	X	X	X		
Treatment of Prisoners: Activities Disallowed					
#100 Tobacco Deprivation	X		X	X	
#101 Exercise Deprivation			X	X	
#102 Inadequate Recreational Opportunities				X	
Treatment of Prisoners: Transfers					
#103 Prisoners Transferred to Countries Practicing Torture	X	X			
#104 Failure to Recall Prisoners Who Have Been Tortured after Their Transfer to Other Countries	X	X			

(continued)

TYPE OF WAR CRIME	GWB	CL	TB	FC	FP
#105 Inhumane Transfer of Prisoners			X	X	
#106 Failure to Notify Prisoners in Advance of Transfers				X	
Treatment of Prisoners: Complaints, Representatives, and Discipline					
#107 Failure to Allow Prisoners to Complain About Captivity Conditions	X	X	X	X	X
#108 Failure to Respond to Complaints of Prisoners Alleging Torture			X		
#109 Failure to Allow Prisoners to Elect Representatives			X	X	X
#110 Repeated Punishment			X	X	X
#111 Punishment for Offenses Not Applied to American Soldiers			X	X	X
#112 Corporal Punishment			X	X	
#113 Confinement Without Daylight			X	X	
#114 Unequal Treatment of Disciplined Prisoners			X	X	
#115 Punishment Exceeding Thirty Days			X	X	
#116 Discipline Without Following Procedures			X	X	
Treatment of Prisoners: Juridical Aspects					
#117 Failure to Treat Captured Belligerents as Prisoners of War	X	X	X		
#118 Secret Detainees	X	X	X		
#119 Failure to Advise Prisoners of Their Right to Counsel	X	X	X		
#120 Denial of Right to Counsel	X	X	X		
#121 Failure to Try Accused Prisoners in a Regularly Constituted Court	X	X			
#122 Sentencing Without Having a Regularly Constituted Court	X	X			
#123 Failure to Use a Competent Tribunal to Determine Whether to Detain Prisoners	X	X			

(*continued*)

TYPE OF WAR CRIME	GWB	CL	TB	FC	FP
#124 Prisoners Have Been Forced to Renounce Their Rights			X		
#125 Depriving Prisoners of Identity Documents			X	X	
#126 Failure to Disseminate Geneva Convention Provisions	X	X	X	X	
#127 Failure to Post the Geneva Conventions			X		
#128 Failure to Translate the Geneva Conventions for Prisoners			X		
#129 Failure to Publicly State How Prisoners Are to Be Handled	X	X	X		
#130 Failure to Transmit Legal Documents to or from Prisoners			X		
#131 Failure to Allow Visits between Lawyers and Prisoners	X	X	X		
#132 Failure to Put Prisoners on Trial in Impartial Tribunals	X	X	X		
#133 Forced Self-Incrimination	X	X			
#134 Failure to Provide Speedy Trials	X	X			
#135 Denial of the Right to Call Witnesses	X	X	X	X	
#136 Failure to Advise Prisoners of Geneva Convention Rights	X	X	X	X	
#137 Failure to Facilitate Selection by Prisoners of Their Attorneys		X	X		
#138 Failure to Allow the United Nations to Provide Attorneys for Prisoners	X	X			
#139 Failure to Provide Attorneys Free Access to Prisoners			X		
#140 Failure to Provide Privacy During Visits Between Attorneys and Prisoners			X		
#141 Failure to Translate Legal Documents for Prisoners			X		
#142 No Right of Appeal	X	X	X		

(continued)

TYPE OF WAR CRIME	GWB	CL	TB	FC	FP
#143 Failure to Inform Prisoners Promptly of Charges Against Them	X	X	X		
#144 Failure to Inform Prisoners' Attorneys of Charges Against Prisoners Whom They Represent					
#145 Secrecy in Judicial Proceedings	X	X	X		
#146 Failure to Prosecute Those Responsible for Prisoner Deaths			X	X	
#147 Absolving Liability for Redress	X				
#148 Refusal to Allow Cross-Examinations	X	X	X		
#149 Failure to Provide Appropriate Legal Advice to Military Commanders Regarding Prisoners	X	X	X		
#150 Failure to Prosecute Commanding Officers for Taking No Action to Stop Abuse against Prisoners			X		
#151 Failure of Commanding Officers to Report Offenses against Prisoners to Superiors			X	X	
#152 Failure of Commanding Officers to Ensure That Subordinates Understand Geneva Convention Obligations Regarding Prisoners	X	X	X	X	
#153 Failure of Commanding Officers to Prevent or Stop Subordinates from Mistreating Prisoners			X	X	
#154 Failure of Commanding Officers to Discipline or Prosecute Subordinates Who Mistreat Prisoners			X	X	
#155 Attempting to Justify Torture	X	X	X		
#156 Failure to Arrest and Prosecute Torturers		X	X	X	

(*continued*)

TYPE OF WAR CRIME	GWB	CL	TB	FC	FP
#157 Failure to Investigate Allegations of Torture			X	X	
#158 Refusal to Cooperate in Investigations and Prosecutions of Torturers			X	X	
#159 Failure to Compensate Victims of Torture	X	X	X		
#160 Admission of Statements Resulting from Torture into Evidence	X	X	X		
Treatment of Prisoners: Relations Between Prisoners and Outside Groups					
#161 Refusal to Allow the Red Cross Access to Prisoners		X	X		
#162 Failure to Establish a Central Prisoner of War Agency	X	X			
#163 Failure to Request Assistance from a Humanitarian Organization	X	X			
#164 Prisoners Prevented from Contacting the Red Cross and the Red Crescent Society			X		
#165 Parcels to Prisoners Disallowed			X		
#166 Failure to Allow Prisoners to Complain to UN Bodies			X		
#167 Failure to Share Inquest Investigations with the UN			X		
#168 Failure to Provide Opportunities for Nongovernmental Organizations to Assist the Religious and Other Needs of Prisoners		X	X		
#169 Denial of Access of UN Agencies to Places of Departure, Passage, Arrival, and Incarceration		X	X		
#170 Failure to Allow UN Officials to Attend Arraignments		X	X		
Treatment of Prisoners: Repatriation					
#171 Failure to Repatriate Prisoners Promptly	X	X	X		
#172 Failure to Repatriate Seriously Ill or Wounded Prisoners	X	X	X		

(continued)

285

Appendix 7.1 (*continued*)

TYPE OF WAR CRIME	GWB	CL	TB	FC	FP
Treatment of Prisoners: Contact with Families					
#173 Denial and Delay of Correspondence Between Prisoners and Their Families	X	X	X		
#174 Prisoners Have Not Been Allowed to Send Telegrams			X		
#175 Failure to Compensate Dependents of Fatal Victims of Torture	X	X			
Treatment of Prisoners: Discrimination					
#176 Sexual Abuse of Females					X
#177 Women Confined in Same Prison Facility as Men			X		
#178 Women Internees Searched by Men				X	X
#179 Discrimination Based on Nationality, Race, or Religion	X	X	X	X	X
#180 Elder Abuse			X	X	
Treatment of Prisoners: Children					
#181 Transfer of Children from Their Home Countries		X	X		
#182 Failure to Obtain Permission from Parents or Guardians for Transfer of Their Children			X		
#183 Incarceration of Children in the Same Quarters as Adults			X		
#184 Failure to Provide Education for Imprisoned Children			X		
#185 Withholding Parental Contact from Child Detainees			X		
#186 Failure to Inform Parents of the Whereabouts of Detained Children			X		
#187 Refusal to Allow Child Detainees to Receive Information			X		
#188 Failure to Protect Child Detainees from Abuse			X	X	

(*continued*)

TYPE OF WAR CRIME	GWB	CL	TB	FC	FP
#189 Failure to Provide Social Programs for Child Detainees to Deal with Prison Abuse			X		
#190 Failure to Establish Programs to Prevent Prison Abuse of Child Detainees			X		
#191 Failure to Investigate Abuse of Child Prisoners			X	X	
#192 Failure to Prosecute Prison Personnel Who Abuse Child Detainees			X		
#193 Failure to Provide Recreational Activities for Child Prisoners			X		
#194 Inhumane Treatment of Child Detainees	X	X	X	X	X
#195 Indefinite Detainment of Children	X	X			
#196 Failure to Allow Parents to Visit Child Detainees		X	X		
#197 Failure to Allow Child Prisoners to Have Legal Counsel	X	X	X		
#198 Failure to Provide an Impartial Tribunal for Child Prisoners	X	X			
#199 Failure to Provide Speedy Trials for Child Prisoners	X	X			
#200 Failure to Provide Post-Confinement Social Programs for Abused Child Prisoners	X	X			
#201 Presumption of the Guilt of Child Prisoners Before Trials	X	X	X		
#202 Failure to Promptly Inform Child Prisoners of Charges against Them	X	X	X		
#203 Forcing a Child Prisoner to Incriminate Himself			X	X	X
#204 Failure to Allow Witnesses to Testify on Behalf of Child Prisoners	X	X	X		
#205 Failure to Allow Appeals from Legal Proceedings of Child Prisoners	X				

(continued)

TYPE OF WAR CRIME	GWB	CL	TB	FC	FP
Treatment of Prisoners: Disappearances					
#206 Extraordinary Renditions	X	X			
#207 Issuance of Executive Orders Authorizing Enforced Disappearances	X				
#208 Failure to Prosecute Those Responsible for Enforced Disappearances	X	X			
#209 Sending Prisoners to Countries Where Enforced Disappearance Is Likely	X	X			
#210 Failure to Disclose Basic Information About Victims of Enforced Disappearance to Appropriate Authorities		X			
#211 Failure to Disclose Basic Information about Victims of Enforced Disappearance to Family and Legal Representatives		X	X		
#212 Failure to Provide Verification of Release of Disappeared Detainees	X	X	X		
#213 Failure to Inform Rendered Persons of the Reasons for Their Disappearance, Investigation of Their Disappearance, and Plans for Their Future	X	X	X	X	
#214 Failure to Release Disappeared Persons	X				
#215 Failure to Return the Bodies of Those Who Die While Disappeared to Next of Kin		X	X		
#216 Failure to Provide Reparation and Compensation to Victims of Enforced Disappearance	X	X			
#217 Failure to Cooperate with NGOs Seeking to Rescue Victims of Enforced Disappearance	X				

(*continued*)

288

TYPE OF WAR CRIME	GWB	CL	TB	FC	FP
Occupation: Re-Establishing Public Order					
#218 Failure to Re-Establish Public Order and Safety	X	X	X	X	X
#219 Complicity with Pillage			X	X	X
#220 Failure to Apprehend and Prosecute Looters		X	X	X	
#221 Failure to Provide Security for Hospitals			X	X	X
#222 Intimidation of Civilians from Living Ordinary Lives			X	X	X
#223 Failure to Stop the Theft of Cultural Property		X	X	X	
#224 Failure to Protect Journalists	X	X	X	X	
Occupation: Civil and Political Conditions					
#225 Failure to Respect the Legal Framework	X	X	X	X	
#226 Failure to Allow Self-Government	X	X			
#227 Failure to Recognize Local Courts		X			
Occupation: Criminal Justice Problems					
#228 Unwarranted Interrogation of Civilians		X	X	X	
#229 Collective Punishment	X	X	X	X	
#230 Cruel Treatment of Civilians				X	X
#231 Unjustified Arrest of Children		X	X	X	X
#232 Unjustified Internment		X	X	X	
#233 Transfer to Countries That Persecute Political Opinions		X			
#234 Failure to Observe Existing Penal Laws		X			
#235 Penalties Imposed for Past Acts		X			
#236 Disproportionate Penal Servitude	X	X			

(continued)

289

Appendix 7.1 (*continued*)

TYPE OF WAR CRIME	GWB	CL	TB	FC	FP
#237 Interned Persons, Prisoners of War, and Common Criminals Accommodated and Administered Together			X		
#238 Failure to Account for Missing Persons			X		
#239 Failure to Ensure Fair Trials of Repatriated Prisoners	X	X	X		
Occupation: Economic and Financial Conditions					
#240 Confiscation of Private Property	X	X			
#241 Lowering Tax Revenues		X			
#242 Secret Contract Awards		X			
#243 Diversion of State Property for Nonmilitary Operations		X			
#244 Privatizing State Assets		X			
#245 Failure to Maintain Material Conditions of State Property		X			
#246 Mass Unemployment		X			
#247 Failure to Provide Re-Employment Opportunities		X			
#248 Unnecessary Destruction of Private Property			X		
#249 Unnecessary Destruction of State Property			X	X	
#250 Failure to Provide Necessities of Daily Living		X			

(*continued*)

TYPE OF WAR CRIME	GWB	CL	TB	FC	FP
Occupation: Discrimination					
#251 Failure to Respect Religious Convictions		X			
#252 Ethnosectarian Discrimination		X	X		
#253 Discrimination in Awarding Contracts		X			
#254 Gender Discrimination		X			
#255 Dishonoring Women				X	X
#256 Discrimination Against Nominal Members of a Political Party		X			
#257 Arrest of Persons for Pre-Occupation Political Opinions		X		X	
Occupation: Social and Cultural Problems					
#258 Failure to Respect Family Honor				X	X
#259 Withholding News from Family Members			X	X	
#260 Charging for Formerly Free Government Services		X			
#261 Failure to Reopen Schools		X			
#262 Failure to Restore Cultural Property Damaged by Military Operations		X			
Occupation: Health Conditions					
#263 Providing Insufficient Food	X	X			
#264 Providing Insufficient Medical Supplies	X	X			
#265 Reduction in the Quality of Medical Care		X	X		
#266 Reduction in the Quality of Public Health		X	X		

(continued)

Appendix 7.1 (*continued*)

TYPE OF WAR CRIME	GWB	CL	TB	FC	FP
Occupation: The Role of Outside Organizations					
#267 Flouting UN Recommendations	X	X	X		
#268 Failure to Accept Relief Organizations		X			
#269 Failure to Disseminate the Fourth Geneva Convention Text to Occupation Personnel	X	X	X		

Key: GWB = decision by George W. Bush

    CL = decision by Cabinet-level officials

    TB = order by top military brass

    FC = order by a military commander in the field

    PC = action by lower-ranking military personnel in the field

ABBREVIATIONS

ABC	American Broadcasting Corporation
ACLU	American Civil Liberties Union
AFP	Agence France Press
AIDS	acquired immune deficiency syndrome
AK-47	Avtomat Kalashnikova-47
AP	Associated Press
ARB	Administrative Review Board
Art.	Article
AWOL	absent without leave
BBC	British Broadcasting Corporation
C$	Canadian dollars
CBC	Canadian Broadcasting Corporation
CIA	Central Intelligence Agency
Civil & Political Rights Covenant	International Covenant on Civil and Political Rights
CNN	Cable News Network
CPA	Coalition Provisional Authority
CRC	Convention on the Rights of the Child
CRRB	Combined Review and Release Board
CSRT	Combatant Status Review Tribunal
Cultural Property Convention	Convention for the Protection of Cultural Property in the Event of Armed Conflict
DC	District of Columbia
DIA	Defense Intelligence Agency
DOD	U.S. Department of Defense

ECRB	Enemy Combatant Status Board
EKG	electrocardiogram
Enforced Disappearances Convention	International Convention for the Protection of All Persons from Enforced Disappearance
ERF	emergency response force
FBI	Federal Bureau of Investigation
Geneva Convention, 1929	Convention for the Amelioration of the Conditions of the Wounded and Sick in Armies in the Field
Geneva I	Convention for the Amelioration of the Condition of the Wounded and Sick in Armed Forces in the Field
Geneva II	Convention for the Amelioration of the conditions of Wounded, Sick, and Shipwrecked Members of the Armed Forces at Sea
Geneva III	Convention Relative to the Treatment of Prisoners of War
Geneva IV	Convention Relative to the Protection of Civilian Persons in Time of War
Hague II	Convention with Respect to the Laws and Customs of War on Land
Hague IV	Convention Respecting the Laws and Customs of War on Land and Its Annex: Regulations Concerning the Laws and Customs of War on Land
Hague V	Convention Respecting the Rights and Duties of Neutral Powers and Persons in Case of War on Land
Hague IX	Convention Concerning Bombardment by Naval Forces in Time of War
HIV	human immunodeficiency virus
ICC	International Criminal Court
ICJ	International Court of Justice
Incendiary Weapons Protocol	Protocol on Prohibitions or Restrictions on the Use of Incendiary Weapons
IRA	Irish Republican Army
IRF	immediate response force
ISAF	International Security Assistance Force
Kellogg-Briand Pact	General Act for the Renunciation of War
LAT	*Los Angeles Times*
Mercenaries Convention, 1993	International Convention against the Recruitment, Use, Financing and Training of Mercenaries

MNF-I	Multinational Force-Iraq
MRE	meal ready to eat
NATO	North Atlantic Treaty Organization
NGO	nongovernmental organization
Nuremberg Charter	Charter of the International Military Tribunal
NYT	*New York Times*
OEF	Operation Enduring Freedom
ORHA	Office of Reconstruction and Humanitarian Assistance
POW	prisoner of war
POW Convention	Geneva Convention of 27 July 1929 Relative to the Treatment of Prisoners of War
Protocol 1	Protocol Additional to the Geneva Conventions of 12 August 1949, and Relating to the Protection of Victims of International Armed Conflicts
Radioactive Waste Convention	Joint Convention on the Safety of Spent Fuel Management and on the Safety of Radioactive Waste Management
Red Crescent	Red Crescent Society
Red Cross	International Committee of the Red Cross
Red Cross Convention	Convention for the Amelioration of the Condition of the Wounded in Armies in the Field
Torture Convention	Convention Against Torture and Other Cruel, Inhuman or Degrading Treatment or Punishment
UN	United Nations
U.S.	United States
USA	United States of America
USA Patriot Act	Uniting and Strengthening America by Providing Appropriate Tools Required to Intercept and Obstruct Terrorism Act
U.S.S.	United States Steamship
WP	*Washington Post*

SOURCES

The following citations are abbreviated. For full citations, see References.

War Crime #1. Waging Aggressive War. Barber (2007); Cohn (2008); *Guardian* (2001); Liste (2008); Woodward (2003: 81); Worthington (2007: 2).

War Crime #2. Aiding Rebels in a Civil War. Cordesman (2008); Fletcher (2008); M. Gordon (2007); Hersh (2004a: 142–143, 157; chap. 4, part I); Johnson (2008); N. Parker (2008b); Partlow (2007); Sanger (2007); Susman (2008c); United Press International (2008); Wax and de Young (2006); Williams (2007a); Woodward (2003: 77–78).

War Crime #3. Threatening Aggressive War. Bush (2003b); Carter (2007).

War Crime #4. Planning and Preparing for a War of Aggression. Bacevich (2008); R. Baker (2004); Bush and Herskowitz (2001); Congress (2008); Danner (2007); C. Ferguson (2008: 24); Ricks (2006: 60–62, 75); Scahill (2007a: 269); Smith (2005a, b); Suskind (2003; 2006); Woodward (2003: 35, 49; 2004: 30–chap. 3; 2006: 52–53, 81, 106); Worthington (2007: 1).

War Crime #5. Conspiracy to Wage War. AP (2008i, p); Barzanji (2007); Chandrasekaran (2006: 291); de Bendern (2008); Fraser (2008); *Hürriyet* (2008); Reuters (2008e); Roberts and de Bendern (2008); Shanker and Schmitt (2004); Susman and Comert (2008); Tao (2008); Tavernise (2007); Tyson and Wright (2007); Woodward (2004: 137, chap. 33); Zavis (2008d).

War Crime #6. Propaganda for War. Barstow (2008); Daniel (2008); Danner (2007); Doyle (2008); Greenstock (2008); Hersh (2004a: chap. 4–5); McClellan (2008a, b); Pincus (2005); Prados (2004); Revolutionary Association of the Women of Afghanistan (2007); Ricks (2002; 2006:

chap 4–5); *Sunday Times* (2005); Suskind (2003: 96; 2008); Tannenhaus (2003); Woodward (2006: 97).

War Crime #7. Failure to Observe the Neutrality of a Hospital. AP (2001); BBC (2004); Chandrasekaran (2006: 238); Dawn (2001); Haddad (2003); Miles (2006); Schuman (2004); UN (2004).

War Crime #8. Destruction of Undefended Targets. Chandrasekaran (2006: 48–49); Godoy (2003); Herring and Rangwala (2006: 191); Reporters Without Borders (2008); Sizemore and Kimberlin (2006), cited in Scahill (2007a: 148); Wilkinson (2003).

War Crime #9. Bombing of Edifices Devoted to Art, Charity, Religion, and Science. ABC (2004); Allawi (2007: 246, 339); Benoist (2003); Chandrasekaran (2004; 2006: 180); Gordon and Trainor (2007); Mrone and Saadi (2004); NewsMax (2004); Scahill (2007a: 185).

War Crime #10. Failure to Compensate. Chandrasekaran (2006: 48–49); Herring and Rangwala (2006: 191); Smith (2008: 158); Wilkinson (2003).

War Crime #11. Naval Bombardment of Undefended Buildings, Dwellings, Towns, and Villages. Conetta (2002a); Human Rights Watch (2003b: n.59–91); West (2003).

War Crime #12. Bombing of Neutral Countries. Amini and De Luce (2003); AP (2002; 2008n); Bannerman (2008); Block (2006); Burke and Gul (2006); Daragahi (2008); Faiez and King (2008); Gettleman and Schmitt (2008); *Gulf Daily News* (2008); Haas (1991); *Mother Jones* (2008); Khan (2008); Musharraf (2006); *NYT* (2008a); Prusher (2003); Rohde (2008); Schmitt and Gordon (2008); Warrick and Wright (2008); Wright and Warrick (2008); Yousafzai and Moreau (2008b).

War Crime #13. Failure to Observe the Neutrality of Hospital Employees. Jamail (2004a); Oppel (2004). The former's testimony was later presented to the International Commission of Inquiry on Crimes against Humanity Committed by the Bush Administration.

War Crime #14. Failure to Respect the Neutrality of a Voluntary Aid Society. Arraf et al. (2004); Baker (2001); Center for Economic and Social Rights (2005: chap. 6); Gannon (2001); McCarthy (2004a); Mishra (2005); Woodward (2003: 247, 272).

War Crime #15. Hostile Acts on the Ground Directed at a Museum. Thurlow (2005).

War Crime #16. Indiscriminate Attacks Against Civilians. ABC (2005); AFP (2008h, k); Al-Taee and Negus (2005); AP (2008d); Allawi (2007: 244); Amnesty International (2005); Brown (2006); Bugliosi (2008: 160, 243); Conetta (2002a); Faramarzi (2004); C. Ferguson (2008: 380); Gall (2008b); Graham (2003); Herold (2003); Hersh (2004a: 49, 149–150, 362); Human Rights Watch (2003b: n.31); Independent (2001); Iraq Body Count (2005: 14); Kahl (2007: 16–18); McCarthy (2004b); Mulrine (2008a, b); Oppel (2008); E. Parker (2008); Perry (2008b); Qader-Saadi

(2004); Rassbach (2007); Ricks (2006: 380); Rondeaux (2008); Roug and Smith (2006); Schmitt (2003); Schofield (2006); Smith (2008: 159); Susman and Ahmed (2008); Therolf and Hameed (2008); Tait (2008); Theroff and Salman (2008); Tyson (2008); U.S. Department of Defense (2004a); Wahidy (2007); White (2006); Williams (2007a); World Tribunal on Iraq (2005); Worthington (2007: 109, 142); Zavis (2008e); Zavis and Rasheed (2008); Zielbauer (2006b).

War Crime #17. Failure to Protect Cultural Property. AP (2008o); Gerstenblith (2004); Newbart (2003); World Tribunal on Iraq (2005); Zavis (2008a).

War Crime #18. Use of Arms and Projectiles to Cause Superfluous Injury. Adriaensens (2005); Amnesty International (2005); Chandrasekaran (2006: 165); C. Ferguson (2008: 10–11); Fick (2007); Ricks (2006: 125); Shimoyachi (2004); Van Moorter (2004); Wiseman (2003); Woodward (2003: 301–302); World Tribunal on Iraq (2005); Worthington (2007: 6); Wright (2007).

War Crime #19. Use of Napalm. Buncombe (2003); Savidge (2003).

War Crime #20. Use of White Phosphorous. Allawi (2007: 339); Popham (2005).

War Crime #21. Use of Depleted Uranium Weapons. Jamail (2005); Mackay (2003b); Stickler (2007); Van Moorter (2004); Shimoyachi (2004); World Tribunal on Iraq (2005).

War Crime #22. Killing or Wounding Civilians Treacherously. AP (2008j); Luscombe (2008); Parker (2007b); Zielbauer (2006a, b).

War Crime #23. Failure to Accept the Surrender of Combatants. Hersh (2004a: 129, 263, 402–403); Monbiot (2003); Worth (2006); Worthington (2007: 83).

War Crime #24. Pillage. Eakin (2008b); Enders (2003); C. Ferguson (2008: 110, 238); Loughlin (2003); Red Cross Report (2004: 390, 401); Reed (2003); Ricks (2006: 176); Rieckhoff (2007).

War Crime #25. Failure to Attend to the Wounded. Gall (2008b); Kramer (2007); Zucchino (2008a).

War Crime #26. Failure to Provide Proper Burials to Enemy Soldiers Killed in Combat. AP (2007c); CNN (2005a); Rose (2004a); Wypijewski (2006); Zucchino (2008a).

War Crime #27. Excessive Targeting of Civilians. Ahmed (2003); Allawi (2007: 134); Catagnus et al. (2005); Center for Economic and Social Rights (2005: chap. 6); Faiez and King (2008); C. Ferguson (2008: 10–14, 383, 385); Fick (2007); Gall (2008a); Gall and Wafa (2008); Hersh (2004a: 116–117, 158, 269–270, 282); Human Rights Watch (2003b: 58, n.31, n.237); Juhl (2008); LaVella (2003); Manning (2007); Massing (2008a); Mishra (2005); Parker (2007a); Price, Neff, and Crain (2004); Raghavan and Fainaru (2007); Rashid (2004); Rayment (2004); Ricks

(2006: 403–404); Scahill (2007a: 139–140, chap. 16); Scotsman (2008); Smith (2007); Susman (2008a); Wright (2007).

War Crime #28. Failure to Notify Authorities of Bombardments. Friedman (2005); Moreau and Hosenball (2008); Schmitt and Mazetti (2008).

War Crime #29. Indiscriminate Naval Bombardments. Carvin (2008: 133); Center for Economic and Social Rights (2005: Chap 6); Human Rights Watch (2003b: n.31); Woodward (2003: 166, 208).

War Crime #30. Naval Bombardments Without Warning. Shanker and Schmitt (2003); Woodward (2003: 165, 203); Worthington (2007: 21).

War Crime #31. Extrajudicial Executions. Brown (2006); Faiez and King (2008); C. Ferguson (2008: 12); Hersh (2004a: 159, 269–270); Israel (2006); *Mother Jones* (2008); Schofield (2006); Sujo (2002); Woodward (2003: 141, 256; 2006: 152, 386); Worthington (2007: 27, 120).

War Crime #32. Reprisals Against Innocent Civilians. AP (2004b); Allawi (2007: 276, 277, 281, 339); Aylwin-Foster (2005); Center for Economic and Social Rights (2005: chap. 8); Chandrasekaran (2006: 311–312); Cockburn (2006: 125–126); Conetta (2002a); Filkins (2003); Gettleman (2004c); Godoy (2003); Herring and Rangwala (2006: 94); Hersh (2004a: 49, 149–150, 362); Human Rights Watch (2004b); Keath (2004a); Kerley (2006); Maguire and Lines (2005); Perry (2007b, d, 2008e); Rath (2008); Ricks (2006: 266, 332); Sanchez (2008b); Scahill (2007a: 114, 143); Shiner (2005); Smith (2007b: 179); Tahboub (2003); Vick (2007); Wells (2001); Woodward (2006: 230); Zielbauer (2007b); Zucchino (2008a, b).

War Crime #33. Depriving Civilians of Food and Drinking Water. Arraf et al. (2004); Badrani (2004); Fainaru (2004); Sengupta (2004); Youssef and Kerkstra (2004); Worthington (2007: 6).

War Crime #34. Excessive Military Force. Krickmeyer (2005); Perry (2007a); Raghavan and Fainaru (2007); Ricks (2006: 252, 403); Zucchino (2008b, c).

War Crime #35. Failure to Provide Battlefield Officers with Appropriate Legal Advice. Clarke (2004: 24); Sanchez interview.

War Crime #36. Failure to Prosecute Commanding Officers for Failure to Stop Battlefield Offenses. Figueroa (2007); Perry (2007e; 2008e, f); Rath (2008); Smith (2008: 159); White (2008e); Zielbauer (2007a).

War Crime #37. Failure of Commanding Officers to Report Battlefield Offenses to Their Superiors. Carter (2008); Perry (2008a, d, e); White (2008e); Whitcomb (2008).

War Crime #38. Failure of Commanding Officers to Ensure That Subordinates Understand Geneva Convention Obligations Regarding the Conduct of Warfare. Perry (2008d, e); Rath (2008); Smith (2008: 155–157).

War Crime #39. Failure of Commanding Officers to Prevent Subordinates from Plotting War Crimes on the Battlefield. Perry (2008d, e); Rath (2008).

War Crime #40. Failure of Commanding Officers to Discipline or Prosecute Subordinates Who Commit War Crimes on the Battlefield. AP (2008k); C. Ferguson (2008: 384); Perry (2007a; 2008a, e); Rashid (2004); White (2008e); Worth (2006); Zucchino (2008b, d).

War Crime #41. Funding War Mercenaries. Bowman (2008); Broder (2007); Brooks (2007); De Young (2007); Fainaru (2007a); Fisk and Carrell (2004); Fisk and Cockburn (2004); Franklin (2004); Hersh (2004a: 44–45); Human Rights Watch (2004a: 28–29); McCoy (2006: chap. 4 n.81); T. Miller (2007); Nordland, Yousafzai, and Dehghanpisheh (2002); *NYT* (2007b); Partlow and Pincus (2007); Raghavan and Fainaru (2007); Reuters (2008b); Risen (2007); Scahill (2007a: 76); Smucker (2002); Stephen (2004); Woodward (2003: 298–299, 315–317); Yoshino (2008); Zavis (2008b).

War Crime #42. Mercenaries Have Engaged in Combat. AP (2007a; 2008r); Daragahi and Salman (2008); Fainaru (2007b); C. Ferguson (2008: 380); Herring and Rangwala (2006: 192); Keath (2004b); T. Miller (2006: 168–171); *NYT* (2007b); Pelton (2006: 33, 114–115, 147–154, 157–165); Perry (2007c); Raghavan and Fainaru (2007); Scahill (2007a: chap. 8, 10; 2007b); Schumacher (2006: 167); Verma (2008).

War Crime #43. Inhumane Treatment. Alden (2005); Austen (2008); Fay/Jones Report (2004: 993, 1005–1006, 1024–1025, 1070, 1074, 1076–1078, 1080–1082, 1084, 1088–1094); Golden (2005b); Gordon (2006); Greenwald (2008); Hersh (2004a: 1, 4, 7–8, 13, 36–39, 41–42, 47, 49–51); Higham and Stephens (2004); Kurnaz (2008); C. Levin (2008); A. Lewis (2004); McCoy (2006: chap. 4 n.48); Margulies (2007: 17, 86–87, 215, 218); Miles (2006: 48); O'Neill (2005: 2007); Physicians for Human Rights (2005; 2008); Ratner and Ray (2004: 37, 62, 65); Red Cross Report (2004: 392, 395); Rose (2004a); Saar and Novak (2005: 190); Sands (2008a); Schmidt Report (2005: 19, 21); Smith (2007a; 2007b: 185, 283, 286); Synovitz (2008); Taguba Report (2004: 416, 418); Van Natta (2003); Weinstein (2007a); Worthington (2007: 82, 133, 207, 224, 229, 245); *WP* (2007); Zagorin and Duffy (2005).

War Crime #44. Depriving Prisoners of Their Property. Cambanis (2004); DIA Report (2004); Fay/Jones Report (2004: 1089); Fisher (2004a); Hersh (2004a: 15, 54); Margulies (2007: 185); Monbiot (2003); Red Cross Report (2004: 390, 401); Rose (2004a); Saar and Novak (2005: 113); Williams (2007); Worthington (2007: 84–85, 225).

War Crime #45. Religious Mistreatment. AFP (2008b); BBC (2005b, c); Bowser (2005); Butler (2008); Eggen (2007a); Eggen and White (2005); Fay/Jones Report (2004: 1081); Higham (2004); Higham and Stephens (2004); Kurnaz (2008); Leonnig (2005); Margulies (2007: 36, 67, 139); Miles (2006: 3, 107, 126); Monbiot (2003; 2008); Physicians for Human Rights (2008: 83); Rasul and Iqbal (2004); Ratner and Ray (2004: 38,

60); Red Cross Report (2004: 398); Ricks (2006: 402); Rivera (2005); Rose (2004a); Sageman (2008); Sands (2008a); Schmitt (2005); Serrano and Danieszewski (2005); Shah (2008); Smith (2007b: 9, 190, 197); A. Sullivan (2008); *Sydney Morning Herald* (2004); *Telegraph* (2008); Worthington (2007: 88, 133, 176, 195). On May 9, 2005, *Newsweek* published an article alleging that a Guantánamo guard tried to flush a Qur'an down the toilet (Michael Isikoff and John Barry, "SouthCom Showdown"), after which riots broke out in Afghanistan and other countries. The result was an apology by Mark Whitaker ("The Editor's Desk," *Newsweek*, May 23, 2005), though several independent complaints from detainees, including the Tipton Three, alleged that the Qur'an was placed in a toilet bucket. Former Chaplain James Yee (2005: chap. 7, 42, 49, 69, 75, 78) provides a thorough inventory of offensive actions in his autobiography.

War Crime #46. Displaying Prisoners. Buruma (2008); Fay/Jones Report (2004: 1024, 1071–1072, 1074, 1076, 1079–1080, 1083, 1091); Fisher (2004a); Gourevich and Morris (2008); Hersh (2004a: 37); Higham and Stephens (2004); Margulies (2007: 87); Monbiot (2003); Gourevitch and Morris (2008); Physicians for Human Rights (2005; 2008: 84); Ratner and Ray (2004: 48); Rose (2004a); Schmidt Report (2005: 19); Taguba Report (2004: 416); Williams (2007); Worthington (2007: 82); Wypijewski (2008).

War Crime #47. Denial of Decent Burial of Prisoners. Margulies (2007: 136); Miles (2006: 43–46, chap. 4); Monbiot (2003); Gourevitch and Morris (2008).

War Crime #48. Cruel Treatment. AP (2008a); Arnin (2008); Butler (2008); CBC (2008a); Elliott (2003); Fay/Jones Report (2004: 989, 1004–1005, 1024–1025, 1070, 1072–1081, 1083, 1091); Gourevitch and Morris (2008); Greenwald (2008); Higham and Stephens (2004); *Jurist* (2008); Mazzetti (2007); McClellan (2008a); McCoy (2006: chap. 4 n.69); *The Observer* (2008); Parenti (2004); Physicians for Human Rights (2005; 2008: 76–77); Rasul and Iqbal (2004); Ratner and Ray (2004: 41, 55, 61); Red Cross Report (2004: 392–393, 398); Ricks (2006: 239–240, 259); Rose (2004a); Shane, Johnson, and Risen (2007); Sharrock (2008); Shiner (2005); Smith (2007b: chap. 3, 185, 225–226); Taguba Report (2004: 416–417); Van Natta (2003); Warrick (2008b); Worthington (2007: 85–89, 108, 131, 133–134, 192–198, 202, 228); Yee (2005: 63).

War Crime #49. Outrages upon Personal Dignity. Fay/Jones Report (2004: 989, 1004–1006, 1024–1025, 1070–1071, 1073–1075, 1078–1080, 1082, 1089); Golden (2005b); Gourevich and Morris (2008); Greenwald (2008); Hamrah (2007); Hersh (2004a: 5, 22–23, 38, 54, 133–136, 215–216); Higham and Stephens (2004); Markon and White (2008); Margulies (2007: 5); Mazzetti (2008c); McClellan (2008a); Physicians for Human Rights (2005; 2008: 82–83); Rasul and Iqbal (2004); Ratner and

Ray (2004: 49, 54); Red Cross Report (2004: 391–392); Ricks (2006: 273); Saar and Novak (2005: 192, 224, 227); Sands (2008a); Schmidt Report (2005: 8, 16, 19); Schmitt and Jehl (2004); Shiner (2005); Smith (2007b: 56, 202, 206); Taguba Report (2004: 416, 419); Warrick (2008a); White (2008c); Williams (2007); Worthington (2007: 84–89, 97, 131, 140, 174–177, 186, 198, 205, 207, 219); Yee (2005: 63, 70, 76, 110, 112–113, 217); Younge (2004).

War Crime #50. Reprisals against Prisoners. AP (2006); Butler (2008); Fay/Jones Report (2004: 1075, 1094); Golden (2005b; 2007b; 2008); Jaffer (2008); Leonnig (2008); Lewis (2006b); Margulies (2007: 216); Miles (2006: 61); Sanchez interview (2008); Schmidt Report (2005: 10); Sharrock (2008); Smith (2007b: 9–10, 133, 201); *Sydney Morning Herald* (2004); Yee (2005: 70–71, 85).

War Crime #51. Interrogation Beyond Name, Rank, and Serial Number. Barry et al. (2004); Eggen (2008a); Fay/Jones Report (2004: 1084); Hirsh (2004); Mayer (2005a, b); McClellan (2008a); McCoy (2006: chap. 4 n.52).

War Crime #52. Coercive Techniques. AP (2008h); Eggen (2008a); Fay/Jones Report (2004: 993); Hersh (2004a: 4, 8); Jaffer (2008); Margulies (2007: 123–125); Mazzetti (2007); Miles (2006: 46); Monbiot (2003); Ratner and Ray (2004: 42, 42, 56); Red Cross Report (2004: 391–392); Scahill (2007a: chap. 15); Warrick (2008b); Williams (2008g); Worthington (2007: 132, 225).

War Crime #53. Threats and Unpleasant Treatment. Austin (2008); BBC (2005d); Benjamin (2006); DIA Report (2004); Eggen (2008a); Fay/Jones Report (2004: 1080–1081, 1084–1088, 1095); Gilson (2006); Hersh (2004a: 15, 46–63, 197, 236, 257, 273, 280; 2004b); Human Rights Watch (2004a: 13); Margulies (2007: chap. 2, 5); McCoy (2006: chap. 4 n.53, 58); Miles (2006: xii); Physicians for Human Rights (2005; 2008: 79–80); Priest and Gellman (2002); Rasul and Iqbal (2004); Ratner and Ray (2004: 39, 41–42, 44–45, 55–56, 59–60, 62); Red Cross Report (2004: 392–393, 395, 397); Rose (2004a); Rosenberg (2008a); Saar and Novak (2005: 162, 172, 197, 221); Sands (2008a, interview); Schmidt Report (2005: 7–9, 11–12, 14–15, 17, 19, 21–22); Smith (2007b: 201, 286); A. Sullivan (2008); Suskind (2006: 230); Taguba Report (2004: 417–418); Worden (2004); Worthington (2007: 93–94, 109, 131–132, 136, 168–169, 173–177, 179, 190, 192–198, 207, 225, 253; 2008b); Yee (2005: 76, 113, 217).

War Crime #54. Systematic Insults. Golden (2005b); Miles (2006: chap. 3); Red Cross Report (2004: 391); Schmidt Report (2005: 19, 21); Worthington (2007: 132).

War Crime #55. Torture. Ackerman (2008); AP (2008g); Baker and Warrick (2007); Berger (2008a); Butler (2008); Center for Economic and Social

Rights (2005: chap. 7); Champagne (2008); Eggen (2007b; 2008a, c, d); Eggen and Pincus (2007); Eggen and Warrick (2007); Froomkin (2008a, b, c); Golden (2005b); Greenburg, Rosenberg, and de Vogue (2008); Hersh (2004a: 16–17, 47–50, 64; 2004b); Human Rights Watch (2005a); Jaffer (2008); Johnston (2006); Kendall (2008); Leonnig (2008); Lithwick (2008); Margulies (2007: 121–125); Markon and White (2008); Mayer (2005b, 2008b); McClatchy News Service (2008); McClellan (2008a); McCoy (2006: chap. 4n.24, 27, 33); Melia (2008a); Mikkelson (2008); Miles (2006: part II); Miller (2008a, b); Miller and Schmitt (2007); Müller (1991); Nathan (2008); Nebehay (2007); *NYT* (2008b); Priest (2005b); Physicians for Human Rights (2005; 2008: 84–85); Priest and Gellman (2002); Red Cross Report (2004: 391); Rozen (2008); Sands (2008a, b); Sengupta (2005); Shane (2008a, b); Shiner (2005); Smith (2007b: 133, 249–250); Taguba Report; Thomas and Hirsh (2005); Voice of America (2008); White and Tate (2008); Worthington (2007, 95–98, 168, 174–177, 179–180, 185–190, 192–198, 202, 204–207, chap. 16).

War Crime #56. Taking Hostages. Bazzo (2004); Benjamin (2006); Center for Economic and Social Rights (2005: chap. 7); DIA Report (2004); Herring and Rangwala (2006: 187); Provance (2006); Ricks (2006: 236).

War Crime #57. Failure to Prevent Torture. AP (2005a); Berger (2008b); Bloche and Marks (2005); Champagne (2008); Eggen (2008a); Eggen and Pincus (2007); Lifton (2004); Mayer (2005b); Mayer (2005a, b); McClellan (2008); Miles (2006: chap. 6); Miller and Schmitt (2007); Red Cross Report (2004); Schlesinger Report (2004); Shane (2008a, b); Woodward (2003: 77; 2006: 80–81); Worthington (2007: 174); Zernike (2004).

War Crime #58. Complicity or Participation in Torture. AFP (2008d); Bloche and Marks (2005); Champagne (2008); Eggen and Warrick (2007); Leonnig (2008); Lifton (2004); Mayer (2005a, b); Miles (2006: chap. 3); Red Cross Report (2004); Schlesinger Report (2004); Sands (2008a); Shane (2008a, b); Worthington (2007: 207); Zernike (2004).

War Crime #59. Failure to Protect Prisoners from Intimidation. Canadian Press (2008d); Fay/Jones Report (2004: 1080–1081, 1088); Golden (2005b); McClellan (2008a); Miles (2006: chap. 3); Physicians for Human Rights (2005); Smith (2007b: 213, 259–260).

War Crime #60. Use of Weapons Against Prisoners. Conover (2005); Fay/Jones Report (2004: 1083, 1085, 1092); Greenwald (2008); McClellan (2008a); Physicians for Human Rights (2005); Rasul and Izbal (2004); Red Cross Report (2004: 394–395, 399–400); Ricks (2006: 273, 280, 398); Rose (2004a); *Sydney Morning Herald* (2004); Taguba Report (2004: 417); Worthington (2007: 93, 109, 136, 176–177; 2008b).

War Crime #61. Inadequate Food. Bonner (2005); Fay/Jones Report (2004: 1075); Higham and Stephens (2004); Jaffer (2008); Margulies (2007:

186); Mikolashek Report (2004: 660); Miles (2006: 58, 91, 105–111, 114, 195–107); Rasul and Iqbal (2004); Ratner and Ray (2004: 40–41, 43, 60); Red Cross Report (2004: 392); Rose (2004a: 1); Smith (2007b: 185); Stack and Drogin (2005); *Sydney Morning Herald* (2004); Worthington (2007: 132, 235).

War Crime #62. Inadequate Clothing. Eggen and Pincus (2007); Fay/Jones Report (2004: 993, 1005–1006, 1024–1025, 1070, 1074–1078, 1080–1082, 1084, 1088–1092, 1094); Hersh (2004a: 27); Higham and Stephens (2004); Jaffer (2008); Margulies (2007: 65, 178, 182); Miles (2006: 111); Rasul and Iqbal (2004); Ratner and Ray (2004: 38); Red Cross Report (2004: 392); Taguba Report (2004: 418).

War Crime #63. Inadequate Shelter. Chandrasekaran (2006); Fay/Jones Report (2004: 1061); Golden (2008); Human Rights Watch (2008a); Jaffer (2008); Margulies (2007: 176–177, 254); Miles (2006: 58, 111–112); Ratner and Ray (2004: 36, 39); Red Cross Report (2004: 392–393, 395, 397); Saar and Novak (2005: 65); Taguba Report (2004: 418); Yee (2005: 50–53);

War Crime #64. Cramped Housing. Astill (2004); Conover (2005); Golden (2008); Hersh (2004a: 39); Martin (2004); Mikolashek Report (2004: 659); Miles (2006: 49, 111); Ratner and Ray (2004: 66); Ricks (2006: 260); Rose (2004a); Saar and Novak (2005: 51); Schmitt and Golden (2008); Taguba Report (2004: 426); Yee (2005: 51).

War Crime #65. Close Confinement. AFP (2008e); Conover (2005); Golden (2008); Hersh (2004a: 1, 4, 13, 27, 35, 37, 39, 54); Human Rights Watch (2008a); Margulies (2007: 137, 176); Martin (2004); McCoy (2006: chap. 6 n.8); Miles (2006: 44, 49, 111); Ratner and Ray (2004: 66); Rose (2004a); Saar and Novak (2005: 51); Synovitz (2008); Yee (2005: 51).

War Crime #66. Internment on Ships at Sea. Greenwald (2008); Margulies (2007: 45); Mikolashek Report (2004: 723–726); Ratner and Ray (2004: 52, 55); Seeley (2001); Smith (2007b: 247, 249, 283); Worthington (2007: 82, 109–110, 146).

War Crime #67. Internment in Penitentiaries. Monbiot (2003); Smith (2007b: 246).

War Crime #68. Inadequate Heating. AP (2008a); Bonner (2005); Conover (2005); Fay/Jones Report (2004: 1093, 1095); *Guardian* (2004); Margulies (2007: 64, 117, 132–134, 136, 176, 186, 207, 215); Miles (2006: 91); Red Cross Report (2004: 392); Smith (2007b: 202); Stack and Drogin (2005); *Sydney Morning Herald* (2004); Yee (2005: 52).

War Crime #69. Inadequate Lighting. AP (2008a); Bonner (2005); Conover (2005); Fay/Jones Report (2004: 1093, 1095); *Guardian* (2004); *Jurist* (2008); Margulies (2007: 64, 117, 132–134, 136, 176, 186, 207, 215); Miles (2006: 91); Red Cross Report (2004: 392); Smith (2007b: 202); Stack and Drogin (2005); *Sydney Morning Herald* (2004); Yee (2005: 52).

War Crime #70. Habitual Diet Ignored. BBC (2005a); Buncombe, Huggler, and Doyle (2004); Fay/Jones Report (2004: 1081); Higham and Stephens (2004); Ratner and Ray (2004: 60); Smith (2007b: 195); *USA Today* (2005a).

War Crime #71. Prisoners Disallowed from Food Preparation. Margulies, personal communication, November 3, 2007; Miles (2006: 109–111); Physicians for Human Rights (2008: 75–76); Smith (2007b: 190, 288), personal communication, January 31, 2008; Yee (2005: 98).

War Crime #72. Solitary Confinement. AP (2008c, g); Fay/Jones Report (2004: 1025, 1071, 1093–1095); Glaberson (2008); Hersh (2004a: 13); Human Rights Watch (2008a); *Jurist* (2008); Margulies (2007: 37); McClellan (2008a); Melia (2008b); Miles (2006: 105); Ratner and Ray (2004: 58); Red Cross Report (2004: 392, 398); Strasser and Whitney (2004: 165–169); Synovitz (2008).

War Crime #73. Prisoners Not Allowed to Eat Together. Glaberson (2008); Golden (2007a); Margulies, personal communication, November 3, 2007; Monbiot (2003); Saar and Novak (2005: 205); Saifee (2008).

War Crime #74. Lack of Prison Canteens. See the fact sheet, as reprinted in Ratner and Ray (2004: 147–149); Smith, personal communication, January 31, 2008; Williams (2008m).

War Crime #75. Prisoners Not Allowed to Receive Funds to Purchase Personal Items. See the fact sheet, as reprinted in Ratner and Ray (2004: 147–149); Hosenball (2008); Monbiot (2003); Clive Stafford Smith (2007b: 155); Smith, personal communication, January 31, 2008.

War Crime #76. Mistreatment of Wounded Prisoners. Hersh (2004a: 8, 14, 28, 31, 35–36, 41–43); Jaffer (2008); Monbiot (2008); Rose (2004a); Smith (2007b: 155–166, 201).

War Crime #77. Killing and Wounding Prisoners Treacherously. Benjamin (2006); Hersh (2004a: 43); Leonnig (2007); Miles (2006: chap. 4, esp. 72); Ricks (2006: 233, 281–282); Whitmire (2005); Yee (2005: 109).

War Crime #78. Unhygienic Housing. Hersh (2004a: 2, 27, 35); Margulies (2007: 71, 205, 211); Mikolashek Report (2004: 660, 705); Miles (2006: 61, 101, 107, 111–112); Ratner and Ray (2004: 36, 56, 62); Red Cross Report (2004: 392); Saar and Novak (2005: 51); Schmitt and Golden (2008); Smith (2007b: 186); Worthington (2007: 176, 233); Yee (2005: 51, 60, 63).

War Crime #79. Water Deprivation. Golden (2005b); Hersh (2004a: 27); Ratner and Ray (2004: 61); Saar and Novak (2005: 228); Sharrock (2008); Smith (2007b: 186); Yee (2005: 70).

War Crime #80. Unhealthful Incarceration. Ackerman (2004); Fay/Jones Report (2004: 1075); Gorman (2008a); Hersh (2004a: 14); Human Rights First (2006a); McGovern (2008); Miles (2006: chap. 5);

Physicians for Human Rights (2008); Press Association (2008); Ratner and Ray (2004: 40); Rose (2004b: 52–53); Saar and Novak (2005: 66–68); Saifee (2008); Smith (2007a; 2007b: 138–140, 188, 190, 194–202, 207, 217–219); A. Sullivan (2008); Williams (2007f); Worthington (2008b); Yee (2005: 100).

War Crime #81. Murder. AFP (2008f); AP (2008q); Barnes and Yoshino (2008); Butler (2008); R. Edwards (2008b); Fay/Jones Report (2004: 1001, 1024, 1077–1078, 1114); Freeman (2008); Gibney interview; Golden (2005b); Hersh (2004a: 43–44, 260); Human Rights First (2006a); Kniazkov (2003); Margulies (2007: 17, 136, 229); McClellan (2008a); McCoy (2006: chap. 4 n.42); Melia (2008a); Mikolashek Report (2004: 655); Miles (2006: 43–45, chap. 4); Partlow and Finer (2006); Perlstein (2008); Perry (2007b); Ratner and Ray (2004: 53); Red Cross Report (2004: 400, 404); Sengupta (2005); Sharrock (2008); R. Smith (2005); Squitieri and Moniz (2004); Taguba Report (2004: 425, 427–428); Whitmire (2005); Woodward (2003: 97, 101); Worden (2004); Worthington (2007: 1, 188–190, 235, 245).

War Crime #82. Mutilation. AP (2008o); Fay/Jones Report (2004: 1076, 1082); Freeman (2008); Miles (2006: 125); Schmidt Report; Smith (2007b: 71); Worthington (2007: 82, 87–89, 96–97, 176, 185, 192–193, 225, 233).

War Crime #83. Reckless Endangerment of Health in Prison. Ackerman (2004); AP (2008h); Cageprisoners (2008); El Khabar (2008a); Fay/Jones Report (2004: 1081–1082, 1086); Gorman (2008b); Higham and Stephens (2004); Hersh (2004a: 6, 22, 26, 34–35, 43–45, 54); Jaffer (2008); Jamail (2004b); Jehl and Schmitt (2004); Margulies (2007: 136); Mayer (2008b); McClellan (2008a); Miles (2006: chap. 3–4); Nicholl (2008); Physicians for Human Rights (2008: 81); Priest (2005a); Rasul and Iqbal (2004); Ratner and Ray (2004: 45, 59–60, 63, 67); Red Cross Report (2004: 391–393, 395–397); Rose (2004a); Saar and Novak (2005: 102, 135); Sands (2008a); Sharrock (2008); Shiner (2005); H. Siddiqui (2008); Smith (2007b: 155–166, 174); A. Sullivan (2008); Taguba Report (2004: 417); Tenet (2007); Whitmire (2005); Williams (2007b); Wilson (2005); Worthington (2007: 82, 87–89, 96–97, 176, 185, 192–193, 225, 233).

War Crime #84. Involuntary Experimentation. Barry et al. (2004); Bloche and Marks (2005); Congress (2008b); Hersh (2004a: 16–17, 20, 46–68); Mayer (2005a, 2008b); McCoy (2006: chap. 4 n.46); Monbiot (2008).

War Crime #85. Reckless Endangerment of Health During Transfers. Dehghanpisheh, Barry, and Gutman (2002); S. Edwards (2008a); Glaberson (2008); Greenwald (2008); Kurnaz (2008); Margulies, personal communication, November 3, 2007; Meek (2005); Physicians for Human Rights

(2008: 74–75); Press Association (2008; Red Cross Report (2004: 391, 393); Ricks (2006: 259, 357); Rose (2004a); Warrick (2008b); Worthington (2007: 85, 125); Yee (2005: 149).

War Crime #86. Denial of Medical Care. AFP (2008l); Ebrahim (2008); Fay/Jones Report (2004: 1080, 1082, 1093); Gibney interview; Gorman (2008b); Hersh (2004a: 14, 43); Jaffer (2008); Keller (2008); *Khadr v Bush*, Appendix G; Markon (2008a); Mikolashek Report (2004: 705, 711–714); Miles (2006: chap. 3–5, esp. 53–54, 61–62, 100–101); Miller and Schmidt (2007); Physicians for Human Rights (2008: 85–87); Priest and Gellman (2002); Ratner and Ray (2004: 44–46, 60); Risen (2006); Saar and Novak (2005: 52–56, 74); Sharrock (2008); Smith (2007a, b: 139, 194, 198, 207–208, 211, 214); Taguba Report (2004: 417); Williams (2007b, f); Williams, personal communication, December 31, 2007; Wilson (2005); Yee (2005: 101).

War Crime #87. Failure to Provide Treatment for Mentally Incompetent Prisoners. Conover (2005); Fay/Jones Report (2004: 1080); Hersh (2004a: 2); Human Rights Watch (2007d; 2008a); Jehl and Lewis (2004); Margulies (2007: 66); Miles (2006: 103–105); Saar and Novak (2005: 52–56, 74); Smith (2007b: 166); Thompson (2008); Yee (2005: 100–102).

War Crime #88. Locating a Prison in a Combat Zone. Fay/Jones Report (2004: 1042); Mikolashek Report (2004: 658–659); Miles (2006: 113); Red Cross Report (2004: 403); Schlesinger Report (2004: 63, 77).

War Crime #89. Inadequate Nutrition. Mayer (2008b); Miles (2006: 108); Physicians for Human Rights (2008: 75–76); Ratner and Ray (2004: 60); Rose (2004a); Wypijinski (2008).

War Crime #90. Inadequate Infirmary, Surgical, and Hospital Care. Ebrahim (2008); Gorman (2008a); Kurnaz (2008); *Lancet* (2004); Markon and White (2008); Miles (2006: 53–54, 61–62, 100–101); Monbiot (2008); Sullivan (2008b).

War Crime #91. Failure to Provide Care for the Disabled. Barnes (2008); Kurnaz (2008); *Lancet* (2004); Monbiot (2008).

War Crime #92. Failure to Issue Proper Medical Records. Gorman (2008a, b); A. Lewis (2004); Lifton (2004); Miles (2006: 69, 100–101); Priest (2005a); Ratner and Ray (2004: 45); Worthington (2007: 245).

War Crime #93. Failure to Weigh Prisoners. Mikolashek Report (2004: 711); Miles (2006: 109); Smith (2007b: 209–211).

War Crime #94. Failure to Detect or Treat Contagious Diseases Properly. Abbas (2008); AP (2008i); Gorman (2008a); Miles (2006: 102–103, chap. 5); Perry (2008f).

War Crime #95. Failure to Provide Appropriate Medical Records upon Release. Miles (2006: 100–101); Rashid (2003); Susman and Salman (2008); Warrick (2008b).

War Crime #96. Failure to Properly Annotate Death Certificates. Jehl and Golden (2005); A. Lewis (2004); Miles (2006: 69, 100–101); Ratner and Ray (2004: 45); Red Cross Report (2004: 390); White (2005b); Worthington (2007: 245); Wyjipewski (2008).

War Crime #97. Failure to Properly Investigate Causes of Prisoner Deaths. Ebrahim (2008); Jehl and Golden (2005); Margulies (2007: 17); Miles (2006: chap. 4, 6).

War Crime #98. Violating Medical Ethics. AP (2007b); Bloche and Marks (2005); Church Report (2005); N. Lewis (2004); Lifton (2004); Mayer (2005b, 2008b); McCoy (2006: 149, chap. 4 n.90, chap. 5 n.12, 65); Miles (2006: 53–65); Physicians for Human Rights (2005; 2008: 85–87); Ratner and Ray (2004); Red Cross Report (2004); Schlesinger Report (2004); Slevin and Stephens (2004); Xenakis (2008).

War Crime #99. Failure to Rehabilitate Victims of Torture. Arrabyee (2008); Dawn (2004); Physicians for Human Rights (2008); Saar and Novak (2005: 218); Stockman (2007).

War Crime #100. Tobacco Deprivation. Lewis and Johnston (2004); Ratner and Ray (2004: 147–149); Red Cross Report (2004: 394); Saar and Novak (2005: 168–169, 223); Smith (2007b: 147); White (2008f).

War Crime #101. Exercise Deprivation. CBC (2008a); Edwards (2008c); Hersh (2004a: 11–12); Human Rights Watch (2008a); A. Lewis (2004); Margulies (2007: 212); Press Association (2008); Ratner and Ray (2004: 56); Rose (2004a); Schmitt and Golden (2008); Worthington (2007: 131, 134); Yee (2005: 54, 60).

War Crime #102. Inadequate Recreational Opportunities. CBC (2008a); Golden (2007a); *Jurist* (2008); Margulies (2007: 213); Red Cross Report (2004: 398); Saar and Novak (2005: 65, 209); Sale (2008); Smith (2007b: 130, 136–137); Synovitz (2008); Yee (2005: 54, 60).

War Crime #103. Prisoners Transferred to Countries Practicing Torture. Austen (2008); Barry et al. (2004); Berger (2008b); Bush (2006b); Common Dreams (2008); El Khabar, (2008b); Farley (2008); Glaberson (2007b); Greenwald (2008); Grey (2006); *In re Guantánamo Detainee Cases*; Jaffer (2008); Jehl and Johnson (2005); Mayer (2005b); Norton-Taylor and Campbell (2008); Margulies (2007: 4, 186–187, 198); Mayer (2005b); McCoy (2006: chap. 4 n.26); Priest and Gellman (2002); Ratner and Ray (2004: 8, 49–51); Smith (2007b: chap. 3, 151, 245–246, 250); Suskind (2006: 76, 187); C. Smith (2005); White (2007c, 2008g); Williams (2007g).

War Crime #104. Failure to Recall Prisoners Who Have Been Tortured after Their Transfer to Other Countries. Jehl (2004b); Priest and Gellman (2002).

War Crime #105. Inhumane Transfer of Prisoners. Amnesty International (2006b); Baldauf (2008); Constable (2004); Hersh (2004a: 54); Margulies

(2007: 35, 43, 185, 192); Physicians for Human Rights (2008: 74–75); Rasul and Iqbal (2004); Ratner and Ray (2004: 36); Rose (2004a); Yee (2005: 146).

War Crime #106. Failure to Notify Prisoners in Advance of Transfers. Pelley (2005); Rose (2004a); Weinstein (2007b).

War Crime #107. Failure to Allow Prisoners to Complain about Captivity Conditions. Greenwald (2008); Hersh (2004a: 25); *In re Guantánamo Detainee Cases*; Margulies (2007: chap. 4); Schmitt (2008c); Smith (2007b: 10, 190–203, 216–217, 287, 289); *Sydney Morning Herald* (2004); Yee (2005: 75).

War Crime #108. Failure to Respond to Complaints of Prisoners Alleging Torture. Herring and Rangwala (2006: 186–187); Margulies (2007); Ratner and Ray (2004); Smith (2007b).

War Crime #109. Failure to Allow Prisoners to Elect Representatives. Margulies, personal communication, November 3, 2007.

War Crime #110. Repeated Punishment. McClellan (2008a); Monbiot (2008); Physicians for Human Rights (2008: 81–82); Red Cross Report (2004: 390–393, 398); Smith (2007b: 155, 186, 197; Worthington (2007: 86).

War Crime #111. Punishment for Offenses Not Applied to American Soldiers. Rose (2004a); Smith (2007b: 9–10).

War Crime #112. Corporal Punishment. Fay/Jones Report (2004: 1075–1076, 1081, 1083, 1095); McClellan (2008a); Monbiot (2008); Ratner and Ray (2004: 36); Saar and Novak (2005: 134); Ratner and Ray (2004: 36); Rose (2004a); Saar and Novak (2005: 134); Smith (2007b: 9–10, 197).

War Crime #113. Confinement Without Daylight. AP (2008c); Ebrahim (2008); Glaberson (2008); Human Rights Watch (2008a); *Jurist* (2008); Physicians for Human Rights (2008: 77–78); Ratner and Ray (2004: 58); Red Cross Report (2004: 392–393, 398); Schmitt and Jehl (2004); Smith (2007b: 207); Worthington (2007: 131–134, 225).

War Crime #114. Unequal Treatment of Disciplined Prisoners. Edwards (2008c); Ratner and Ray (2004: 36, 60); Saar and Novak (2005: 65); Smith (2007b: 190, 195, 203, 213).

War Crime #115. Punishment Exceeding Thirty Days. AP (2008c); Edwards (2008c); Golden (2008); Human Rights Watch (2004a: 13); Margulies (2007: 142, 218); McCoy (2006: chap. 4 n.53); Meyer (2007); Schmitt and Jehl (2004); Smith (2007b: 133, 190, 227); Synovitz (2008); Worthington (2007: 201, 214).

War Crime #116. Discipline Without Following Procedures. Edwards (2008c); Fay/Jones Report (2004: 1005, 1071); Higham and Stephens (2004); Human Rights Watch (2008a); Rose (2004a); Smith (2007b: 9–10, chap. 8).

War Crime #117. Failure to Treat Captured Belligerents as Prisoners of War. BBC (2002, 2005d); Jaffer (2008); Margulies (2007); Ratner and Ray (2004: 3, 19); Williams (2007d).

War Crime #118. Secret Detainees. Amnesty International (2006a); AP (2005b); Barry et al. (2004); BBC (2005d); Berger (2008b); Crispin (2008); Edwards (2008c); Eggen and Pincus (2007); Fay/Jones Report (2004: 990, 1044); Golden (2008); Hersh (2004a: 54); Hosenball (2008); Human Rights First (2004; 2005); Jaffer (2008); Lewis (2005); Margulies (2007: 4, 10, 177–181); Marty (2006); Mayer (2005b); Mazzetti (2007; 2008b); McCoy (2006: chap. 4 n.26); Miles (2006: 45); Priest (2005b); Priest and Gellman (2002); Ratner and Ray (2004: 75, 135); Red Cross Report (2004: 389); Ricks (2006: 199); Schmitt and Shanker (2004); Smith (2007b: chap. 9, 285–286, 289); Smith, personal communication, May 18, 2008; Taguba Report (2004); Whitlock (2007); Worthington (2007: 88).

War Crime #119. Failure to Advise Prisoners of Their Right to Counsel. Saar and Novak (2005: 76); Yee (2005: 47).

War Crime #120. Denial of Right to Counsel. Ratner and Ray (2004: 75, 85, 139); Rosenberg (2008c); Saar and Novak (2005: 23); Smith (2007b: 13, 152, 286–287, chap. 4); Williams (2008f, l, m); Worthington (2007: 230); Yee (2005: 47).

War Crime #121. Failure to Try Accused Prisoners in a Regularly Constituted Court. BBC (2007); Human Rights First (2008b); Klapper (2008).

War Crime #122. Sentencing Without Having a Regularly Constituted Court. ACLU (2008a); Arango (2007); Denbeaux and Denbeaux (2006); Gall (2008d); Glaberson (2007c, d); Hersh (2004a: 13–14); Human Rights First (2008b); Klapper (2008); Leonnig (2007); M. Levin (2008); Margulies (2007: chap. 8, 176); Miles (2006: xii, 116); Nebehay (2007); Ratner and Ray (2004: 11); Ricks (2006: 238); Smith (2007b: 152, 286–287); Taguba Report (2004); Williams (2007b, d).

War Crime #123. Failure to Use a Competent Tribunal to Determine Whether to Detain Prisoners. Greenwald (2008); Meyer (2007); Miles (2006: 11–16, 125); Rose (2004a); T. Sullivan (2008); *Sydney Morning Herald* (2004); Worthington (2007: 262; 2008b).

War Crime #124. Prisoners Have Been Forced to Renounce Their Rights. Golden (2008); Hersh (2004a: 4, 6, 27, 37, 54); Margulies (2007: 192); Ripley (2004); Smith (2007b: 106, 166, 256, 287).

War Crime #125. Depriving Prisoners of Identity Documents. Levy and Scott-Clark (2003); Harding (2004); Mikolashek Report (2004: 726–728); Moffeit (2004); Clive Stafford Smith, personal communication, May 18, 2008; Taguba Report (2004); Tuttle (2008).

War Crime #126. Failure to Disseminate Geneva Convention Provisions. BBC (2002); Mikolashek Report (2004: 726–728); Miles (2006: 49, 52); Monbiot (2003).

War Crime #127. Failure to Post the Geneva Conventions. Monbiot (2003); Smith (2007b: 230).

War Crime #128. Failure to Translate the Geneva Conventions for Prisoners. AP (2008k); Fishback (2005); Klein (2007); Yee (2005: 102, 120).

War Crime #129. Failure to Publicly State How Prisoners Are to Be Handled. Margulies (2007: 71); Sutton (2008a); White (2007b); White, Pincus, and Tate (2008).

War Crime #130. Failure to Transmit Legal Documents to Prisoners. Edwards (2008c); Golden (2008); Glaberson (2007b); Kendall (2008); Mazzetti (2007); McCoy (2006: chap. 5 n.63); Meyer (2008d, e); Priest and Gellman (2002); Ratner and Ray (2004: 79); Smith (2007a, b: 9, 128–129, 132, 287); Sutton (2008a); White (2007b); White, Pincus, and Tate (2008); Williams (2007d, 2008j).

War Crime #131. Failure to Allow Visits Between Lawyers and Prisoners. AP (2008f); Bazelon and Lithwik (2008); Bush (2003a; 2006a); Davis (2007); El Akkad (2008); Ephron (2008); Falkoff (2007); Gilson (2006); Glaberson (2007a, d); *International Herald Tribune* (2006); Leonnig (2007); D. Levin (2008); Margulies (2007: 163); Mazzetti and Shane (2008); Melia (2008c); Meyer (2007); *NYT* (2008c); Murphy (2008a); Ratner and Ray (2004: 85); Savage (2007); Smith (2007b: chap. 4, 93–99, 123); U.S. Department of Defense (2003); White (2008a); White, Pincus, and Tate (2008); Williams (2007c, e; 2008c, h, m); Worthington (2008a, b).

War Crime #132. Failure to Put Prisoners on Trial in Impartial Tribunals. ACLU (2008a); Denbeaux et al. (2008); Greenwald (2008); Human Rights Watch (2004a: 32–33; 2008b); M. Levin (2008); Margulies (2007: 42); McCoy (2006: chap. 4 n.31, 5n.64); Monbiot (2008); Rasul and Iqbal (2004); Ratner and Ray (2004: 56, 59); Smith (2007b: 135); White (2008b); Williams (2008d, l); Worden (2004); Worthington (2007: 239–240).

War Crime #133. Forced Self-Incrimination. ACLU (2008a); Golden (2008); Golden and Rohde (2008); Ratner and Ray (2004: ix, 22, 72, 74, 78, 80); Rondeaux, White, and Tate (2008); Williams (2008g); Worthington (2008a).

War Crime #134. Failure to Provide Speedy Trials. Gall (2008d); Glaberson (2007b); *International News* (2008); Leonnig (2007); Saar and Novak (2005: 95–96); Schmitt and Golden (2008); Rondeaux, White, and Tate (2008); Smith (2007b: 151); Smith and Salman (2007); Susman (2008c); Synovitz (2008); White (2007a); Williams (2007d; 2008m).

War Crime #135. Denial of the Right to Call Witnesses. Gall (2008dc); M. Levin (2008); Melia (2008d); Nebehay (2007); O'Neill (2007); Smith (2007b: 92, 152); White, Pincus, and Tate (2008); Williams (2007d; 2008b); Worthington (2007: 265–266; 2008d).

War Crime #136. Failure to Advise Prisoners of Geneva Convention Rights. Gilson (2006); Taguba Report (2004: 418).

War Crime #137. Failure to Facilitate Selection by Prisoners of Their Attorneys. Melia (2008b); Reidy (2008); Rosenberg (2008f); Smith (2007b: 11, chap. 4); Sullivan (2008a); White (2008a); Williams (2008a, f, m); Worthington (2008b).

War Crime #138. Failure to Allow the United Nations to Provide Attorneys for Prisoners. See Margulies (2007) and Smith (2007b).

War Crime #139. Failure to Provide Attorneys Free Access to Prisoners. Glaberson (2007a); Human Rights First (2008b: #204); Loney (2008); McCoy (2006: chap. 5n.63); Smith (2007b: 9, 132); Sullivan (2008b); White (2007b).

War Crime #140. Failure to Provide Privacy During Visits Between Attorneys and Prisoners. Ratner and Ray (2004: 77); Smith (2007b: 12); Sutton (2008a); White, Pincus, and Tate (2008); Worthington (2007: 264).

War Crime #141. Failure to Translate Legal Documents for Prisoners. AFP (2008h); Loney (2008); Smith (2007a); Williams (2008m).

War Crime #142. No Right of Appeal. Human Rights First (2008b: #4-5); Saar and Novak (2005: 160); Williams (2008l).

War Crime #143. Failure to Inform Prisoners Promptly of Charges against Them. Arango (2007); Cambanis (2004); Gilson (2006); Golden (2008); Greenhouse (2008); Jaffer (2008); Leonnig (2007); Ricks (2006: 238); Schmitt and Golden (2008); Smith (2007b: 88, 152); Smith and Salman (2007); Synovitz (2008); Taguba Report (2004); Weinstein (2007b); Williams (2007c, m).

War Crime #144. Failure to Inform Prisoners' Attorneys of Charges against Prisoners Whom They Represent. Arango (2007).

War Crime #145. Secrecy in Judicial Proceedings. Freeze (2006); Glaberson (2007d); Greenhouse (2008); Human Rights First (2008b: 204); Jehl and Schmitt (2004); Leonnig (2007); M. Levin (2008); Meyer (2008b, c); Smith (2007b: 152, 288); Sullivan (2008b); Williams (2007d; 2008l, m).

War Crime #146. Failure to Prosecute Those Responsible for Prisoner Deaths. Ackerman (2004); AP (2008w); Human Rights First (2006a: 3); Martin (2004); Miles (2006: chap. 4, 6); Red Cross Report (2004: 400); Sharrock (2008); Worthington (2007: 190).

War Crime #147. Absolving Liability for Redress. Congress (2008c); Robinson (2008); Schidgen (2005); *USA Today* (2005b).

War Crime #148. Refusal to Allow Cross-Examinations. M. Levin (2008); Ratner and Ray (2004: 75); Rosenberg (2008d); White, Pincus, and Tate (2008); Williams (2008m); Worthington (2008a).

War Crime #149. Failure to Provide Appropriate Legal Advice to Military Commanders Regarding Prisoners. Davey (2005); Eggen (2008b); Elliott (2003); Fay/Jones Report (2004: 1015); Harvey and Schoomaker

(2005); Hersh (2004a: 41–42); A. Lewis (2004); Martin (2004); McClellan (2008a); McCoy (2006: 123); Red Cross Report (2004: 400); Ross and Salomon (2004); Schmidt Report (2005: 8, 11); Schmitt (2008b); Williams (2008c); Williams, personal communication, April 3, 2008; Wypijewski (2008); Worthington (2007: 174).

War Crime #150. Failure to Prosecute Commanding Officers for Taking No Action to Stop Abuse against Prisoners. Fay/Jones Report (2004: 1071, 1091, 1110–1101, 1113); Ricks (2006: 260); Hersh (2004a: 42); Mayer (2008a); Miles (2006: chap. 3); Priest (2005a); Red Cross Report (2004: 400); White (2005a); Schmidt Report (2005: 8, 11); Smith (2007b: 287); Williams (2008c); Williams, personal communication, April 3, 2008; Yee (2005: 115).

War Crime #151. Failure of Commanding Officers to Report Offenses against Prisoners to Superiors. Fay/Jones Report (2004: 1005–1006, 1011, 1092, 1109, 1111); Hersh (2004a: 26); Human Rights Watch (2005c); *NYT* (2007a); Ricks (2006: 260); Saar and Novak (2005: 161); Sanchez (2008a); Schmitt (2008b); Taguba Report (2004: 418); *WP* (2007).

War Crime #152. Failure of Commanding Officers to Ensure That Subordinates Understand Geneva Convention Obligations Regarding Prisoners. Elliott (2003); Fay/Jones Report (2004: 989, 1005–1006, 1071, 1111, 1113); B. Ferguson (2008); Jehl and Schmitt (2004); Karpinski (2005); M. Levin (2008); Lichtblau and Shane (2008); Margulies (2007: 5); McCoy (2006: chap. 4 n.69, 76); Mikolashek Report (2004: 650–654); *NYT* (2007a); Schmidt Report (2005: 1); Shane, Johnson, and Risen (2007); Williams (2008m); Worden (2004); Worthington (2007: 203); *WP* (2007); Yee (2005: 112, 132).

War Crime #153. Failure of Commanding Officers to Prevent or Stop Subordinates from Mistreating Prisoners. AFP (2008d); Danner (2004); DIA Report (2004); Elliott (2003); Fay/Jones Report (2004: 989, 1007, 1092, 1113–1114); Gourevitch and Morris (2008); Harvey and Schoomaker (2005); Jehl and Schmitt (2004); Johnson (2008); Margulies (2007: 17, 215); Mayer (2008b); McClellan (2008a); *NYT* (2007a); Ricks (2006: 260, 282); Schlesinger Report (2004); Schmidt Report (2005: 16); Schmitt (2008b); Williams (2008c); Williams, personal communication, April 3, 2008; *WP* (2007); Yee (2005: 115).

War Crime #154. Failure of Commanding Officers to Discipline or Prosecute Subordinates Who Mistreat Prisoners. Eggen (2008b, d); Eggen and Pincus (2007); A. Lewis (2004); Mazzetti (2007); Miller and Schmitt (2007); New York University (2008); Shane, Johnson, and Risen (2007); Singh and Jaffer (2007); Worth (2006).

War Crime #155. Attempting to Justify Torture. Congress (2008b); Denbeaux et al. (2008); Eggen and Pincus (2007); Eggen and Warrick (2007); Eggen and White (2005); Faith (2008); Froomkin (2008a); Golden (2005b); A. Lewis (2004); Meyer (2007); Ratner and Ray (2004: 85); Sands interview; Shane (2008b); White (2008b); Williams (2008e); Williams, personal communication, April 3, 2008.

War Crime #156. Failure to Arrest and Prosecute Torturers. Baker and Warrick (2007); Denbeaux et al. (2008); Golden (2005b); *In re Guantánamo Detainee Cases*; Hersh (2007); Jehl (2004a); Mayer (2008a, b); Priest (2005a); Taguba Report.

War Crime #157. Failure to Investigate Allegations of Torture. Baker and Warrick (2007); Eggen and Pincus (2007); Eggen and Warrick (2007); Nebehay (2007); Priest (2005b); UN Commission on Human Rights (2005); White (2008b).

War Crime #158. Refusal to Cooperate in Investigations and Prosecutions of Torturers. Baldauf (2008); C. Ferguson (2008: 298, 392); McDoom (2008); Monbiot (2008); New York University (2008); White (2008g); Williams (2008m); Worthington (2008b).

War Crime #159. Failure to Compensate Victims of Torture. Congress (2008c); Davis (2008); Denbeaux et al. (2008); Eggen (2008d); El Khabar (2008a); Farley (2008); *In re Guantánamo Detainee Cases*; Lasseter (2008a, b); Melia (2008a); Meyer (2007); Ratner and Ray (2004: 42–43); Rouse (2008); White (2008b); White, Pincus, and Tate (2008); Worthington (2007: 209–214).

War Crime #160. Admission of Statements Resulting from Torture into Evidence. AFP (2008c); Danner (2004); Davies (2006); *The Economist* (2008a); Golden (2008); Harvey (2008); Hentoff (2008); Higham (2004); Jehl and Lewis (2004); Jehl and Schmitt (2004); Human Rights First (2008b: 4); Kendall (2008); Klapper (2008); Klein (2008); Margulies, personal communication, November 9, 2007; Markon (2008a); Mazzetti (2007); Miles (2006: xii, 45, 54–55, 127); Priest and Gellman (2002); Ratner and Ray (2004: 40, 61); Schmitt and Shanker (2004); Taguba Report; Vine (2008).

War Crime #161. Refusal to Allow the Red Cross Access to Prisoners. Congress (2008d); Fisher (2004b); Margulies, personal communication, November 9, 2007; Smith (2007b: 288); Worthington (2007: 321).

War Crime #162. Failure to Establish a Central Prisoner of War Agency. See citations of Amnesty International, Human Rights First, Human Rights Watch, and the International Committee of the Red Cross in the References.

War Crime #163. Failure to Request Assistance from a Humanitarian Organization. Fisher (2004b).

War Crime #164. Prisoners Prevented from Contacting the Red Cross and the Red Crescent Society. Margulies, personal communication, November 9, 2007.

War Crime #165. Parcels to Prisoners Disallowed. AP (2008t); Golden (2008); Grey (2006); Iraqi Red Crescent Organization (2007); Margulies (2007: 71, 142, 205, 211); Margulies, personal communication, November 9, 2007; Monbiot (2003); Priest (2005b); Red Cross Report (2004: 389; 2006); UN Commission on Human Rights (2005); Wypijewski (2008).

War Crime #166. Failure to Allow Prisoners to Complain to UN Bodies. Miles (2006: chap. 4); Physicians for Human Rights (2008: 87); Clive Stafford Smith, personal communication, February 20, 2008.

War Crime #167. Failure to Share Inquest Investigations with the UN. Ebrahim (2008); Golden (2008); Margulies, personal communication, November 9, 2007.

War Crime #168. Failure to Provide Opportunities for Nongovernmental Organizations to Assist the Religious and Other Needs of Prisoners. Canadian Press (2008b).

War Crime #169. Denial of Access of UN Agencies to Places of Departure, Passage, Arrival, and Incarceration. Gilson (2006); Greenwald (2008); Nebehay (2007); Clive Stafford Smith, personal communication, February 20, 2008; UN Commission on Human Rights (2005).

War Crime #170. Failure to Allow UN Officials to Attend Arraignments. A. Lewis (2004).

War Crime #171. Failure to Repatriate Prisoners Promptly. AFP (2008j); Al-Qiri (2008); Al-Sahwa (2008); AP (2008c, w); Arango (2007); Baldauf (2008); BBC (2005d); Butler (2008); Denbeaux and Denbaux (2006); El Khabar (2008c); Fay/Jones Report (2004: 1043, 1008); Glaberson (2007b); Golden (2005b); Golden and Rohde (2008); Gray (2008); Herring and Rangwala (2006: 188); Hersh (2004a: 14, 30–31); Human Rights Watch (2004a: 32–33); Jaffer (2008); Kurnaz (2008); Lasseter (2008a, b); Margulies (2007: 66–67, 226); Mayer (2005a, b, 2008b); McCoy(2006: chap. 5 n.59); Miles (2006: 50); Miller (2002); Monbiot (2003; 2008); Red Cross Report (2004); Rose (2004a); Saar and Novak (2005: 193, 208); Savage (2007); Smith (2007b: 91, 156–157, 203, 256, 287); Synovitz (2008); U.S. Department of Defense (2006); Vaznis (2008); White (2008d); Whoriskey (2008); Williams (2007g; 2008e, h-l); Woodward (2003: 67); Worth (2008); Worthington (2008c).

War Crime #172. Failure to Repatriate Seriously Ill or Wounded Prisoners. Cageprisoners (2008); Ebrahim (2008); R. Edwards (2008a); Gall (2008c); Golden (2005b); Gorman (2008a); *LAT* (2008); McGuirk (2007); Meyer (2008a); Miles (2006: chap. 4–5); Patterson (2007); Rietig (2008); Tuttle (2008); Williams (2007d).

War Crime #173. Denial and Delay of Correspondence Between Prisoners and Their Families. Amnesty International (2006a: 13); CNN (2005a);

Constable (2004); Ebrahim (2008); *Guardian* (2005); Kreickenbaum (2004); Mackay (2003a); Margulies (2007: 205); Monbiot (2003); Ratner and Ray (2004: 60); Ricks (2006: 199, 238); Rose (2004a); Saar and Novak (2005: 47); Salam (2006); *Sydney Morning Herald* (2004); Weinstein (2007a); White (2007b); Williams (2008g).

War Crime #174. Prisoners Have Not Been Allowed to Send Telegrams. CBC (2008a); Gall (2008c, e); Rosenberg (2008e); Smith (2007b: 132, 141, 203); Sutton (2008b).

War Crime #175. Failure to Compensate Dependents of Fatal Victims of Torture. Austen (2007); Jehl and Schmitt (2004); Muir (2007); Rouse (2008).

War Crime #176. Sexual Abuse of Females. Ackerman (2004); BBC (2005d); Booth (2008); Chandrasekaran (2006: 101); Fay/Jones Report (2004: 1074, 1091); Golden (2005b); Novak and Waller (2004); Miles (2006: 124); Provance (2006); Taguba Report.

War Crime #177. Women Confined in Same Prison Facility as Men. Booth (2008); Fay/Jones Report (2004: 1086); Miles (2006: 124); Red Cross Report (2004: 398); Taguba Report (2004: 455).

War Crime #178. Women Prisoners Searched by Men. Ackerman (2004); BBC (2005d); Chandrasekaran (2006: 101); Fay/Jones Report (2004: 1074, 1091); Golden (2005b); Miles (2006: 124); Novak and Waller (2004); Provance (2006); Taguba Report.

War Crime #179. Discrimination Based on Nationality, Race, or Religion. Ratner and Ray (2004: 5); Smith (2007b: 142); Williams (2008a); Woodward (2003: 114, 121–122); Worthington (2007: 102, 104, 129, 140, 229); Yee (2005).

War Crime #180. Elder Abuse. Dodds (2005); Hersh (2004a: 2); Mariner (2002); Ratner and Ray (2004: 67); Saar and Novak (2005: 124–126); Smith (2007b: 151).

War Crime #181. Transfer of Children from Their Home Countries. Astill (2004); Canwest (2008); Conover (2005); Constable (2004); Farley (2007); Greenwald (2008); Hersh (2004a: 371); Jamison (2005: 127, 136); Red Cross Report (2004: 390–391); Saar and Novak (2005: 47, 114); Smith (2005, 2007b: 152–151).

War Crime #182. Failure to Obtain Permission from Parents or Guardians for Transfer of Their Children. Astill (2004); BBC (2005d); Conover (2005); Constable (2004); Farley (2007); Smith (2005, 2007b: 245).

War Crime #183. Incarceration of Children in the Same Quarters as Adults. Fay/Jones Report (2004: 1082–1083, 1086); Higham and Stephens (2004); Keller (2008); Provance (2006); Smith (2007b: 142); Wilson (2006).

War Crime #184. Failure to Provide Education for Imprisoned Children. Wilson (2006).

War Crime #185. Withholding Parental Contact from Child Detainees. Farley (2007); Hersh (2004a: 369); Ratner and Ray (2004: 68).

War Crime #186. Failure to Inform Parents of the Whereabouts of Detained Children. Astill (2004); Farley (2007); Ricks (2006: 199); Ratner and Ray (2004: 68); C. Smith (2005); Smith (2007b: 230); Suskind (2006: 230); Taguba Report (2004: 416).

War Crime #187. Refusal to Allow Child Detainees to Receive Information. Canadian Press (2008c); Farley (2007); Wilson (2006).

War Crime #188. Failure to Protect Child Detainees from Abuse. AP (2008a); Astill (2004); Benjamin (2006); Farley (2007); Fay/Jones Report (2004: 1083, 1086, 1090); *Jurist* (2008); Keller (2008); Melia (2008a); Smith (2007b: 190); Williams (2008f, m).

War Crime #189. Failure to Provide Social Programs for Child Detainees to Deal with Prison Abuse. Farley (2007); *Jurist* (2008); Margulies (2007: 67).

War Crime #190. Failure to Establish Programs to Prevent Prison Abuse of Child Detainees. AP (2008t); Benjamin (2006); Farley (2007); Fay/Jones Report (2004: 1083, 1086, 1090); Margulies (2007: 67); Williams (2008m).

War Crime #191. Failure to Investigate Abuse of Child Prisoners. Benjamin (2006); Farley (2007); Fay/Jones Report (2004: 1086); Keller (2008); Noronha (2008).

War Crime #192. Failure to Prosecute Prison Personnel Who Abuse Child Detainees. Benjamin (2006); Farley (2007); Fay/Jones Report (2004: 1086); Keller (2008); Melia (2008a); Shephard (2007).

War Crime #193. Failure to Provide Recreational Activities for Child Prisoners. Canadian Press (2008c); Smith (2007b: 130, 136–137); Wilson (2006).

War Crime #194. Inhumane Treatment of Child Detainees. AP (2004a, 2008h); Benjamin (2006); Constable (2004); S. Edwards (2008a); Farley (2007); Fay/Jones Report (2004: 1083, 1086, 1090); Higham and Stephens (2004); *Jurist* (2008); *Khadr v Bush*, Appendix G; Melia (2008a); C. Smith (2005; 2007b: 147, 345); Tietz (2006); Williams (2008m); Worthington (2008d).

War Crime #195. Indefinite Detainment of Children. Farley (2007); Hersh (2004a: 371); *Jurist* (2008); Williams (2008m).

War Crime #196. Failure to Allow Parents to Visit Child Detainees. Farley (2007); Ricks (2006: 199).

War Crime #197. Failure to Allow Child Prisoners to Have Legal Counsel. Farley (2007); *Jurist* (2008); Pine (2008); Shephard (2007); Smith (2007b: 152).

War Crime #198. Failure to Provide an Impartial Tribunal for Child Prisoners. Farley (2007); Glaberson (2007d); Margulies (2007: 42); Melia

(2008b); Reidy (2008); Rosenberg (2008f); Shephard (2008a); Smith (2007b: 135); White (2008a, b); Williams (2008a, f, I, m).

War Crime #199. Failure to Provide Speedy Trials for Child Prisoners. Farley (2007); *Jurist* (2008); Williams (2008l).

War Crime #200. Failure to Provide Post-Confinement Social Programs for Abused Child Prisoners. Human Rights Watch (2007c); *Jurist* (2008); Margulies (2007: 67); Sanders (2006).

War Crime #201. Presumption of the Guilt of Child Prisoners Before Trials. Farley (2007); Smith (2007b: 152); Williams (2007c).

War Crime #202. Failure to Promptly Inform Child Prisoners of Charges against Them. Farley (2007); Smith (2007b: 152).

War Crime #203. Forcing a Child Prisoner to Incriminate Himself. Farley (2007); Melia (2008a); U.S. Department of Defense (2004b); Williams (2007c).

War Crime #204. Failure to Allow Witnesses to Testify on Behalf of Child Prisoners. Farley (2007); Melia (2008a); Smith (2007b: 152); Williams (2007e, 2008m); Worthington (2008b).

War Crime #205. Failure to Allow Appeals from Legal Proceedings of Child Prisoners. Saar and Novak (2005: 160).

War Crime #206. Extraordinary Renditions. Booth (2008); Froomkin (2008b); Grey (2006); Horton (2008a); Jehl (2005); Marty (2006); Monbiot (2003); Smith (2007b: 230); Worthington (2007: chap. 16).

War Crime #207. Issuance of Executive Orders Authorizing Enforced Disappearances. Bush's Executive Order of January 18, 2002; Red Cross Report (2004: 389).

War Crime #208. Failure to Prosecute Those Responsible for Enforced Disappearances. Priest (2005a).

War Crime #209. Sending Prisoners to Countries Where Enforced Disappearance Is Likely. Grey (2006); *Ottawa Recorder* (2008); Smith (2007b: 245, 283); Whitlock (2005); Worthington (2007: chap. 16).

War Crime #210. Failure to Disclose Basic Information About Victims of Enforced Disappearance to Appropriate Authorities. BBC (2005d); Whitlock (2005).

War Crime #211. Failure to Disclose Basic Information About Victims of Enforced Disappearance to Family and Legal Representatives. BBC (2005d).

War Crime #212. Failure to Provide Verification of Release of Disappeared Detainees. Margulies (2007: 192); Priest (2005a).

War Crime #213. Failure to Inform Rendered Persons of the Reasons for Their Disappearance, Investigation of Their Case, and Plans for Their Future. Margulies (2007: 64, chap. 10).

War Crime #214. Failure to Release Disappeared Persons. Smith (2007b: 289).

War Crime #215. Failure to Return the Bodies of Those Who Die While Disappeared to Next of Kin. Margulies (2007: 136); Miles (2006: 89).

War Crime #216. Failure to Provide Reparation and Compensation to Victims of Enforced Disappearance. Gans (2007); Saar and Novak (2005: 208); Susman and Salman (2008).

War Crime #217. Failure to Cooperate with NGOs Seeking to Rescue Victims of Enforced Disappearance. *The Economist* (2008a); Human Rights First (2004); Human Rights Watch (2005b); Red Cross Report (2004: 402).

War Crime #218. Failure to Re-Establish Public Order and Safety. Allawi (2007: 94, 157–159, 165, 170, 175, 189, 202, 372–374, 379); Amnesty International (2003); Anon. (2008a, b); Aylwin-Foster (2005); Burns (2008); Center for Economic and Social Rights (2005: chap. 5–6); Chandrasekaran (2006: 22, 31, 46, 69, 84, 100–101, 190, 326); Ciezadlo (2005); Constable (2003); Diamond (2005: 46); Fallows (2004); C. Ferguson (2008: chap. 3–4, 96–97, 373–374, chap. 6–7, 418–419, 436–437, 463, 476); FitzGerald (2002); Galbraith (2004a, b); Gall (2008a); Glasser (2002); Gordon and Trainor (2006); Herring and Rangwala (2006: 188–189, 216); Human Rights Watch (2003a: 23); Massing (2008); Parker (2008a); Parker and Redha (2008); Perito (2007); Public Broadcasting System (2008); Raghavan and Fainaru (2007); Rashid (2004); Salman (2008); Susman (2007); Woodward (2003: 317); Zavis (2008c, g).

War Crime #219. Complicity with Pillage. Allawi (2007: 118, 162, 184, 188, 258–260, 262, 359, chap. 19); Chandrasekaran (2006: 51); Cockburn (2006: 75); Corbin (2008); C. Ferguson (2008: xi); Fick (2007); Galbraith (2004a); Harriman (2005); Judah (2003); Rodenbeck (2003); Scahill (2007a: 86); Wright (2007).

War Crime #220. Failure to Apprehend and Prosecute Looters. Allawi (2007: 115, 367–368); Chandrasekaran (2006: 288); Eakin (2008a); Enders (2003); C. Ferguson (2008: xi, 96, chap. 3, 297, 306); Guggenheim (2004); Ricks (2006: 275).

War Crime #221. Failure to Provide Security for Hospitals. Center for Economic and Social Rights (2005: chap. 6); Galbraith (2004a); Judah (2003); Van Moorter (2004).

War Crime #222. Intimidation of Civilians from Living Ordinary Lives. C. Ferguson (2008: 316–317, 385); Gall (2008a); Gans (2007); Gordon (2008b); Harriman (2007); Human Rights Watch (2004b); Massing (2008a); Oppel (2006); Ricks (2006: 233–235); Rieckhoff (2007); Van Moorter (2004).

War Crime #223. Failure to Stop the Theft of Cultural Property. AP (2008o); Derhally (2008); C. Ferguson (2008: 111, 117–118, 137); Herring and Rangwala (2006: 217); Judah (2003); McElroy (2008); Ricks

(2006: 176–178); Rodenbeck (2003); World Tribunal on Iraq, (2005); Zavis (2008a).

War Crime #224. Failure to Protect Journalists. AFP (2008a); Allawi (2007: 154–155, 270, 380); Arango (2007); Arie (2005); CBC (2008b); Canadian Press (2008a); Chandrasekaran (2006: 152–153, 300); Cockburn (2006: 135); Coghlan (2008); C. Ferguson (2008: 261, 345, 390–391); Gall (2008d); Herring and Rangwala (2006: 27, 62–65); *LAT* (2008); Massing (2004); Poole (2005); Qader-Saadi (2007); Scahill (2007a: 120–121, 139–140); Smith (2007b: chap. 7); Susman (2008b); World Tribunal on Iraq (2005); Worthington (2007: 143); Zavis and Rasheed (2008).

War Crime #225. Failure to Respect the Legal Framework. Ahmed (2004); Allawi (2007: 433–434); Center for Economic and Social Rights (2005: chap. 13); Chandrasekaran (2006: 101, 268); C. Ferguson (2008: 327–328, 332–333); Gall (2008a); Herring and Rangwala (2006: 228); Liptak (2004); Massing (2008a); Mishra (2005); Patel (2004); Scahill (2007a: 80; 2008b); *Sydney Morning Herald* (2005); Verlöy (2003); Worthington (2007: 123, 244, 251).

War Crime #226. Failure to Allow Self-Government. Allawi (2007: 86, 88, 91, 102, 105–106, 110–111, 119–120, 139, 164, 167, 169, 187, 191, 201–202, 212, 221, 224, 304); Burns and Shanker (2004); Center for Economic and Social Rights (2005: chap. 4); Cockburn (2006: 161); Deen (2008); Diamond (2005: 37, 50, 140); Dreazen and Cooper (2004); *The Economist* (2008); C. Ferguson (2008: 34–35, 42, 141, 266–275, 474); Galbraith (2004b); Gall (2008a); Haynes (2008); Herring and Rangwala (2006: 16, 33, 86–89, 110–111); Leopold (2004); Massing (2008); Mishra (2005); Paley and De Young (2008); E. Parker (2008); Parker and Hameed (2008); Rashid (2004); Reuters (2008a); Scahill (2007a: 86); Shanker and Schmitt (2004).

War Crime #227. Failure to Recognize Local Courts. AFP (2008a); Allawi (2007: 433–434); Herring and Rangwala (2006: 88, 188–190); Parker (2008c); Reuters (2008d); Schmitt and Golden (2008); Smith and Salman (2007).

War Crime #228. Unwarranted Interrogation of Civilians. Allawi (2007: 167); Chandrasekaran (2006: 274); C. Ferguson (2008: 391); Massing (2008a).

War Crime #229. Collective Punishment. Center for Economic and Social Rights (2005: chap. 8); Efron (2005); Filkins (2003); World Tribunal on Iraq (2005).

War Crime #230. Cruel Treatment of Civilians. Allawi (2007: 167); C. Ferguson (2008: 316–317, 385); Human Rights Watch (2004b); Massing (2008a); Rashid (2004); Whitmire (2005).

War Crime #231. Unjustified Arrest of Children. Rashid (2004); Worthington (2007: 252).

War Crime #232. Unjustified Internment. AFP (2008j); Worthington (2007: 246).

War Crime #233. Transfer to Countries That Persecute Political Opinions. Grey (2006); Hersh (2004a: 44–45); Human Rights Watch (2004a: 28–29); McCoy (2006: 143, chap. 4 n.81); Worthington (2007: 148).

War Crime #234. Failure to Observe Existing Penal Laws. Ballavia (2007); Chandrasekaran (2006: 268); Gans (2007); Golden and Rohde (2008); Harriman (2007).

War Crime #235. Penalties Imposed for Past Acts. See CPA Orders 1 and 2 in www.cpa-iraq.org/regulations.

War Crime #236. Disproportionate Penal Servitude. Worthington (2007: chap. 16).

War Crime #237. Interned Persons, Prisoners of War, and Common Criminals Accommodated and Administered Together. Hersh (2004a: 32); McCoy (2006: chap. 4 n.56); Worden (2004); Worthington (2007: chap. 16).

War Crime #238. Failure to Account for Missing Persons. Worthington (2007: 226, 266).

War Crime #239. Failure to Ensure Fair Trials of Repatriated Prisoners. Bowman (2008); Rondeux, White, and Tate (2008).

War Crime #240. Confiscation of Private Property. Allawi (2007: 372); *Arab News* (2008); Constable (2003); De Young (2008); Herring and Rangwala (2006: 114, 187); Londoño (2008); Massing (2008); Pelton (2006: 112–113); Rashid (2004); Ricks (2006: 275).

War Crime #241. Lowering Tax Revenues. Baker (2004); Herring and Rangwala (2006: 226–227); Jackson (2008); Milbank and Pincus (2003); Pelton (2006: 113).

War Crime #242. Secret Contract Awards. AFP (2008g); Allawi (2007: 364); Harriman (2005; 2007); Herring and Rangwala (2006: 249); Warde (2004).

War Crime #243. Diversion of State Property for Nonmilitary Operations. Center for Economic and Social Rights (2005: chap. 13); Center for Public Integrity (2006: 287, 289); Chandrasekaran (2006: 326); Harriman (2005; 2007); Herring and Rangwala (2006: 241–243, 248, 257); Juhasz (2006); Pelton (2006: 113); Scahill (2007a: 88).

War Crime #244. Privatizing State Assets. Allawi (2007: 196–197, 264); Center for Economic and Social Rights (2005: chap. 13); Center for Public Integrity (2006: 287); Chandrasekaran (2006: 133–143, 253); C. Ferguson (2008: 310); Galbraith (2004b); Herring and Rangwala (2006: 225, 227–229); Juhasz (2006); Pelton (2006: 113); Scahill (2007a: 88); World Tribunal on Iraq (2005).

War Crime #245. Failure to Maintain Material Conditions of State Property. Allawi (2007: 248, 258); Chandrasekaran (2006: 23, 35–37, 45, 51, 190, 326); Cha (2004); Chatterjee and Docena (2003/2004);

C. Ferguson (2008: chap. 3, 296–311); Harriman (2007); Hedgepeth and Paley (2008); Massing (2000b); Perry (2008c); Schildgen (2005); Zavis (2008p).

War Crime #246. Mass Unemployment. Center for Economic and Social Rights (2005: chap. 12); C. Ferguson (2008: 148, 310, 314, 342, 345); Herring and Rangwala (2006: 222); Van Moorter (2004); Whitney (2008).

War Crime #247. Failure to Provide Re-Employment Opportunities. CBC (2003); Chandrasekaran (2006: 236); C. Ferguson (2008: 290, 302); Galbraith (2004b); Herring and Rangwala (2006: 73–74, 238); Sale (2003); Spinner (2004); UN (2004b).

War Crime #248. Unnecessary Destruction of Private Property. C. Ferguson (2008: 388, 392); Herring and Rangwala (2006: 27); Human Rights Watch (2004b); Ricks (2006: 233–235); Wilkinson (2003).

War Crime #249. Unnecessary Destruction of State Property. Daily War News (2004); Silvey (2004).

War Crime #250. Failure to Provide Necessities of Daily Living. Allawi (2007: 374–376); Booker (2008); Center for Economic and Social Rights (2005: chap. 9); Cockburn (2006: 83, 86); Colt (2008); Danner (2004); C. Ferguson (2008: 92–94, 296–311, 334, 351, 397, 420–421, 431–432, 468); FitzGerald (2002); Galbraith (2004a, b); Gordon (2008a); J. Gordon (2007); Herring and Rangwala (2006: 56–71, 91–92, 216); *Iraq Oil Report* (2008); Massing (2008a); Miller (2008); Mu (2008); Rashid (2004); Whitney (2008); Witte (2006); Yoshino (2008).

War Crime #251. Failure to Respect Religious Convictions. Allawi (2007: 384).

War Crime #252. Ethnosectarian Discrimination. C. Ferguson (2008: 356, 422, 430).

War Crime #253. Discrimination in Awarding Contracts. Allawi (2007: 253); BBC (2008b); Center for Economic and Social Rights (2005: chap. 13); Cha (2004); Chandrasekaran (2006: 317); Chatterjee and Docena (2003/2004); C. Ferguson (2008: 298–301, 306–307); Galbraith (2004b); Herring and Rangwala (2006: 77, 227, 236–237, 240).

War Crime #254. Gender Discrimination. Cockburn (2006: 197–198); Mishra (2005); Rashid (2004).

War Crime #255. Dishonoring Women. Herring and Rangwala (2006: 217); Rashid (2004); Spring and Kaplow (2008); World Tribunal on Iraq (2005).

War Crime #256. Discrimination Against Nominal Members of a Political Party. Allawi (2007: 376); Chandrasekaran (2006: 79); C. Ferguson (2008: 152, 156); Herring and Rangwala (2006: 111).

War Crime #257. Arrest of Persons for Pre-Occupation Political Opinions. Allawi (2007: 337, 376, 383); Gall (2008a); Worthington (2007: chap. 16).

War Crime #258. Failure to Respect Family Honors. Allawi (2007: 186, 433–434); Mishra (2005).

War Crime #259. Withholding News from Family Members. C. Ferguson (2008: 321); Gettleman (2004a); Herring and Rangwala (2006: 188); Massing (2008); Red Cross Report (2004: 388–389); Ricks (2006: 199); Sharnberg (2005).

War Crime #260. Charging for Formerly Free Government Services. Chandrasekaran (2006: 242).

War Crime #261. Failure to Reopen Schools. Allawi (2007: 267, 382); Center for Economic and Social Rights (2005: chap. 11); C. Ferguson (2008: 156, 159, 422); Harriman (2007).

War Crime #262. Failure to Restore Cultural Property Damaged by Military Operations. Chandrasekaran (2006: 190, 326).

War Crime #263. Providing Insufficient Food. Allawi (2007: 312, 376); Center for Economic and Social Rights (2005: chap. 11); C. Ferguson (2008: 159); Fowler (2005); Van Moorter (2004).

War Crime #264. Providing Insufficient Medical Supplies. Chandrasekaran (2006: 237, 247, 326); Galbraith (2004a, b); Integrated Regional Information Networks (2004b); Massing (2008b); Van Moorter (2004).

War Crime #265. Reduction in the Quality of Medical Care. Center for Economic and Social Rights (2005: chap. 10); Chandrasekaran (2006: 237, 326); C. Ferguson (2008: 158, 345, 374); Galbraith (2004b); Gettleman (2004b); Whitney (2008).

War Crime #266. Reduction in the Quality of Public Health. Allawi (2007: 372); Center for Economic and Social Rights (2005: chap. 10); Chandrasekaran (2006: 295, 326); C. Ferguson (2008: 420, 422, 469); U.N. Food and Agriculture Organization (2003); Galbraith (2004a); Goode (2008); Gordon (2008a); Herring and Rangwala (2006: 267); Integrated Regional Information Networks (2004a); Soriano and Komarow (2004); Van Moorter (2004); World Tribunal on Iraq (2005); Zavis (2008e).

War Crime #267. Flouting UN Recommendations. Allawi (2007: 359); Diamond (2005: 54–58); C. Ferguson (2008: 295, 299, 319–320); Van Moorter (2004).

War Crime #268. Failure to Accept Relief Organizations. Clark (2003); Miles (2006: 113); Red Cross Report (2004); Rodenbeck (2003).

War Crime #269. Failure to Disseminate the Fourth Geneva Convention Text to Occupation Personnel. See CPA Orders in www.cpa-iraq.org/regulations.

REFERENCES

Abbas, Ala. (2008). "Guantánamo Detainee Denied Treatment for AIDS." Jurist, March 28.

ABC. (2004). "Four Iraqis Killed, 15 Injured in Fallujah." ABC News, July 1.

———. (2005). "Five Iraqi Civilians Wounded in US Chopper Attack." ABC News, March 14.

Ackerman, Elise. (2004). "Afghanistan Probe Implicated Abu Ghraib Interrogators." Knight-Ridder News Service, August 21.

Ackerman, Spencer. (2008). "How the Pentagon Turned an Interrogation Resistance Program into a Blueprint for Torture." *Washington Independent*, June 21.

Adriaensens, Dirk. (2005). *White Phosphorous, Daisy Cutters, Depleted Uranium, Thermobaric Bombs, Clusterbombs, Napalm…The US Uses WMD against Civilians*. Montréal: Center for Research on Globalization.

African Press International. (2008). Rwandan Gov't Accuses Mitterand Administration of Plotting Genocide. http://www.africanpress.worldpress.com; accessed August 6, 2008.

Agence France Press. (2008a). "AP Photographer in Iraq to Be Freed." Agence France Press, April 16.

———. (2008b). "Bush Sends Apology Over Korea Shooting in Iraq." Agence France Press, May 20.

———. (2008c). "Ex-Guantánamo Prosecutor to Testify for Suspect: Lawyer." Agence France Press, February 22.

———. (2008d). "FBI Sought to Oppose Torture at Guantánamo: Report." Agence France Press, May 21.

———. (2008e). "Lawyer for Guantánamo Inmate Urges Pakistan Gov't Help." *Agence France Press*, June 2.

———. (2008f). "Marine to Stand Trial over Detainee Killing in Iraq." *Agence France Press*, May 14.

———. (2008g). "New US Military Contractor Overbilling Scandal in Iraq Looms." *Agence France Press*, June 21.

———. (2008h). "US Air Strike Kills Six in Iraq." *Agence France Press*, March 23.

———. (2008i). "US Court Rejects Canadian's Guantánamo Appeal." *Agence France Press*, June 21.

———. (2008j). "US Holds German at Military Base in Afghanistan." *Agence France Press*, April 19.

———. (2008k). "US-Led Force Kills Eight Civilians in Afghanistan." *Agence France Press*, August 11.

———. (2008l). "US Orders Medical Care for Jailed Pakistani Scientist." *Agence France Press*, August 12.

Ahmed, Aijaz. (2003). "The War of Occupation." *Frontline*, March 29.

Ahmed, Asso, and Tina Susman. (2008). "Iraq Wants U.S. to Intervene to Stop Turkey's Incursion." *Los Angeles Times*, February 26, 2008.

Ahmed, Kamal. (2004). "Iraqis Lose Right to Sue Troops Over War Crimes." *Observer*, May 23.

Al-Qiri, Mohammed. (2008). "Relatives of Guantánamo and Bagram Detainees Stage Sit-In at the Parliament." *Yemen Observer*, February 10.

Al-Sahwa. (2008). "In Solidarity with Guantánamo Detainees, Yemenis to Hold Sit-In." alsahwanet.net, May 25.

Al-Taee, Awadh, and Steve Negus. (2005). "Sunnis Feel Full Force of Lightning Strike." *Financial Times*, June 29.

Alden, Edward. (2005). "Cheney Cabal Hijacked US Foreign Policy." *Washington Post*, October 20.

Allawi, Ali A. (2007). *The Occupation of Iraq: Winning the War, Losing the Peace*. New Haven, CT: Yale University Press.

American Civil Liberties Union. (2008a). "ACLU Sues to Uncover Records Detailing Torture and Abuse of Guantánamo Prisoners." aclu.org, March 13.

———. (2008b). "Credibility of U.S. Justice System at Stake as Military Commissions Proceed." aclu.org, March 12.

Amini, Mohammad, and Dan De Luce. (2003). "Basra Hit by Bombardment." *Guardian*, March 21.

Amnesty International. (2003). *Looting, Lawlessness and Humanitarian Consequences*. London: Amnesty International, April 11.

———. (2005). *Iraq: Civilians under Fire*. London: Amnesty International.

———. (2006a). *Beyond Abu Ghraib: Detention and Torture in Iraq*. London: Amnesty International.

———. (2006b). *Report on Rasul Kudaev*. January 25.

Anonymous. (2008a). "I Went AWOL and Could Have Been Shot." *Los Angeles Times*, April 10.

————. (2008b). "Some Tea, a Smoke, a Look Down Gun Barrel." *Los Angeles Times*, April 10.

Arab News. (2008). "Iraq: US Is Digging in for the Long Haul." arabnews. com, May 6.

Arango, Tim. (2007). "Case Lays Bare the Media's Reliance on Iraq Journalists." *New York Times*, December 14.

Arie, Sophie. (2005). "Dueling Views of the Sgrena Shooting." *Christian Science Monitor*, May 5.

Arnin, Akhtar. (2008). "Two Ex-Guantánamo Detainees to Sue US." *Daily Times* (Pakistan), May 14.

Arraf, Jane, et al. (2004). "War-Wracked Fallujans Seek Aid." CNN.com, November 15.

Arrahyee, Nasser. (2008). "Yemen Guarantees to 'Reform' Its Men from Guantánamo." *Yemen Observer*, June 10.

Associated Press (2001). "Taliban Say Hospital Hit." Associated Press, October 23.

————. (2003a). "Iranian Oil Ministry Building Near Iraq Hit by Missile." Associated Press, March 21.

————. (2003b). "Spanish Judge Indicts Osama Bin Laden, 34 Others for Terrorism." Associated Press, September 17.

————. (2004a). "Two Children Among Abused Prisoners: Report." Fairfax-Digital, May 8.

————. (2004b). "U.S. Launches 'Vigilant Resolve'." Associated Press, April 5.

————. (2005a). "Gonzales: U.S. Has Little Control Over Foreign Prisoner Torture," Associated Press, March 7.

————. (2005b). "U.S. Has Detained 83,000 in Anti-Terror Effort." Associated Press, November 15.

————. (2006). "Red Cross Expects to Visit Top Terror Suspects during Guantánamo Visit." Associated Press, September 20.

————. (2007a). "2 Afghan Private Security Firms Shut Down." *Los Angeles Times*, October 12.

————. (2007b). "Doctors Decry the Role of US Military Medicine in War on Terror." Associated Press, September 7.

————. (2007c). "Soldier Found Guilty of Rape, Murder." CNN, August 4.

————. (2008a). "Afghan Detainee Asks to Boycott Trial at Guantánamo Bay, Demands 'Justice and Fairness'." *International Herald Tribune*, March 13.

————. (2008b). "Canadian Facing Trial at Guantánamo Accuses US Military Interrogators of Abuse." Associated Press, March 19.

————. (2008c). "Chinese Muslims Issue Plea for Freedom as Guantánamo Release Stalls." *International Herald Tribune*, March 19.

————. (2008d). "Eight Policemen Killed in Operation in Afghanistan." *Hindustan Times*, January 24.

————. (2008e). "Gitmo Detainees Not Told of Rights." *The Australian*, July 24.

————. (2008f). "Guantánamo Judge May Suspend Trial for Canadian Detainee." Associated Press, May 8

————. (2008g). "Judge Says Hamdan Can Swap Notes With Fellow Guantánamo Detainees." *Wall Street Journal*, May 2.

————. (2008h). "Lawyers for Bin Laden Driver on Trial at Guantánamo Raise New Abuse Claims." *International Herald Tribune*, April 5.

————. (2008i). "Military: Turkish Jets Have Struck Kurdish Rebel Target in Northern Iraq." Associated Press, June 8.

————. (2008j). "Military Lawyer for Guantánamo Detainee: Evidence Suggests US Soldiers Committed War Crimes." *International Herald Tribune*, March 20.

————. (2008k). "NATO General Called to Testify." *Los Angeles Times*, May 31.

————. (2008l). "Official Defends Bush's CIA Limits." *Los Angeles Times*, July 23.

————. (2008m). "A Package of News Briefs from the Caribbean," *Miami Herald*, January 30.

————. (2008n). "Pakistan Militants Target NATO." *Los Angeles Times*, June 23.

————. (2008o). "Syria Returns Stolen Marble Artifact to Iraq." Associated Press, July 4.

————. (2008p). "Turkey Strikes Targets in Iraq." *Los Angeles Times*, March 30.

————. (2008q). "2 US Soldiers Face Murder Charges." *Los Angeles Times*, August 3.

————. (2008r). "U.K. Rights Group: U.S. Has Photographic Evidence of Torture." *USA Today*, June 11.

————. (2008s). "UN Panel Criticizes US War Crimes Charges for Guantánamo Minors." *International Herald Tribune*, June 7.

————. (2008t). "U.N. Rights Expert Can't Visit U.S. Detainees." *Los Angeles Times*, March 12.

————. (2008u). "US Military Orders Court-Martial for Contractor in Iraq." Associated Press, May 11.

————. (2008v). "US Tells UN Has about 500 Detained Juveniles in Iraq, 10 in Afghanistan." May 19.

————. (2008w). "Yemenis Protest Against Their Government, US Over Continued Guantánamo Detentions." Associated Press, February 10.

Association of the Bar of the City of New York. (2004). *Human Rights Standards Applicable to the U.S.'s Interrogation of Detainees*. New York: Association of the Bar of the City of New York.

Astill, James. (2004). "Cuba? It Was Great, Say Boys Freed from US Prison Camp." *Guardian*, March 6.

Austen, Ian. (2007). "Canada Reaches Settlement with Torture Victim." *New York Times*, January 26.

———. (2008). "Canadian Military Has Quit Turning Detainees Over to Afghans." *New York Times*, January 24.

Austin. (2008). "The Guantánamo Six." *The Economist*, February 16.

Australian Broadcasting Commission. (2007). "Hicks's Father Slams Release Conditions." Australian Broadcasting Commission News, March 31.

Aylwin-Foster, Nigel. (2005). "Changing the Army for Counterinsurgency Operations." *Military Review*, November–December.

Bacevich, Andrew J. (2008). "The 'Long War' Fallacy." *Los Angeles Times*, May 13.

Badrani, Fadhil. (2004). "Taking Cover in Falluja." BBC, November 8.

Baker, David R. (2004). "Bechtel's 2003 Revenue Breaks Company Record: Iraq Rebuilding Contracts Help S. F. Firm Reverse a 3-Year Slump." *San Francisco Chronicle*, April 20.

Baker, Mark. (2001). "Red Cross Depots in Flames as US Aircraft Strike Again." *Miami Herald*, October 27.

Baker, Peter, and Joby Warrick. (2007). "CIA Seeks Investigations of Ex-Officer's Claims: Waterboarding Statements Raise Concern." *Washington Post*, December 22.

Baker, Russ. (2004). "Bush Wanted to Invade Iraq If Elected in 2000." Guerrilla News Network, October 27.

Baldauf, Scott. (2008). "Former Guantánamo Prisoner Asks U.S. to Review Its Founding Ideals." *Christian Science Monitor*, February 8.

Ballavia, David. (2007). *House to House: An Epic Memoir of War*. New York: Free Press, 2007.

Bannerman, Lucy. (2008). "Abu Laith Al-Libi, Al-Qaeda Chief in Afghanistan, Killed in Missile Attack." *New York Times*, February 1.

Barber, Julian. (2007). "Mistrial Ends Watada Court-Martial: War Objector May Have to Be Tried Again." *Seattle Post-Intelligencer*, February 7.

Barnes, Cory. (2008). "Guantánamo Bay Guards Think Khadr's a 'Good Kid.' " Canadian Broadcasting Corporation, June 3.

Barnes, Julian E., and Kimi Yoshino. (2008). "U.S. Captives Allegedly Killed." *Los Angeles Times*, January 30.

Barry, John, et al. (2004). "The Roots of Torture." *Newsweek*, May 24.

Barstow, David. (2008). "Message Machine: Behind TV Analysts, Pentagon's Hidden Hand." *New York Times*, April 20.

Barzanji, Yahya. (2007). "Turkey Sends Troops into Northern Iraq, Official Says." *New York Sun*, December 18.

Bazelon, Emily, and Dahlia Lithwik. (2008). "A Few Good Soldiers: More Members of the Military Turn Against the Terror Trials." slate.com, May 14.

Bazzo, Mohammed. (2004). "U.S. Using Some Iraqis as Bargaining Chips." *Newsday*, May 26.

BBC. (2002). "'Too Nice' Guantánamo Chief Sacked." BBC, October 16.

————. (2004). "US Strikes Raze Falluja Hospital." BBC, November 6.

————. (2005a). "Abu Ghraib Inmates Recall Torture." BBC, January 12.

————. (2005b). "'Religious Abuse' at Guantánamo." BBC, February 10.

————. (2005c). "US Guantánamo Guard Kicked Koran." BBC News, June 4.

————. (2005d). "US Held Youngsters at Abu Ghraib." BBC, March 11.

————. (2007). "Trial of David Hicks a 'Charade'." Asia-Pacific BBC, July 25.

————. (2008a). "Pakistan Fury at Deadly US Strike." BBC, June 11.

————. (2008b). "US Spending in Iraq Ignored Rules." BBC, May 25.

Begg, Moazzam. (2006). *Enemy Combatant: A British Muslim's Journal to Guantánamo and Back*. London: Free Press.

Benjamin, Mark. (2006). "U.S. Accused of Kidnapping Family Member of Iraqi Detainees." informationliberation.com, July 14.

Benoist, Annick. (2003). "Iraq's Heritage in Jeopardy." Middle East Online, March 27.

Benvenisti, Eyal. (2004). *The International Law of Occupation*. Princeton, NJ: Princeton University Press.

Berger, Peter. (2008a). "No Torture. No Exceptions." *Washington Monthly*, March.

————. (2008b). "The Body Snatchers." *Mother Jones*, March/April.

Berntsen, Gary, and Ralph Pezzullo. (2005). *Jawbreaker: The Attack on Bin Laden and Al Qaeda: A Personal Account by the CIA's Key Field Commander*. New York: Crown.

Bloche, M. Gregg, and Jonathan H. Marks. (2005). "When Doctors Go to War." *New England Journal of Medicine*, January 6.

Block, Melissa. (2006). "Armitage Denies Making 'Stone Age' Threat." *All Things Considered*, National Public Radio, September 22.

Bonner, Raymond. (2005). "Detainee Says He Was Tortured in U.S. Custody." *New York Times*, February 13.

Booker, Christopher. (2008). "What Afghanistan Needs Is Infrastructure." *Telegraph*, July 6.

Booth, Jenny. (2008). "Female 'Terror' Scientist Aafia Siddiqui Facing US Court after Extradition." Times Online.com, August 5.

Bowman, Michael. (2008). "Congress Details Massive Use of Private Contractors in Iraq." Voice of America, August 12.

Bowser, Betty Ann. (2005). "Allegations of Abuse." *The Newshour with Jim Lehrer*, PBS, June 3.

Broder, John M. (2007). "Report Says Firm Sought to Cover Up Iraq Shootings." *New York Times*, October 2.

Brooks, Rosa. (2007). "Mercenaries R Us." *Los Angeles Times*, September 21.

Brown, Drew. (2006). "Officials Say U.S. Troops Used Appropriate Force in Iraqi Raid." *Miami Herald*, June 2.

Brubaker, Jack. (2004). "Bush Meets with Amish." *Lancaster New Era*, July 16.

Bugliosi, Vincent. (2008). *The Prosecution of George W. Bush for Murder*. New York: Vanguard Press.

Buncombe, Andrew. (2003). "U.S. Admits It Used Napalm Bombs in Iraq." *Independent*, August 10.

Buncombe, Andrew, Justin Huggler, and Leonard Doyle. (2004). "Abu Ghraib: Inmates Raped, Ridden Like Animals, and Forced to Eat Pork." *Independent*, May 22.

Burke, Jason, and Imtiaz Gul. (2006). "The Drone, the CIA and a Botched Attempt to Kill Bin Laden's Deputy." *Guardian*, January 15.

Burns, John F. (2002). "Threats and Responses: The Manhunt." *New York Times*, September 30.

———. (2008). Interview, Charlie Rose. PBS, April 9.

Burns, John F., and Thom Shanker. (2004). "U.S. Finds a Legal Basis to Retain Force in Iraq." *New York Times*, March 27.

Buruma, Ian. (2008). "Ghosts." *New York Review of Books*, June 26.

Bush, George W. (2001). "Military Order #13 (Detention, Treatment, and Trial of Certain Non-Citizens in the War Against Terrorism)." November 13.

———. (2002a). "Humane Treatment of al Qaeda and Taliban Detainees." whitehouse.com, February 7.

———. (2002b). "President Bush Outlines Iraqi Threat." whitehouse.com, October 7.

———. (2003a). "President Bush, Prime Minister Blair Discuss War on Terrorism." whitehouse.com, July 17.

———. (2003b). "War on Terror." whitehouse.com, March 8.

———. (2006a). "President Discusses Creation of Military Commissions to Try Suspected Terrorists." whitehouse.com, September 6.

———. (2006b). "Press Conference of the President." whitehouse.com, September 15.

———. (2007). "Interpretation of the Geneva Conventions Common Article 3 as Applied to a Program of Detention and Interrogation Operated by the Central Intelligence Agency." July 20.

Bush, George W., and Mickey Herskowitz. (2001). *Charge to Keep: My Journey to the White House*. New York: Harper.

Butler, Desmond. (2008). "Former US Detainee Testifies of Abuse." Associated Press, May 21.

Bybee, Jay S. (2002a). "Application of Treaties and Laws to al Qaeda and Taliban Detainees." U.S. Department of Justice, January 19.

———. (2002b). "Potential Legal Constraints Applicable to Interrogations of Persons Captured by U.S. Armed Forces in Afghanistan." U.S. Department of Justice, February 26.

———. (2002c). "Standards of Conduct for Interrogation Under18USC §§2340-2340A." U.S. Department of Justice, August 1.

———. (2002d). "Status of Taliban Forces Under Article IV of the Third Geneva Convention of 1949." U.S. Department of Justice, February 7.

Cable News Network. (2001). "Bush: Bin Laden 'Prime Suspect'. " CNN.com, September 17.

———. (2005a). "A Progress Report: The Iraq War." CNN.com, July 22.

———. (2005b) "U.S. Soldiers Reprimanded for Burning Bodies: Cremating Taliban Fighters Showed Poor Judgment, Military Says." CNN.com, November 26.

———. (2006a). "Annan: Shut Guantánamo Prison Camp." CNN.com, February 17.

———. (2006b). "Hussein Executed with 'Fear in His Face'." CNN.com, December 30.

Cageprisoners. (2008). "Military Doctors Infect Gitmo Detainee with HIV." rinf.com, January 31.

Cambanis, Thanassis. (2004). "Iraqi Detentions Fuel Anti-US Sentiment." *Boston Globe*, March 28.

Canadian Broadcasting Corporation. (2003). "Former U.S. Administrator Blasts U.S. Post-War Actions in Iraq." cbc.ca, November 26.

———. (2008a). "Guantánamo Prisoners to Get Phone Access." cbc.ca, March 12.

———. (2008b). "Journalists' Murders Most Likely to Go Unsolved in Iraq: Report." cbc.ca, April 30.

Canadian Press. (2008a). "Afghan BBC Journalist Found Dead in Afghanistan a Day After He Went Missing." *Canadian Press*, June 8.

———. (2008b). "France Urges U.S. Treat Canadian Guantánamo Detainee Omar Khadr as Minor." *Canadian Press*, January 24.

———. (2008c). "Guantánamo Guards Seize 'Lord of the Rings' Script from Khadr." *Canadian Press*, April 11.

———. (2008d). "U.S. Army Deserter Seeks Refugee Status." *Edmonton Sun*, September 7.

Canwest News Service. (2008). "Canada Didn't Want Khadr Sent to Guantánamo: A Report." canada.com, April 17.

Carter, Chelsea. (2008). "Marine Cleared on Charges of Covering up Iraq Killings." *New York Times*, June 5.

Carter, Jimmy. (2007). Interview, Charlie Rose. PBS, October 11.

Carvin, Stephanie. (2008). "Linking Purpose and Tactics: America and the Reconsideration of the Laws of War During the 1990s." *International Studies Perspectives*, May.

Catagnus, Sergeant Earl, Sergeant Bard Z. Edison, Lance Corporal James D. Keeling, and Lance Corporal David A. Moon. (2005). "Infantry Squad Tactics: Some of the Lessons Learned During MOUT in the Battle for Fallujah." *Marine Corps Gazette*, September.

Center for Constitutional Rights. (2007). "Donald Rumsfeld Charged with Torture During Trip to France." Center for Constitutional Rights, October 26.

Center for Economic and Social Rights. (2005). *Beyond Torture: U.S. Violations of Occupation Law in Iraq*. Brooklyn, NY: Center for Economic and Social Rights.

Center for Public Integrity. (2006). "U.S. Contractors Reap the Windfalls of Post-War Reconstruction," in Richard Falk, Irene Gendzier, and Robert Jay Lifton, eds., *Crimes of War: Iraq*. New York: Nation Books, 279–292.

Cha, Ariana Eunjung. (2004). "Iraqi Experts Tossed With the Water Workers Ineligible to Fix Polluted Systems." *Washington Post*, February 27.

Champagne, Noiselle. (2008). "Lawyers Say Mauritanian Was Tortured in Guantánamo." Reuters, March 10.

Chandrasekaran, Rajiv. (2004). "Anti-U.S. Uprising Widens in Iraq; Marines Push Deeper into Fallujah: Cleric's Force Tightens Grip in Holy Cities." *Washington Post*, 8.

———. (2006). *Imperial Life in the Emerald City: Inside Iraq's Green Zone*. New York: Vintage.

Chao, Elaine L. (2003). "Children in the Crossfire: Prevention and Rehabilitation of Child Soldiers." www.dol.gov, May 7.

Chatterjee, Pratap, and Herbert Docena. (2003/2004). "Occupation, Inc." *Institute for Southern Studies*, Winter.

Church, Vice Admiral Albert T., III. (2005). *Detention Operations and Interrogation Techniques*. U.S. Department of the Navy, March.

Ciezadlo, Annia. (2005). "What Iraq's Checkpoints Are Like." *Christian Science Monitor*, March 7.

Clark, General Wesley K. (2003). "Iraq: What Went Wrong." *New York Review of Books*, October 23.

Clark, Ramsey. (1992). *The Fire This Time: U.S. War Crimes in the Gulf*. New York: Thunder's Mouth Press.

Clarke, Richard. (2004). *Against All Enemies: Inside America's War on Terror*. New York: Free Press. The quote about "kicking ass" appears on page 24.

Cockburn, Patrick. (2006). *The Occupation*. New York: Verso.

———. (2008). *Muqtada: Muqtada Al-Sadr, The Shia Revival, and the Struggle for Iraq*. New York: Scribner.

Coghlan, Tom. (2008). "Afghanistan Journalist in Torture Claim." *Telegraph*, May 19.

Cohn, Marjorie. (2008). "Afghanistan: The Other Legal War." AfterNet, August 1.

Cole, David. (2008). "The Brits Do It Better." *New York Review of Books*, June 12.

Colt, Ned. (2008). "Iraq's Biggest Aid Agency? Muqtada Al-Sadr & Co." worldblog.com, April 16.

Common Dreams. (2008). "Human Rights Groups Address European Parliament on Resettlement of Guantánamo Detainees Who Fear Torture in Home Countries." commondreams.org, February 28.

Conetta, Carl. (2002a). *Operation Enduring Freedom: Why a Higher Rate of Civilian Bombing Casualties*. Cambridge, MA: Project on Defense Alternatives.

———. (2002b). *Strange Victory: A Critical Appraisal of Operation Enduring Freedom and the Afghanistan War*. Cambridge, MA: Project on Defense Alternatives.

Conover, Ted. (2005). "In the Land of Guantánamo." *New York Times Magazine*, June 29.

Constable, Pamela. (2003). "Land Grab in Kabul Embarrasses Government: Mud Homes Razed to Make Room for Top Afghan Officials." *Washington Post*, September 16.

———. (2004). "An Afghan Boy's Life in U.S. Custody." *Washington Post*, February 12.

Corbin, Jane. (2008). "BBC Uncovers Lost Iraq Billions." BBC, June 11.

Cordesman, Anthony H. (2008). "A Civil War Iraq Can't Win." *New York Times*, March 30.

Cornwell, Susan. (2008). "Condoleezza Rice Defends Guantánamo." *International Herald Tribune*, June 1.

Crider, Cory. (2008). "Guantánamo Children." *Guardian*, July 21.

Crispin, Shawn W. (2008). "US and Thailand: Allies in Torture." *Asia Times* (Hong Kong) (atimes.com), January 25.

Curran, John. (2008). "Vermont Candidate to Prosecute Bush If She Wins." Associated Press, September 19.

Daily War News. (2004). "Today in Iraq." dailywarnews.blogspot.com, July 31.

Daniel, Douglass K. (2008). "Study: False Statements Preceded War." Associated Press, January 22.

Danner, Mark. (2004). "Abu Ghraib: The Hidden Story." *New York Review of Books*, October 7.

———. (2007). "The Moment Has Come to Get Rid of Saddam." *New York Review of Books*, November 8.

Daragahi, Borzou. (2008). "Iran Says U.S. Aids Rebels at Its Borders." *Los Angeles Times*, April 15.

Daragahi, Borzou, and Raheem Salman. (2008). "Grieving Iraqis Want Honor First, Not Money." *Los Angeles Times*, May 4.

Davey, Monica. (2005). "An Iraqi Police Officer's Death: A Soldier's Varying Accounts." *New York Times*, May 23.

Davies, Nicholas J. S. (2006). "Bush Confesses to War Crimes." onlinejournal.com, September 11.

Davis, Morris D. (2007). "Why I Quit as Chief Prosecutor at Guantánamo." *Miami Herald*, December 16.

———. (2008). "Unforgiveable Behavior, Inadmissible Evidence." *New York Times*, February 17.

Dawn. (2001). "Bombs Leave Children in Shock, Destroy Radio." dawn.com, October 27.

———. (2004). "32 Guantánamo Returnees Freed." dawn.com, April 4.

de Bendern, Paul. (2008). "Turkish Army Says It Strikes PKK in Northern Iraq." Reuters, April 16.

De Young, Karen. (2007). "Other Killings by Blackwater Staff Detailed." *Washington Post*, October 2.

———. (2008). "A Dark Shade of Green Zone." *Washington Post*, January 5.

Deen, Thalif. (2008). "Can Iraq PM Undermine Bush's Plan and Survive?" *Sunday Times*, July 27.

Dehghanpisheh, Babak, John Barry, and Roy Gutman. (2002). "The Death Convoy of Afghanistan." *Newsweek*, August 26.

Denbeaux, Mark, and Joshua Denbeaux. (2006). *Report on Guantánamo Detainees: A Profile of 517 Detainees Through Analysis of Department of Defense Data.* South Orange, NJ: Seton Hall University.

Denbeaux, Mark, et al. (2008). *Captured on Tape: Interrogation and Videotaping of Detainees at Guantánamo.* South Orange, NJ: Seton Hall University.

Derhally, Massoud A. (2008). "Jordan Returns 2,466 Artifacts Looted from Iraq Museum." bloomberg.com, June 23.

Diamond, Larry. (2005). *Squandering Victory: The American Occupation and the Bungled Effort to Bring Democracy to Iraq.* New York: Holt.

Dodds, Paisley. (2005). "Tales of Abuse, Forced Confessions in Guantánamo Testimonies." Associated Press, May 31.

Dowd, Maureen. (2008). "Voting for a Smile." *New York Times*, January 6.

Doyle, Leonard. (2008). "Pentagon Propaganda Over Torture and Iraq Revealed." *Independent*, April 21.

Dreazen, Yochi, and Christopher Cooper. (2004). "Lingering Presence: Behind the Scenes, U.S. Tightens Grip on Iraq's Future." *Wall Street Journal*, May 13.

Dworkin, Ronald. (2008). "Why It Was a Great Victory." *New York Review of Books*, August 14.

Eakin, Hugh. (2008a). "The Devastation of Iraq's Past." *New York Review of Books*, August 14.

———. (2008b). "Iraqi Files in U.S.: Plunder or Rescue?" *New York Times*, July 1.

Ebrahim, Zofeen. (2008). "Ailing Guantánamo Prisoner May Die, Says Lawyer." Inter Press Service, February 7.

Economist, The. (2008a). "Bending the Rules: The High Cost of Guantánamo Bay." *The Economist*, July 19.

———. (2008b). "Blood in Basra and Beyond." *The Economist*, April 19.

Edwards, Richard. (2008a). "Ex-Guantánamo Captive 'Who Was Tortured'." *Telegraph*, February 22.

———. (2008b). "Guantánamo Defendant Calls Trial Illegal." canada.com, March 12.

Edwards, Steven. (2008a). "Khadr Affidavit Alleges Rape Threat, Other U.S. Abuses." *National Post* (Canada), March 17.

———. (2008b). "Pentagon's Head of Guantánamo Trials Resigns." Canwest, February 25.

———. (2008c). "'There Is No Punishment at Guantánamo … and This Is Not a Prison." Canwest, February 7.

———. (2008d). "Was Omar Khadr Coerced?" *National Post*, March 14.

Efron, Sonni. (2005). "US Backs Away from Afghan Aerial Spraying." *Los Angeles Times*, January 22.

Eggen, Dan. (2007a). "FBI Reports Duct-Taping, 'Baptizing' at Guantánamo." *Washington Post*, January 3.

———. (2007b). "Hill Briefed on Waterboarding." *Washington Post*, December 9.

———. (2008a). "Bush Approved Meetings on Interrogation Techniques: President's Comments to ABC News Prove Top-Level Involvement in Allowing Harsh Coercion." *Washington Post*, April 12.

———. (2008b). "Justice Dept. 'Cannot' Probe Waterboarding, Mukasey Says." *Washington Post*, February 8.

———. (2008c). "Justice Official Defends Rough CIA Interrogations: Severe, Lasting Pain Is Torture, He Says." *Washington Post*, February 17.

———. (2008d). "White House Pushes Waterboarding Rationale: Administration May Be Trying to Shore up Prosecution of Terrorism Suspects." *Washington Post*, February 13.

Eggen, Dan, and Walter Pincus. (2007). "FBI, CIA Debate Significance of Terror Suspect: Agencies Also Disagree On Interrogation Methods." *Washington Post*, December 18.

Eggen, Dan, and Joby Warrick. (2007). "CIA Destroyed Videos Showing Interrogations." *Washington Post*, December 7.

Eggen, Dan, and Josh White. (2005). "Inmates Alleged Koran Abuse: FBI Papers Cite Complaints as Early as 2002." *Washington Post*, May 26.

———. (2008). "Administration Asserted an Exception on Search and Seizure." *Washington Post*, April 4.

El Akkad, Omar. (2008) "Khadr Trial Judge Relieved of Duties." *Globe and Mail*, May 31.

El Khabar. (2008a). "Algerian Former Prisoner at Guantánamo Lodges Complaint Against U.S. Government." *El Khabar*, July 29.

———. (2008b). "CIA Deports 14 Terrorism Suspects from Guantánamo Bay to Jordan." *El Khabar*, April 15.

———. (2008c). "US Government Behind Failing Agreement on Algerian Prisoners in Guantánamo Base." *El Khabar*, April 3.

Elias, Richard. (2008). "Eight Men Sue Britain Over 'Illegal Detention." scotsman.com, April 20.

Elliott, Andrea. (2003). "Interrogations; Unit Says It Gave Earlier Warning of Abuse in Iraq." *New York Times*, June 14.

Enders, David. (2003). "Getting Back on the Grid." *Baghdad Bulletin*, June 10.

Englehart, Tom. (2008). "The Afghan Pipeline You Don't Know About." *The Nation*, July 7.

Ephron, Dan. (2008). "Gitmo Grievances." *Newsweek*, May 26.

Esposito, John L., and Dalia Mogahed. (2008). *Who Speaks for Islam? What a Billion Muslims Really Think*. New York: Gallup Press.

Evans, Robert. (2008). "U.N. Experts Rap U.S. 'Cruelty' to Child Prisoners." Reuters, June 8.

Faiez, M. Karim, and Laura King. (2008). "Pakistan Condemns U.S. Strike from Afghanistan." *Los Angeles Times*, March 14.

Fainaru, Steve. (2004). "After Recapturing N. Iraqi City, Rebuilding Starts from Scratch." *Washington Post*, September 19.

———. (2007a). "Guards in Iraq Cite Frequent Shootings." *Washington Post*, October 3.

———. (2007b). "Warnings Unheeded on Guards in Iraq." *Washington Post*, December 24.

Falkoff, Marc. (2007). "Politics at Guantánamo: The Former Prosecutor Speaks." jurist.law.pitt.edu/forum/2007/11, November 2.

Fallows, James. (2004). "Blind into Baghdad." Atlantic, January/February.

Faramarzi, Scheherezade. (2004). "U.S. Aircraft Reportedly Kills 40 Iraqis." Associated Press, May 19.

Farley, Maggie. (2007). "Guantánamo Inmate Center of Debate." *Los Angeles Times*, June 24.

———. (2008). "U.S. to Reopen Canadian's Torture Case." *Los Angeles Times*, June 6.

Fay, Major General George R., and Lieutenant General Anthony R. Jones. (2004). *Investigation of Intelligence Activities at Abu Ghraib*. U.S. Department of the Army, August. [Fay/Jones Report]. Pagination in sources corresponds to text in Greenberg and Dratel, eds., *The Torture Papers*.

Feith, Douglas. (1985). "Law in the Service of Terror." *National Interest*.

———. (2008). Testimony before the House Judiciary Committee, July 15.

Ferguson, Barbara. (2008). "FBI Wrestling a 'Good News, Bad News' Predicament." *Arab News*, May 26.

Ferguson, Charles H. (2008). *No End in Sight: Iraq's Descent into Chaos*. New York: Public Affairs.

Fick, Nathaniel. (2007). *One Bullet Away: The Making of a Marine Officer*. Boston: Mariner Books.

Figueroa, Teri. (2007). "General Frees Another Marine Convicted of War Crimes." *North Country Times*, August 11.

Filkins, Dexter. (2003). "Tough New Tactics by U.S. Tighten Grip on Iraq Towns." *New York Times*, December 6.

Fishback, Captain Ian. (2005). "A Matter of Honor." *Washington Post*, September 28.

Fisher, Ian. (2004a). "Inmate Recounts Hours of Abuse by U.S. Troops." *New York Times*, May 5.

————. (2004b). "Prison Rosters; Searing Uncertainty for Iraqi's Missing Loved One." *New York Times*, June 1.

Fisk, Robert, and Severin Carrell. (2004). "Occupiers Spend Millions on Private Army of Security Men." *Independent*, March 29.

Fisk, Robert, and Patrick Cockburn. (2004). "Deaths of Mercenaries Hidden from View." *The Star* (Johannesburg), April 13.

FitzGerald, Frances. (2002). "George Bush & The World." *New York Review of Books*, September 26.

Fletcher, Holly. (2008). *Mujahadeen-e-Khalq (MEK) (aka People's Mujahedin of Iran or PMOI)*. New York: Council on Foreign Relations.

Food and Agriculture Organization of the United Nations. (2003). "Crop, Food Supply and Nutrition Assessment Mission to Iraq." September 23.

Fowler, Jonathan. (2005). "Expert: Malnutrition Affects Iraqi Kids." Associated Press, March 30.

Franklin, Jonathan. (2004). "US Hires Mercenaries for Iraq Role." *Guardian*, March 5.

Fraser, Suzan. (2008). "Turkish Jets Bomb Northern Iraq, Targetting Kurdish Rebels for 3rd Straight Night." *San Diego Union*, May 12.

Freeman, Clive. (2008). "Documentary of US 'War Crimes' Shocks Europe." Ireland Online (iol.com), May 26.

Freeze, Colin. (2006). "Release Sought of Khadr Interrogation Footage." *Globe and Mail*, May 31.

Friedman, Herbert A. (2005). "Psychological Operations in Afghanistan." psywarrior.com, May 5.

Froomkin, Dan. (2008a). "General Accuses WH of War Crimes." *Washington Post*, June 21.

————. (2008b). "We Tortured and We'd Do It Again." *Washington Post*, February 6.

————. (2008c). "White House Torture Advisers." *Washington Post*, April 10.

Galbraith, Peter W. (2004a). "How to Get Out of Iraq." *New York Review of Books*, May 13.

————. (2004b). "Iraq: The Bungled Transition." *New York Review of Books*, September 23.

Gall, Carlotta. (2008a). "Afghan Leader Criticizes U.S. on Conduct of War." *New York Times*, April 26.

————. (2008b). "Afghan Militants Killed in Airstrikes, U.S. Says." *International Herald Tribune*, July 17.

————. (2008c). "Detainees in Afghanistan Get a Video Link to Their Families." *International Herald Tribune*, April 13.

————. (2008c). "Time Runs Out for an Afghan Held by the U.S." *New York Times*, February 5.

————. (2008d). "Video Link Plucks Afghan Detainees from Black Hole of Isolation." *New York Times*, April 13.

Gall, Carlotta, and Abdul Waheed Wafa. (2008). "10 Die in Mistaken Afghan Fire Fight." *New York Times*, January 25.

Gannon, Kathy. (2001). "Kabul Awakes to the Aftermath of Another Night's Heavy Bombing." *Guardian*, October 27.

Gans, Janessa. (2007). "Guards Who Hurt Us." *Los Angeles Times*, October 6.

Gerstenblith, Patty. (2004). *Legal Damage Control for Iraq's Looted Cultural Heritage: The Need for U.S. Import Restrictions*. Pittsburgh: Jurist Legal Intelligence (www.juristlaw.pitt.edu/forum), February 23.

Gettleman, Jeffrey. (2004a). "As U.S. Detains Iraqis, Families Plead for News." *New York Times*, March 7.

———. (2004b). "Chaos and War Leave Iraq's Hospitals in Ruins." *New York Times*, February 14.

———. (2004c). "In Falluja Cease-Fire, the Battle Still Rages." *International Herald Tribune*, April 14.

Gettleman, Jeffrey, and Eric Schmitt. (2008). "U.S. Forces Fire Missiles into Somalia at a Kenyan." *New York Times*, March 4.

Gibney, Alex. (2008). Interview, *Now*. PBS, March 7.

Gilson, Dave. (2006). "'Why Am I in Cuba?'" *Mother Jones*, September/October.

Glaberson, William. (2007a). "Court Tells U.S. to Reveal Data on Detainees at Guantánamo." *New York Times*, July 21.

———. (2007b). "Hurdles Frustrate Effort to Shrink Guantánamo." *New York Times*, August 9.

———. (2007c). "Reserve Officer Criticizes Process of Identifying 'Enemy Combatants' at Guantánamo." *New York Times*, June 23.

———. (2007d). "Witness Names to Be Withheld from Detainees." *New York Times*, December 1.

———. (2008). "Detainee Challenges Guantánamo by Describing Life." *New York Times*, July 16.

Glasser, Susan B. (2002). "US Backing Helps Warlord Solidify Power." *Washington Post*, February 18.

Godoy, Julio. (2003). "U.S. Govt Accused of War Crimes Against Journalists." Inter Press Service, April 12.

Golden, Tim. (2005a). "American Filmmaker Held by the U.S. Military in Iraq for 7 Weeks Is Released." *New York Times*, July 7.

———. (2005b). "In U.S. Report, Brutal Details of 2 Afghan Inmates' Deaths." *New York Times*, May 20.

———. (2007a). "Guantánamo Detainees Stage Hunger Strike." *New York Times*, April 9.

———. (2007b). "Naming Names at Gitmo." *New York Times*, October 21.

———. (2008). "Foiling U.S. Plan, Prison Expands in Afghanistan." *New York Times*, January 7.

Golden, Tim, and David Rohde. (2008). "Afghans Hold Secret Trials for Men That U.S. Detained." *New York Times*, April 10.

Goldsmith, Jack, III. (2004). "Draft of an Opinion Concerning the Meaning of Article 49 of the Four Geneva Convention as It Applies in Occupied Iraq." U.S. Department of Justice, March 19.

———. (2007). *The Terror Presidency: Law and Judgment Inside the Bush Administration*. New York: Norton. (The quote about "conspiracy to commit a war crime" appears on page 68).

Gonzales, Alberto. (2001a). "Decision Re Application of the Geneva Convention on Prisoners of War to the Conflict with Al Qaeda and the Taliban." whitehouse.com, September 25.

———. (2001b). "Decision Re Application of the Geneva Convention on Prisoners of War to the Conflict with Al Qaeda and the Taliban." whitehouse.com, January 25.

Goode, Erica. (2008). "War Takes Toll on Baghdad Psychiatric Hospital." *New York Times*, May 20.

Gordon, Joy. (2007). "Iraq: Follow the Money." *Le Monde Diplomatique*, April.

Gordon, Michael R. (2006). "Career Crisis Hovers Over Guantánamo Commander." *Charlotte Observer*, June 19.

———. (2007). "The Former-Insurgent Counterinsurgency." *New York Times*, September 2.

———. (2008a). "In Sadr City, Basic Services Falter." *New York Times*, April 22.

———. (2008b). "U.S. Begins Erecting Wall in Sadr City." *New York Times*, April 18.

———. (2007). *Cobra II: The Inside Story of the Invasion and Occupation of Iraq*. New York: Vintage.

Gordon, Michael R. and Bernard E. Trainor. (2006). "Dash to Baghdad Left Top U.S. Generals Divided." *New York Times*, March 13.

Gorman, H. Candace. (2008a). "A Sickening Truth at Guantánamo." salon.com, March 14.

———. (2008b). "Judge Decides Guantánamo Prisoner's Health Problems Are His Own Fault." huffingtonpost.com, April 18.

Gourevitch, Philip, and Errol Morris. (2008). *Standard Operating Procedure*. New York: Penguin.

Graham, Bradley. (2003). "U.S. Moved Early for Air Supremacy." *Washington Post*, July 20.

Gray, Andrew. (2008). "US Efforts to Close Guantánamo at Standstill—Gates." Reuters, May 21.

Greenberg, Karen J., and Joshua L. Dratel, eds. (2005). *The Torture Papers: The Road to Abu Ghraib*. New York: Cambridge University Press.

Greenburg, Jan Crawford, Howard L. Rosenberg, and Ariane de Vogue. (2008). "Bush Aware of Advisors' Interrogation Talks: President Says He Knew His Senior Advisers Discussed Tough Interrogation Methods." ABC News, April 11.

Greenhouse, Linda. (2008). "Bush Appeals to Justices on Detainees Case." *New York Times*, February 15.

Greenstock, Jeremy. (2008). Interview, "Charlie Rose." PBS, May 14.

Greenwald, Glenn. (2008). "Standards of American Justice Under George W. Bush." salon.com, January 2.

Grey, Stephen. (2006). *Ghost Plane: The True Story of the CIA Torture Program*. New York: St. Martin's Press.

Guardian. (2001). "Bush Rejects Taliban Offer to Hand Bin Laden Over." *Guardian*, October 14.

———. (2004). "After Abu Ghraib." *Guardian*, September 20.

———. (2005). "The One Left Behind." *Guardian*, February 19.

Gude, Ken. (2008). "Bush's Botched Military Commissions." *Guardian*, August 6.

Guggenheim, Ken. (2004). "Iraq's Looting Appears More Serious Year After War." Associated Press, March 14.

Gulf Daily News. (2008). "Deal Lets US Drones Raid Bin Laden." *Gulf Daily News*, July 3.

Haas, Michael. (1991). *Genocide by Proxy: Cambodian Pawn on a Superpower Chessboard*. Westport, CT: Praeger.

———. (2008). *International Human Rights: A Comprehensive Introduction*. London: Routledge.

Haddad, Subhy. (2003). "Eyewitness: Visiting Baghdad's Wounded." BBC News, March 25.

Hamrah, A. S. (2007). "It's Not Torture, It's Sex." *Los Angeles Times*, July 30.

Harding, Iuke. (2004). "'I Will Always Hate You People': Family's Fury at Mystery Death." *Guardian*, May 24.

Harriman, Ed. (2005). "So, Mr. Bremer, Where Did All the Money Go?" *Guardian*, July 7.

———. (2007). "Where Has All the Money Gone?" *London Review of Books*, October 13.

Harvey, Francis J., and Peter J. Schoomaker. (2005). "Detainee Deaths." National Review Online, September 22.

Harvey, Frank P. (2008). "Guantánamo Bay Recidivism: How Concerned Should We Be?" *Chronicle Herald*, June 5.

Haynes, Deborah. (2008). "Iraq Minister: US Combat Troops to Pull Out in Three Years Under New Deal." Timesonline.com, August 14.

Haynes, William J., II. (2002). "Counter-Resistance Strategies." Department of Defense, November 27.

Hedgpeth, Dana, and Amit R. Paley. (2008). "U.S. Says Contractor Made Little Progress on Iraq Projects." *Washington Post*, July 28.

Hentoff, Nat. (2008). "How Our Attorney General Defines 'Justice'." *Durand Daily Democrat*, June 21.

Herold, Marc W. (2003). *Dossier on Civilian Victims of United States' Aerial Bombing*. Durham, NH: Whittemore School of Business and Economics, March 9.

Herring, Eric, and Glen Rangwala. (2006). *Iraq in Fragments: The Occupation and Its Legacy*. Ithaca, NY: Cornell University Press.

Hersh, Seymour M. (2004a). *Chain of Command*. New York: Penguin.

———. (2004b). "The Gray Zone: How a Secret Pentagon Program Came to Abu Ghraib." *New Yorker*, May 24.

———. (2007). "The General's Report." *New Yorker*, June 25.

Hicks, David. (2004). "The David Hicks Affidavit." *Sydney Morning Herald*, December 10.

Higgins, Alexander G. (2004). "Red Cross: Iraq Abuse Widespread, Routine." Associated Press, May 11.

Higham, Scott. (2004). "A Look Behind the 'Wire' at Guantánamo: Defense Memos Raised Questions About Detainee Treatment as Red Cross Sought Changes." *Washington Post*, June 13.

Higham, Scott, and Jose Stephens. (2004). "New Details of Prison Abuse Emerge: Abu Ghraib Detainees' Statements Describe Sexual Humiliation and Savage Beatings." *Washington Post*, May 21.

Hill, General James T. (2002). "Counter-Resistance Strategies." U.S. Department of the Army, October 25.

Hirsh, Michael. (2004). "A Tortured Debate." *Newsweek*, June 21.

Horton, Scott. (2008a). "The U.S. Isn't Like to Try Bush Administration Officials for War Crimes—But It's Likely That a European Country Will." *New Republic*, June 19.

———. (2008b). "Which Came First: Memos or Torture?" *Los Angeles Times*, April 21.

Hosenball, Mark. (2008). "Is This Terror on Trial?" *Time*, June 16.

Hughes, Langston. (1938). *Let America Be America Again*. New York: Vintage, reissued 2004.

Human Rights First. (2004). *Ending Secret Detentions*. New York: Human Rights First.

———. (2005). *Behind the Wire: An Update to Ending Secret Detentions*. New York: Human Rights First.

———. (2006a). *Command Responsibility: Detainee Deaths in U.S. Custody in Iraq and Afghanistan*. New York: Human Rights First.

———. (2006b). *Trials Under Military Order: A Guide to the Rules for Military Commissions*. New York: Human Rights First.

Human Rights Watch. (2003a). *Hearts and Minds: Post-War Civilian Deaths in Baghdad Central by U.S. Forces*. New York: Human Rights Watch.

———. (2003b). *Off Target: The Conduct of the War and Civilian Casualties in Iraq*. New York: Human Rights Watch.

———. (2004a). *The Road to Abu Ghraib*. New York: Human Rights Watch.

———. (2004b). *Sidelined: Human Rights in Postwar Iraq.* New York: Human Rights Watch.

———. (2005a). *Leadership Failure: First Hand Account of Torture of Iraqi Detainees by the U.S. Army's 82nd Airborne Division.* New York: Human Rights Watch.

———. (2005b). *List of "Ghost Prisoners" Possibly in CIA Custody.* New York: Human Rights Watch.

———. (2005c). "New Accounts of Torture by U.S. Troops: Soldiers Say Failures by Command Led to Abuse." *Human Rights News*, September 12.

———. (2007a). *Caught in the Whirlwind: Torture and Denial of Due Process by the Kurdistan Security Forces.* New York: Human Rights Watch.

———. (2007b). *Ghost Prisoner: Two Years in Secret CIA Detention.* New York: Human Rights Watch.

———. (2007c). *The Omar Khadr Case: A Teenager Imprisoned at Guantánamo.* New York: Human Rights Watch.

———. (2007d). *The "Stamp of Guantánamo": The Story of Seven Men Betrayed by Russia's Diplomatic Assurances to the United States.* New York: Human Rights Watch.

———. (2008a). *Locked Up Alone: Detention Conditions and Mental Health at Guantánamo.* New York: Human Rights Watch.

———. (2008b). "US: Move New Guantánamo Cases to Federal Courts." *Human Rights Watch*, March 10.

Hürriyet. (2008). "Turkish Army Confirms Air Strikes Against PKK Camps in N. Iraq." *Hürriyet*, May 2.

Independent. (2001). "US Heavy Bombers Pound Taleban." *Independent*, November 1.

Integrated Regional Information Networks. (2004a). "Inadequate Sewage Disposal Blamed for Hepatitis Outbreak." Integrated Regional Information Networks, June 1.

———. (2004b). "Patients Complain of Medical Shortage." Integrated Regional Information Networks, January 22.

International Commission of Inquiry on Crimes Against Humanity Committed by the Bush Administration. (2006). *The Bush Crimes Commission Hearings.* New York: International Commission.

International Committee of the Red Cross. (2004). *Report of the International Committee of the Red Cross on the Treatment by the Coalition Forces of Prisoners of War and Other Protected Persons by the Geneva Conventions in Iraq During Arrest, Internment and Interrogation.* Geneva: International Committee of the Red Cross [Red Cross Report]. Pagination in sources corresponds to text in Greenberg and Dratel, eds., *The Torture Papers.*

———. (2006). "Families of Detainees in Afghanistan and Iraq Desperate for News." Geneva: International Committee of the Red Cross, April 25.

International Herald Tribune. (2006). "Stuck in Guantánamo." *International Herald Tribune*, April 22.

International News (Karachi). (2008). "Afghan Courts Convict Dozens." *International News*, April 17.

Iraq Body Count. (2005). *A Dossier of Civilian Casualties 2003-2005*. Oxford: Oxford Research Group.

Iraq Oil Report. (2008). "The Iraq Oil Circus Comes to Washington." *Iraq Oil Report*, April 11.

Iraqi Red Crescent Organization. (2007). *The Internally Displaced People in Iraq: Update 26*. September 16.

Isikoff, Michael, and John Barry. (2005). "SouthCom Showdown." *Newsweek*, May 9.

Israel, Ministry of Foreign Affairs. (2006). "Israel Supreme Court Decision on Targeting Terrorist Operatives." December 20.

Jackson, Derrick C. (2008). "Big Oil and the War in Iraq." boston.com, June 24.

Jaffer, Maisam. (2008). "Guantánamo Bay Detainees Released." *Muslim News* (UK), January 25.

Jamail, Dahr. (2004a). "Fallujah Doctors Report U.S. Forces Obstructed Medical Care in April." *New Standard*, May 21.

———. (2004b). "The Horror Story of Sadiq Zoman." *New Standard*, May 5.

———. (2005). "What Have We Done?" *Iraq Dispatches*, August 5.

Jamison, Melissa. (2005). "Detention of Juvenile Enemy Combatants at Guantánamo Bay: The Special Concerns of Children." *University of California at Davis Journal of Juvenile Justice, Law and Policy*.

Jehl, Douglas. (2004a). "G.I. in Abu Ghraib Abuse Is Spared Time in Jail." *New York Times*, November 3.

———. (2004b). "U.S. Action Bars Right of Some Captured in Iraq." *New York Times*, October 25.

———. (2005). "Questions Left by C.I.A. Chief on Torture Use." *New York Times*, March 18, 2005.

Jehl, Douglas, and Tim Golden. (2005). "CIA Is Likely to Avoid Charges in Most Prisoner Deaths." *New York Times*, October 23.

Jehl, Douglas, and David Johnson. (2005). "Rule Change Lets CIA Freely Send Suspects Abroad to Jails." *New York Times*, February 6.

Jehl, Douglas, and Neil A. Lewis. (2004). "The Prisoners; U.S. Military Disputed Protected Status of Prisoners Held in Iraq." *New York Times*, May 23.

Jehl, Douglas, and Eric Schmitt. (2004). "Officer Says Army Tried to Curb Red Cross Visits to Prison in Iraq." *New York Times*, May 19.

Johnson, Carrie. (2008). "Ashcroft Testifies on Interrogation Policy: Letter of Law Was Followed, He Says." *Washington Post*, July 26.

Johnson, Scott. (2008). "Dilemma of the Horn." *Newsweek*, April 21.

Johnston, David. (2006). "At a Secret Interrogation, Dispute Flared Over Tactics." *New York Times*, September 10.

Jones, Seth G., and Martin C. Libicki. (2008). *How Terrorist Groups End: Lessons for Counter Al Qa'ida*. Santa Monica, CA: RAND.

Judah, Tim. (2003). "The Fall of Baghdad." *New York Review of Books*, May 15.

Juhasz, Antonia. (2006). "In Iraq, It's the Oil, Stupid." *Topeka Capitol Journal*, January 21.

Juhl, Bushra. (2008). "13 Die in Overnight Clashes in Iraq." Associated Press, April 12.

Jurist. (2008). "Report from Guantánamo: Mohammed Jawad Is Another Teen Growing up in Detention." Jurist, May 19.

Kahl, Colin H. (2007). "In the Crossfire of the Crosshairs? Norms, Civilian Casualties, and U.S. Conflict in Iraq." *International Security*, January.

Karpinski, Janis. (2005). *One Woman's Army: The Commanding General of Abu Ghraib Tells Her Story*. New York: Miramax Books.

Keath, Lee. (2004a). "Around 1,361 Iraqis Killed in April's Violence, 10 Times the U.S. Death Toll." Associated Press, April 30.

———. (2004b). "Shi'ite Cleric Pulls Back Militias." Associated Press, April 12.

Keaton, Jamey. (2008). "European Envoy: Shut Guantánamo Soon." Associated Press, June 25.

Keller, Michael. (2008). *Torture Central: E-Mails from Abu Ghraib*. Lincoln, NE: iUniverse.

Kendall, Frank. (2008). "Not Quite the Thing to Do Here." *Human Rights First*, July 14.

Kerley, David. (2006). "Military General Urging Less Force, More Sensitivity in Iraq." ABC News, June 7.

Kessler, Ronald. (2007). *The Terrorist Watch: Inside the Desperate Race to Stop the Next Attack*. New York: Random House.

Khan, Habibullah. (2008). "Residents: Missile Strike Hits Pakistan Village." Associated Press, May 14.

Klapper, Bradley S. (2008). "Red Cross: Progress in U.S. Detention." *Fort Wayne Journal Gazette*, January 30.

Klein, Benjamin. (2008). "'High Value' Detainee Transferred to Guantánamo from CIA Custody." *Jurist*, March 15.

Klein, Naomi. (2007). "The US Psychological Torture System Is Finally on Trial." *Guardian*, February 23.

Kniazkov, Maxim. (2003). "Military Charges Eight Marines with Abusing Prisoners in Iraq." *FairfaxDigital*, October 20.

Koelbl, Susanne. (2007). "The Taliban Kill More Civilians Than NATO." Der Spiegel Online, September 24.

Kramer, Andrew E. (2007). "Helicopter Gunfire Kills Iraqi Civilians, Days After Sadr City Battle." *New York Times*, October 24.

Kreickenbaum, Martin. (2004). "Guantánamo Prisoners 'Locked Up in a World of Shadows'." World Socialist Web Site, May 28.

Krickmeyer, Ellen. (2005). "U.S. Airstrikes Take Toll on Civilians: Eye Witnesses Cite Scores Killed in Marine Offensive in Western Iraq." *Washington Post*, December 24.

Kristof, Nicholas D. (2008). "The Truth Commission." *New York Times*, July 6.

Kurnaz, Murat. (2008). *Five Years of My Life: A Report from Guantánamo.* Berlin: Rowohlt.

Lancet. (2004). "Call for Full Enquiry into Role of Medical Staff at Abu Ghraib." *Lancet*, August.

Lasseter, Tom. (2008a). "Exploiting Abuse." *Seattle Times*, June 21.

———. (2008b). "Freed Captives Get No 'Sorry'." *Seattle Times*, June 19.

LaVella, Leonard. (2003). *Operation Enduring Freedom Time Sensitive Targeting Process Study.* Air Combat Command Analysis Division, Directorate of Requirements, August 25.

Leonnig, Carol. (2005). "Desecration of Koran Has Been Reported Before." *Washington Post*, May 18.

———. (2007). "Evidence of Innocence Rejected at Guantánamo." *Washington Post*, December 5.

———. (2008). "Ex-Afghanistan Detainee Alleges Torture by U.S." *Washington Post*, March 29.

Leopold, Evelyn. (2004). "Iraq Resolution Gives Wide Powers to U.S. Forces." Reuters, May 24.

Lever, Sharon. (2005). "Jurisdiction for 'Material Support' Crimes: Factual Illustrations." *United States Attorneys' Bulletin*, July.

Levin, Carl. (2008). Opening Statement at Hearings of the Senate Armed Services Committee. June 17.

Levin, Daniel. (2004). "Legal Standards Applicable Under 18USC§§2340-2340A." U.S. Department of Justice, December 30.

Levin, Myron. (2008). "Making a Case Against Tribunals." *Los Angeles Times*, January 5.

Levy, Adrian, and Cathy Scott-Clark. (2003). "One Huge US Jail." *Guardian*, March 19.

Lewis, Anthony. (2004). "Making Torture Legal." *New York Times*, July 15.

Lewis, Neil A. (2004). "Red Cross Finds Detainee Abuse in Guantánamo." *New York Times*, November 30.

———. (2005). "French Details Emerge on Harsh Methods at Guantánamo." *New York Times*, January 1.

———. (2006a). "German Prosecutor Asked to Investigate Rumsfeld." *New York Times*, November 14.

———. (2006b). "Red Cross Officials to Visit Prisoners at Guantánamo." *New York Times*, September 20.

Lewis, Neil A., and David Johnston. (2004). "New F.B.I. Files Describe Abuse of Iraq Detainees." *New York Times*, December 21.

Lichtblau, Eric, and Scott Shane. (2008). "FBI Reported Abuses Against Detainees: But Review Says 'War Crimes File' Was Ignored." *New York Times*, May 20.

Lifton, Robert Jay. (2004). "Doctors and Torture." *New England Journal of Medicine*, July 29.

Liptak, Adam. (2004). "Who Would Try Civilians of U.S.? No One in Iraq." *New York Times*, May 26.

Liste, Philip. (2008). "Articulating the Nexus of Politics and Law: War in Iraq and the Practice Within Two Legal Systems." *International Political Sociology* (2): 38–55.

Lithwick, Dahlia. (2008). "The Fiction Behind Torture Policy." *Newsweek*, August 4.

Londoño, Ernest. (2008). "Frustration and Deceit on U.S.-Iraqi Patrol in Mosul." *Washington Post*, May 10.

Loney, Jim. (2008). "Logistics, Secrecy Hamper Guantánamo Trials." Reuters, July 13.

Los Angeles Times. (2008). "Al Jazeera Journalist Is Freed After 6 Years at Guantánamo." *Los Angeles Times*, May 2.

Loughlin, Sean. (2003). "Rumsfeld on Looting in Iraq: 'Stuff Happens'." CNN, April 12.

Luscombe, Richard. (2008). "Shadowy Tactics of US Troops in Iraq." *The Scotsman*, February 11.

Mackay, Neil. (2003a). "First Letters from Briton Now Facing the Death Penalty at Camp X-Ray." *Sunday Herald*, July 6.

———. (2003b). "US Forces' Use of Depleted Uranium Is 'Illegal'." *Sunday Morning Herald*, March 20.

Maguire, Keith, and Andy Lines. (2005). "Bush Plot to Bomb Arab Ally: Madness of War Memo." *Daily Mirror*, November 22.

Manning, Michael. (2007). "Iraq: Hidden Human Costs." *New York Review of Books*, December 20.

Margulies, Joseph. (2007). *Guantánamo and the Abuse of Presidential Power*. New York: Simon & Schuster.

Mariner, Joanne. (2002). "Geriatric Terrorists on Guantánamo." *Counterpunch*, November 7.

Markon, Jerry. (2008a). "Guantánamo Judge Blocks Use of Some Statements." *Washington Post*, July 22.

———. (2008b). "Moussaoui Deprived of Constitutional Rights, Attorneys Say: Appeal Seeks to Overturn Guilty Plea, Life Sentence Because of Evidence Kept Secret, Counsel Choice Denied." *Washington Post*, February 15.

Markon, Jerry, and Josh White. (2008). "Detainee Describes Treatment: Lawyers for Another Captive Released Interrogation Tapes." *Washington Post*, July 16.

Martin, Susan. (2004). "Report Steers Clear of Interrogators' Boss." *St. Petersburg Times*, May 8.

Marty, Dick. (2006). *Alleged Secret Detentions in Council of Europe Member Countries*. Strasbourg: Council of Europe.

Massing, Michael. (2004). "Unfit to Print?" *New York Review of Books*, June 24.

———. (2008a). "As Iraqis See It." *New York Review of Books*, January 17.

———. (2008b). "Embedded in Iraq." *New York Review of Books*, July 17.

Mayer, Jane. (2005a). "The Experiment." *New Yorker*, July 11.

———. (2005b). "Outsourcing Terror." *New Yorker*, February 14.

———. (2008a). "The Battle for a Country's Soul." *New York Review of Books*, August 14.

———. (2008b). *The Dark Side: The Inside Story of How the War on Terror Turned into a War on American Ideals*. New York: Random House.

Mazzetti, Mark. (2007). "Rules Lay Out CIA's Tactics in Questioning," *New York Times*, July 21.

———. (2008a). "'03 U.S. Memo Approved Harsh Interrogations," *New York Times*, April 2.

———. (2008b). "C.I.A. Secretly Held Qaeda Suspect, Official Says," *New York Times*, March 15.

———. (2008c). "Letters Give C.I.A. Tactics a Legal Rationale," *New York Times*, April 27.

Mazzetti, Mark, and Scott Shane. (2008). "Tapes' Destruction Hovers Over Detainee Cases," *New York Times*, March 28.

McCarthy, Rory. (2004a). "US Denies Need for Falluja Convoy," *Guardian*, November 15.

———. (2004b). "Wedding Party Massacre: Iraqis Claim More than 40 Killed in US Helicopter Attack." *Guardian*, May 20.

McClatchy News Service. (2008). "Ex-Med. Resident Writes from Guantánamo About CIA Torture." *Baltimore Sun*, January 22.

McClellan, Scott. (2008a). Testimony Before the House Judiciary Committee. June 20.

———. (2008b). *What Happened: Inside the Bush White House and What's Wrong with Washington*. New York: Public Affairs.

McCoy, Alfred W. (2006). *A Question of Torture: CIA Interrogation, from the Cold War to the War on Terror*. New York: Holt.

McDoom, Opheera. (2008). "Sudan's Ex-Guantánamo Prisoners Demand Payout." Reuters, January 26.

McElroy, Steven. (2008). "Looted Antiquities Returned to Iraq." *New York Times*, June 23.

McGovern, Ray. (2008). "Iniquities of War, Iniquities of Life." consortium-news.com, January 31.

McGuirk, Rod. (2007). "Australia to Pressure U.S. on Gitmo Inmate." *Washington Post*, February 6.

Meek, James. (2005). "'They Beat Me from All Sides.'" *Guardian*, January 14.

Melia, Michael. (2008a). "Abuse Claims Complicating Gitmo Trials." Associated Press, March 15.

———. (2008b). "Guantánamo Detainees Spread Word to Boycott Trials." Associated Press, May 9.

———. (2008c). "Judge Removes Legal Adviser from Guantánamo Case." Associated Press, May 11.

———. (2008d). "Secret Evidence Bogs Down Gitmo Hearings." Associated Press, February 9.

Meyer, Josh. (2007). "FBI Works to Bolster Cases on Al Qaeda." *Los Angeles Times*, October 21.

———. (2008a). "Court Rules in Favor of Detainee." *Los Angeles Times*, June 24.

———. (2008b). "Defending 'the Most Hated Man in the World'." *Los Angeles Times*, May 25.

———. (2008c). "Judge Allows Guantánamo Inmates to Testify." *Los Angeles Times*, July 15.

———. (2008d). "Judge Urges 9/11 Suspects to Accept Legal Help." *Los Angeles Times*, July 10.

———. (2008e). "9/11 Plotters Tell Judge of Legal Woes." *Los Angeles Times*, July 11.

Mikkelson, Randall. (2008). "Guantánamo Trials Called Tainted by Coercion." Reuters, March 10.

Mikolashek, Lieutenant General Paul T. (2004). *Inspection Report on Detainee Operations*. Washington, DC: Department of Defense [Mikolashek Report]. Pagination in Sources corresponds to text in Greenberg and Dratel, eds., *The Torture Papers*.

Milbank, Dana, and Walter Pincus. (2003). "U.S. Administrator Imposes Flat Tax System on Iraq." *Washington Post*, November 2.

Miles, Steven H. (2006). *Oath Betrayed: Torture, Medical Complicity and the War on Terror*. New York: Random House.

Miller, Greg. (2002). "Many Held at Guantánamo Not Likely Terrorists." *Los Angeles Times*, December 22.

———. (2007). "Bush Signs Rules for CIA Interrogators." *Los Angeles Times*, July 21.

———. (2008a). "CIA Chief Confirms Use of Waterboarding." *Los Angeles Times*, February 6.

———. (2008b). "Waterboarding Is Still an Option." *Los Angeles Times*, February 7.

Miller, Greg, and Richard B. Schmitt. (2007). "CIA Doesn't Torture, Bush Says." *Los Angeles Times*, October 6.

Miller, Judith. (2008). "Stuck in the Middle." *Los Angeles Times* (Sunday Opinion Section), April 20.

Miller, T. Christian. (2006). *Blood Money: Wasted Billions, Lost Lives, and Corporate Greed in Iraq*. New York: Little Brown.

———. (2007). "Contractors Outnumber Troops in Iraq." *Los Angeles Times*, July 4.

Mishra, Pankaj. (2005). "The Real Afghanistan." *New York Review of Books*, March 10.

Moffeit, Miles. (2004). "Skipped Autopsies in Iraq Revealed." *Denver Post*, May 21.

Monbiot, George. (2003). "One Rule for Them." *Guardian*, March 25.

———. (2008). "Guantánamo Crimes Made World Less Safe." *Pakistan Observer*, May 16.

Montgomery, Devin. (2008). "Guantánamo Detainee Files Rights Commission Complaint against US." *Jurist*, August 8.

Moreau, Ron, and Mark Hosenball. (2008). "Pakistan's Dangerous Double Game." *Newsweek*, September 22.

Mother Jones. (2008). "Bombs Away!" *Mother Jones*, March/April.

Mrone, Bassern, and Abdul-Qader Saadi. (2004). "US Bombs Fallujah Mosque; More than 40 Worshippers Killed: Revolutionary Violence Engulfs Iraq." Associated Press, April 7.

Mu Xuequan. (2008). "Report: Hundreds of U.S.-Funded Reconstruction Contracts in Iraq Terminated." chinaview.cn, April 29.

Muir, Hugh. (2007). "Saudi Four Back Compensation Campaign for Torture Victims." *Guardian*, June 25.

Müller, Ingo. (1991). *Hitler's Justice: The Courts of the Third Reich*. Cambridge, MA: Harvard University Press.

Mulrine, Anna. (2008a). "Operating by the (Law) Book." *U.S. News & World Report*, June 9.

———. (2008b). "A Struggling Coalition of the Willing and the Not-So-Willing." *U.S. News & World Report*, June 16.

Murphy, Brett. (2008a). "Guantánamo Lawyers Ask Court to Restrict Prosecution Contact with Detainees." Jurist, March 18.

———. (2008b). "UK Law Lords Reject Bid for Inquiry into Legality of Iraq War." Jurist, April 9.

Musharraf, Pervaiz. (2006). *In the Line of Fire: A Memoir*. New York: Free Press.

Nathan, Debbie. (2008). "A Nightmare World of Torture and Prison Guard Suicides: Confessions of a Gitmo Guard." Counterpunch, February 26.

Nebehay, Stephanie. (2007). "UN Rights Envoy Suspects CIA of Guantánamo Torture." Reuters, July 14.

———. (2008). "Guantánamo War Crimes Trials Fall Short—Arbour." Reuters, June 11.

Neumeister, Larry (2008). "Court: U.S. Gov't Can't Block Detainee Photos Release." Associated Press, September 22.

New York Times. (2007a). "Abu Ghraib Swept Under the Rug." *New York Times*, August 30.

———. (2007b). "Subcontracting the War." *New York Times*, October 1, 2007.

———. (2008a). "Strike from Afar: How Would 'Over the Horizon' Counter-terrorism Work in Iraq? Look at Somalia." *New York Times*, May 3.

———. (2008b). "The Suffering of Soldiers." *New York Times*, May 11.

———. (2008c). "Unnecessary Harm." *New York Times*, February 13.

New York University. (2008). *By the Numbers: Findings of the Detainee Abuse and Accountability Project*. New York: Center for Human Rights and Global Justice, School of Law.

Newbart, Dave. (2003). "U. of C. Experts Decry Looting of Iraqi Sites." *Chicago Sun-Times*, June 12.

NewsMax. (2004). "U.S. Bombs 'Mosque' Fortress; Violence Spreads in Iraq." NewsMax.com, April 7.

Nicholl, David. (2008). "Giving up the Ghost: Detainees, Doctors and Torture." Jurist, March 15.

Nordland, Rod, Sami Yousafzai, and Babak Dehghanpisheh. (2002). "How Al Qaeda Got Away." *Newsweek*, August 19.

Noronha, Charmaine. (2008). "Teen's Lawyer Releases Guantánamo Video in Plea for Freedom." *Associated Press*, July 16.

Norton-Taylor, Richard, and Duncan Campbell. (2008). "Fresh Questions on Torture Flights Spark Demands for Inquiry." *Guardian*, March 10.

Novak, Viveca, and Douglas Waller. (2004). "New Abuse Charges." *Time*, June 20.

Observer, The. (2008). "All Great Music Is Political." *Guardian*, May 18.

O'Neill, Brendan. (2005). "After Guantánamo." BBC, January 25.

O'Neill, Sean. (2007). "The London Chef Who Was Forsaken for Five Years in Guantánamo." *London Times*, June 16.

Oppel, Richard A., Jr. (2004). "Early Target of Offensive Is a Hospital." *New York Times*, November 8.

———. (2006). "Premier Accuses U.S. of Attacking Civilians in Iraq." *New York Times*, June 2.

———. (2008). "U.S. Military Says Soldiers Fired on Civilians." *New York Times*, July 28.

Ossenova, Katerina. (2007). "Spain Judge says Bush and Iraq War Allies Should Face War Crimes Charges." Jurist, March 20.

Ottawa Recorder. (2008). "2 Algerians Sent from Gitmo Missing." *Ottawa Recorder*, July 14.

Paley, Amit R., and Karen De Young. (2008). "Iraqis Condemn American Demands." *Washington Post*, June 11.

Pape, Robert. (2008). *Dying to Win: The Strategic Logic of Suicide Terrorism*. London: Allen Lane.

Parenti, Christian. (2004). "Torture Claims Mark US Media Campaign in Iraq." *Guardian*, April 23.

Parker, Edmund. (2008). "Iraq: Sadrists Mobilise Against Occupation." greenleft.org.au, June 15.

Parker, Ned. (2007a). "At Least 5 Iraqi Civilians Are Killed by U.S. Troops." *Los Angeles Times*, November 28.

———. (2007b). "U.S. Army Sniper's Murder Trial Begins in Baghdad." *Los Angeles Times*, November 7.

———. (2008a). "Between War and Peace, an Uneasy Calm." *Los Angeles Times*, July 28.

———. (2008b). "U.S. Is Entangled in Shi'ite Rivalry." *Los Angeles Times*, March 30.

———. (2008c). "U.S. Sway in Iraq Wanes as Maliki's Power Grows." *Los Angeles Times*, September 16.

Parker, Ned, and Saif Hameed. (2008). "Iraqis Protest U.S. Security Talks." *Los Angeles Times*, May 31.

Parker, Ned, and Usama Redha. (2008). "Basra Breathes a Little Easier But Can't Relax." *Los Angeles Times*, May 31.

Partlow, Joshua. (2007). "Many Trainees Are Complicit with 'Enemy Targets'." *Washington Post*, September 4.

Partlow, Joshua, and Jonathan Finer. (2006). "Group Says It Abducted Missing GIs; 3 Americans Charged in Iraqi Deaths." *Washington Post*, June 20.

Partlow, Joshua, and Walter Pincus. (2007). "Iraq Bans Security Contractor." *Washington Post*, September 18.

Patel, Mayur. (2004). "The Legal Status of Coalition Forces in Iraq After the June 30 Handover." asil.org, March.

Patterson, Kevin. (2007). "Talk to Me Like My Father." *Mother Jones*, July/ August.

Paust, Jordan J. (2005). "Executive Plans and Authorizations to Violate International Law Concerning Treatment and Interrogation of Detainees." *Columbia Journal of Transnational Law*, v. 43.

———. (2007). *Beyond the Law: The Bush Administration's Unlawful Responses in the "War" on Terror*. New York: Cambridge University Press.

Pelley, Scott. (2005). "CIA Flying Suspects to Torture?" CBS News, March 6.

Pelton, Robert Young. (2006). *Licensed to Kill: Hired Guns in the War on Terror*. New York: Crown.

Perito, Rorbert. (2007). *Reforming the Iraqi Interior Ministry, Police, and Facilities Protective Service*. Washington, DC: U.S. Institute of Peace.

Perlstein, Deborah. (2008). Testimony to the House Committee on the Judiciary, July 25.

Perry, Tony (2007a). "Convicted Marine Is Spared Prison Sentence," *Los Angeles Times*, July 21.

———. (2007b). "Marine Is Charged with Murder in Fallouja Death," *Los Angeles Times*, August 21.

———. (2007c). "Marines to Investigate Afghanistan Shooting," *Los Angeles Times*, October 12.

———. (2007d). "Marines Were Ordered to Be More Violent, Witness Says," *Los Angeles Times*, July 15.

———. (2007e). "Three Marine Officers Issued Censures in Haditha Slayings," *Los Angeles Times*, September 6.

———. (2008a). "Charges Against Marine Dropped," *Los Angeles Times*, June 18.

———. (2008b). "Court Martial Not Advised for Marine in Iraq Deaths," *Los Angeles Times*, July 15.

———. (2008c). "Four Years Later." *Los Angeles Times*er, Fallouja Rises Again from the Ashes of War," *Los Angeles Times*, March 21.

———. (2008d). "Marine Cleared in Haditha Case," *Los Angeles Times*, March 29.

———. (2008e). "Marine to Stand Trial in Haditha Killings," *Los Angeles Times*, January 1.

———. (2008f). "Marines Contempt Charges Dropped." *Los Angeles Times*, September 24.

———. (2008g). "Seeking Truth in Haditha Killings," *Los Angeles Times*, February 19.

Pew Research Center for the People and the Press. (2007). "America's Image in the World: Findings from the Pew Global Attitudes Project: Remarks of Andrew Kohut to the U.S. House Committee on Foreign Affairs; Subcommittee on International Organizations, Human Rights, and Oversight." Washington, DC: Pew Center for People and the Press, March 14.

Philbin, Patrick F., and John Yoo. (2001). "Possible Habeas Corpus Jurisdiction Over Aliens Held in Guantánamo Bay, Cuba." U.S. Department of Justice, September 28.

Physicians for Human Rights. (2005). *Break Them Down: Systematic Use of Psychological Torture by U.S. Forces.* Cambridge, MA: Physicians for Human Rights.

———. (2008). *Broken Laws, Broken Lives: Medical Evidence of Torture by US Personnel and Its Impact.* Cambridge, MA: Physicians for Human Rights.

Pincus, Walter. (2005). "British Intelligence Warned of Iraq War: Blair Was Told of White House's Determination to Use Military Against Hussein." *Washington Post*, May 13.

Pine, Sean. (2008). "Omar Khadr: A Most Peculiar Young Offender." *Globe and Mail*, March 22.

Poole, Oliver. (2005). "'Worst War Crime' Committed by US in Iraq." *Telegraph*, May 27.

Popham, Peter. (2005). "US Forces 'Used Chemical Weapons' During Assault on City of Fallujah." *Independent*, November 8.

Prados, John. (2004). ed., *Hoodwinked: The Documents That Reveal How Bush Sold Us a War*. New York: New Press.

Press Association (2008). "Guantánamo Man 'Breaking Down'." Press Association (UK), February 7.

Price, Jay, Joseph Neff, and Charles Crain. (2004). "Mutilation Seen Around the World." *News and Observer* (Raleigh, NC), July 25.

Priest, Dana. (2005a). "CIA Avoids Scrutiny of Detainee Treatment." *Washington Post*, March 3.

———. (2005b). "Wrongful Imprisonment: Anatomy of a CIA Mistake." *Washington Post*, December 4.

Priest, Dana, and Barton Gellman. (2002). "U.S. Decries Abuse But Defends Interrogations: 'Stress and Duress' Tactics Used on Terrorism Suspects Held in Secret Overseas Facilities." *Washington Post*, December 26.

Provance, Samuel. (2006). "Testimony Before Congress." New York: Human Rights First (humanrightsfirst.info/pdf/06214-usls-provance-statement. pff).

Prusher, Illene R. (2003). "Errant US Missile Raises Ire of Turkish Villagers." *Christian Science Monitor*, March 25.

Public Broadcasting System. (2004). "Son of Al Qaeda." Frontline, April 21.

———. (2008). "Bush's War." Frontline, March 17–18.

Qader-Saadi, Abdul. (2004). "Fallujah Death Toll for Week More Than 600." Associated Press, April 12.

———. (2007). "Iraqi Kurdistan's Downward Spiral." *Middle East Quarterly*, Summer.

Raghavan, Sadarsan, and Steve Fainaru. (2007). "U.S. Repeatedly Rebuffed Iraq on Blackwater Complaints." *Washington Post*, September 23.

Rashid, Ahmed. (2004). "The Mess in Afghanistan." *New York Review of Books*, February 12.

Rashid, Harood. (2003). "Guantánamo Prisoners Speak Out." *Guardian*, November 24.

Rassbach, Elsa. (2007). "The War on Terror Is a Mockery." *Z Magazine*, November.

Rasul, Shafig, and Asif Iqbal. (2004). Letter to Members of the Senate Armed Services Committee. May 13. Reprinted in Ratner and Ray, *Guantánamo*, 150–154.

Rath, Arun. (2008). "Rules of Engagement." Frontline, February 19.

Ratner, Michael, and Ellen Ray. (2004). *Guantánamo: What the World Should Know*. White River, VT: Chelsea Green.

———. (2008). "Think Again: Geneva Conventions." *Foreign Policy*, March/April.

Rayment, Sean. (2004). "US Tactics Condemned by British Officers." *Telegraph*, April 11.

Reed, Ishmael. (2003). "Iraqi Slaughter, Mayhem and Plunder." *Counterpunch*, June 9.

Regular, Arnon. (2003). "'Road Map Is a Life Saver for Us,' PM Abbas Tells Hamas." *Ha'aretz*, June 27.

Reidy, Aisling. (2008). "Watching Jawad." hwr.org, March 21.

Reporters Without Borders. (2008). "RSF Petitions International Humanitarian Fact-Finding Commission Over Bombing of Iraqi State Television." International Freedom of Expression Exchange, Canada (canada.ifex. org), May 24.

Reuters. (2008a). "Canada Premier Sued Over Guantánamo Inmate." *New York Times*, August 8.

———. (2008b). "Iran Government Faces Credibility Test: U.S. General." Reuters, September 22.

———. (2008c). "Iraq Lawmakers Want US Forces out as Part of Deal." Reuters, June 5.

———. (2008d). "Iraq's Sadrists Demand U.S. Release Former Minister." *Washington Post*, March 4.

———. (2008e). "Turkey Shells Kurdish Rebel Positions in N. Iraq." Reuters, February 21.

Revolutionary Association of the Women of Afghanistan. (2007). "Communiqué on International Human Rights Day." rawa.org, December 10.

Ricks, Thomas E. (2002). "Some Top Military Brass Favor Status Quo in Iraq." *Washington Post*, July 28.

———. (2006). *Fiasco: The American Military Adventure in Iraq*. New York: Penguin.

———. (2007). Interview, *Charlie Rose*. PBS, November 12.

Rieckhoff, Paul. (2007). *Chasing Ghosts: Failures and Facades in Iraq: A Soldier's Perspective*. New York: NAL Caliber.

Rietig, Thomas. (2008). "US Authorities Hand over German Held in Afghanistan." Associated Press, May 31.

Ripley, Amanda. (2004). "Redefining Torture." *Time*, June 13.

Risen, James. (2006). *State of War: The Secret History of the CIA and the Bush Administration*. New York: Free Press.

———. (2007). "Contractors Face Combat-Related Stress After Iraq." *New York Times*, July 5.

Rising, David. (2006). "CIA Kidnapping Case: Germany Issues Warrants for 13." Associated Press, January 31.

Rivera, Ray. (2005). "Suspicion in the Ranks." *Seattle Times*, January 9–16.

Roberts, Kristin, and Paul de Bendern. (2008). "Bush Calls for Quick End to Turkish N. Iraq Operation." Reuters, February 27.

Robinson, Dan. (2008). "Former POWs Continue Efforts for Compensation from Iraq." Voice of America, June 18.

Rodenbeck, Max. (2003). "Bohemia in Baghdad." *New York Review of Books*, July 3.

Rogge, John (1959). *Why Men Confess*. New York: Nelson.

Rohde, David. (2008). Interview, Charlie Rose. PBS, July 1.

Rondeaux, Candace (2008). "Civilian Airstrike Deaths Probed: 78 Have Died in Three Incidents This Month Alone, Afghan Officials Say" *Washington Post*, July 25.

Rondeaux, Candace, Josh White, and Julie Tate. (2008). "Afghan Detainees Sent Home to Face Closed-Door Trials." *New York Times*, April 13.

Rose, David. (2004a). "How We Survived Jail Hell." *The Observer*, March 14.

———. (2004b). Guantánamo: *America's War on Human Rights*. London: Faber and Faber.

Rosen, Mir. (2008). Interview, NewsHour. PBS, March 11.

Rosenberg, Carol. (2008a). "Abuse Allegations Cloud Coming War Court Cases." *Miami Herald*, March 13.

———. (2008b). "ACLU Taps Legal Talent to Defend Alleged Terrorists." *Miami Herald*, April 5.

———. (2008c). "Held 6 Years, Al Qaeda Suspect Sees Lawyers." *Miami Herald*, February 26.

———. (2008d). "Pentagon to Challenge Interview of 9/11 Suspect." *Miami Herald*, February 19.

———. (2008e). "Report Was Wrong: Detainee Didn't Get Call from Sudan." *Miami Herald*, May 25.

———. (2008f). "Saudi Terror Suspect: Military Trials a 'Sham'." *Miami Herald*, April 9.

Ross, Brian, and Alexandra Salomon. (2004). "Intel Staff Cites Abu Ghraib Cover-Up." ABC News, May 18.

Roug, Louise, and Doug Smith. (2006). "War's Iraqi Death Tolls Tops 50,000." *Los Angeles Times*, June 25.

Rouse, Beverly. (2008). "Family of Iraqi Man Killed by Soldiers Gets £3 Payout." *Independent*, July 12.

Rozen, Laura. (2008). "Central Intelligence Anxiety." *Mother Jones*, March/April.

Rumsfeld, Donald. (2002a). "Detainee Interrogations." U.S. Department of Defense, December 2.

———. (2002b). "Memorandum for Chairman of the Joint Chiefs of Staff, re Status of Taliban and Al Qaeda." U.S. Department of Defense, January 19.

———. (2003a). "Counter-Resistance Techniques." U.S. Department of Defense, January 15.

———. (2003b). "Counter-Resistance Techniques in the War on Terrorism." U.S. Department of Defense, April 16.

———. (2003c). "Working Group Report on Detainee Interrogations in the Global War on Terrorism." U.S. Department of Defense, April 4.

Ruthven, Malise. (2008). "The Rise of the Muslim Terrorists." *New York Review of Books*, May 29.

Saar, Erik, and Viveca Novak. (2005). *Inside the Wire: A Military Intelligence Soldier's Eyewitness Account of Life at Guantánamo*. New York: Penguin.

Sageman, Marc. (2008). *Leaderless Jihad: Terror Networks in the Twenty-First Century*. Philadelphia: University of Pennsylvania Press.

Saifee, Seema. (2008). "Guantánamo's Uighurs: No Justice in Solitary." Jurist, March 28.

Salam, Mullah Abdul. (2006). *Broken Chains of Guantánamo* (currently in translation).

Sale, Jonathan. (2008). "Passed/Failed: An Education in the Life of Moazzam Begg, Ex-Guantánamo Bay Detainee." *Independent*, March 6.

Sale, Richard. (2003). "Iraqi CPA Fires 28,000." United Press International, November 21.

Salman, Raheem. (2008). "The View from the Shi'ite South." *Los Angeles Times*, April 10, 2008.

Sanchez, Lieutenant General Ricardo S. (2008a). Interview, Charlie Rose. PBS, May 16.

———. (2008b). *Wiser in Battle: A Soldier's Story*. New York: HarperCollins.

Sanders, Jackie. (2006). "Statement by Ambassador Jackie W. Sanders, Alternate U.S. Representative to the UN for Special Political Affairs, on the Report of the Secretary-General on Children and Armed Conflict, in the Security Council." Washington, DC: U.S. Department of State, November 28.

Sands, Philippe.(2008a). "The Green Light." *Vanity Fair*, April.

———. (2008b). Interview, Bill Moyers Journal. PBS, May 9.

———. (2008c). *The Torture Team: Rumsfeld's Memo and the Betrayal of American Values*. New York: Palgrave Macmillan.

Sanger, David E. (2007). "Bush Is Said to Approve More Aid to Iraqi Sunnis Battling Extremist Groups." *New York Times*, September 2.

Savage, David G. (2007). "High Court Debates Rights of Guantánamo Detainees." *Los Angeles Times*, December 6.

Savidge, Martin. (2003). "Protecting Iraq's Oil Supply." CNN, March 22.

Scahill, Jeremy. (2007a). *Blackwater: The Rise of the World's Most Powerful Mercenary Army*. New York: Avalon.

———. (2007b). "Blackwater's Loopholes." *Los Angeles Times*, November 15.

Scharnberg, Kirsten. (2005). "U.S. Raids Test Iraqi Patience." *Chicago Tribune*, June 15.

Schildgen, Bob. (2005). "Why We Should Pay War Reparations to Iraq." *San Francisco Chronicle*, November 6.

Schlesinger, James R., et al. (2004). *Final Report of the Independent Panel to Review DoD Detention Operations*. Washington, DC: Independent Panel [Schlesinger Report].

Schmidt, Lieutenant General Randall. (2005). *Investigations into FBI Allegations of Detainee Abuse at Guantánamo Bay, Cuba, Detention Facility.* U.S. Department of Defense [Schmidt Report]. Pagination in Sources corresponds to text in Greenberg and Dratel, eds. *The Torture Papers.*

Schmitt, Eric. (2003). "High-Tech Fighter Pilots Recount Exploits." *New York Times,* April 25.

———. (2005). "U.S. Tells How Quran Was Defiled." *San Francisco Chronicle,* June 4.

———. (2008a). "FBI Called Slow to Join Terror Fight." *Los Angeles Times,* May 9.

———. (2008b). "Military Tactics Worried FBI Interrogators." *Los Angeles Times,* May 21.

———. (2008c). "Pentagon Drops Post in Pakistan for Top General." *New York Times,* May 9.

Schmitt, Eric, and Tim Golden. (2008). "U.S. Planning Big New Prison in Afghanistan." *New York Times,* May 17.

Schmitt, Eric, and Michael R. Gordon. (2008). "Leak on Cross-Border Chases from Iraq." *New York Times,* February 4.

Schmitt, Eric, and Douglas Jehl. (2004). "M.P.'s Received Orders to Strip Iraqi Detainees." *New York Times,* May 18.

Schmitt, Eric, and Mark Mazetti. (2008). "Bush Said to Give Orders Allowing Raids in Pakistan." *New York Times,* September 10.

Schmitt, Eric, and Thom Shanker. (2004). "Prison Abuse: Rumsfeld Issued an Order to Hide Detainee in Iraq." *New York Times,* June 17.

Schofield, Matthew. (2006). "Iraq Police Report Details of Civilians' Deaths at Hands of U.S. Troops." *Miami Herald,* March 19.

Schor, Elena. (2008). "Obama Might Pursue Criminal Charges Against Bush." *Guardian,* September 3.

Schumacher, Colonel Gerald. (2006). *A Bloody Business: America's War Zone Contractors and the Occupation of Iraq.* St. Paul, MN: Zenith Press.

Schuman, Miles. (2004). "Falluja's Health Damage." *The Nation,* December 13.

Schwartz, Emma. (2008). "How the Trials Will Work." *U.S. News & World Report,* February 25.

Schweich, Thomas. (2008). "Is Afghanistan a Narco-State?" *New York Times,* July 27.

Scotsman. (2008). "Two Die in Afghanistan Protests." scotsman.com, May 11.

Seeley, Katherine Q. (2001). "A Nation Challenged: The Detention Campus; U.S. to Hold Taliban Detainees in the 'the Least Worst Place'." *New York Times,* December 28.

Sengupta, Kim. (2004). "Onslaught in Samarra Escalates in 'Dress Rehearsal' for Major US Assault on Rebels." *Independent,* October 3.

———. (2005). "Anger as American Troops Kill Four Inmates in Jail Riot." *Independent,* February 2.

Serrano, Richard, and John Danieszewski. (2005). "Dozens Have Alleged Koran's Mishandling." *Los Angeles Times*, May 22.

Sevastopulo, Demetri. (2008). "Former Navy Legal Chief Condemns Guantánamo 'Cruelty.'" *Financial Times*, June 21.

Shah, Amir. (2008). "Hundreds of Afghans Protest Over Quran Shooting." *Associated Press*, May 26.

Shane, Scott. (2008a). "Inside the Interrogation of a 9/11 Mastermind: After Harsh Tactics, Gentler Methods Elicited Details About Al Qaeda." *New York Times*, June 22.

———. (2008b). Interview, Charlie Rose. PBS, June 23.

Shane, Scott, David Johnson, and James Risen. (2007). "Secret U.S. Endorsement of Severe Interrogations." *New York Times*, October 4.

Shanker, Thom, and Eric Schmitt. (2003). "Threats and Responses: Hearts and Minds: Firing Leaflets and Electrons, U.S. Wages Information War." *New York Times*, February 23.

———. (2004). "Pentagon Expects Long-Term Access to Key Iraq Bases." *New York Times*, April 19.

Sharrock, Justine. (2008). "Am I a Torturer?" *Mother Jones*, March/April.

Shephard, Michelle. (2007). "Khadr's Canadian Lawyer Barred from Hearing." *Toronto Star*, October 31.

———. (2008a). "Judge Orders Release of Gitmo Interrogation Tap, Suggests Canadian Questioner Knew of Prior Abuse." *Toronto Star*, June 26.

———. (2008b). "Khadr's Military Interrogation Faces Scrutiny." *Toronto Star*, March 25.

Shimoyachi, Nao. (2004). "Depleted Uranium Shells Decried: Citizens Find Bush Guilty of Afghan War Crimes." *Japan Times*, March 14.

Shiner, Philip. (2005). "A New International Legal Order." *American Journal of International Law*.

Siddiqui, Haroon. (2008). "Families Sue over Guantánamo Bay Suicides." *Guardian*, June 11.

Siddiqui, Latafat Ali. (2008). "American Paid $500,000 to Pakistan for Arrest of Canadian." *Dawn*, May 14.

Silvey, Robert. (2004). "Halliburton Bad News Disappears." *Rubicon*, July 29.

Singh, Amrit, and Jameel Jaffer. (2007). *Administration of Torture: A Documentary Record from Washington to Abu Ghraib and Beyond*. New York: Columbia University Press.

Sizemore, Bill, and Joanne Kimberlin. (2006). "Blackwater: When Things Go Wrong." *Virginian-Pilot* (Hampton Roads), July 26.

Slevin, Peter, and Joe Stephens. (2004). "Detainees' Medical Files Shared: Guantánamo Interrogators Access Criticized." *Washington Post*, June 10.

Slater, Dan. (2008). "Gitmo Judge Delays Hamdan Trial, Awaits High Court Decision." *Wall Street Journal*, May 19.

Smith, Clive Stafford. (2005). "The Kids of Guantánamo Bay." *Cageprisoners*, June 15.

——. (2007a). "America's Legal Black Hole." *Los Angeles Times*, October 5.

——. (2007b). *Eight O'Clock Ferry to the Windward Side: Seeking Justice in Guantánamo Bay*. New York: Nation Books.

Smith, Doug. (2007). "U.S. Airstrike Kills at Least 11 in Iraq." *Los Angeles Times*, October 24.

Smith, Doug, and Raheen Salman. (2007). "Maliki Prods U.S. to Hand Over Condemned Trio." *Los Angeles Times*, November 12.

Smith, Michael. (2005a). "How the Leaked Documents Questioning War Emerged from 'Britain's Deep Throat'." *Sunday Times*, June 26.

——. (2005b). "The War Before the War." *New Statesman*, May 30.

Smith, R. Jeffrey. (2005). "Interrogator Says U.S. Approved Handling of Detainee Who Died." *Washington Post*, April 13.

Smith, Thomas W. (2008). "Protecting Civilians ... or Soldiers? Humanitarian Law and the Economy of Risk in Iraq." *International Studies Perspectives*, May.

Smucker, Philip. (2002). "How Bin Laden Got Away." *Christian Science Monitor*, March 4.

Sorensen, Theodore. (2008). "No Torture. No Exceptions." *Washington Monthly*, March.

Soriano, Cesar G., and Steven Komarow. (2004). "Poll: Iraqis Out of Patience." *USA Today*, April 28.

Spiegel, Peter, and Josh Meyer. (2008). "Basis for Offshore Prison Is Undercut." *Los Angeles Times*, June 13

Spinner, Jackie. (2004). "U.S. Criticized for Dismissing Iraqi Companies in Reconstruction." *Washington Post*, February 9.

Spring, Silvia, and Larry Kaplow. (2008). "Sacrificed to the Surge." *Newsweek*, April 14.

Squitieri, Tom, and Dave Moniz. (2004). "Prison Probe Finds More Abuse." *USA Today*, May 31.

Stack, Megan, and Bob Drogin. (2005). "Detainee Says U.S. Handed Him Over for Torture." *Los Angeles Times*, January 13.

Stephen, Andrew. (2004). "America: The U.S. Military Now Puts Machine Guns in the Hands of Mercenaries." *New Statesman*, April 26.

Stickler, Angus. (2007). "Depleted Uranium Weapons–A BBC Investigation." BBC Radio (Internet version), August 21.

Stockman, Farah. (2007). "Nationality Plays Key Role in Detainee Release: More Saudis Are Freed from Guantánamo." *Boston Globe*, November 2

Strasser, Steven, ed. (2004). *The Abu Ghraib Investigations: The Official Reports of the Independent Panel and the Pentagon on the Shocking Prisoner Abuse in Iraq*. New York: Public Affairs.

Stringer, David. (2008). "Report: 8 Former Guantánamo Detainees Sue British Government." Associated Press, April 20.

Sujo, Aly. (2002). "We're Ready to Unleash More Hellfire." *New York Post*, November 11.

Sullivan, Andrew. (2008). "Inside Guantánamo." *Atlantic*, January.

Sullivan, Stacy. (2008a). "Osama Bin Laden's Media Director Puts on a Show at Guantánamo." huffingtonpost.com, May 14.

———. (2008b). "Sabotage in Guantánamo: How the 9/11 Suspects Are Trying to Exploit the Major Flaws in the Military Commissions Implemented by the Bush Administration." salon.com, July 15.

Sullivan, Thomas P. (2008). "Held by the U.S. in Iraq and Guantánamo." *New York Times*, June 8.

Sunday Times. (2005). "The Secret Downing Street Memo." *Sunday Times*, May 1.

Suskind, Ron. (2003). *The Price of Loyalty: George W. Bush, the White House, and the Education of Paul O'Neill*. New York: Simon & Schuster.

———. (2006). *The One Percent Doctrine: Deep Inside America's Pursuit of Its Enemies Since 9/11*. New York: Simon & Schuster.

———. (2008). *The Way of the World: A Story of Truth and Hope in an Age of Extremism*. New York: HarperCollins.

Susman, Tina. (2007). "They're on Speaking Terms with Danger." *Los Angeles Times*, October 21.

———. (2008a). "Clashes Kill More than 20 in Sadr City." *Los Angeles Times*, April 10.

———. (2008b). "Iraq: Murdering the Messengers." *Los Angeles Times*, May 10.

———. (2008c). "Iraqis Languish in Crowded Jails." *Los Angeles Times*, September 22.

———. (2008d). "Sadr Rejects Order to Disarm." *Los Angeles Times*, March 30.

———. (2008e). "U.S. Fights But Tries Not to Offend." *Los Angeles Times*, May 7.

Susman, Tina, and Cesar Ahmed. (2008). "Security Volunteers Quit Posts Near Baghdad." *Los Angeles Times*, February 17.

Susman, Tina, and Yesim Comert. (2008). "Turks Invade Iraq, Clash with Kurds." *Los Angeles Times*, February 23.

Susman, Tina and Raheem Salman. (2008). "A Martyr and More in His Mother's Eyes." *Los Angeles Times*, March 6.

Sutton, Jane. (2008a). "Security Rules Stall Guantánamo Defense Efforts." Reuters, May 20.

———. (2008b). "U.S. Says Some Guantánamo Prisoners Can Phone Home." Reuters, March 12.

Sydney Morning Herald. (2004). "The David Hicks Affidavit." *Sydney Morning Herald*, December 10.

———. (2005). "US Detentions Abuse Iraq Mandate: UN." *Sydney Morning Herald*, December 5.

Synovitz, Ron. (2008). "Afghanistan: Kabul Seeks Release of More Bagram Detainees." Radio Free Europe, May 11.

Taguba, Major General Antonio. (2004). *Article 15-6 Investigation of the 800th Military Police Brigade* [Taguba Report]. Pagination in Sources corresponds to text in Greenberg and Dratel, eds., *The Torture Papers*.

Tahboub, Dima Tareq. (2003). "The War on Al-Jazeera: The US Is Determined to Suppress the Independent Arab Media." *Guardian*, October 4.

Tait, Paul. (2008). "U.S. Says 9 Accidentally Killed." Reuters, February 4.

Tannenhaus, Sam. (2003). "Bush's Brain Trust." *Vanity Fair*, July 1.

Tao, Feng. (2008). "Turkish Army Strikes PKK Targets in Northern Iraq." *Xinhua*, April 27.

Tavernise, Sabrina. (2007). "Turkey Bombs Kurdish Militants in Northern Iraq." *New York Times*, December 17.

Telegraph. (2008). "US Forces Apologise After Soldier Uses Koran for Target Practice." *Telegraph*, May 19.

Tenet, George. (2007). *At the Center of the Storm: My Years in the CIA*. New York: HarperCollins.

Therolf, Garrett, and Said Hameed. (2008). "Errant U.S. Airstrike Kills 9 in Iraq." *Los Angeles Times*, February 4.

Therolf, Garrett, and Raheem Salman. (2008). "U.S. Raid on Home Leaves Three Civilians Dead." *Los Angeles Times*, February 6.

Thomas, Evan, and Michael Hirsh. (2005). "Torture and Terror." *Newsweek*, November 22.

Thompson, Mark. (2008). "America's Medicated Army." *Time*, June 16.

Thurlow, Matthew D. (2005). "Protecting Cultural Property in Iraq: How American Military Policy Comports with International Law." *Yale Human Rights and Development Law Journal*, January.

Tietz, Jeff. (2006). "The Unending Torture of Omar Khadr." *Rolling Stone*, August.

Tuttle, Ross. (2008). "Gitmo Trials Rigged." *The Nation*, March 10.

Tyson, Ann Scott. (2008). "Afghan Commandos Emerge: U.S.-Trained Force Plays Growing Role in Fighting Insurgents." *Washington Post*, April 19.

Tyson, Ann Scott, and Robin Wright. (2007). "U.S. Helps Turkey Hit Rebel Kurds in Iraq: Intelligence Role Could Complicate Diplomacy." *Washington Post*, December 18.

United Kingdom. (2005). "The Secret Downing Street Memo." *Sunday Times*, May 1.

United Nations. (2004a). "UN Human Rights Expert Calls on Coalition Authorities to Allow Iraqi Detainees to Challenge Lawfulness of Detention." UN Press Release, May 5.

———. (2004b). "U.N. Special Advisor Lakhar Brahimi on the Political Situation in Iraq." *U.N. Observer and Special Report*, April 15.

United Nations, Assistance Mission in Iraq. (2004). *Iraqi Media Monitoring.* November 22.

———. (2007). *Human Rights Report.* April 1–June 30.

United Nations, Commission on Human Rights. (2005) "UN Experts Address Concerns Regarding Guantánamo Bay Detainees." Geneva, June 23.

United Press International. (2008). "U.S. and Iraq in Talks over PMOI." upi. com, June 21.

United States, Central Intelligence Agency. (2002a). *Iraq's Weapons of Mass Destruction Programs,* October 4 (the "White Paper").

———. (2002b). *National Intelligence Estimate: Iraq's Continuing Programs for Weapons of Mass Destruction,* October 1 (classified).

United States, Congress. (2005). *An Oversight Hearing on Pre-War Intelligence Relating to Iraq.* Washington, DC: Senate Democratic Policy Committee, June 26.

———. (2008a). "Hearings of the House Judiciary Committee." June 17.

———. (2008b). "Hearings of the Senate Armed Services Committee." June 17, as summarized in *Kat's Korner* (available at http://katskornerofthe-commonills.blogspot.com).

———. (2008c). "Rockefeller Announces Committee Approval of the 2009 Intelligence Authorization Bill: Legislation Revives Important Provisions Vetoed by the President Including a Ban on CIA Enhanced Interrogation Techniques." Senate Select Committee on Intelligence, May 1.

———. (2008d). *Intelligence Authorization Act for Fiscal Year 2009: Report.* May 1.

United States, Department of Defense. (2003). "Background Briefing on Military Commissions." Office of the Assistant Secretary of Defense for Public Affairs, July 3.

———. (2004a). *Report of Violations of the Geneva Convention and the International Laws of Land Warfare.* Defense Intelligence Agency, June 18 [DIA Report].

———. (2004b). "Summary of Evidence for Combatant Status Review Tribunal–Khadr, Omar Ahmed." Combatant Status Review Tribunal, Guantánamo Naval Base, August 31.

———. (2006). "Detainee Transfer Announced." October 12.

United States, Department of State. (2006). "Statement by Ambassador Jackie W. Sanders, Alternate U.S. Representative to the UN for Special Political Affairs, on the Report of the Secretary-General on Children and Armed Conflict, in the Security Council." U.S. Department of State, November 28.

United States, Director of National Intelligence. (2006). *Trends in Global Terrorism: Implications for the United States.* Washington, DC: Office of the Director of National Intelligence, April.

United States, Special Inspector General for Iraq Reconstruction. (2008). *Quarterly Report and Semiannual Report to the United States Congress.*

Washington, DC: Government Printing Office. Relevant figures are in Table 2.3.

USA Today. (2005a). "Abu Ghraib Inmate Fingers Graner Before Trial's Close." *USA Today*, January 11.

———. (2005b). "Supreme Court Declines to Hear POW Case." *USA Today*, April 25.

Van Moorter, Geert. (2004). "One Year After the Fall of Baghdad: How Healthy Is Iraq?" Health-Now.com, April 28.

Van Natta, Don, Jr. (2003). "Questioning Terror Suspects in a Dark and Surreal World." *New York Times*, March 9.

Vaznis, James. (2008). "At Hub Hearing, Lawyers Press Case of Guantánamo Detainees: Tell Congress Clients Innocent, Conditions Awful." *Boston Globe*, March 27.

Verlöy, André. (2003). "Oil Immunity? Government Denies Charges That Bush Helped Oil Companies in Iraq." *New York Herald Sun*, October 30.

Verma, Sonia. (2008). "Federal Judge Rules Iraq 'Gang-Rape Victim' Can Seek Trial in US." *The Times* (London), May 12.

Vick, Karl. (2007). "Witness Describes Iraq Killing." *Washington Post*, September 1.

Vine, David. (2008). "Introducing the Other Guantánamo." *Asia Times* (Hong Kong) (atimes.com), April 17.

Voice of America. (2008). "Guantánamo Detainee Accuses US Military of Torture." Voice of America, June 21.

Wahidy, Farzana. (2007). "Afghan Civilians Reportedly Killed More by U.S., NATO than Insurgents." Associated Press, June 25.

Warde, Ibrahim. (2004). "Iraq: A License to Loot the Land." *Le Monde Diplomatique*, May 2.

Warrick, Joby. (2008a). "Administration Says Particulars May Trump Geneva Conventions." *Washington Post*, April 27.

———. (2008b). "Detainees Allege Being Drugged, Questioned: U.S. Denies Using Injections for Coercion." *Washington Post*, April 22.

———. (2008c). "Lawmakers Urge Special Counsel Probe of Harsh Interrogation Tactics." *Washington Post*, June 8.

Warrick, Joby, and Robin Wright. (2008). "Unilateral Strike Called a Model for U.S. Operations in Pakistan." *Washington Post*, February 19.

Washington Post. (2007). "Pentagon Justice." *Washington Post*, September 2.

———. (2008a). "The Imprecise Meaning of War." *Washington Post*, July 3.

———. (2008b). "A Tale of Abuse." *Washington Post*, January 17.

———. (2008c). "Workable Terrorism Trials: A Special Federal Court Could Balance Fundamental Rights and National Security Needs." *Washington Post*, July 27.

Watkinson, David. (2008). "Guantánamo Bay Detainee Speaks at Cathedral." *Lancashire Telegraph*, March 19.

Wax, Emily, and Karen de Young. (2006). "U.S. Secretly Backing Warlords in Somalia." *Washington Post*, May 17.

Weinstein, Henry. (2007a). "Judge Says Detainee in Afghan War May Seek Freedom." *Los Angeles Times*, July 19.

———. (2007b). "Judge Says U.S. Must Alert Lawyer on Detainee Transfer." *Los Angeles Times*, October 4.

Wells, Matt. (2001). "How Smart Was This Bomb?" *Guardian*, November 19.

West, Andrew. (2003). "Some 800M to Hit Iraq in First 48 Hours." *The Sun-Herald*, January 26.

Whitaker, Mark. (2005). "The Editor's Desk." *Newsweek*, May 23.

Whitcomb, Dan. (2008). "Charges Dropped Against Marine in Haditha Case." Reuters, March 28.

White, Josh. (2005a). "Abu Ghraib Tactics Were First Used at Guantánamo." *Washington Post*, July 14.

———. (2005b). "Documents Tell of Brutal Improvisation by GIs." *Washington Post*, August 3.

———. (2006). "Marines Say Rules Were Followed: Sergeant Describes Hunt for Insurgents in Haditha, Denies Coverup." *Washington Post*, June 11.

———. (2007a). "11 Detainees Returned to Home Nations." *Washington Post*, November 5.

———. (2007b). "Detainee's Lawyers Fear That Mail Is Uselessly Slow at Guantánamo." *Washington Post*, October 12.

———. (2007c). "Judge Orders U.S. Not to Transfer Detainee." *Washington Post*, October 10.

———. (2008a). "Guantánamo Detainee Rejects Court Procedure." *Washington Post*, April 30.

———. (2008b). "Defendants' Lawyers Fear Loss of Potential Evidence at Guantánamo Bay." *Washington Post*, February 14.

———. (2008c). "From Chief Prosecutor to Critic at Guantánamo." *Washington Post*, April 29.

———. (2008d). "Guantánamo Man in Suicide Bombing: US." *Sydney Morning Herald*, May 9.

———. (2008e). "No Murder Charges Filed in Haditha Case." *Washington Post*, January 4.

———. (2008f). "U.S. Boosts Its Use of Airstrikes in Iraq." *Washington Post*, January 17.

———. (2008g). "U.S. May Have Taped Visits to Detainees: Foreign Countries Sent Interrogators." *Washington Post*, August 5

White, Josh, and Del Quentin Wilber. (2008). "Guantánamo Detainee to File Habeas Petition." *Washington Post*, June 26.

White, Josh, and Julie Tate. (2008). "Charges Dropped Against 9/11 Suspect: His Statements Were the Result of Abusive Interrogation, Officials Say." *Washington Post*, May 14.

White, Josh, Walter Pincus, and Julie Tate. (2008). "Rules for Lawyers of Detainees Are Called Onerous: Fair, Adequate Defense Questioned." *Washington Post*, February 13.

Whitehouse, Sheldon. (2008). "Whitehouse Criticizes Justice Department Advice Condoning Torture." Press Release of Senator Whitehouse, February 13.

Whitlock, Craig. (2005). "CIA Ruse Is Said to Have Damaged Probe in Milan: Italy Allegedly Misled on Cleric's Abduction." *Washington Post*, December 6.

———. (2007). "From CIA Jails, Inmates Fade into Obscurity: Dozens of 'Ghost Prisoners' Not Publicly Accounted for." *Washington Post*, September 27.

Whitmire, Tim. (2005). "Short Sentences, Dismissals Show Wartime Murder Prosecutions Hard." Associated Press, June 5.

Whitney, Mike. (2008). "Hunkering Down in Afghanistan, Watching 'NATO Bleed to Death on the Afghan Plains'." *Online Journal*, July 7.

Whoriskey, Peter. (2008). "Man Acquitted in Terror Case Faces Deportation: Lawyers Criticize Effort as Retribution from U.S." *Washington Post*, March 2.

Wilkinson, Jeff. (2003). "In Tikrit, US Destroys Homes of Suspected Guerrillas." *Miami Herald*, November 13.

Williams, Carol J. (2007a). "18 Iraqis Killed in U.S. Raid in Baghdad." *Los Angeles Times*, August 25.

———. (2007b). "Britain Wins Release of 4 Men at Guantánamo." *Los Angeles Times*, December 8.

———. (2007c). "Case Could Turn on Eyewitness." *Los Angeles Times*, November 9.

———. (2007d). "Detainee Can Make POW Case." *Los Angeles Times*, December 6.

———. (2007e). "Detainee Lawyers See Stacked Deck." *Los Angeles Times*, November 13.

———. (2007f). "Guantánamo Bay Detainee, 68, Dies of Cancer." *Los Angeles Times*, December 31.

———. (2007g). "Guantánamo Detainees Face an Uncertain Future." *Los Angeles Times*, December 9.

———. (2008a). "3rd Guantánamo Detainee to Boycott Trial." *Los Angeles Times*, April 11.

———. (2008b). "Detainee Lawyer Says Death Was Possibly by Friendly Fire," *Los Angeles Times*, April 12.

———. (2008c). "Gitmo Tribunal Rules Limit Disclosures," *Los Angeles Times*, April 2.

———. (2008d). "Guantánamo Criticism Intensifies," *Los Angeles Times*, June 11.

———. (2008e). "Guantánamo Detainee to Be Charged," *Los Angeles Times*, June 4.

———. (2008f). "Guantánamo Trial Delayed Amid Prisoner's Protests," *Los Angeles Times*, March 13

————. (2008g). "Hamdan Helped Ben Laden Succeed, Agent Says," *Los Angeles Times*, July 26.

————. (2008h). "Hamdan's Lawyer Says Advisor Is Exerting Illegal Sway for Political Ends," *Los Angeles Times*, March 28

————. (2008i). "Judge Critical of War Crimes Case Is Ousted," *Los Angeles Times*, May 31.

————. (2008j). "Jury Is Out for Hamdan—and the Tribunal Process," *Los Angeles Times*, August 4.

————. (2008k). "New Incentive Dangled at Guantánamo," *Los Angeles Times*, August 3.

————. (2008l). "Officer Calls Sept. 11 Cases Tainted," *Los Angeles Times*, June 5.

————. (2008m). "U.S. Accused of Doctoring Tribunal Evidence," *Los Angeles Times*, March 14.

Williams, Kayla. (2007). *Love My Rifle More than You: Young and Female in the US Army*. New York: Norton.

Wilson, Jamie. (2005). "Hunger Strikers Allege 'Force Feed Torture' in Guantánamo." *Guardian*, October 21.

Wilson, Richard J. (2006). *Children in Armed Conflict: The Detention of Children at* Guantánamo *Bay, and the Trial for War Crimes by Military Commission of Omar Khadr, a Child*. Washington, DC: Eminent Jurists Panel on Terrorism, Counter-Terrorism and Human Rights.

Wiseman, Paul. (2003). "Cluster Bombs Kill in Iraq, Even After Shooting Ends." *USA Today*, December 16.

Witte, Griff. (2006). "Halliburton Cited for Iraq Overhead: Costs in Oil Contract Called Extreme." *Washington Post*, October 25.

Wolfowitz, Paul. (2004a). "Administrative Review Procedures for Enemy Combatants in the Control of the Department of Defense at Guantánamo Naval Base, Cuba." U. S. Department of Defense, May 11.

————. (2004b). "Order Establishing Combatant Status Review Tribunal." U.S. Department of Defense, July 7.

Woodward, Bob. (2003). *Bush at War*. New York: Simon & Schuster.

————. (2004). *Plan of Attack*. New York: Simon & Schuster.

————. (2006). *State of Denial*. New York: Simon & Schuster.

————. (2008). *The War Within: Secret White House History, 2006–2008*. New York: Simon & Schuster.

Worden, Leon. (2004). "Brig. Gen. Janis Karpinski." *The Signal* (Santa Clarita, CA), July 4.

World Tribunal on Iraq. (2005). *Declaration of the Jury of Conscience*. Istanbul, June 25.

Worth, Robert F. (2006). "US Military Braces for Flurry of Criminal Cases in Iraq." *New York Times*, July 9

————. (2008). "Yemen's Deals With Jihadists Unsettle the U.S." *New York Times*, January 28.

Worthington, Andy. (2007). *The Guantánamo Files: The Stories of the 774 Detainees in America's Illegal Prison.* London: Pluto Press.

———. (2008a). "Afghan Hero Who Died in Guantánamo: The Background to the Story." Counterpunch, March 13.

———. (2008b). "Guantánamo Trials: Where Are the Terrorists?" huffingtonpost. com, February 8.

———. (2008c). "Italy's Forgotten Prisoners at Guantánamo." Counterpunch, June 24.

———. (2008d). "Torture Allegations Dog Guantánamo Trials." Huffington Post, March 21.

Wright, Evan. (2007). *Generation Kill: Devil Dogs, Iceman, Captain America, and the New Face of American War.* Berkeley: Caliber.

Wright, Robin, and Joby Warrick. (2008). " U.S. Steps Up Unilateral Strikes in Pakistan." *Washington Post*, March 27.

Wypijewski, JoAnn. (2006). "Conduct Unbecoming." *Mother Jones*, January/ February.

———. (2008). "The Final Act of Abu Ghraib." *Mother Jones*, March/April.

Xenakis, Stephen N. (2008). "No Torture. No Exceptions." *Washington Monthly*, March.

Xinhua. (2008). "U.S. Military Says It keeps 21,000 Detainees in Iraq." *Xinhua*, August 2.

Yee, James. (2005). *For God and Country: Faith and Patriotism Under Fire.* New York: Public Affairs.

Yoo, John. (2001). "The President's Constitutional Authority to Conduct Military Operations Against Terrorists and Nations Supporting Them." U.S. Department of Justice, September 25.

———. (2002). Letter Regarding "The Views of Our Office Concerning the Legality, Under International Law, of Interrogation Methods to Be Used on Captured Al Qaeda Operatives." U.S. Department of Justice, August 1.

Yoo, John, and Robert J. Delahunty. (2002). "Application of Treaties and Laws to Al Qaeda and Taliban Detainees." U.S. Department of Justice, January 9.

Yoshino, Kim. (2008). "Protests and Violence Lead to Vehicle Ban in Diyala." *Los Angeles Times*, January 5.

Younge, Gary. (2004). "US Soldiers Sent Home for Beating Prisoners of War." *Guardian*, January 6.

Yousafzai, Sami, and Ron Moreau (2008a). "The Taliban's Baghdad Strategy." *Newsweek*, August 4.

———. (2008b). "Where 'The Land Is on Fire'. " *Time*, June 16.

Youssef, Nancy A., and Patrick Kerkstra. (2004). "US, Iraqi Forces Take Control of Samarra." *Kentucky News*, October 1.

Zagorin, Adam, and Michael Duffy. (2005). "Inside the Interrogation of Detainee 063." *Time*, June 20.

Zavis, Alexandra. (2008a). "Ancient Civilization ... Broken to Pieces." *Los Angeles Times*, January 22.

———. (2008b). "Army Interpreter Sentenced at Court-Martial." *Los Angeles Times*, June 24.

———. (2008c). "In Iraq, U.S. Apologizes for Soldier Using Koran in Target Practice." *Los Angeles Times*, May 19.

———. (2008d). "Iraq to Help Turkey Fight Rebels." *Los Angeles Times*, July 11.

———. (2008e). "Iraqis Say U.S. Attacked Citizen Guards." *Los Angeles Times*, February 16.

———. (2008f). "Power-Starved Iraq Goes Solar." *Los Angeles Times*, July 14

———. (2008g). "Sons of Iraq? Or Baghdad's Sopranos." *Los Angeles Times*, May 20.

Zavis, Alexandra, and Saif Rasheed (2008). "Iraqi Police, U.S. at Odds Over Helicopter Assault." *Los Angeles Times*, May 23.

Zernike, Kate. (2004). "Only a Few Spoke Up on Abuse as Many Soldiers Stayed Silent." *New York Times*, May 22.

Zielbauer, Paul von. (2006a). "Account of 4 G.I.'s Accused of Killing Civilians, Tell of How Iraqi Raid Went Wrong." *New York Times*, August 7.

———. (2006b). "G.I.'s Say Officers Ordered Killing of Young Iraqi Men." *New York Times*, August 3.

———. (2007a). "The Erosion of a Murder Case Against Marines in the Killing of 24 Iraqi Civilians." *New York Times*, October 6.

———. (2007b). "Marines Punish 3 Officers in Haditha Case." *New York Times*, September 6.

Zucchino, David. (2008a). "Army Colonel Again Criticized Marine Unit." *Los Angeles Times*, January 23.

———. (2008b). "Marine Shooter Seeks Immunity in Afghan Case." *Los Angeles Times*, January 11.

———. (2008c). "Marine Testifies He Saw No Enemy Fire." *Los Angeles Times*, January 9.

———. (2008d). "Unit Cleared in Afghan Killings." *Los Angeles Times*, May 24.

LEGAL CITATIONS

In addition to the court cases cited in Table 6.2, the following are cited in the text:

Acree v Iraq (04-820), 2005

Al-Hussayen v United States (393 F.3d 902), 2004

Al-Odah v United States (321 F.3d 1134), 2003

Al-Odah v United States (Civil Action No. 02-828 Memorandum Opinion), 2004

Ali v Rumsfeld 06-0145 (TFG), 2007

American Civil Liberties Union v Department of Defense (339 F.2d 501), 2004

Associated Press v Department of Defense (1:05-CV-03941-JSR), 2006

Arar v Ashcroft (414 F. Supp F.2d 250), 2006

Bismullah v Gates (06-1197), 2007

Boumediene v Bush (06-1195), 2008

Burton v Livingston (791 F.2d 97), 1986

Demore v Kim (538 U.S. 510), 2003

Doe v Gonzales (546 U.S. 1301), 2005

El-Maghraby v Ashcroft (200 U.S. Dist Lexis 21434 ED, NY), 2005

El-Masri v Tenet (479 F.3d 296), 2006

Gates v Bismullah (501 F.3d 178), 2007

Hamdan v Rumsfeld (126 S.Ct. 2749), 2006

Hamdi v Rumsfeld (542 U.S. 507), 2004

Hawkins v Holloway (326 F.3d 777), 2003

Humanitarian Law Project v Dept. of the Treasury (380 F.2d 1134), 2006

Hutton v Finney (437 U.S. 678), 1978

In re Guantánamo *Detainee Cases* (355 F.2d 443), 2005

Ireland v United Kingdom (5310/71), 1978

Jama v INS (22 F.2d 353), 1998

Judiciary Committee v Miers (08-0409 (JDB), 2008.

Kar v Bush (dismissed), 2005

Khadr v Bush (377 F.2d 102), 2005

Kiyemba v Bush (1:05-CV-01509-UNA), 2008

Lhanzom v Gonzales (430 F.3d 833), 2005

Lopez v Gonzales (U.S. 05-547), 2007

Lucien v Peters (107 F.3d 873), 1997

Marbury v Madison (5 U.S. 137), 1803

Maxwell v Mason (668 F.2d 361), 1981

Miranda v Arizona (384 U.S. 436), 1966

Olmstead v United States (277 U.S. 438), 1928

Parhat v Gates (06-1397), 2008

Public Committee Against Torture in Israel v Government of Israel (769/02), 2006

Rasul v Bush (542 U.S. 466), 2004

Rasul v Myers (U.S. 08-235), 2008

Rochin v California (342 U.S. 165), 1952

Tachiona v Mugabe (234 F.2d 401), 2002

Tillery v Owens (907 F.2d 418), 1990

Trop v Dulls (356 U.S. 86), 1958

Youngberg v Romeo (457 U.S. 307), 1982

Zadvydas v Davis (533 U.S. 678), 2001

INDEX

About the Author

MICHAEL HAAS is Professor Emeritus of Political Science at the University of Hawaii and Chairman of the International Academic Advisory Board of the University of Cambodia. He played a role in stopping the secret funding of the Khmer Rouge by the administration of President George H. W. Bush. He has taught political science at the University of London, Northwestern University, Purdue University, and the University of California, Riverside. He is the author or editor of 33 books on human rights, including *International Human Rights* (2008), *International Human Rights in Jeopardy* (2004), *The Politics of Human Rights* (2000), *Improving Human Rights* (Praeger, 1994), and *Genocide by Proxy* (Praeger, 1991).